D1485129

"*Thirty Years in a W te Haze* is a new benchmark
library… Egan's blunt, hard-won wisdom about
sometimes personal costs of following your dreams provides a level of
insight and humanity seldom found in the heights of the alpine world. This
is a must-read account of a sport and a storied skier's intertwined history."

— **PETER KRAY**, Author of *American Snow* and *The God of Skiing*

"Rarely if ever has the ski bum life been told as authentically and
honestly as in *Thirty Years in a White Haze*. Written with remarkable candor
and introspection, the book is a chronicle of his nearly primal pursuit of
skiing. From the tension of sibling rivalry to the realities of an athlete
getting older, Dan Egan and Eric Wilbur have penned a fearless personal
and cultural history of one of the most dynamic eras in skiing. Not only
is it a must-read for fans of the sport—especially those whose
jackets are patched with duct tape—it's a page-turning
confessional of a career spent on multiple edges."

— **STEVE CASIMIRO**, former Editor of *Powder Magazine*
and Founder of *Adventure Journal*

"Dazzling! A fascinating read by one of the world's gutsiest adventurers…
It's hard to tell what Dan Egan is better at—exploring the
world's most fascinating and dangerous places or putting into words
what his adventures mean to him and to the rest of us."

— **PATRICK CREADON**, Award-Winning Filmmaker and Director
of *SKI BUM: The Warren Miller Story*

"In *Thirty Years in a White Haze*, Dan Egan and Eric Wilbur take readers
from the highs of success to rock bottom lows. You don't have to be a
skier to appreciate Egan's humanity as he navigates obstacles on the
mountain and off, personal and professional, at home and abroad.
Egan honors pioneers in the US ski industry, his family, his peers. Each
chapter tells a different story; however, the theme remains the same:
rise from your challenges, live your heart out, and be true to yourself."

— **JANET LOVE MORRISON**, Award-Winning Author,
and Goodwill Ambassador for Friends to Mankind

"…just when you think you know what Dan is all about, you turn around and discover something about him you never imagined. During my childhood years, Dan was an East Coast born-and-bred 'extreme skier'—harkening back to Scott Schmidt, Glen Plake, Mike Hattrup and the rest of the Stump-era-shredders…. Within skiing, Dan saw the bigger picture of the 'industry' and that it could be something bigger than just a personal portfolio of contest results and films segments. He found a way to leverage skiing to give back to others… And now comes *Thirty Years in a White Haze*, and Dan has done it again…
The guy is a ski legend in ways I never knew! Enjoy the read!"

— **MIKE NICK**, Pro Skier, X Games Medalist

"You know when you read something and have no doubt that the person writing it was there for it all… That is this book, for sure. *Thirty Years in a White Haze* is truly authentic. You can tell Dan lived, breathed, and loved extreme skiing his entire career, and put his life on the line time after time, and lived to tell the story… This book is the raw, truthful, and candid accounts he experienced as a skier. Dan is a true storyteller."

— **JUSTIN KOSKI**, Executive Director of the
US Ski and Snowboard Hall of Fame

"Along his drool-worthy journey, Dan meets 'iconic' personalities—skiers, resort operators, film-makers, promoters, etc.— who played pivotal roles in making the ski sport a lifestyle that so many world-wide have embraced. International figures like Stein Erickson, Wayne Wong, Sylvan Saudan, Patrick Vallencant, Tom Corcoran, Harry Leonard, and Warren Miller are just a few of the many people who we meet in White Haze. Beyond the amazing experiences readers get to enjoy through the Egans' exploits, the book also serves as a must-read primer in ski history, covering the evolution of the sport from the early days of freestyle skiing—known once as hot dog skiing—to today's 'disciplines'of Extreme and Big Mountain. A great read that every committed skier— no matter what your level of expertise—will want to read."

— **BERNIE WEICHSEL**, Ski Bum,
Show Promoter, and Industry Gadfly!

"In [*Thirty Years in a White Haze,*] it's easy to root for what's brave and human and hang on every word as Dan finds what matters most in the chaos and darkness of a storm. This is a universal tale, honestly and skillfully told by a good and kind fellow traveler."

— **DAN COONEY**, Founder of The Cooney Company and former Commercial Director of the US Sailing Team

"Dan Egan, alongside his brother John, was a big, famous deal in the world of skiing for several decades. One of *THE* most colorful characters in an already colorful industry, this book about his spectacular career and life is not to be missed. Even if you don't ski, to read about a man who lived life to his fullest, is an inspiration to help you also live your life to the fullest. Not only that, much like you hope an adventure story to be, *Thirty Years in a White Haze* is one hell of a page-turner."

— **KRISTEN ULMER**, former Best-in-the-World Pro Skier, and Author of *The Art of Fear*

"As I approached the summit of Mt. Elbrus with my husband in June 2005, we were in a raging storm just below the summit, and Rob spoke with graveness about the situation Dan Egan had endured in 1990 on this same mountain. Now, in *Thirty Years in a White Haze*, the world has the firsthand account of Dan's struggle to survive in a small snow cave he dug by hand, solo on the highest peak in Europe. Like Dan, I have traveled to ski in remote places around the world. I agree with his sentiment that, while skiing nearly killed him, it also saved him."

— **KIT DESLAURIERS**, First Person to Ski the Seven Summits, 2x World Freeskiing Champion, and Member of U.S. Ski and Snowboard Hall of Fame

"Since emerging as a pioneer of skiing in the 1980s, Dan Egan has been central to the sport's colorful, ever-evolving history. With *Thirty Years in a White Haze*, Egan and Wilbur have laid a graceful set of tracks through this landscape, taking readers to the icy edge of the wilderness and back."

— **NATHANIEL VINTON**, Author of *The Fall Line: America's Rise to Ski Racing's Summit*

"Dan's passion for skiing and the skiing life is as infectious as it is undeniable. He lays it all out here. The discovery of something that so captures you that it shapes the rest of your life: from the places you live, the jobs you take, and the friends you keep, to some of the best and worst decisions you ever make. The breadth of Dan's adventures is vast and impressive. Being a similarly infected, if less adventurous, skier, it all rang true to me. The names, locations, and details are different, but I recognized many of the people I've known, places I've been, things I've done, wished I'd done, and wished I hadn't. And so, probably, will you."

— **RON LEMASTER**, Ski Writer, Photographer, and Educator

"Whether Dan was racing to Bermuda in brutally rough seas, or traversing difficult terrain in the wilderness, he relied on his experience and instinct to survive and, most importantly, trusted in others... What sets Dan's story apart from so many sports enthusiasts who dream about great adventures is he actually went out and reached for the ultimate ski and sailing expeditions. And, even better, he filmed many of these stories for everyone to enjoy. Dan Egan's story is one of inspiration, spirituality, and the appreciation of human kindness... Every sentence of this story keeps you glued to the narrative. It is an amazing story that takes you from one amazing episode to another. Bravo!"

— **GARY JOBSON**, America's Cup Hall of Famer

"As a kid, I looked up to Dan Egan the pro skier, a pioneer of mind-blowing extreme skiing. As an adult, I looked up to Dan, the entrepreneur, turning his skiing passion into businesses. However, it wasn't until I read this book that I realized how crazy Dan's adventures actually were!...If you ever dreamed of becoming a lifelong ski bum, this is your chance to make it happen without leaving your couch...These stories are told as if passed around the bar at the end of a ski day, backed by Dan's infectious sense of humor and first-hand perspective."

— **JASON LEVINTHAL**, Entrepreneur and Founder of Line and J skis

Thirty Years in a White Haze

Photograph by Jen Bennett

Dan Egan wasting another perfectly productive day skiing. Location: Big Sky, Montana

Thirty Years in a White Haze

Dan Egan and Eric Wilbur

Degan Media, Inc.
Campton, NH

Published by Degan Media, Inc.

Color Hardcover ISBN-13: 978-1-7364927-4-1
Color Paperback ISBN-13: 978-1-7364927-1-0
Ebook ISBN-13: 978-1-7364927-3-4

First edition (paperback): March 2021

Book design: Eddie Vincent, ENC Graphic Services
Cover design by Christopher Wait and Deirdre Wait, ENC Graphic Services
Front cover photograph of Dan Egan skiing in Val d'Isère, France, by Dave Roman
Back cover photographs: film strip photos: Photo 1 by Dave Roman,
Photo 2 by Jen Bennett, Photo 3 by Ian Anderson, Photo 4 by Wade McCoy;
main photo of Dan Egan, as well as his "About the Author" photo by Kathryn Costello

Chapter Illustrations created by:
Senan Gorman (World Map, 2, 4, 8, 9, 10, 13, 24, 36, 43)
Kimberley Kay (3, 5, 11, 12, 14, 15, 16, 18, 19, 20, 22,
28, 29, 30, 31, 32, 34, 37, 38, 39, 41, 42, 44)
Nancy Griswold (21)
Priscilla Christie (23, 26, 33)
Martina Diez-Routh (6, 7, 35, 40)
Tom Day (25, 27)
Blair Boettger (1, 17)

Degan|media

Published by Degan Media, Inc.
PO Box #988, Campton, NH, 03233
https://dan-egan.com/
https://www.white-haze.com/

Dedications

Dan dedicates this book to his namesakes who have gone before him . . .

Daniel E. Gillis
(Uncle, and Mary Ellen Gillis' twin brother)

Daniel E. Gillis
(Cousin)

Daniel E. Egan
(Brother)

Eric dedicates this book to his wife,
Kathleen Karcher Wilbur,
for her devotion and support.

Dan Egan skiing in Cappadocia, Turkey, for Warren Miller's *Steeper and Deeper*

Table of Contents

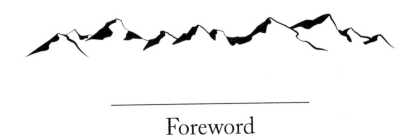

Foreword

by Tony Horton

IT'S SO FASCINATING HOW MEETING one person can steer your life in a completely new direction. Meeting Dan Egan did that for me. Maybe it's a New England thing—we hit it off almost immediately and the symbiotic relationship made it easy to brainstorm and collaborate on various projects. We were just a couple of entrepreneurs looking to work together and have a positive effect on others. From my appearances on his TV show to ski retreats at Squaw Valley and funky hills like Sugar Bowl in Tahoe, CA, Dan provided opportunities for me that altered my life dramatically. Dan has always strived for a BIG life, and he never hesitates to share that with others, so you can reach outside your comfort zone and succeed.

My skiing was inspired by Tony Sr. (aka Big Tone), who decided that the Horton family would be skiers mid-way through the 1960s. I still have the old oak wooden skis he used growing up in the 1940s. Ski tech hadn't advanced much when I first started skiing—rock-hard black lace-up leather boots, cable bindings, and wood skis with metal edges—a slight upgrade from the all-wood ski my dad used in his South Attleboro, MA, neighborhood.

Truth be told, I hated skiing when my pops first dragged me to a local hill called Song Mountain in Central New York. I was just five years old when Big Tone attempted to help me figure out how to stand up (and *not* sit down) on a J-Bar. When a lift operator handed me the spring-loaded metal pole with a two-by-four attached at the bottom to drag me up the hill, the concept did not compute. The result was young TJ (my nickname given to me by my grandmother) in a heap, facedown in the snow and crying.

Over time fear was replaced by excitement at the thought of strapping on a pair of skis and tearing down a mountain on a snowy winter's day. The problem was, I couldn't get my ski skills to catch up to my enthusiasm, from childhood through college, and into my early thirties, I improved very little. In all that time I had no more than half a dozen formal lessons, because I was stubborn and thought I'd figure it out all on my own. My poor habits caught up to me in the winter of 1978, at Smuggler's Notch in northern Vermont, my sophomore year in college. After two days of rain followed by a bunch of snow I found myself flailing down a trail called Freefall on Madonna Mountain at Smuggs. Unbeknownst to me, all the "moguls" that day were actually frozen tree stumps concealed by a thin layer of fresh wet snow. I was demonstrating my worst Stein Eriksen ski technique, which consisted of being in the back seat, legs glued together, with my arms apart or behind me. The flailing came to an abrupt end when my right knee came in direct contact with one of those rock-hard tree stumps. Blam! Shattered patella. No cell phones in those days, so the ski patrol had a tough time finding me. After about an hour and a half of sitting in the snow in a whiteout waiting for the sled, my now-frozen feet were becoming a bigger problem than my shattered kneecap.

Trust me when I tell you that in that moment, I was convinced my skiing days were over. Not because of the accident, but honestly because I felt I wasn't cut out for it. Surgery, a cast from my toes to my hip, rehab, and a knee that can predict the weather, and I was sure skiing was in the rearview mirror. As I muddled my way through The University of Rhode Island, I think I strapped on my skis only twice more, at the Yawgoo Valley Ski Area in Exeter, RI.

Everything changed for me when I met Dan Egan on July 30, 1994, at my sister Kit's wedding. What was Dan Egan doing at my sister's wedding? Turns out, Kit's fiancé Dan Caldicott and Dan Egan where close friends and co-captains on the Babson College soccer team. I knew of Dan and his brother John from the annual Warren Miller ski movies, narrated by Warren, at the Santa Monica Civic center in Santa Monica, CA. I attended every year. I was mesmerized by what the Egans could do on a pair of skis, and where they traveled, too. To me, their skill level was on par with NASA astronauts going to the moon and back.

My new brother-in-law, Danny, knew I was a skier and had been encouraging me to join Dan Egan on one of his adventures, but after watching these guys on film, hucking cliffs in places like Squaw Valley, California; Chamonix, France; and Valle Nevado, Chile, I thought, no way in hell was I up for that kind of extreme skiing. However, on the dance floor of my sister's wedding, Dan Egan decided to recruit me for one of his X-Team ski camps. I humored Dan, saying I'd sign up for an X-Team camp, but truthfully, it sounded way too treacherous for me.

However, every winter I thought more about it, so finally I phoned and peppered Egan with questions—lot and lots of questions. How much does it cost? Do you have to jump off of cliffs? Can you be an intermediate skier to sign up? Has anyone ever been injured or killed at one of these camps? Tell me more about the other coaches. Where do they hold these X-Team camps? How many people attend? Will I be the only intermediate skier? I finally pulled the trigger in January of 1998, for the Red Mountain camp in BC.

In 1998 you didn't need a passport to cross the Canadian border—a good thing, because I didn't have one. A forty-one-year-old grown man without a passport. This tells you a lot about me in 1998. I had traveled only to parts of the U.S., Tijuana in Mexico, and Vancouver Island as a trainer for the movie *The 13th Warrior*. I flew to Spokane, WA, rented a car, and drove the 402 miles to Rossland, BC. After getting lost three times, I finally arrived after 10 p.m. The other X-Team attendees had already eaten dinner and were telling tales of past camps in Alaska, New Zealand, and all over Europe.

I didn't know a soul, but was lucky enough to wave to Dan between his duties to get us to the hill before it opened. I hopped on a chair with other X-Team campers and engaged in small talk, but once at the top the entire group, coaches and all, bolted down the mountain. Right then, I start having flashbacks to the fifth grade, as the last kid picked for dodgeball. Without a trail map I ended up on a narrow, bump-covered, double-black, rodeo run. I was skiing in the back seat going way too fast, and launched off a cat track. The impact on landing knocked the air out of me, caused a yard sale, and tweaked my right wrist.

During lunch, I ended up sitting next to another first-time X-Teamer and learned that he, too, was petrified—we became instant friends. After lunch it was time for the "Ski Off." The Ski Off is designed to help the five coaches figure out your degree of skill, so you can be placed into groups. Each group had names like Cornice, Couloir, Northface, and Headwall. After skiing in front of thirty-five strangers, I was placed in the lowest group.

Three days and five incredible coaches later, I was transformed. I was no Tommy Moe, but I'd learned about equipment, body position, edge angle, attitude, adapting to terrain, beer, and met a ton of friends. On day one I was ready to leave—by Sunday afternoon I was sky-high, fired up, and ready to sign up for the next camp, which I did.

When the first flakes start to fall every year, I think of that conversation I had with Dan on the dance floor of my sister's wedding, and how it changed my life forever. Over the years, I attended fourteen more camps in Grand Targhee, Wyoming; Squaw Valley, California; and Valle Nevado, Chile. It was Dan Egan who dragged me to my first heli-trip, and because of him, I've been on dozens since. The X-Team turned me into a real skier; before meeting them, I'd purposely stay indoors on powder days because I had no idea how to ski in all that snow. My fellow X-Team camper and friend, John Nicolich, once told me that, "It's not very often you get to choose a defining moment in your life." He was referencing my good fortune through the health and fitness industry, as it was through my life choices from which my best-selling fitness series—P90X®; P90X2®; P90X3®; Ten Minute Trainer®; and most recently, my twenty-two-minute military-inspired workout, 22 Minute Hard Corps®—were developed and have allowed me to experience and enjoy my time in the mountains with Dan and the X-Team.

The character of Joe Powder was developed by artist Nick Lyons in Val d'Isère, France in the 1980s. He based the character on an American skier named Russell Blair. His art was featured on posters and greeting cards throughout the resort, sold in local shops, and found in chalets and hotels throughout Val d'Isère and Tignes, France.

My brother John and I first met Nick Lyons in 1990 at one of the local hangouts for après ski, the Perdix Blanche bar and restaurant. It was there, drinking, laughing, and rehashing ski adventures with international ski bums that Nick would pull his inspiration for Joe Powder. Joe Powder could always go one better, ski steeper, deeper, and pull off feats only dreamt about by mortals.

In the winter of 1991, I commissioned Nick to give me Joe Powder's ultimate run for my multi-projector slide show tour "Worldwide and Wild" in which I toured ski shows, ski shops, and small theaters. Nick used images of me and John skiing for his inspiration to create Joe Powder's ultimate run.

Sprinkled through this book are the illustrations (and the images that inspired them) of Joe Powder's ultimate run. I hope Nick's drawings inspire readers to seek their own ultimate runs.

—Dan Egan

Photograph by Dave Roman

In the days before speed flying, ski base jumping, and wingsuits, Nick Lyons knew Joe Powder's ultimate run would start in a hot air balloon.

Introduction

by Dan Egan

IN MAY OF 2000, MY brother John and I were in northeastern Canada, on the frozen coast of Ungava Bay on the Arctic Ocean in Nunavik, in a blinding windstorm. I had gotten separated from my group and was seeking shelter from the wind against a big piece of ice. John, Dean Decas, and cameraman Eric Scharmer were with the Inuit guides, a hundred or so yards away. And I was shaking from a flashback of being lost in a snowstorm on Mount Elbrus in Russia, ten years earlier.

We were on a twenty-day trip to make a television documentary on adventure tourism in northern Quebec. Our objective was to traverse east on the Torngat Mountain range from the coast of Ungava Bay to the Labrador

Peninsula. Our main goal was to ski Tower Mountain, a stand-alone, sphinx-like pyramid on the border with Labrador.

We were traveling by snowmobile and living with the Inuit, building igloos at night, fishing for Arctic char to complement our meals, ski touring, and climbing the endless mountain chutes along the way. A year earlier, John and I had spoken about a reunion trip back to Mount Elbrus, but decided a new adventure would be a better way to celebrate, rather than going back to the site of such tragic loss. So I organized this trip, through a grant provided by a partnership with the Canadian and Quebec offices of tourism, to document and discover whether ski touring would be possible in this frozen land.

However, here I was hunkered down in another wild storm—scared, unable to find my way in the Arctic, remembering Elbrus. It has been difficult for me to speak of the isolation I feel when surrounded in clouds, wind, and snow in the mountains, or in fog on the open ocean while sailing. My body tenses up, my breathing gets short, and I start to think of what will happen if I can't find the others or a path forward.

As a pro skier, coach, guide, and sailor, I have found myself in these conditions many times over the years, since being trapped for over thirty-eight hours, lost in the storm that killed a dozen climbers on Elbrus. Even today, thirty years later, the sensation remains very personal; I haven't found a way to express the panic that builds in situations like this. Often, being the one in charge, I mask my fear with confidence and a gentle urgency to move myself and my companions toward safety.

Our trip to Ungava Bay was our second trip up north. Two years earlier, we traveled to Baffin Island, the largest island in Canada, to ski the fjords along the Davis Straight. We stayed on Broughton Island in a small research hut and traveled by snowmobile across the frozen sea to the coast of Baffin to tour, climb, and ski. I liked the North. It's a world wrapped in snow and ice that brings you back in time.

Since the mid-1980s, John and I built a reputation for skiing the world's remote locations. We traveled throughout the Eastern Bloc at the end of the Cold War, skied with Kurds in Turkey during Desert Storm, pioneered heli-skiing in Chile, skied the Martial Glacier above the Drake Passage on the southern tip of Argentina, snuck into Lebanon to ski in the mid-1990s, as well as skiing the classic lines and resorts across Europe and North America.

Together, John and I have chalked up more than fifty first descents, launched off cliffs the height of twelve-story buildings, and skied more than our share of pristinely perfect powder snow on mountain peaks around the globe. Our mountain antics were documented by filmmakers and writers, and shared on VHS tapes, cable television shows, magazines, and books years before the advent of the X-Games, half-pipes, terrain parks, GoPro, YouTube, or social media.

The brother angle played well. John, six years my elder, was my childhood hero. His bold personality and life-on-the-edge attitude left me searching for a way to gain his attention and confidence. And I found it in the marketing of our brand as "The Egan Brothers" through films, television shows, merchandise, and sponsorships which I managed and produced.

Growing up in a large family—my parents, Marlen and Robert, had seven children—embedded a work ethic and goal-setting standard that lives deep within me and all of my siblings. Mary-Ellen, Bob, John, Sue, Ned, and Mike are each fiercely independent souls with big hearts and a belief system of service to others. I love them all. They have all supported me in the good times and in the hard times, but most of all they have accepted my rough edges and all that comes along with them. There is nothing like family for creating tension, releasing emotion, and caring. I've never found a replacement for it and trust me I have looked.

Skiing is timeless and simple, which is why I love it—the satisfaction and joy of gliding on, over, and through snow. This all started for me as a young boy. Every fall, just after Halloween, we'd trek to the attic as a family and haul down all the boots and clothing, bring the skis up from the basement, and turn our living room into a ski shop. Boots were tried on, bindings adjusted, and poles handed out. Whatever fit automatically became yours. Then we'd begin waxing our skis in the basement, place our gear by the cellar door, and wait for snow.

We lived on a hill, so when snow fell we'd ski and ride the yellow Snurfer down the hill, over the jumps, then run back to the top for another run. On Saturdays we'd load up the car, head toward the Howard Johnson's parking lot at the exit to the highway, and board the Blizzard Ski Club bus for New Hampshire. I took ski lessons until I was sixteen. We were taught by the Europeans at the Paul and Paula Volar Ski School at Mount Sunapee and Cannon Mountain, as well as at the Egon Zimmerman Ski School at Blue Hills, just a few miles from my family's home in Milton, Massachusetts.

In the 1970s, Bob and John always had cool gear. I remember when they got their orange Olin Mark IV skis—plus Jet Stix, an extension for the back of the boots that would allow you to lean back and do freestyle tricks. My sister Mary-Ellen was an expert skier as well, and would challenge us younger kids to turning contests—she was the queen of quick turns, feet locked together, smooth and flawless. In high school, when I finally got new skis and boots that fit, my world opened up. The skills I'd learned from ski school expanded to skiing the woods, moguls, and racing down icy runs.

Skiing fostered two main things for me: independence and confidence. The independence was forced on me by my two older brothers refusing to wait for a ten-year-old kid. The confidence grew over time, knowing one day I would catch 'em. Once I was a senior in high school, having been tested by Bob and his friends on the Norwich University Ski Patrol (where he went to school) and at Sugarbush Resort (where John was a ski bum), I finally had my first taste of the wild side of life and what real skiing felt like off the beaten path. My skills were coming up to their standards.

I jumped my first real cliff at Mad River Glen Ski Area in Vermont. In the early 1980s, the landings were flat. I was skiing with one of John's ski bum friends, Tim Ritson. It was a fresh powder day and he was showing me all the cliff drops in the woods. He was telling me, out West you can do this and ski away from the cliffs—it was steeper and deeper. Since that day, I've been hooked on the thrill of heading toward the edge of a cliff and flying off it. I've come to call it "the eternal now," when everything slows down and then, *bang*! you land in a pillow of snow. That day with Tim, I got a taste of that feeling and wanted more.

Meeting, skiing and working with Warren Miller was fuel for my life. His films provided me with a platform, a way to belong to the industry I could never have foreseen. He introduced me to the art of filmmaking, storytelling, and how to distribute the end product. The door he opened became a path to many possibilities for my ideas, passion, and drive. He once told me: when I skied, I should think about the beauty of the place and my role in it—which was to complement the surroundings, to be the exclamation point on the mountain. His many examples have been inspiration for this book, my films, articles, and career.

Thirty Years in a White Haze is more than a ski story. Yes, at the center are our snow adventures, but more importantly, this is an attempt to show the historical connections and generational ties through our family. We also explore the roots of extreme skiing in the 1980s, how it is forever tied to the freestyle movement, which started with Stein Erikson in the 1950s, on to the hotdoggers of the 1970s, and brings to life the people who shaped extreme skiing in the 1980s and 1990s. It was a wild, fun, and impactful time in the ski industry when skiers went from straight to shaped skis, dark blue conservative skiwear to Day-Glo one-piece suits, and letting long hair fly, free of helmets.

My co-author Eric Wilbur and I decided to tell this story through the third person viewpoint. We believe telling the story from that perspective allowed more space for the many voices, thoughts, and recollections of people who were interviewed to be heard and understood.

This story also expresses how the 1990 Degré7 expedition to Mount Elbrus affected my life. I've come to believe trauma doesn't shape your life, rather, it dictates it. Being lost in a storm with winds blowing over a hundred miles per hour, trudging through five-foot-plus deep snow, and digging a snow cave in the battle to survive on one of the precipitous Seven Summits of the world while being separated from my brother, all formed internal reactions I couldn't control for years afterward.

Walking off that mountain alive on May 3, 1990, was the beginning of my adult life as I know it today. I was twenty-six years old; for the next thirty years, I've had to learn to restructure the patterns caused by that traumatic experience. That trip has touched every aspect of my life: relationships with my siblings, especially John; the ending of my marriage in 2001; post-divorce relationships; business and financial decisions, especially when I've felt threatened; and where and why I ski the locations I do today.

That trip brought me closer to God and helped me understand the deep and rich roots of faith that run through the generations of my family. It also created my wonderful, rewarding, sober life, which is a constant cycle of discovering who I am. *Thirty Years in a White Haze* is my story of how skiing almost killed me and saved me, all at the same time. I hope you enjoy it.

Prologue

"To the roots of the mountains I sank down;
the earth beneath barred me in forever."

Jonah 2:6

DAN EGAN WAS IN THE belly of Mount Elbrus, shivering in a snow cave he figured would become his tomb. Like Jonah, he ignored his inner voice and was swallowed by the big fish, a mountainous consumer, tediously digesting his fear into an awakening.

At 18,500 feet, Russia's Elbrus, a dormant volcano just west of the Black Sea and north of Russia's border with Georgia, is the highest peak in Europe. An estimated twenty-five to thirty people die each year attempting to summit the mountain. Elbrus is one of the Seven Summits in the classic mountaineering challenge: scaling the highest peak on each of the world's seven continents. Seven Summits is an exclusive club only a few hundred people have managed to join.

Elbrus has a higher annual death toll than Mount Everest, despite the list of tragic stories that emerge from the highest peak in the world, many of which have been made into riveting documentaries of triumph and loss. There were eleven deaths on Mount Everest in 2019, one of the deadliest years in the mountain's recorded climbing history. But as recently as 2016, thirty climbers were estimated to have died in attempts on Elbrus in a single year. In 2004, forty-eight perished trying to reach the summit.

The Elbrus ascent is steep and icy. Abrupt storms and sub-zero

1

temperatures lead to frostbite and hypothermia. Its history of bad weather has frustrated climbers for centuries. And in 1990, this was where Dan Egan found himself, pinned down by a massive snowstorm, digging a snow cave in a fight for his life.

At the time, the Caucasus mountain range, between the Black and Caspian Seas, was still a geographical characteristic of the former Soviet Union. It was also a world away—both in distance and culture—from Dan's home in suburban Boston, Massachusetts.

Thousands of miles to the west, the Boston public school system, which Dan's grandfather had helped steer through its most volatile period, was throttling down toward summer break. The South Boston Yacht Club, where Dan inherited his passion for sailing from his father, was bustling with spring fever. It was the time of year when Dan usually made an annual pilgrimage to Mount Washington's Tuckerman Ravine in New Hampshire, about four hours north of the Blue Hills Ski Area, which was less than half an hour's drive from Boston, making it the ski area nearest to any major metro area in the United States. Both Blue Hills and New Hampshire were responsible for luring at least two generations of Egans into the sport of skiing. But, that year, Dan was in a snow cave on Elbrus. It was his sister Mary-Ellen's birthday. His former Babson College soccer friends were gathered to dedicate a memorial to a teammate on the very same day. The Blue Hills, Tuckerman's, and home were far, far away.

Dan's brother John was far below, in the storm raging on Elbrus. The brothers had traveled there with cameraman Tom Day to help document an expedition consisting of twenty-three people from nine countries. Filmmaker Warren Miller had discovered John while skiing at Vermont's Sugarbush Resort in 1978. After Dan joined John on the big screen in 1985, they branded themselves as "The Egan Brothers" as they chased the news on snow to places like the Berlin Wall, Yugoslavia, and the Persian Gulf War, lugging their skis along for narratives that would redefine the genre. It had become quite a ride around the world. That John and Dan were separated on Mount Elbrus was certainly an uncommon exception to their usual tight bond.

"Let's follow CNN," Dan had told Miller, a proposal for documenting the sort of skiing on film that eventually led to John and Dan's careers paralleling the geopolitical landscape of the 1980s and 1990s. After all, as Miller often quoted Hannes Schneider, "If everyone skied, there would be no wars." What better way to deliver the peace-seeking promises of skiing than to showcase the sport on film in some of the world's most renowned front lines?

By 1995, the Egan brothers had appeared in more Warren Miller productions than any other skiers. While Dan was hallucinating, vomiting blood, and fighting for his life on Mount Elbrus, it was likely that somebody was enjoying watching him and his brother ski in tandem on a VHS tape, rewinding a favorite scene over and over, awed by the two skiers at the forefront of extreme sports as they hucked cliffs and skied mountain steeps. Whenever the Egan brothers appeared on film, it was together—where one went the other would follow, skiing back-to-back and side-by-side.

But there was no John in Dan's hastily created cave, only a Russian guide who was doing his best to save the life of an American he didn't know.

There was startling diversity among the climbers on that trip, many of whom found their way to Elbrus via a sweepstakes from Degré7, the French winter sports outfitter founded by Patrick Vallençant. Recognized as the grandfather of extreme skiing, Vallençant, who hailed from Chamonix, the Alps region known for its extraordinary mountain challenges, had died the previous year in a climbing accident.

This expedition to Elbrus had been coordinated by those left in charge of his clothing line. The purpose was to film The Egan Brothers performing their outstanding extreme skiing abilities. Wearing Degré7 skiwear, they would hike up the eastern peak, which could take nine hours, then perform their daredevil skiing down the challenging forty-five-degree slopes. So far, it wasn't going well.

The language barrier crippled the expedition from the start, which wasn't helped by the group's disparity of skills and experience, ranging from Chamonix mountain guides to recreational mountaineers. Members of the expedition had been living on the mountain in a refuge at fourteen thousand feet for three days, getting acclimated to the altitude. There were thirteen separate expeditions heading up Elbrus on May 2, 1990—destined to become one of the most disastrous days in the mountain's climbing history.

The weather had been inconsistent in the days leading up to the climb. On the night of May 1, a storm raged briefly but broke by morning. So, with skies clearing, the guides decided to push for the summit. In what would turn out to be a major mistake, Dan left John and Tom behind and made way for the top of the mountain, eager for the opportunity to bask in the accomplishment. It was a decision that would ultimately leave him stranded, facing a long, cold, hungry stretch of time, uncertain whether he would survive.

As Dan continued his climb, oblivious to the impending danger, John and Tom found themselves turned back by the storm's resurgence and were forced to rescue three less-experienced members of the expedition, lower down on the mountain. Somehow, they found the refuge amid the storm, where they joined the others who'd managed to find it, as well.

"The storm came up from the bottom of the mountain," John would later say. "I saw it coming up, and when it got to us, I knew it was still going up and only getting worse."

But the storm had yet to reach Dan. He was climbing with Alfred Jimenez-Segarra, a Spanish member of the expedition who'd won his way to Elbrus after purchasing a Degré7 beanie from a sports store in Brussels. At eighteen thousand feet, they were laboring through the deep snow and thin air, twenty steps at a time before pausing to catch their breath. But clear skies beckoned, drawing them onward. Fooled by blind ambition and the clear skies, Dan continued to climb, focused on the summit. Both he and Jimenez-Segarra ignored the storm threat approaching from below.

They were only 150 feet beneath the summit when, rationalizing they ought to lighten their loads, they dropped their packs. The thought that their contents might save their lives never crossed their minds. Instead, as the wind increased and ominous clouds gathered, Dan and Alfred ignored common sense.

Their celebration at the summit was short. They were blanketed by a deep, dark, white haze. After hours of climbing, both were confused, tired, and without their packs. Luckily, they were not alone. A Russian guide who introduced himself as Sasha could not believe the ecstasy Dan and Alfred displayed upon reaching the summit, and probably wondered why the pair could not understand the horrific situation about to confront them all. He convinced them to immediately come with him, insisting they abandon their backpacks; to risk a search for them would also pose the risk of losing Sasha, who was searching for missing members of an Italian expedition he'd been leading. With snow swirling, breathing becoming more difficult, and their senses deteriorating, Dan and Alfred chose to follow Sasha and his fellow Russian climbers, feeling confident they could make the refuge, fourteen thousand feet below.

As they traversed, the situation grew worse. The group took themselves out onto the middle of a glacier for ease of travel, its blue ice as solid as granite. But there were crevasses in the ice, major cracks; avoiding them led to mass confusion and they were soon lost—though the Russians wouldn't admit it. One of the climbers fell through a crevasse, forcing Sasha to rescue him. As the storm grew and raged, emotions bubbled to near panic. Nobody knew what to do. Nobody seemed confident in moving forward any longer.

The Russians made it clear it was time to stop. It was time to dig in and wait out the storm. Dan couldn't understand what was happening or what they were doing, and didn't know how to help. One of the Russians hit him on the back and pleaded with him to help dig. So, with the only tools he had—an ice axe and his hands and feet—Dan punched, kicked, and clawed his way into the snowy mountainside.

He dug, and dug, and dug . . .

As Dan understood it, he was digging a snow cave for other members of the expedition. But he was tired and nobody was helping—he seemed to be building it by himself for three other people. Dan became frustrated and grew even more tired. He returned to the cave and started kicking again, unsure what everyone else was doing to take shelter. Nobody tapped him on the shoulder and asked him to rest. Nobody offered to help.

After digging alone for four and a half hours, Dan laid down in his snow cave. Snow piled up outside, reaching five and a half feet. Wind was whipping, over one hundred miles an hour. Dan was vomiting blood and began experiencing hallucinations when, out of nowhere, Sasha dropped into his cave. "I was having a white-light experience and it got interrupted by a six-foot-four Russian," Dan said.

Dan Egan was in the belly of Mount Elbrus, swallowed by Jonah's whale in the form of Elbrus's mountain peaks. It was climbing and skiing such mountain peaks where he'd previously discovered a sense of purpose—a calling, as he considered it, to aspire to the highest level of success in his chosen sport: extreme skiing. And now he was confronting this calling on quite different terms—surviving a storm the likes of which he had never experienced.

Destiny? Perhaps.

"Our path from Boston to the highest peaks around the world was born out of a combination of how our parents raised us—to be independent, confident, and steadfast in our pursuits," Dan said, "mixed with our personal connections from our childhood into our twenties, just because we loved to ski and were willing to risk career, relationships, and security for the simple pleasure of gliding on, over, and through snow." Because, according to Dan, there's no other good reason why two kids from Milton, Massachusetts, would go on to ski around the world, become icons of the Alpine community, and define a generation of extreme sports.

"It has always amazed me how our pursuit expanded before us at every turn, even when it was hard or the path forward was unclear due to financial reasons, or in the face of other people's expectations of how life should be, rather than what life could be. I was like a dog with a bone," Dan said. "Once

I saw what my brother had done with his move to Vermont in the '70s to be a ski bum, that vision of breaking outside the boundaries of a 'normal life,' I wanted to taste it too—soak it all in and blow it wide open into something bigger. The idea that I could do it with him—my older brother—subconsciously, that was the motivation behind it all."

The Egan Brothers *were* extreme skiing in the 1980s and '90s. Extreme skiing demonstrated a fearless energy that spoke of and to the Egans' sense of adventure, shared with the help of emerging videotape technology—what future generations would experience through YouTube and GoPro cameras. VHS technology moved film watching from the theater into the home, changing not only the way viewers consumed skiing as a form of entertainment, but also how they learned more exciting ways to ski.

Dan and John helped bring the extreme mantra from the mountains to Madison Avenue. Cameras followed the Egans to places never before skied, as they made first descents in Turkey, Canada, and Greenland, and used their love for skiing to inspire peace in places like Yugoslavia, Romania, and Russia. To this day, they are considered among the most influential skiers of their generation.

It was not only his love of extreme skiing but his heartfelt desire to be an emissary for peace, love, and understanding that ultimately brought Dan to Mount Elbrus, where he found himself in a snow cave facing death and coming to terms with the realities of his career choice. Instead of achieving the personal and career success he had anticipated, this excursion would turn out to be the beginning of everything else, as he would one day discover.

And the Lord commanded the fish, and it
vomited Jonah onto dry land.
Jonah 2:10

Joe Powder launches out of a hot air balloon to start his ultimate run off the mountain summit.

John jumping into space during Warren Miller's *Born to Ski* in Slovenia.

Chapter One

STANDING IN THE HALL OF FAME

JOHN EGAN SPENT THE FIRST ten minutes of his speech revisiting some of the moments that made him worthy of being honored in 2017 with an induction into the U.S. Ski and Snowboard Hall of Fame, at a ceremony in Stowe, Vermont. The induction was a tribute the pioneer of extreme skiing shared with his brother, Dan. Co-inducted, they became the first siblings to receive the nod as a pair since the Hall's first class in 1956.

John's acceptance speech first and foremost paid tribute to Dan, his younger brother by six years, with whom he'd formed "The Egan Brothers," an extreme skiing duo who helped make skiing a marketable form of entertainment. Together, they would go on to star in more than a dozen films for Warren Miller, the high-ranking chieftain of winter sports movies. John thanked his friend Dennis Ouellette, who in 1976 enticed the fellow ski bum at the Sugarbush Resort in Vermont to take his first journey out West: a ski trip Ouellette would finance in exchange for John's promise to work at his New York apple orchard that summer. John next recalled how he'd met Montpelier, Vermont, native Tom Day in a lift line at Squaw

Valley, leading to a partnership resulting in John and Tom spending more time in the mountains than anybody else over the next four decades.

When it was Dan's turn to step up to the podium, he had his own gaggle of people to thank, along with a more extensive chronicle of stories to share, more than doubling the time his brother had spoken. Glancing around as he approached the podium, Dan marveled at the audience. Gathered in the ballroom were dozens of the most influential individuals in the skiing and snowboarding communities: the athletes, promoters, and executives who helped define the sports.

Dan and John had reached the peak: they were now Hall of Famers. Their influence on skiing, filmmaking, and apprenticeships reverberated from their childhood roots in Boston to the revered halls of the U.S. Ski and Snowboard Hall of Fame—physically located in Ishpeming, Michigan, the birthplace of organized skiing in the United States. They were two of the most notable extreme skiers to emerge from 1980s. They'd changed how the public consumed the sport—in their own homes—thanks to the birth of the VCR. Indeed, the Egan brothers were more influential in the sport of skiing than most skiers competing on the World Cup circuit, simply because—thanks to the VCR and videotape—they'd become household names. They were a known commodity, a "brand," and therefore more easy for the average skier to relate to than an Olympic gold medalist.

Dan stepped to the stage, grinning like a master of ceremonies rather than the object of attention. As the applause settled down he opened his speech, conveying the kind of awe felt by audiences watching him and his big brother sail off snow-covered cliffs. He gave tribute to the man who inspired his career, the one who'd just stepped away from the microphone, emotion welling up in a moment of incredulity as if he couldn't fathom how he'd followed in his older brother's footsteps. Again.

"John Egan!" he shouted into the microphone, as if asking for an encore from the crowd, his voice filled with a reverence that defined their history together. The moment spoke of impassioned influence and admiration, despite the recent rocky pavement that brought them there. It was a recognition without resentment.

Later in his speech, Dan thanked his brother again: "It has been an awesome journey, my brother. I've had a front row seat to learn from one of the best skiers on the planet, and I love you so much, mate." The room was silent for a moment, experiencing the reciprocity between the brothers on the highest stage of their careers.

"John is such an icon to so many people," Dan later reflected. "For me, it was a summing-up, because I was paying him back and expressing how much he means to me. I was giving him his due. I think he stands on his own. I had always thought he could have been invited into the Hall without me."

Several years earlier, Hall of Fame board member Mike Bisner wanted to nominate the Egan brothers for the Hall, but there was a problem—at the time, Hall of Fame bylaws stated that only one person could be admitted each year, precluding a pair from being nominated under one submission. That seemed to leave the possibility of the brothers being honored together out in the cold. But Bisner recognized the importance of the branding the Egans had contributed to the sport as a pair, and struggled with the policy.

"Basically, I had to get the bylaws changed to allow two people under one nomination," Bisner said. "When John was first presented as a possible nomination the year before, Justin Koski [director of the Hall of Fame] said, 'Well, just have them go under separate nominations and, when the chips fall, we'll see who gets in and who doesn't.' I replied, 'It would be a travesty to put the two Egan brothers in separate nominations and have one get in and one not get in.'"

Bisner's relationship with the Egans dates back to when Dan worked for him at the St. Moritz Ski Shop in Wellesley, Massachusetts, where he gave Dan, then sixteen years old, equipment to teach windsurfing. Later, Bisner sponsored the brothers in his role as vice president of marketing at Salomon. He was always a keen observer of the passion Dan and John expressed through their skiing. "So, I had to actually present to the executive committee that, in certain circumstances, it would be proper to allow two individuals when their accomplishments were interlinked. Together, the sum of the two parts equaled greater than two individual accomplishments. I was able to sell this to the Hall, get it passed and the bylaws changed. Which meant I could move forward with nominating John and Dan together."

The Hall of Fame has always been a family affair. Twin brothers Phil and Steve Mahre, World Cup and Olympic legends, were honored separately in 1981 and 1984. Tamara McKinney, winner of eighteen World Cup races, was inducted in 1984; her half-brother Steve, the first speed-skier to break 120 miles per hour, was thus honored in 2017, over thirty years later. Nordic skiers Magnus and Hermond Bakke were both honored individually in the same year, 1972, but their skiing careers weren't characterized by the sort of kinship that made Dan and John, who were attached to each other by their souls, refer to themselves as "The Siamese Twins of Skiing."

"I think it was appropriate for the Egan brothers, and really set the tone," Bisner said.

For John, who served as chief recreation officer at Sugarbush Mountain Resort, the nomination was an important factor in moving his career forward at the Vermont ski resort he has long called home. "How do you keep doing new things to keep your career alive?" John asked. "So, how do I keep Sugarbush interested in having me? I can't rest on my laurels and say, 'Oh yeah, I was a great ski bum in the '70s, '80s, and '90s.'"

But, being "Hall of Famer John Egan" helped to officially classify him as an even more attractive source for sponsorship and counsel. The designation helped rejuvenate his status in Warren, Vermont, and boost his relevance.

Dan first proposed the idea of seeking out a Hall of Fame nomination from a sponsor like Bisner to John's wife, Barbara, during a family reunion he hosted at his New Hampshire home. What he didn't expect was Barbara's admission that she'd already taken care of the application—for John, and John only.

Dan was taken aback. Certainly, John Egan's career alone might have warranted admission as one of the most recognizable ski movie stars of his generation—he remains the only man to ever compete at the world pro mogul and race tours in the same year—but it is The Egan Brothers, as a duo, that people remember making first descents around the world wearing Day-Glo suits, goofily jumping off the Berlin Wall in skis, and barely escaping the rules of gravity at Grand Targhee, Wyoming. It seemed like Barbara's oversight was just something Dan would have to sit with.

When the names for the Hall of Fame class of 2016 were released later that year, the list included icons such as freestyle legend Genia Fuller, publisher Harry Kaiser, Olympic-medalist snowboarder Chris Klug, and executive David Ingemie. But there was no John Egan.

With some trepidation about being rejected again when applying the following year, Barbara and John called Dan in a panic. From Dan's end, it seemed like his sudden recognition was one of convenience, and he was hesitant to get involved. John Egan and Dan Egan, in their own individual rights, are ambassadors of the sport. But The Egan Brothers, as a tandem, helped write the playbook for a pivotal stretch in skiing history.

"I had wrestled with this," Dan said. "I had gotten to a point where I was happy for John. John should be in the Hall of Fame. He's an amazing guy, an amazing skier. I had envisioned myself sitting there, watching him get into the Hall of Fame, and I was going to be fine. I would just do it later. I was fine with that, too, because I would finally get to do it as myself. So, I had come to peace with this."

Only ten days before the application deadline, Dan was in the midst of covering the thirty-fifth America's Cup in Bermuda, running a $4 million sponsorship for Sperry, which required all of his focus. He declined to get involved. "I said, 'I hope John gets in the Hall of Fame. He deserves to be in the Hall of Fame. But I've got a life, and I'm living it. Good luck.'"

In response, John and Barbara had a card up their collective sleeve: Bisner wanted to nominate *both* John and Dan.

"Bisner called minutes after I got off the phone with them and delivered a message: 'Help me get this application fucking done.' That was a brilliant move on their part, because Bisner has been a mentor of mine ever since I was fourteen," Dan said. "He'd helped me. He'd given me sponsorships. Every time he was at Head or Salomon, he was there for The Egan Brothers. I could not say no to Mike Bisner."

Bisner knew John's intentions may have lacked the necessary follow-through the year before. Yet, with Dan's perspective and input on the new application, Bisner thought he could actually pull it together before the deadline. Besides, his prodding had gotten the Hall of Fame to change its bylaws. "I just stuck my neck out there and changed the bylaws to make this happen," Bisner said. "So, I told Dan, 'You've got to get involved with this fucking thing.'"

Dan took a three-day break from the America's Cup, locked himself up and focused for the first time on putting their careers into perspective. Who were "The Egan Brothers"? What did The Egan Brothers do, anyway? How could Dan even begin to define their importance to the ski industry? They didn't win any gold medals. They didn't invent anything essential to the sport. How, then, had two ski bums gotten such acclaim around the world?

Bisner started the application with: "The Egans' career followed the geopolitical and geographical landscape of the 1980s and 1990s." This gave Dan the denotation he was seeking. He started to understand the importance of the locations and the timing of how he and John had skied the most remote regions of the world, including war-torn areas.

"That line freed me. Because that's what we did. We went to the Berlin Wall. We went to Red Square. We skied with the Kurds in 1991. We were in Yugoslavia the week before the war started. We were part of the 1993 Middle East Peace Ski in Lebanon. And after they murdered Ceaușescu, we went to Romania. We were on it."

With that in mind, Dan was able to add the details Bisner was seeking for the application. "It also helped me realize that the Hall of Fame wasn't about what I was *doing*, it was about what I *had done*. It was about what I'd done with John. Everything he did post-Dan Egan was not in my application, because it wasn't relevant. Neither was anything I did post-John Egan relevant. Our relevancy was '88–'95." The Hall of Fame qualification was about The Egan Brothers. It was not whatever other worthwhile accomplishments each had on his own. With that in mind, Dan wrote about how, twenty years later, nobody hosts more Warren Miller films throughout the country than the Egans.

"We're still paid to talk to audiences," he said. "Why? Because we can tell great stories, like Warren did. The fact that we are intertwined with Warren makes people often say to me, 'Hey, you and your brother are the Warren Miller skiers, right?' We are storytellers."

Storytelling is a trait Dan and John both acknowledge being passed down from their grandfather, Dr. Frederick Gillis, the former superintendent of the Boston Public School Department and a master orator in his own right. On Sunday mornings, the Egans would sit and listen to him tell stories about his time in World War I, tales that would make all seven of the Egan siblings feel as if they were right there with him in battle.

Perhaps some of their grandfather's spirited wartime tales inspired the competitiveness in his grandsons. Dan still bristles at the fact that John rarely mentions him when he tells his own story—there is brotherly animosity, for sure. But that was nothing, compared to the Post sisters: the same year Bisner helped rewrite the rules, it not only helped John and Dan get inducted together, but also Marion and Ellen Post, twin sisters who excelled in freestyle skiing in the '70s—their relationship was decidedly icier. "Those two don't even talk," John said. "They had to be separated at the event. Pretty intense.

"Dan and I have always appeared like we have a great relationship. We both like the same things, both look the same, act the same, and have the best Boston accents. But we're different people. We operate differently, and we expect different things from relationships. Those differences come out in little ways that upset him about my personality and upset me about his personality. That's a sibling thing. It's been going on for centuries, I think."

The inherent conflict has tugged at their Siamese souls throughout their careers. John was, ultimately, on the mountain for the fun of it, while Dan saw opportunity at every angle, always looking for chances to market The Egan Brothers into another sponsorship or appearance. Dan was manic in keeping to the schedule sponsors dictated. John would be two days late for a photo shoot just because the skiing had been good. "That's where I was. I was in it to have a good life, not to make a name," John said. "I've always been in it for the skiing and pushing my own personal limits."

As Dan sees it, though, while John was able to open a lot of doors throughout their careers, it was he who had the savvy to hold them open for the opportunities that awaited. "Having me in the mix made a lot of things possible for him," Dan said. "And what he'd done previously made it all possible for me. So it was a very synergistic relationship."

Albeit, like any relationship, there were fault lines, something John's architectural expertise sees as the recipe for their strength, as a duo. "In construction, when you build a house, there has to be stress on the frame or it just won't be strong in the end," John said. "There has to be stress on the growth of a business, too, otherwise you don't test what it can do and come out with the best product or service, or whatever you're providing. I feel my knowing that enhanced our relationship, because there was some stress there."

There would be further contention as the Hall of Fame induction ceremony grew closer, including an argument over the guest list and John's failure to hand out the "Egan Brothers" stickers and hats Dan created as gifts. John wasn't looking to recreate The Egan Brothers that evening, he told Dan, even if it was set in that brand's honor.

Either way, it was a night honoring both Dan and John Egan—The Egan Brothers—as among the most "prominent athletes and snow-sport builders, whose accomplishments showcase American skiing and snowboarding."

As John put it, in his speech that night, "Not bad for a couple of ski bums from Boston."

Chapter Two

THE HIGHEST HILL IN BOSTON

RISING TO 330 FEET ABOVE sea level, the Bellevue Hill neighborhood of West Roxbury is the highest point in both the city of Boston and Suffolk County. Bellevue Hill offers panoramic views, from the skyline of downtown Boston all the way to Boston Harbor. The omnipresence of a pale green water tower serves as a beacon, a compass for residents and commuters navigating the West Roxbury Parkway.

It is fitting that the Gillis family lived at the highest point in the immediate Boston neighborhood—a precursor to the heights that a pair of its offspring would one day conquer throughout their careers. There is a relative steepness that steadily increases as Bellevue Hill Road intersects with the West Roxbury Parkway, so there's little surprise that this is the site of the first Egan turns on snow. This was also where Mary Ellen Gillis and her five brothers skied down the median strip of the parkway, back in the 1930s and '40s. Bellevue Street ends in an oval about a block long, where it meets with Bellevue Hill Road and Bellevue Hill Park, where a path to the water tower above resembles a medieval passage to the castle-like tower at the top of the hill. All six of the Gillis siblings shared a single pair of wooden skis, a limited resource that would lay the foundation for one of the many passions that filtered through the household.

On a blank wall in her kitchen, flanked by a built-in bench, Grandmother Ellen created a painting of the Gillis family tree, documenting the lineage of Gillises from one generation to the next. A marriage was identified by an "M," a death with a "D," each with the date next to the names. At the top of the family tree is Frederick James Gillis, father of the aforementioned six children and, over time, grandfather to thirty-four of their offspring. His wife, Ellen, originally hailed from South Dakota, where her mother and father had perished in a prairie fire. After that tragedy, she went to live in Washington, D.C., with her uncle, Monsignor William J. Kerby, who helped organize the sociology department at Trinity College. (Pope John Paul II held a mass in Msgr. Kerby's honor, on the Kerby Lawn at the school, during a visit to the U.S. in 1979.) In 1910, Msgr. Kerby was among the founders of the National Conference of Catholic Charities, one of the largest charity networks in the United States, and was selected as the organization's first executive secretary.

Frederick's clan was immersed in Catholicism and teaching. Two of his brothers were priests, while Frederick went on to create a landmark career, structuring the Boston education system. There's a graduation photo of young Frederick in his Boston College yearbook, in 1916. In it, he stares into the camera, his auburn hair parted back. "This is a remarkable picture of a remarkable fellow," reads the detail. "Its [sic] that big word because it is just like him, as he's never been seen—painfully serious. And would again that our photographer had caught him at himself, for then you would be assured of here seeing 'Freddie' as in memory we shall always remember him—smiling."

Frederick earned a full scholarship to BC upon graduation from Boston Latin in 1912, the first Latin High School graduate to earn the four-year Cardinal O'Connell Scholarship. He also became the first Boston resident to earn the Knights of Columbus scholarship to Catholic University, where he began his teaching career and earned his M.A. before heading overseas in August, 1917, to serve in World War I with the American Expeditionary Force. He saw action in France as a lieutenant in the 103rd infantry, Yankee Division. During the war, Gillis, part of a platoon known as "The Invincibles," was wounded in combat—the victim of a gas attack in May of 1918, and by machine gun fire two months later—and was promoted to First Lieutenant for bravery in action. Shortly after his return to the U.S., in August of 1919, he was praised in a speech by his former commanding officer, before the Charitable Irish Society in Boston, as being "the gamest and pluckiest soldier I ever saw."

After exiting the service, he and Ellen purchased a small colonial in West Roxbury and started a family; Mary Ellen and her twin brother, Daniel, were born on Sept. 23, 1928. Mary Ellen was to be the only female sibling; having five brothers forced her to develop a certain tenacity, but she also benefitted from the protective nature of Fred, Bill, Joe, and David. Her twin was the first "Danny" added to the family tree. Baby Danny couldn't pronounce "Mary Ellen," so called her "Marlen," and the nickname stuck. Not that she played favorites, but Ellen Gillis wasn't shy about classifying Mary Ellen and Danny as her most pleasant babies. Of all the boys, she always said Danny was the nicest and easiest to deal with. Yet, his name would carry a sort of ominous presence in the family.

During World War II, with all the older brothers off serving, Danny and Marlen had the run of the Gillis household. Danny took the opportunity to publish the monthly "Gillis Times," reporting on the activities of the family, both at home and abroad in the war—only one of Danny's entrepreneurships during the 1940s. The West Roxbury neighborhood came to depend on his egg route, a surplus he provided via the chickens he singlehandedly raised in the family's backyard.

In 1946, Danny introduced Marlen to his new friend, Robert Egan. Soon enough, Marlen found herself in a pickle, as two boys now wanted her hand for the junior prom at Boston Latin High School. It was a tough decision, made easier by Danny: "Go with Egan, he'll never let you down," he said.

"My twin brother was an extrovert and had lots of friends," Marlen said. "I was an introvert and didn't have many. My twin brother liked Robert, so why not?"

Over the years, as they dated, they often skied together—slowly, Marlen said—at the Blue Hills Ski Area, which opened in 1949 on the beautiful woodlands of the Blue Hills Reservation in Milton. In 1954, they married—but there was a loved one sadly missing: Danny Gillis.

Marlen's twin brother had been reported missing off the coast of Florida on November 27, 1950, after a routine squadron training flight originating from a Jacksonville airbase. Flying single-seat, propeller-powered Douglas A-1 Skyraider aircraft, the Air Force pilots were practicing bombing runs over the ocean. A flare had been tossed into the water and the planes were dive-bombing it. Danny made his run, but was never seen or heard from afterward. An extensive air and sea search began immediately, but was discontinued by mid-December.

The loss of her brother hit Marlen hard, creating a grief she tended to bury, not so much hiding from the awful truth, but as her way of coping with an event from which she never truly recovered. An envelope from the War Department arrived, addressed to her father, stuffed with the death announcement, telegrams from congressmen telling of the search, and photos of Danny. She tucked both the envelope and her feelings away for decades, apart from the home she was building for her own family. Never able to share the depth of these memories with her children, she simply tucked the event away and moved on with her life.

"We all knew about her brother," her oldest son, Bob, said. "But he wasn't dinner conversation."

Photo albums rife with images of Danny were for the most part hidden away. When Marlen's children came across them, they were stunned at their inability to recognize young Danny standing beside their mother, grandfather, and grandmother. It really wasn't until, years later, when an uncle created a book dedicated to his lost brother, filling a loose-leaf binder with information detailing Danny's life, that the younger generation began learning about Danny. The book, a tribute to a man the Egan children never knew, made them wish they had.

Memorial masses were held simultaneously, in both Massachusetts and Florida, on Dec. 16, 1950. "D" was added to Danny's name on the family tree. Eight more names would be added over the next twenty years, as Marlen and Robert increased the Egan family. One of them, an infant named Danny in honor of Marlen's twin brother, died. The loss of sons named Daniel became a recurrence in the family, something Dan Egan would notice, years later. "Almost all of the Dannys in the family had 'D's next to them," Dan said. "With the exception of my cousin and myself, they all died before the age of twenty-four."

One person who did talk about Danny all the time was Ellen, who regaled her grandchildren with stories about her late son's businesses in the neighborhood. Sunday mornings at the Gillis house were akin to a tribal conference, with Frederick and Ellen holding roundtables of discussion and storytelling. Their grandfather's sessions often lasted for hours, as he repeatedly told of his exploits in World War I. "We used to sit around and listen to him tell stories that made you feel like you were in France liberating a town or something with him," John said.

It was during these sessions that they learned about "The Invincibles," their grandfather's war wounds, and how this valued education made him the man he was. Sometimes he'd whip out the helmet of the German soldier he'd shot through the neck during the war, a hole marking the bullet's exit at the top.

It was an easy, one-mile walk from the Egan household in West Roxbury to their grandparents' home, where the Egan children knew they would be tested by a consummate educator. After Ellen filled their bellies in the kitchen, it was off to be with Frederick, who always had skill-nurturing projects for the kids, giving them anything broken—from toasters to lawnmowers—to see if they could figure out how to fix them. These chores also included the carpentry skills that would become a defining portion of John's life.

At the time, John's schooling was more exemplified by his ability to avoid it, rather than his bringing home good grades. In response, Frederick made him build a treehouse in order to learn the math classes he was skipping. The treehouse-building lesson became foundational for John's stints as a carpenter in his ski-bumming days, as well as when building his home in Vermont. "Learning how to build is something my grandpa taught me," he said. "He taught me how to get through life, really. He was an amazing orator, a great storyteller. Really, just one of the best adult listeners I've ever encountered." Those were also the traits Grandpa Gillis put to work in the challenging circumstances of his reign as Boston school superintendent during the emotionally explosive times in the city's racial history.

After World War I, Gillis's education continued. In 1917, he earned a Master of Arts from Catholic University, a Master of Foreign Service degree from Georgetown University in 1922, and a Doctor of Philosophy from B.C. in 1930. By the time he was elected assistant superintendent in 1935, his extensive teaching experience already included posts at Catholic University, Boston University, the Massachusetts State Extension, and the Catholic Summer School at Cliff Haven, in New York. He joined the teaching staff at Boston College in 1932 as head of the department of education.

In August of 1960, the Boston School Committee elected him superintendent at a time when Boston schools were growing exponentially. During his three years at the helm of the school system, the issue of racial segregation came to the forefront.

By 1963, Boston public schools boasted a then-record enrollment of 93,500 students, seven hundred more than the previous year. In response, the city added five hundred teachers, began $22.8 million in school construction projects, and initiated a number of other programs to attempt to swallow the onslaught. But size wasn't the looming controversy with which Gillis had to deal. Boston was about to embark on its own war within its communities divided by race.

"The school department never differentiates between children," Gillis told the *Boston Globe*, just weeks before his retirement in 1963. "They are coming here to be taught. All are accepted on an equal basis and are treated as individuals regardless of race, color, or creed. They are entrusted to the public school system for an education."

Gillis's theory on how to integrate the schools could have led to a different outcome in terms of the city's forced-bussing debacle. Before the courts stepped in, Gillis had begun integrating schools at the kindergarten level, with the thought of growing integrated classes through the years. But all of Gillis's policies would be wiped out with the implementation of forced bussing. Gillis wrote, in the superintendent's annual report in 1963, "The public school, I believe, is the touchstone for the beginnings of a new generation for whom the words 'Emancipation Proclamation' will have full meaning—for a generation entitled to a way of life equal in every respect to the one enjoyed by their white brothers."

Gillis's advocacy for African American education wasn't exactly roundly applauded. At the same time Boston was suffering from racial growing pains, the school committee found itself locked in a battle with the NAACP over alleged segregation in the schools.

Gillis was set to retire from his post at the time the controversy started brewing, but he made it imminently clear that segregation, de facto or otherwise, should not exist in the Boston public school system. In the closing days of his tenure, he became increasingly concerned over the possible effects the controversy might have in the elementary grades.

"These young children are feeling the effects of this issue," he told the *Boston Globe* on Sept. 19, 1963, "which I assure you never existed nor ever will exist in the Boston schools."

For nearly a decade, the Boston School Committee lay dormant in addressing its racially imbalanced school system. In his June 1974 ruling, in Morgan v. Hennigan, Judge W. Arthur Garrity ordered the implementation of the Massachusetts State Board of Education's drastic "Master Plan," updated from the document originally written by Frederick Gillis, to achieve racial balance in public schools. The board of education's Master Plan required students from primarily white neighborhoods to be bussed to schools in

23

primarily black neighborhoods, and vice versa. Kids from all parts of the city who had never been on a school bus, having been able to walk to their neighborhood school, were now required to take designated busses to schools farther from home, where they were separated from familiar surroundings, teachers, and peers, in a misguided effort to integrate the schools.

Gillis, long since retired, sat on the sidelines of the debate in frustration. "He was anti-forced bussing," Dan said. His "open enrollment plan," as laid out in his original Master Plan, would have allowed families to send their children to any school in the city. "This option would have been much more palatable to the public and far less costly than forced bussing. But Garrity showed little interest. He gave the city only eleven weeks to prepare for the biggest social experiment in its history," Gillis said. Worse, six days after the court order, Garrity unabashedly admitted he had not read the Master Plan prior to ordering its implementation.

"My dad was against forced bussing," Marlen said. "And look what it did to the city. He was really stressed about it. He wanted it done gradually, over time."

On Sept. 12, 1974, the beginning of forced bussing was met with widespread protest, especially in South Boston's Irish-Catholic neighborhood. Hundreds of white demonstrators—children and their parents—pelted a caravan of twenty school busses carrying students from nearly all-black Roxbury to all-white South Boston. The police wore riot gear. Over the first week and a half of Boston's bussing, twenty-five people were injured, twenty-four assaulted, and seventy-two arrested. Twenty-seven busses in total were stoned in neighborhood protests.

Fred J. Gillis, Jr., Frederick's son, taught at South Boston High School in 1974, where he dealt with metal detectors and befriended teachers from Roxbury who were being threatened. Fred Jr.'s daughter, Cheryl (Gillis) Lane, began her career as a gym teacher at West Roxbury High School (Westie) in 1976 and worked there until the school closed in 2019. "The thing people forget is that, prior to bussing, kids rode public transportation or walked to their local school," she said. "My grandfather's plan would have continued to use public transportation rather than shipping kids all over the city. Boston didn't need school busses until forced bussing. But, for the most part, the kids from all across the city attending Westie got along. We were outside of the negative reactions my dad was witnessing in Southie."

Dan was only ten years old when bussing began, but even so, he felt the racial tensions in the Boston neighborhoods. In his own experience, riding the T and walking through those neighborhoods to the South Boston Yacht Club (SBYC) was a traumatizing game of hurdling over and through racial barriers. "Kids hanging on the corners would stop me and ask, 'Where do you hang? What corner do you hang on?' And press me on racial issues," Dan said.

Bob took the bus to the SBYC, and bystanders pelted the windows with rocks. It became apparent over the years that he and his people were very much outsiders in the South Boston neighborhood. He recalled, "One day, I'm at the yacht club when some local Southie kids said, 'There are two black kids at Carson Beach, we've got to run them off.' I'm like, why? It never struck me as an odd thing."

Growing up two miles from Dorchester, on the Mattapan line, instilled a level of fear in the Egan household; they were never really sure if an outburst from racial tensions would eventually reach their front door. "I knew the boundaries were blurred," Dan said, "and I knew that answering those aggressive questions I was getting was critical to my getting where I was going. So I became a survivor as a kid, surviving the family structure and then surviving the South Boston structure from a young age."

Photograph by Wade McKoy

Joe Powder lands on the peak and makes a few turns, power sliding towards the edge to judge time and distance before the next take off.

Dan power sliding towards the edge.

26

Chapter Three

GROWING UP EGAN

THE EGAN HOUSEHOLD IN WEST Roxbury was bursting at its seams. Robert and Marlen had so far welcomed six children into the world: Mary-Ellen, Bob, John, Daniel, and Sue, tragically losing Daniel Edward, born March 16, 1960, as an infant. On January 31, 1964, Robert and Marlen welcomed their sixth child, another Daniel, named in honor of both Marlen's brother and her son. The middle name, Russell, Marlen's mother's maiden name, was a subtle but powerful differentiator. Marlen would tell Dan, years later, that Russell was her favorite name. "I wanted to call you 'Russ,'" he remembered her saying in a rare moment of openness. Marlen told him, "My mother's family always stayed close, even after the prairie fire, and I always credited her character to both her Midwestern roots and the Monsieur's unyielding faith."

Despite never having met his brother or uncle, Dan said he's always felt a connection with them. "There's always been a sadness in me," he said. "I never knew where it came from. But after some intense work, I kind of identified the source of it. My mom never speaks about her twin and I'm the only one who ever counts Danny, the baby, as a family member. There were eight Egan kids, not seven." Marlen, as she had with her brother, suppressed her emotions over losing her child, but this did not stop her from bestowing the name to another child, even if the name Daniel did carry the burden of a legacy in the Gillis-Egan household.

Another Danny, a cousin who'd earned a full-ride scholarship as the goalie for the Boston College hockey team, died in a car crash after celebrating at Mary Ann's, a bar in the Cleveland Circle area that abuts the Chestnut Hill campus. In all, there are three "D"s next to Dannys on the Gillis family tree, two of whom had died in their early twenties. Dan never misunderstood the weight of this, nor did he ignore the fact that his own choices in life might influence or affect his mother. So it came as no surprise to Dan when, at the age of twenty-six, he was clinging to sanity and life in a snow cave on a mountainside in Russia.

The Egan Brothers' iconic scenes on film were a far cry from how John and Dan learned to ski. Whether under the watchful eye of their father, who chaperoned bus trips from the Boston area to New Hampshire's Mount Sunapee where they were members of the Blizzard Ski Club, or at home in West Roxbury, the brothers were irrepressible. They dragged snow from the Mobil station at the end of Richwood Street and piled it on a picnic table in the backyard for some shenanigans. They made frequent trips to North Conway, N.H., where they stayed at the Oxen Yoke Inn on Kearsarge Road while taking lessons at nearby Cranmore Mountain. After the family moved to Milton, in 1968, and purchased a fourteen-room, seven-bedroom home for $44,000, they began frequenting the nearby Blue Hills ski area, where Marlen and Robert had had some of their first dates.

There was a decided difference in each of the Egan children's edges. Some of those edges depended on where they'd spent the most time, growing up. Dan moved to Milton in kindergarten and has only slight memories of the home in West Roxbury. But that was where his older siblings, Mary-

Ellen, Bob, John, and Sue began defining themselves, in both hobbies and social interactions. For Bob and John, interests swayed toward the world of motorized minibikes and go-carts, one of which could hit sixty miles an hour. For Dan and his younger brothers, Ned and Mike, interests shifted once their roots grew in Milton. They were the "varsity crowd," as John put it—more focused on competitive team sports in the community and in school than their older brothers, who were racing various wheeled vehicles down the streets of West Roxbury and Dorchester—neighborhoods the family had left behind. They'd built many of their best childhood memories there, before moving to Milton, which was a tamer (aka, boring) place to live, according to John.

"The years in Milton were spent leaving Milton to be with my buddies from West Roxbury and Dorchester," he said. "The kids we hung out with in Milton . . . we didn't do the sports. We had race cars, and go-carts, and motorcycles. We didn't give a shit about what was going on in what we considered a suburban hell." Drugs, alcohol, cars, speed, overdoses—all played a part in John's upbringing and took a toll on his high school class, which counted six deaths during their junior year's April vacation, including an accident at the Lower Falls of the Neponset River, where John and his buddies liked to spend time.

The diverse group of friends from Boston and Dorchester were known to hang out on the trolley trucks at Lower Mills District, bordering Dorchester and Milton, and would catch rides to Lower Falls on the electric trolley cars of the Ashmont extension Mattapan trolley. They would hang off the back and disengage the electrical connection to make it stop at their will. At some point, someone decided it would be fun to try shooting the rapids at Lower Falls. Until one of them was killed doing so.

"I know my family was pretty worried," John said. "I had buddies who got killed, some while I was playing with them. I always felt pretty comfortable in the range [of danger] where we were playing, but I don't know if I ever paid much attention."

The Egan's driveway in Milton was wide and flat behind the house, where street hockey and basketball games were played. The driveway continued around the house and down the steep hill, where jumps were built for skiing and Snurfing. At the bottom of the hill, where the driveway met the gravel lane, go-carters and bikers would fishtail in a U-turn and zoom back up the driveway.

When Dan turned twelve, John gave him his "wicked loud" go-cart with the McCulloch chainsaw engine, which he'd outgrown. When the brothers outgrew the confines of the driveway, and John and Bob had licenses, they'd drive out to Wood Road, an undeveloped two mile strip that was perfect for bikes and go-carts. Adjacent to a main highway, it was an easy scene for lots of kids to get to, and John knew everyone.

"I was always bumping into other kids doing the same sorts of things in different towns," Dan said. But it was difficult for Dan to comprehend the energy it took to lead a lifestyle like John's. "I didn't expect John to live past twenty," he recalled. "I just didn't. I thought he was too nuts, so I always assumed he just wouldn't. Even once we started skiing, that was always on my mind."

It was with Bob, his older brother by eight years, that Dan found more connection than with John. Their bond stemmed from their father's passion for sailing. Robert was a longtime member of the SBYC, and Dan remembers being about five years old, walking the streets of Southie— from Broadway Station to L Street—to go sailing with Bob, and to attend the SBYC's junior sailing program. Racial tensions were high for students and parents on all sides, from the bitterness and unrest of being forced to attend schools outside their own neighborhoods. Walking those streets was hostile situation, and Dan was frightened.

"He loved the South Boston Yacht Club," Dan said of his father, who'd grown up in the Quincy neighborhood of Squantum and learned to sail off Wollaston Beach, which was about seven miles from the SBYC, which is still located on Columbia Road. Robert was a member of the first sailing team at Boston College, in 1950. Sailing was part of his daily life. Being a member of SBYC made sense to him, because it was close by. He could get a Wednesday afternoon off from Milton Hospital and be soon on his boat—a wooden Herreshoff 12.5 sailboat named "Imp II" (for impulse)—a proximity Robert cherished, even over the option of one of the Bay State's more notable ports. As a kid, Dan wondered why Dad didn't choose a nicer marina. Dad wanted proximity.

Life as a neurologist was time-consuming for Robert, and often left Marlen busy picking up the many pieces of their family life. He cherished his family, but was dedicated to practicing medicine, something the Egan children seemed to understand when their father couldn't make it to a baseball game or wasn't able to take his sons to soccer practice.

"When I talked to patients and colleagues of his, he was well-respected in what he did," Bob said. But when he was with his family, Robert's aura took on another dimension, particularly on the boat. "If you were part of the sailing team, you had a really good relationship with him, because you got your time together on the boat. It didn't seem like he was that absent. He taught us all responsibility and dedication to work, and when he chartered boats, he was a different individual. You could see that side of him. It just didn't come out all the time. He was just a different guy on the boat. The conservative doctor would go away. I think he did a lot of things as a youth on his boats that lined up with what Dan and I did as youths. Unless you sailed with him, you never really got a chance to see it."

Dan recalled racing the "110," a double-ended, long, narrow sailboat class popular in racing during Quincy Bay Race Week, while he was in high school, with his dad as crew. "We were racing off of Wollaston Beach, where Dad grew up," Dan said, "in a south-westerly breeze building to twenty knots with lots of waves. A line had gotten tangled on the bow and was collapsing the spinnaker, so Dad had to crawl out to the bow to untangle it. It was urgent, but while he was clinging on for dear life, I heard howling laughter. I thought, 'Wow my dad is loving this. Is he crazy? Maybe this is where I get it from?' I'd never seen that side of him before."

Aside from accompanying their father, the boys made frequent use of the yacht club. The Egans' home in Milton was right on the Ashmont extension of Boston's public transportation system, so they could easily take the MBTA train to Southie, long before any of them were licensed to drive. Bob and Dan spent summers there, five days a week, instead of going to summer camp. Robert encouraged his sons' enthusiasm for sailing. When Bob turned twelve, his father bought him his own sailboat for $600—a wooden 110, dubbed "Top Hat II," with the sail number 144. The boat gave Bob and Dan their own access to sailing, in addition to SBYC's lineup through the junior sailing program.

"Robert said Bob couldn't have a bike. It was too dangerous. But he bought him a boat," Marlen said.

The 110 was the prevalent racing boat at the time, and while Robert might consider a bicycle more of a danger than an open-sea vessel, that caution was based on how he'd grown up, sailing at Wollaston Beach. Robert, legally blind in one eye, never rode a bike or played organized sports. He was a shy boy with glasses, smart and confident who, at the age of twelve, convinced his father to buy him a small, wooden boat. His first vessel was a Snipe he named "Top Hat." Occasionally, Robert would recall for his boys how he'd won the prestigious Pleon Youth Sailing Championships in Marblehead, on D-Day, 1946. Following the award ceremony, he hopped in his fifteen-and-a-half-foot dingy to sail back home to Squantum Yacht Club in Quincy. After racing all day, winning the championship, and sailing home, navigating through twenty miles of island breaks, rocks, and shifting tides in the dark—in a dingy!—Robert arrived with trophy in hand to find his father pacing up and down the beach, not knowing where Robert had been. "That was over twenty nautical miles in a small, open cockpit dingy—and he did it at sixteen years old. At night," Dan said with a burst of admiration.

Robert began sailing with his son Bob when the boy was only two years old. By the time he was twelve, clearly in the thrall to his father's experience, Bob was sailing from South Boston all the way down to Hull, a ride that took a good couple hours. He often took his sailboat out on the open sea before coming home for dinner.

"If I let my kids take a boat across Boston Harbor at twelve these days,

I'd get arrested," Bob said. By the time Dan was seven, he was already sailing up and down Boston Harbor, and he and Bob raced 110s in Atlantic Coast Conference championships. When Dan turned nine, Bob dragged him to regattas up and down the Massachusetts and Rhode Island coasts.

"Sailing meant I could be with my dad and my older brother, as well as make my own way out of the house," Dan said. "I learned how to be a pretty good sailor, despite all the chaos in Southie."

That chaos, stemming from the bussing period, provided an edge to everything, something he noticed having an effect on Bob from time to time. "I witnessed, as a young boy, Southie kids picking on Bob. They were not his chums. They accepted him all right, but there was an edge to it. Bob was a little kinder and less aggressive than me, so when they picked on me, I would fight those fights," Dan said. "I could beat those kids in sailboat races, but not too often on land. They were tough. I was a wiseass, and that often led my getting chucked off the sea wall or pushed off the dock into the water. But I didn't care.

"One time, my sister Sue was at the yacht club and we went out on the boat. I won the race, and the Southie kids threatened me. So, as I sailed by, I spit at them. We got back to the dock and we fought. They picked me up and threw me over the sea wall. While they were doing that, my sister was like, 'Hey, stop.' I said, 'No it's fine. This is what we do.' It was like we all knew the rules and our roles, so it wasn't necessarily mean or malicious. We were kids and we were all struggling to be who we were, how and where we belonged. I didn't feel like I was abused or picked on. I felt like they were sort of friendly to me, but there were limits to our friendship. And I was different. They didn't really want to win a sailboat race. I did."

The pursuit of sailing brought a different kind of experience into the Milton household, which the rest of the children didn't necessarily care about. "Skiing was something the whole family liked to do," Marlen said. "We didn't all like to sail." Ned, two years younger than Dan, never connected to the sailing experience. Instead, he preferred playing baseball at Eliot Park. John and Sue only occasionally sailed, Mary-Ellen hated it, and Mike was too young to get hooked. Marlen used to help clean the boats, but never discovered the same passion for sailing that her husband and Dan knew. She understood how intense Robert's practice as a neurologist was, and how sailing gave him incomparable release from it. Marlen's strategy was to get all her family members out of the house doing *something*, especially on Saturdays. After spending the first twenty years of their marriage raising children, Marlen found herself with some free time—Saturday mornings alone at home became hers to cherish.

"There was a sense of belonging, to be in this family where you skied on Saturday because Mom needed the day off," Dan said. "She wasn't going to take you to play basketball. She wasn't going to take you to play hockey. You joined the ski club, and you went away. All day. And Dad went, too. That sense of belonging stayed with us, too. Like being in the lodge at Mount Sunapee, brown-bagging lunch and pulling out the bulky-roll sandwich Mom made you and wrapped up with your name on it, so every kid got the right one. You felt like you belonged."

Sailing did give Dan pleasure, but it also left him torn between two worlds. "Looking up to my older brothers, Bob always took me sailing and it was all good. John was out doing his own thing with his group of kids. If I wanted to hang with John's group, I had to become something like them. When we were riding our bikes and kicking trash barrels over, I always felt like Dr. Jekyll and Mr. Hyde. I didn't know if I should be the tough kid or the nice kid."

As Dan puts it, the sixties had a purpose, the seventies had none, and the eighties gave the world a lost generation. "The '60s, of course, were about rebelling, the '70s kids were about music and drugs, but the '80s kids—we didn't have either," he said. "We had shitty music and we didn't know what to do with the drugs. We didn't have a cause and we didn't belong. We saw the end of disco music and eventually the birth of punk rock. We were a really funny generation from that point of view.

"I remember when I won a disco contest in eighth grade. John came into my room and I was playing the album I'd won. He said, 'We don't listen to fucking disco in this house.' And he threw it out the third-floor window like a frisbee. He was pissed. And I was like, 'Oh—I don't fit.' I'd thought I was cool. This was my music, but it was rejected by my brother. There was always that sort of thing. I think those generational events are telling about where we went."

Dan turned sixteen in 1980. He and Bob took part in the Marion-to-Bermuda sailing race, a biennial offshore event from southeastern Massachusetts to Bermuda, a distance of 645 nautical miles. Along with two high school friends, they experienced what would be hailed as the worst storm in the history of the race. One boat sank, leaving the crew waiting eighteen hours in a life raft before being rescued. "We sailed through a huge storm that night," Dan said. "At 3 a.m., I'm at watch, driving the boat up the biggest wave I'd ever seen. I was freaked out and didn't roll the boat down the backside of the wave properly. I dropped that thirty-seven-foot boat into the trough. It woke Jack, my dad's friend and the owner of the boat. Jack was a yeller. He came on deck, looking to rip my head off."

Once in Bermuda, Jack wanted to gauge Dan's feelings. "How'd you like that trip?" he asked. Dan's answer surprised him. He'd loved it. Everything about it. "You loved it?" Jack asked. "You looked miserable most of the time."

"That's how I know I loved it," Dan replied. "That was the essence of loving it for me. It was what I was willing to put myself through. I was willing to sacrifice and suffer to reach the end goal of the achievement."

Chapter Four

EAST COAST CONNECTIONS

IT DIDN'T TAKE LONG AFTER moving to Milton for the Egan household to gain a neighborhood reputation for being the place to hang out. The home garnered the nickname "The Milton Hilton," as the go-to place for family gatherings, neighborhood street hockey, and Wiffle ball games. It was a jungle gym of go-carts, boats, a climbing rope, and trails from the backyard through the woods. There were constant activities for kids of all ages.

"I was five when we moved to Milton," Dan said. "Ned was three, Sue was seven, John was eleven, Bob was thirteen, and Mary-Ellen was fourteen. Mike was born in 1970, after we'd moved, so that set the family dynamics for the older three, the younger three, and then Mike. For Mike, Ned, Sue, and myself, our perspective was Milton. The older kids had left friends behind and were becoming teenagers in a new town."

Ned and Dan didn't have to go far to find friends in a neighborhood loaded with families, many boasting children around their ages. "We had enough for street hockey, baseball, and football teams," Dan said. "When these kids came to our house, they were fascinated by what our older brothers were doing with boats, minibikes, go-carts, and eventually hot rods."

Dan and Ned's crew would go to Eliot Park, the local ballfield, where they'd stay all day; the only unbreakable rule was to be home before dark. It was an independence Robert and Marlen encouraged in their children, born from their acknowledged inability to simultaneously manage all their children's lives. In Milton, the Egans could walk to church, school, and the playground. This forced them to grow up a bit on their own, Marlen lamented, yet her respect and admiration for her children remains, even today.

"All of us had chores," Dan said. "Mom was very organized. She made a chart with each of our names on it, and every week the chart assigned us a different chore. One week would be loading the dishwasher, one week sweeping floors and stairs, one setting the table. And there was no debate, just major consequences if you didn't do it."

Marlen, having grown up with all brothers in a strict household, instinctively knew how to manage her own. "She did more laundry than I can ever imagine," Dan said. "Our socks, underwear, shirts, and pants were all labeled per child, folded, placed in our individual plastic bins, and left on the stairs in the birth order of the family. Plus, each week we worked for Grandpa Gillis: painting the house, working in the garden, trimming hedges, cutting grass, restacking the woodpile, weeding and staining the decks with creosote."

Marlen was the boss and everyone in the Egan family knew it. But even the normally stoic Marlen had a boiling point. "More than a few times, we pushed Mom to the edge," Dan said, "and in those moments, when that happened and she set us straight, there was the realization that without her we would all be lost."

"We didn't have instructions on parenting," Marlen said. "We just had what we grew up with. Each of the children gave us a little bit of a challenge here and there, but I would always stick to my guns."

The constant activity might have been seen by outsiders as chaos, but to the Egans, it was the normal they grew up with. When Bob's future wife, Jackie, dropped by for the first time, she witnessed the free-for-all that was the Egan dinner table. It made her want to crawl under the table and hide, while Robert sat watching her with a grin on his face.

The big backyard was ideal for storing boats during the off-season; the driveway was perfect for the go-cart and big enough for street hockey, basketball, and baseball games, which resulted in a lot of broken windows. In the winter, the boys would take the keel off Bob's boat (which weighed about three hundred pounds) to carry the vessel into the basement for refurbishment. Bob sanded the boat in preparation for painting, while Dan observed, and John collected the fiberglass dust as it fell to the floor. John was not simply tidying up; he intended to package it for sale as itching powder, at school.

The basement workshop was also where Robert displayed his famously meticulous approach to everything he worked on. His insistence on prep work before painting laid the groundwork for Mike's future work as a painter, just as Grandpa Gillis's instructional rounds on building treehouses led John to working in carpentry. It was a level of detail essential for a neurologist, but also instilled a sense of personal responsibility in his children. There was a bond of teamwork and community in the Egan home and its somewhat controlled chaos that helped define the many avenues of life emerging from its doorstep.

Robert loved gathering the family together. Often, after a Sunday dinner, they'd watch one of his 35-millimeter slide shows of skiing, sailing, or a recent trip. "Dad loved having an order to things, so they were coordinated with Mom, right down to carving the Thanksgiving turkey," Dan said. "For Dad, there was pleasure in the fanfare, and even more pleasure in seeing things done correctly."

Robert's allegiance to his core beliefs never wavered, and was even evident during the priest sexual abuse scandal that rocked the Boston archdiocese in the early 2000s. The scandal challenged Dan's faith in the Catholic Church, but not his father's. Dan fumed as his father put money in the collection basket, unsure of what deviousness the money was funding. "My dad and I had many heated conversations over the years, which he would slowly and insistently bring back to faith," Dan said. "He would tell me, 'The Church has created over two thousand years of unwavering faith. You can disagree with certain things, but you can't deny the power of its faith through the years. You are a product of the Church. The world needs an unchanging and unyielding voice of morality.'" The refrain was always the same. *It's the church, Danny, it's the church.* "To experience that blind faith was unbelievable," Dan said. "Even when he had Alzheimer's, if I asked him if he wanted to pray or say a rosary, he would immediately perk up."

The challenges in the family also stemmed from the wide variety of individuals with contrasting tastes and traits. Whereas Sue admits she was shy, it was hardly a characteristic she shared with her siblings, particularly Dan, whose gregarious nature was evident at an early age. In fact, after his first day in third grade, Dan reported to his parents at dinner that he'd had to spend some time in the hallway after his teacher grew exasperated with his constant chattering. "You know, you can't talk in the third grade," he told them.

So, while a certain level of passion pervaded in both skiing and sailing, activities that gave the Egans a sense of familial bonding as well as varying degrees of individual success, other sports and activities were not of lasting interest. For example, while Bob was a successful wrestler at Milton High School, the sport never really caught on for Dan. "I can tell you how many lights there are on every gym's ceiling in the whole Bay State League, because I was getting pinned so often," Dan said, recalling his fleeting days as a middle school wrestler.

Dan and Ned were not only Alpine downhill skiers, they were compelled toward Nordic cross-country racing, which Dan calls the "hardest sport I ever did." Nevertheless, Dan became a two-time skimeister (a skier with the best combined performance in Alpine and Nordic) in the Bay State League. Even when he didn't win, competing in Nordic resulted in some of his finest acts of sportsmanship. One instance was a cross-country race for Milton High, in which he was "doing pretty well," according to his mother. During the race, Dan noticed a competitor from one of the Newton schools taking a wrong turn. Instead of reveling in a competitor's error, Dan called him over and pointed out the correct route.

"The kid beat him," Marlen said, "but Dan was that thoughtful of others." Dan's brand of camaraderie across competitive lines helped form long-lasting bonds. While at Milton High, Dan became embroiled in a rivalry with a racer from Newton North High, named Henry Schniewind, who was considered a "proper ski racer," unlike Dan who was thought of as a rather unconventional, risk-taking skier. Henry became Dan's main competition on the Massachusetts slopes. Henry had spent a few years attending and racing for the Green Mountain Valley School, in Waitsfield, Vermont, where he and his team trained at nearby Sugarbush Ski Resort. Schniewind had raced on the Eastern USSA circuit; at the Eastern Massachusetts State Ski League competition, he was the man to beat.

Egan and Schniewind traded jabs in the form of speed, swapping victories from week to week. They became rivals way before they became friends, but by the late '80s, these two ski racers, respectively from Blue Hills and Prospect Hill became lifelong friends as their ski careers intersected.

With a degree in geology, Henry moved to France where he became an internationally renowned avalanche expert and off-piste ski guide. Today, Schniewind runs Henry's Avalanche Talk, a company that raises awareness of avalanche safety for skiers and riders. Based in Val d'Isère, France, Henry has drawn Dan to this powder paradise every April, where he hosts a variety of his own camps and clinics. "I think it's amazing how two Boston kids whose roots go back to racing against each other in high school have gone on to make a living in the ski industry," Dan said.

Schniewind made waves as soon as he arrived in the French ski world, when he earned a fully certified French Ski Instructor Degree from the Ecole Nationale de Ski et d'Alpinisme (ENSA). Henry passed the ENSA exams in 1993, the first American to obtain the modern-day French "Alpine

Skiing – Educateur Sportif" degree—an unheard-of accomplishment before this Boston kid showed up. "I'm sure, even today, he'd beat me in a ski race," Dan said. "I wouldn't let him know that, but . . ."

The Milton High ski team was born when John, Bob, and a teacher named Paul Ajemian, put it together. Their interest wasn't competitive angst-building, they just wanted to ski more and forming the school team allowed them to ski twice a week at Blue Hills, which was devoid of many luxuries. Participants rarely skied gates and team members were usually off in the woods, trying to ski down to Chickatawbut Road, in the opposite direction from the ski area's base. In its early years, the Milton High ski team wasn't exactly a force to be reckoned with. "I don't think we had more than two or three races the whole time Bob and I were there," John said.

For Ajemian, the club was a way to promote the sport of skiing, not necessarily racing, which started out haphazardly. "Now, it's all about racing," he said. "I don't think any of the boys or girls belonged to a mountain with ski races on a regular basis. Now, for all the successful schools, the majority of their kids are racing up north every single weekend."

Dan was in the eighth grade when John, a junior at Milton High, asked Ajemian if his little brother could race with the team, just to get some practice. Ajemian quickly recognized the talent and skiing insights Dan possessed, an apple not falling far from his supportive older brother's tree. By the time Dan officially joined the Milton High ski team, it had become more organized. The Massachusetts Bay League was in its infancy, with only six teams to its name, but Milton quickly became league champs. At one point, Dan ranked as high as third in the state.

"Milton always seemed to do pretty well," said Ajemian, who required the team to participate in cross-country, in addition to slalom.

Bob Egan helped outfit the team with XC equipment: boots, bindings, and skis. After graduating from Norwich University in 1978, Bob landed a job with Ski Market, hitting it off with the manager in Braintree. He'd landed in the hot spot of the emerging competitive skiing landscape in the '80s—a dream come true for a college graduate. Case in point: Bob was working at

Ski Market at Five Corners in Braintree, only a stone's throw from its direct competition, Ski Town on Wood Road, and Herman's Sporting Goods in the popular South Shore Plaza shopping center.

"It was a very competitive time for ski shops," Dan said. "It was the boom years, really. Ski shops in metropolitan areas were popular then. People were buying their first pairs of skis and boots. The industry was going upscale with snowmaking, lifts, and grooming. It was really the infancy of what we know today as the ski industry, but it demonstrated the maturity of the ski product companies, in terms of how they were handling their sales clinics."

Ski Market would become a New England landmark. Starting as a franchise in Wellesley, Massachusetts, when owner Bob Ferguson opened St. Moritz Sports in 1958, its empire spread to twenty-one stores throughout the region by 1988. After thirteen years in business, Ferguson partnered with Tom Richardson to open the first Ski Market, on Commonwealth Avenue in Boston. Ski Market fulfilled the growing market's need for a discount ski shop. In 1971, the only places to buy ski equipment were high-end, expensive specialty shops. To diversify, Ski Market's owners added bikes to their product line to capitalize on the sleek, lightweight ten-speed craze.

Most important to Dan, Bob's new job gave him another venue where he could hang out with his oldest brother, who he'd desperately missed when he was away at college. "Bob was probably my best friend, as a kid," Dan said. "Then he went off to Norwich University in Vermont, and I really missed him."

As the oldest male among the Egan children, a lot of the responsibility to take care of the younger siblings fell into Bob's lap. He was often called upon to take his younger siblings to practice or host a Cub Scout meeting, at which he would inevitably find himself building pinewood derby cars. Later in life, he impressed his wife and her parents with his ability to easily change their first-born child's diaper. Nothing to it, he figured; he'd been doing it since he was eleven years old.

Among Bob's more memorable tutoring jobs was teaching Dan to drive, perhaps a bit too early. When Marlen remarked a few years later how well

Danny had picked it up, even before getting his license, Bob said, "That's because I've been letting him drive me to and from Vermont since he was thirteen."

"The way they let us run and experiment with our lives, as long as we weren't getting in trouble, and supporting us the whole way, I think really grew independence and our own style in each of us," said Bob.

Bob's willingness to chip in was something John seemed to shy away from. "He was a challenging young man, kind of stuck in between the family structure and making his own life choices," said Bob, who was often called upon to mediate disagreements and differing points of view between his brother and parents. So when Bob left for Norwich, so too did that buffer between the entities, creating some rough waves that rocked the stability of the household. Dan recalls John's teenage years as a chaotic period of fighting in the household. "It was not a pleasant place to be," Dan said. "My other siblings were trying to protect us from that. Bob was eighteen and out of the house; Mary-Ellen, the oldest, was in nursing school at Boston College. She lived in and out of the house, and eventually got kind of tired of being 'the Mom.' Sue, she was squeezed in between John and me, and was very mild. For her, it was kind of like hiding."

Dan was less about hiding than he was trying to get John to notice his worth and his contribution. He wanted validation. "I think wanting that approval was a driving force for me," he said.

After finishing high school, John bolted for Vermont, settling fifteen miles away from his older brother. "I was at Norwich and John was at Sugarbush," Bob said. "He wanted to do things on his own and I think it's a testament to his character. John could've had whatever support he asked for, but he never asked for it. He just went ahead and did for himself."

"As a teenager, I visited John during his early days at Sugarbush," Dan recalls. "It was a world I'd never seen. His group of ski buddies was a wide range of strong individuals, and their love of skiing was like nothing I'd ever experienced before. First of all, they skied every day, in all conditions, top to bottom with no stops. The energy was contagious and complemented by their personalities and looks. They skied in jean jackets, sweaters, ripped-up ski parkas, scarves, wool hats, and stretch pants. Their equipment was beat up, their skis long, and their bindings were cranked to the max so as not to release. I could barely keep up. Some runs, I'd crash in the tight trees and get so tangled up, someone would have to pull me up and out and dust me off. Other times, I'd come around a corner and just watch them rip the icy bumps in complete awe. I came home from that trip with a changing perspective on life and what could be possible."

During those times, Dan's skiing partner wasn't John as often as Bob. "Dan had the ability to think and act and portray himself as much older than he was, so he fit in with my whole crowd just fine," Bob said. "We had a junior ski patrol program at Norwich, so people were used to seeing younger kids hang out with the ski patrol."

During visits north, Dan became an honorary member of that ski patrol. "When Bob started on ski patrol at Norwich, he would come home for Christmas but go back on Christmas night to run ski patrol the next morning . . . and he would take me with him," Dan said. "Even though John was at Sugarbush at the same time, we never saw him. My parents thought it was better for me to be with Bob."

In all, Bob spent seven years with Ski Market, working his way up to running the store. That gave the Egans access to the winter sport, as well as an introduction to summertime recreations, since the outlet also sold bikes and windsurfing gear. Dan hung around the shop from the time he was in his early teens, absorbing how everything worked years before landing a job in the repair shop.

"I did my ninth-grade project on how to make skis, and had great resourcing to do that," Dan said. "Ski Market was a place to gather information, a place for me to explore everything about the industry. It was where I learned how to mount bindings, tune skis, and fix boots. I got to attend all the on-snow demos and test-ski different products. I would snap into an Olin 185 cm ski on the left and a Dynastar 207 cm race ski on the right, and go ski. I learned that I could ski on anything. My skills were progressing to the point where I was, like, give me anything and I can make it work. And I was always around knowledgeable older people and skiers."

Ski Market turned out to be an invaluable place for Dan to learn customer service. He started working in the shop, eventually making his way to the floor, then began marketing tune-ups, explaining the process to customers. Eventually, they let him sell skis. "I did everything but run cash registers," he said. It was the first time he actually felt like he could act and think as an authority on skiing. "If I knew something the consumer didn't, I would explain it," he said. "And I had the confidence, backing, and authenticity of the store to do that."

He learned the retail side of the skiing business, how to host product clinics, and how to create marketing plans. More importantly, Dan got to meet and deal with upper management. He got to know the Fergusons, and once Mike Bisner started as the store manager at St. Moritz in Wellesley, he got to know him, too. Bisner eventually made it all the way to Ski Market's front office before moving on to a notable skiing career of his own, as well as becoming marketing chief for Salomon and president of Head Skis North America. It was the Ski Market connection that would determine how far Dan's own unique skiing career would go.

"I think Dan started working for me even before he had working papers," Bisner said. Bisner's first encounter with Dan and John came one Sunday, when Ski Market employees would load skiers on busses to head up north to the ski mountains. This was during the time of Massachusetts's blue laws, when retail businesses were prohibited from opening their doors on Sundays. "Bob would bring these two little brothers of his, who would kick our ass," Bisner said. "They were young, energetic athletes."

During those Sunday ventures, Dan was constantly breaking his junior skis. *Constantly.* "On his third pair, I said, 'Just take mine and go race,'" Bob said. "He could just shatter a pair of skis because he needed the stiffness and the strength of an adult ski, even though he was a junior. It all kind of picked up for Dan from there."

The Ski Market network would become really important as Dan's career moved forward. "As I'm working at Ski Market, John is becoming a sponsored athlete," Dan said. "Rossignol is coming through and giving John skis, because he's on the pro mogul tour. They know one brother runs the shop while the other has a work apron on and is tuning the skis in the back. But I was developing a lot of connections all the time. My biggest takeaway, in hindsight, is that even as a teenager I had a voice in the sport. It was on a really small level, but I think it contributed to my confidence and what I'm doing today with my presentations, whenever I speak about the sport.

"By the time we made our first movie, all those Ski Market VPs had become marketing directors, sales reps, and bigwigs at Smith, Head, and Volkl, so they knew us and eventually sponsored us. That blew it open. John and I were the hometown kids who'd made good. We had the blessing of the New England ski industry, and were knighted."

Meanwhile, the seeds of the extreme skiing scene, which would become the central defining characteristic of John and Dan's world, were just beginning to grow across the country from films being made in Squaw Valley, California. It was a new way to consume and enjoy skiing, and it was destined for The Egan Brothers.

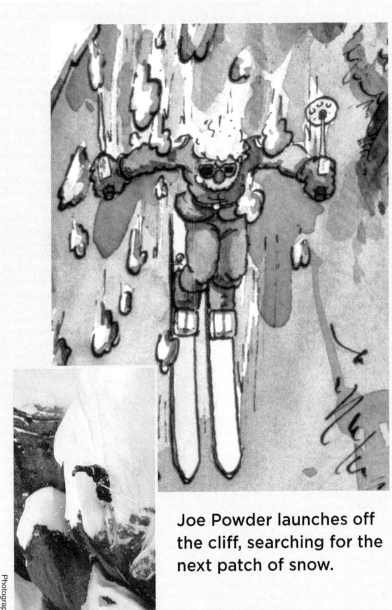

Joe Powder launches off the cliff, searching for the next patch of snow.

Dan jumps into the famed Corbet's Couloir for *North Face's Skiing Extreme II*.

Chapter Five

EXTREME DEBATE

IN THE FALL OF 1988, Dan wanted to sell the newly released film, *Skiing Extreme I,* featuring The North Face Extreme Team, of which Dan and John were members. Walter Driscoll, the accessories buyer at Ski Market, had purchased a case of movies for the retail chain and encouraged Dan to call Bernie Weichsel, owner of BEWI Production, who ran the Boston Ski Show.

Weichsel, a self-proclaimed ski bum who is outgoing and accommodating, and an attraction in his own right, was a U.S. Ski and Snowboard Hall of Fame inductee who shared the stage in Stowe with the Egans in 2017. Weichsel played a central figure in promoting the hotdog movement, beginning with giving the hotdoggers their own forum at ski shows. He'd already realized that this "extreme thing" could be the next wave.

"Walter told me to call Bernie and arrange getting a booth at the Boston Ski Show, so I did," said Dan. "I had never met him, but he answered the phone and spoke to me. By the time I got off the phone, I had a booth and a movie theater at all of his shows up and down the East Coast. He just plugged me right in—said if the retailers exhibiting at the shows were buying this film, then I should be showing it in his theater."

BEWI Productions scheduled ski and snowboard expos that ran annually in Boston, Denver, Seattle, Baltimore, Philadelphia, and New York for almost forty years before selling the properties to Snowsports Industries America in late 2019. Bernie's wildly successful expositions always included exhibits, demonstrations, and equipment sales, and, most important of all, served to generate early-season excitement among skiers and snowboarders, accelerating their interest, purchases, and plans for the impending winter season. Some forty thousand people attend the expo in Boston each year looking to gather information, appraise new gear and clothing, buy season pass lift tickets, or just enjoy the entertainment.

In 1974, Weichsel was hired to run the International Freestyle Skiers Association tour, the first organized professional competitive circuit. He was only twenty-six years old. Extreme skiing could be said to have come from freestyle, with an inherent simplicity in its manifesto to ski where no one had ever skied before, away from the lift lines, groomers, and boundaries that impede the challenge and promise of limitless freedom. Extreme skiing arrived in America at the time ski racing was the proverbial king of the hill—but it had a problem.

"I grew up watching freestyle," recalls Dan. "Wayne Wong at Waterville Valley, hanging with the freestyle kids. The racing crowd was just so uptight and unfriendly, but the freestylers were the opposite."

What freestyle had in common with extreme skiing was its departure from a predictable form of expression. In fact, racing's rather militaristic demand on mimicking form voided expression, thereby opening up massive opportunity to ski freely and imaginatively in the pristine backcountry, as if it were a blank canvas waiting for the artist to transform it with color, texture, shape.

Of course, there's another, more simplistic definition of extreme skiing that warns skiers traversing the most treacherous terrain in the world: *You fall. You die.* This terse definition isn't necessarily accurate, according to Kristen Ulmer, a native of New Hampshire who starred in some twenty ski movies and is, perhaps, the most notable female extreme skier in the industry. Kristin was inducted into the U.S. Ski and Snowboard Hall of Fame in the Class of 2018. She says, in reference to the "extreme" skiing that became popular with viewing audiences, "The word 'extreme' means that the consequence of failure is death. Jumping off a cliff doesn't necessarily mean you're risking your life. Some people would argue that . . . but when I think of extreme skiing, I think of 'you fall, you die.' But those kinds of runs are not often filmed. They're really slow and meticulous and oftentimes we climb the mountains before we ski them. I don't know, necessarily, if that's what we're seeing in the films."

In reality, extreme or big-mountain skiers have been hiking into the backcountry to ski for decades. In New Hampshire, the headwall of Mount Washington's Tuckerman Ravine has long stood as the Northeast's ultimate challenge for having the fiercest weather conditions and most dangerous skiable terrain of any mountain range in the region. Skiing Tuckerman's headwall is as close to extreme skiing as the advanced skier may want to get. Given that it has claimed over twenty-five skiers' lives, it may in fact live up to "you fall, you die."

Perhaps it's no surprise, then, that some of the country's top extreme skiers of the '80s and '90s hailed from New England, where extreme technical skill combines with an ability to handle the extreme elements to forge skiers who might give even the most seasoned skiers out West reason for pause. Names like Doug Coombs, Chris Davenport, Ulmer, the DesLauriers brothers, and the Egan brothers would come to join left-coasters such as Glen Plake and Scot Schmidt in defining the extreme scene, which was driven more by marketing and sponsorship than any "you fall, you die" incidents.

The Western style would be the sort of extreme skiing credited to European skiers, such as Sylvain Saudan, Jean-Marc Boivin, and Patrick Vallençant. The "real" thing, according to the European mountaineers, was born from dangerous landscapes, like that of Chamonix, France, where extremists had to climb and conquer rugged mountainscapes before skiing down them. The American version was more brash. As Peter Oliver summed it up in his *Skiing* magazine article, "Extreme Explained," published in 1990, the "born-in-the-USA" edition of extreme consisted more of selling posters and movies, not to mention skis, clothing, and hairstyles.

"It's not exactly extreme skiing—it's just good for pictures," said Eric Charamel, a leading mountaineer in Chamonix and one of the guides on the Degré7 Elbrus trip in 1990. "People here in Chamonix don't have a lot of interest in it."

Maybe. But, as Oliver wrote, "the French always have a way of getting touchy when Americans reinvent their inventions, or at least rebrand them into something perhaps more appealing to the masses."

Case in point: Saudan, Boivin, and Vallençant weren't exactly household names in thrill-seeking America, where films starring brightly colored daredevils, like the Egans, Schmidt, and Plake, took center stage in the extreme milieu.

"Everybody always wanted to say that extreme skiing was 'you fall, you die'," Dan said. "I don't think it ever was true. Yet, I preached it, of course, as a marketing thing. But really, what we were doing was cliff jumping. We skied a lot of radical stuff, for sure, but compared to Vallençant and Jean-Marc Boivin and the early days of what they were skiing in Europe, it really wasn't the same. Extreme skiing in America was a marketing event featuring great skiers."

So, while there may not be one godfather of extreme skiing, East Coasters often point to the extraordinary skiing of Brooks Dodge, a native of North Conway, N.H., who clocked at least a dozen first descents in Tuckerman Ravine. Dodge competed in the 1952 and 1956 Olympics (he finished fourth in slalom at Cortina, Italy, in '56), but he's best known in New Hampshire. By the 1950s he'd already established skiable routes in Tuckerman Ravine, such as Duchess, Sluice, Cathedral, Icefall, and one that came to be known as Dodge's Drop.

"I set out to devise a different approach to skiing there," Dodge told *Sports Afield* magazine in a 1999 interview, explaining his technique for tackling the ravine, which involved quick, two-pole turns at tight spots on the run. It's a common technique in today's skiing, but was unheard-of back in the 1940s. It was a new way to descend the mountain, and it hooked Dodge with its possibilities. When he began skiing Tuckerman Ravine in the '30s, there were seven established routes. Dodge added twelve more.

Saudan and other Europeans made their names similarly in the more intense mountains of the Alps. It was 1967 when rumors started to circulate around Chamonix, that somebody had attempted—and had prevailed—in a descent on the Spencer Couloir, a treacherous, fifty-five-degree section on the Aiguille de Blaitière. Local guides thought the story foolhardy, particularly since they considered it an impossible stretch to ski without falling to your death. Nevertheless, photos taken from the air captured the confirming set of tracks. Saudan was immediately nicknamed *"Le Skieur de l'Impossible."*

Much as Dodge had done in Tuckerman Ravine, Saudan also developed a new technique in order to conserve his energy and stop himself from accelerating too quickly between turns. Saudan would keep his weight on both skis in a heavy snow and swivel on his heels, thrusting the ski tips back and forth across the fall line. He called it the windscreen wiper turn, a way to maintain balance not only in the deep powder but eventually into the thin strips of snow beckoning from the Spencer Couloir.

Vallençant would also adapt his skiing as he attempted new descents, inventing a technique he called "pedal jumping," a skill that Oliver described as "a combination of edging the uphill ski and planting the downhill pole to gain leverage in order to flip the skis across the near-vertical fall line." Today, such implementations don't exactly seem so—for lack of a better term— extreme. But we need to remember the simplicity of the equipment fifty and more years ago, and what it might be like to consider yourself a skiing pioneer without the benefit of today's advancements, such as shaped skis.

But, back in the United States, the Europeans' feats of mountaineering and first descents went practically unnoticed, as a rebellious, hotdogging flair was starting to catch on. It was here, in the 1970s, when freestyle skiing came on the scene, which some argue was the *real* father of American extreme skiing culture. "When you look at big-mountain freeriding today, you can see it comes out of the roots of freestyle," Dan said. "There's always been this thing about U.S. extreme skiers versus European extreme skiers. I've always disagreed with the suggestion that we were part of the mountaineering culture—no, we belonged with the freedoggers. What you see is the Americanization of the sport. There's nothing in America we don't turn into MTV. We are the glitz and the glamour. So, we took some mountaineering and some freestyle skiing, and then we added extreme and we popularized it. We sold it. We packaged it."

The significance of VHS and videotape in the '80s cannot be overemphasized. Before VHS, television content was viewed in real time. There was no record, pause, or replay for home viewers. VHS gave viewers control over what they wanted to watch and when they wanted to watch it. It was even given a name: time shifting. VHS offered an ideal opportunity for the extreme skiing scene to explode onto the family television screen in a way the freestyle movement never really had.

At Weichsel's ski shows, major retailers, such as Ski Market and Ski Barn, held huge ski sales. Weichsel also invited extreme artists, namely the Egans, to host their own "extreme theaters," complete with slideshows and videos, narrated by Dan, of their ski-jumping off the Berlin Wall and skiing with the Kurds in Turkey. Just outside the theater was a booth where visitors could purchase The Egan Brothers branded Day-Glo gear . . . and videos. VHS was the perfect technology for the skiing industry to deliver extreme skiing—its newest brand of excitement—to millions and millions of American living rooms.

Chapter Six

HOTDOGGING'S ROOTS

HOTDOGGING, ALSO KNOWN AS FREESTYLE skiing, goes back decades. Perhaps most notable of all its forefathers was the legendary Stein Eriksen, who moved to the United States in 1952 after winning Olympic gold in giant slalom and silver in slalom in his native Oslo, Norway. He was a ski instructor at Sun Valley when he began showing off signature techniques not generally suited for the racecourse, like throwing front flips on skis, which would earn him the moniker of "The Father of Freestyle Skiing." It was a technique Eriksen credited to fellow Norwegians Sigmund and Birger Ruud, who introduced him to it. At the end of World War II, the two Norwegians started making exhibition somersaults from regulation jumps—adding a footnote to their Hall of Fame ski-jumping careers.

"So, we built a little kicker out of snow . . . with a sharp transition to it," Eriksen said in the documentary film, *The Legendary Skier.* "We knew how to kind of maneuver in the air and knew that this kicker would give us plenty of air. When the [ski] tips came to the top of the kicker we just jumped up from the skis and tried to tuck and come around. Then [we] developed what I called the layout, kind of a swan dive. And then finally, when I felt I was dropping, I tucked and then landed on my skis. Since then, I always did the layout. That became a trademark. I must have done over a thousand of them without any accident."

In the late 1950s, Eriksen relocated to Sugarbush, Vermont. The young resort, commonly known as "Mascara Mountain," was a winter stomping ground for the rich and famous of New York and New England. One of the signature trails at Sugarbush is "Stein's Run," designed and named for Eriksen.

Sugarbush is an important landmark in Egan skiing history. "Stein's Run at Sugarbush is where I first saw John as the icon he was becoming," Dan said. "I was a young teenager. Bob and I were visiting John one spring, and there was a mogul comp on Stein's Run. It was packed with spectators. The competitors were from Killington, Stowe, Jay Peak, and the like, and when John got ready to go, the place went wild for him. I remember thinking, 'Wow, they know my brother.' He ripped that run on a pair of race skis, in stretch pants, a flannel shirt, and no hat—just wearing goggles, his hair flying as he went by me. I'll never forget it."

By the time of that mogul contest, in the mid 1970s, Eriksen was already a legend, thanks in part to filmmaker John Jay, who featured Eriksen's flips on camera in the '50s, which helped capture the attention of a young generation of skiers looking for adventure outside of racing. That included skiers like Sun Valley's Bob Burns, whom filmmaker Dick Barrymore wrote about in his 1997 autobiography, *Breaking Even*. "Burns's style was unlike any I had seen before. Burns sat back in a permanent toilet bowl position with his hands high over his head, holding sixty-inch poles. He sent his skis straight over the mogul in front of him and when it looked like he would fall flat on his back, he used his strong body to catch up with the skis. No one skied like Burns. Bob Burns was, in 1969, the first of the famous hotdoggers."

Burns was a representative for the K2 ski company, which would go on to finance Barrymore's films, *Eleven Minutes*, and *59 Seconds of Skis and Skiers* which debuted in 1969 as one of the first films to embrace hotdogging. This set the stage for Barrymore's 1972 film, *The Performers*, which would become his landmark production, widely credited with having helped spawn the freestyle movement, if not the true essence and transcendence of the ski-bum lifestyle.

In *The Performers*, five members of the K2 Demonstration Team—John Clendenin, Jim Stelling, Pat Bauman, Bob Griswold, and Charlie McWilliams—crowded into an old red, white, and blue motor home with Barrymore and traveled the U.S., hitting some two dozen ski resorts over three months. The resulting film may be only twenty-six minutes long, but it boasted enough daffys, spread eagles, and back-scratchers from the quintet to signal a new era in skiing. It was the unofficial birth of the "hotdog" skier, as audiences watched different ways of floating through powder, navigating air, and nimbly handling the bumps in ways ski schools of yore never imagined.

"*The Performers* was the great mix," Barrymore said in an interview with MountainZone.com before he died in 2008. "You make a cake out of the same ingredients, and somebody's going to make a great cake, but if you don't have the right ingredients, nobody can make a cake. Well, then, we get five guys that were so different and such great skiers, it was easy for me just to make a film about every skier's dream. To get on a bus and travel all over the United States and ski everywhere for free and get paid for it. They didn't get much, but at least they got their expenses. Those guys worked three months, and I think they got $1,000 apiece. But they got room and board for all of the United States and free skiing. So, those are just the ingredients of the cake and I just kind of mixed it up and threw it in the oven and it came out *The Performers*. But they were the creative force behind it. The five guys that we had, they were the creative force behind that film."

The Performers was perhaps one of the first ski films to inspire repeated viewings, watching five guys immersing themselves in deep powder at Sun Valley, throttling themselves off cliffs at Snowbird, and soaring though the air against a bass-laden soundtrack normally reserved for the far-out freedom of surfing films, rather than the inspired beauty of mountain skiing, on the big screen.

"It helped end the regimentation of European-type skiing and racing," Barrymore said in a 1996 *SKI Magazine* piece chronicling K2's twenty-fifth anniversary tour of *The Performers*. "There was so much excitement in the way *The Performers* skied—going straight down the fall line, sucking up the bumps, and throwing big air."

During the filming, on March 10, 1971, Barrymore put together a hastily organized competition on the Ridge of Bell, at Aspen. Three thousand spectators turned out to watch eighty-nine skiers take part in what was billed as "the first hotdogging contest." The skier who made the fastest, most "showy" run down Bell Mountain would win a new pair of skis.

In the contest, a fall was only judged as such if the skier came to a complete stop. Otherwise, it was considered a "recovery," which meant even the worst "yard sale" on the hill might still garner high scores, based on the individual's ability to get back up quickly. In fact, judges only made up rules as the contest moved along, reacting to the crowd's cheers to gauge performance. Essentially, the K2 Hot Dog Contest played to the crowd in a way that sports revolving around the unforgiving nature of a stopwatch never had.

Aspen instructor Sid Ericksen won the pair of K2 skis for flying over the moguls the fastest. The event was a huge hit with the crowd—except, that is, for the president of Aspen Skiing Corporation, Darcy Brown. Brown caught the wafting scent of marijuana while riding a chairlift over the Ridge at Bell Mountain, and vowed that no hotdog competition would ever again be staged on such a highly visible spot on his mountain.

The event truly considered the birth of freestyle skiing competitions, just two days earlier, involved a bit more organization when the First National Championships of Exhibition Skiing took place at Waterville Valley, New Hampshire. Waterville Valley founder Tom Corcoran and former *Skiing* magazine editor-in-chief Doug Pfeiffer had concocted the idea during a meeting at the Boston ski expo the previous fall. The marriage of the two minds might at first have seemed an odd match for something so revolutionary for those times. Corcoran, a former member of the U.S. Ski Team, founded the Waterville ski area in 1966. The more rebellious Pfeiffer, who, even into his nineties, wears his hair in a looping ponytail, had been hip to the mogul-skiing youngsters finding air at ski resorts across the country. Pfeiffer, once a ski school director at Snow Summit in California, was a groundbreaker in the art of freestyle skiing as early as 1958, when he released his book, *Skiing with Pfeiffer*, which included an illustrated chapter on freestyle skiing stunts.

A headline in the *Boston Globe*, on February 28, 1971, announced a "Daredevil ski contest at Waterville Valley," the writer arguing that the "National Championship of Exhibition Skiing" was a bit misleading for what should have been dubbed the "Waterville Inferno." Sponsored by Chevrolet, *Skiing* magazine, and Waterville Valley, the contest (postponed for a day, thanks to a blinding snowstorm) gave each competitor three runs down a True Grit trail riddled with moguls. The forty competitors were allowed to ski the run however they deemed the flashiest, with the winners taking home a share of the $10,000 in prize money and, to the top finisher, a 1971 Corvette.

"The event turned out to be everything Pfeiffer dreamed freestyle skiing could be," Morten Lund and Peter Miller wrote in a September, 1998, edition of *Skiing Heritage Journal*. "Some two thousand spectators showed up, even in the teeth of a miserable snowstorm. The competitors pulled off moves never seen before by the public, the Polish Donut and the Worm Turn, involving big body contact with the snow. Bob Burns did his hair-raising wheelies; the irrepressible Suzy Chaffee—the only woman entrant—resplendent in red, black, and white tights, cut stylish figures on four-foot double-ended skis. Ignoring the negative vocal comment from the sidelines, she came in fourth overall."

The winner was Hermann Goellner, a native of Austria who became a coach at Killington in 1964 and was a pioneer in the art of the skiing backflip. In 1966, he and fellow Killington ski instructor Tom Leroy performed simultaneous flips on skis—one forward and one backward.

Goellner also composed what would become known as the Moebius Flip, a full twisting front somersault, or reverse back somersault, that served as inspiration for the 1969 film of the same name.

Despite the fact that he won, Goellner's name didn't resonate with the Waterville event. Nor did second-place-prize-winner Ken Tofferi's, of Okemo. The highest praise was reserved for a twenty-one-year-old Canadian freestyler from British Columbia named Wayne Wong, who'd hitchhiked across the States in order to participate in the New Hampshire event. Despite crashing on his first run while trying to land his trademarked "Wong-Banger" (a move he happened upon when his tips got stuck on a sharp transition, allowing him to vault himself forward with his poles), Wong ended up finishing third in the competition, aided by losing a ski during a jump on his final run—undeterred, Wong landed the jump on one ski and skidded to the finish with flair. The following year, Wong wrote to Waterville seeking a job, which he landed, becoming the head coach of the ski area's junior freestyle program.

In 2017, Dan produced *50 Years of Firsts: Waterville Valley*, a documentary which featured footage from the 1971 contest and interviews with Pfeiffer, Wong, Weichsel, and Corcoran, among others. "Producing that film for Waterville Valley was a thrill," Dan said. "It celebrated the pioneers of freestyle who'd shaped the sport that would become my career. Wong was my childhood hero. Pfeiffer had skied and snowboarded in my movie, *Return of the Shred-I*, in 1993, at sixty-five years old. Weichsel had become my mentor, and I grew up skiing at Corcoran's resort."

It was the epoch of a freestyle skiing explosion, emerging from the events in New Hampshire and Aspen. Hotdoggers were now officially on the skiing map. Even the likes of Darcy Brown couldn't stop the sport's popularity from skiing its way onto slopes normally reserved for the more stoic Alpine racing. Freestyle skiing continually evolved its interpretation and definition of itself, finding success by going against the grain. It was the counterculture's avenue into a sport once reserved solely for ultimate precision and conformity.

The freedoggers were just having fun, man. Everyone had their own style, and freedogging's popularity eventually led to bigger, better, badder tricks on the hills. New moves became the norm at each ensuing competition.

But when accidents started happening, that ultimately led to the dark days of the hotdog movement.

Joe Powder refers to airtime as the "eternal now," where time and space collide and one can be at peace.

Photograph by Wade McKoy

For Dan, time stands still on big jumps. Here is Dan jumping off a cliff. John is below in the saddle finishing up his run down the same face.

Chapter Seven

ACCIDENTS HAPPEN

AT AN EVENT CALLED THE "Super Hot Dog Classic" at Steamboat Springs, Colorado, on Feb. 10, 1973, the first shoe dropped on the counter-culture movement that freestyle skiing had brought to the slopes.

Peter Hershon was one of the competitors that day. The twenty-four-year-old from Montreal had feverishly prepared to compete on the circuit the previous summer, training for fourteen hours a week. He'd worked with a gymnastic trainer in Aspen, tinkering with his athletic maneuvers mid-air. He'd met repeatedly with a diving coach in his hometown, learning how to twist and contort his body, hoping to adapt the knowledge to skis. He hit the trampoline day after day. Hershon's diligence produced his 12th-place finish in the 1972 National Freestyle Championship.

What Hershon remembers about the course that day was that it was unusually slow. He was also concerned about the landing area, the runout at the end of the mogul course. It wasn't the typical steep pitch he and other competitors were accustomed to. "A contest like that would never have happened today," he told the *Aspen Times* in 2007.

Nevertheless, Hershon announced his intention to perform a back layout with a spread-eagle, going into a double somersault with his legs tucked. But the slope, as he'd feared upon inspection, was too slow, giving him insufficient takeoff speed. He still managed to perform his tricks mid-air, but he came down on the landing surface too quickly, and his head slammed into the snow. The contest was halted. An ambulance raced Hershon to St. Luke's Hospital in Denver, where he would learn he'd broken two vertebrae. He was paralyzed from the waist down. He would never walk again.

A few days later, at the Rocky Mountain Freestyle Championships at Vail, a skier named Scott Magrino failed to complete a flip in the qualifying round. He also landed on the back of his neck.

He never got up.

According to an account of the incident in *SKI Magazine*, Magrino's injury was due to confusion on the hill. The jumps were being built and taken down amid miscommunication between the organizers of the event, the competition committee, and the Vail ski patrol. The Vail contest consisted of three jumps in a series, two of which competitors had to hit in eliminations. Magrino hadn't had much chance to practice on the second jump, which had an altered kicker. During the competition, he completed a reverse somersault off the first jump, but didn't land quite right and failed to make any sort of adjustment. He flew into the second jump with too much speed, threw a reverse, and overshot the landing. He came down on his neck, severing his spinal cord. Like Hershon, he, too, would be paralyzed for life.

This, of course, frightened ski area operators across the country, leading to war on the freestyle movement. There was talk of banning freestylers altogether, out of fear that younger skiers with no experience or understanding about the risks would start tinkering with jumps and flips all over the mountain. Two experienced aerialists had been paralyzed—what dangers awaited novices?

In true counterculture fashion, there was never really any sort of rule book to begin with. The very nature of freestyle skiing was to show off—putting restrictions on freestylers' means of expression would limit their enthusiasm, but the pull of prize money would surely lead to even more unqualified skiers and even more showing off, with safety taking a backseat. But the alternative was risking further injuries, perhaps death. Jumps needed to be created by qualified personnel. Scoring had to be tailored so the hotdoggers were not going beyond their limits.

This led to the formation of the International Freestyle Skiing Association, which introduced new rules, including the requirement that any freestyler wishing to compete in an IFSA-sanctioned event had to attend a "rules and procedures clinic." Practice runs were mandatory. Judging of aerials was based on form, style, and degree of difficulty, and would be mathematically calculated. In other words, the fun was over. The rules were both a necessity and yet another sign that the party doesn't last forever.

In the winter of 1974, IFSA ran five accident-free events, but by the following winter was turmoil. An elite group of skiers didn't want to follow the organization's new guidelines. They argued that their stunts were important for attracting TV coverage, but were opposed by IFSA sponsors. They teamed up with Salt Lake City lawyer Curtis Oberhansly, "the biggest crook ever," according to Bernie Weichsel, who was IFSA's executive director in 1974. "He took the assets and main competitors out of the group, which collapsed the association," Weichsel said.

The elite skiers' group wound up splitting off from IFSA and forming the Professional Freestyle Associates, which took over the tour the following year. PFA established a handful of sponsor relationships including Midas, *Skiing* magazine, Chevrolet, Palmolive, Colgate, and Camel. That 1974–75 season produced nine meets and $275,000 in prize money—nearly three times the $100,000 purse awarded by IFSA the previous year. ABC televised the PFA World Trophy Tour on its Saturday *Wide World of Sports* program.

The two freestyle circuits competing against each other caused a political battle that spread to the competitors. Some freestylers turned to ballet in search of the freedom of expression now being denied in freestyle competition. Rules and policies created barriers and structure, helping to evolve the sport which would eventually head to the Olympics. But, for all intents and purposes, the hotdogging movement, as initially constituted, was officially over.

"The birth of competitions was what ruined freestyle skiing," Dan Egan said. "Once you start judging, it's the death, not the beginning. I think if you talk to any of the early freedoggers, they would say the same thing. They were all amazing skiers. The only reason for judging was because they thought it was the way to get sponsors and create excitement."

In 1973, two-time Olympic Alpine racer Spider Sabich compared it to surfing, "which originally was big in competition and finally died because of subjective judging." It would turn out to be a prophetic statement. "The freedoggers ran out of runway," Dan said. "They had national coverage and national sponsors, then it started to fall apart. By the end of the '70s, and into the early '80s, the sport changed to disciplines, moguls, aerials, and ballet. You had the pro events, which were fun, head-to-head competition, but the amateur events had way more rules and only one competitor was allowed on the course. This specialization helped the sport organize, but also made it tamer as it headed toward becoming an Olympic competition. They started timing the mogul skiers, added jumps in the middle of the course which then created the zipper line, and the dynamic changed."

The TV viewing audience understood speed—who was fastest to the bottom—and the skiing industry needed predictable outcomes. Both led back to racing. It would take another type of skiing to inject vibrant life into a sport overwhelmed by increasingly dull racing. The extreme skiing movement was waiting in the wings, and with the advent of VHS, its timing couldn't have been better. John and Dan Egan were at the head of the line, ready to take to the snow.

Chapter Eight

REACHING FOR GOALS

IT WAS NOT ONLY SKIING, but also soccer, which gave Dan his distinctive athletic identity, beginning in grade school. He was in the fourth grade when Milton's Glover Elementary School found a new gym teacher, Tom Herget, who would turn out to be more than just a physical education instructor. Herget came on board during the early- to mid-1970s, at a time when soccer was an afterthought in American neighborhoods; there was much more focus on baseball and basketball at town parks across the nation. But Herget had also been appointed as the Milton High School's soccer coach, and wanted to build the soccer team at Glover so he'd have a batch of talent coming up through the school system. He formed Milton Youth Soccer's travel team, which sparked an interest in Dan and his friends.

"My mom drove us to every game," Dan said. "She'd fill the station wagon with all my friends. I can still name almost every kid on that team. We played as a unit, starting then."

Dan was good at soccer, and Herget trained him at a higher level. When the team members were in the sixth grade, Herget had them train with the middle school kids. When the group was in middle school, he had Dan train with the high school team. "Coach Herget was a major influence on me and my friends," Dan said. "He tested our limits while at the same time stressing things like sportsmanship. He never swore. He reinforced manners and taught us to act like gentlemen. He set the bar pretty high. For me, personally, he let me know when I was falling short of his standard."

Dan was in high school when Herget invited him and a few other players to join him on a men's team in Braintree, the town where Herget grew up and where his father was still the athletic director at the high school. "On that team was the Babson College coach, the Boston University coach, the Northeastern University coach, the Boston College coach, and they were all buddies with Herget," Dan said. "Those guys were icons. During that time, Babson won its first national soccer championship. By the time I got to high school, they'd won five. They were a national dynasty."

Babson's soccer excellence had actually begun in 1967, when Bob Hartwell turned a winless team into a playoff squad. By 1975, he'd led the team to its first national championship with a 17–0–1 record. Their success didn't waver once Bill Rogers took over as coach in 1977; Babson won back-to-back titles in 1979 and '80. The soccer field was christened Hartwell-Rogers Field, in their honor.

Seeing Milton's Donny Lake on a Babson national championship team got Dan thinking. He remembered Donny, kicking at his ankles when he was in junior high school, repeating his success when they both played in the summer league. "And I thought, if Donny Lake could play for Babson, I could play for Babson." Since he was training with Rogers, Dan figured maybe the next natural step would be to play for the coach at Babson. Rogers had a different opinion.

"He told me in my junior year in high school that I didn't stand a rat's ass chance in hell of going to Babson with my grades," Dan recalls. "He said he wanted me, but said there was no way I would get admitted."

At the outset, it appeared Rogers might be right. Dan had had four interviews at Babson by his high school senior year, each of them only giving him a lingering hope. Dan's soccer and skiing skills both spoke for themselves. His lagging grades were another story entirely. So Rogers suggested prep school, where Dan could get himself together, after which his athletic and academic self would make him a stronger candidate for college admission. A Milton High college counselor, named Ms. Sears, who'd advised all the Egan siblings, suggested two prep schools to Robert and Marlen, neither of whom were quite sure what to make of Dan's new interest in attending college.

"It was an all-on-my-own initiative," Dan said. "I had wanted to go to a ski academy, like Green Mountain Valley School or Burke Mountain School, but my folks had said no to that a few years earlier. Soccer was my way of being different from John. Ned and I played soccer. It was our thing. Ned was a great goal scorer. He played on all of our youth teams and was part of my high school gang of friends."

At Bridgton Academy, in North Bridgton, Maine, the only all-male, one-year college preparatory school in the country, Dan found what he was looking for—a home for wayward athletes. A sports factory of sorts. "When Bridgton became an option, I posited it to my parents as being all about my grades and going to college. Not sports."

Marlen had been a gym teacher and taught Dan most of his sports. "She taught me basketball and how to ride a bike, and always encouraged us to join teams," Dan said. "And she never let us quit; once we started something, we had to finish." And, she'd grown up in the home of Frederick Gillis, the teacher. Thus, education was always a priority. "She always stressed, if you do your homework each night, you won't have to cram at the last minute," Dan said.

All of the Egans achieved different results in school. Mary-Ellen excelled with her grades. Bob knew that the military environment at Norwich University would provide the structure he needed. John had a more hands-on approach to life; the confinement of the classroom wasn't his thing. Sue was diligent. Dan liked school because it was social. Ned did, too, but he was an "A" student. "If soccer was my way of being different from John, grades were Ned's way of being different from me," Dan said. "He had the athletics, friends, *and* the grades." Mike, six years younger than Dan, was a blend of the best parts of all the others; spirited and kind, but with big shoes to fill, following in the footsteps of his older siblings' accomplishments. Robert and Marlen thought Bridgton, three hours removed from Milton, might be just what Dan needed to get focused.

"I knew Bob had benefited from his Norwich education and training. It was a conscious decision for him to seek that," Dan said. "He and his friends had hinted to me that I might need some structure and goals outside partying and working out."

Marlen saw it as a way to get Robert and Dan to bond. "My dad drove me to Bridgton. Which was amazing," Dan said. "I think it was my mom's way of saying to my dad, 'you deal with him, spend some time with him not on a boat or a chairlift.' I don't think, in high school, my dad came to more than two soccer games. My mom came to every one, but my dad was busy. He liked Bridgton and could see that the combined remote location, academics, and sports might, as he said, 'straighten me out a bit.'"

Bridgton Academy aimed to prepare "students to succeed in college and to do so at schools that might otherwise have felt out of reach." Its athletics program prepared "student-athletes to compete at the college level while successfully balancing academics." It was just the sort of balance Dan needed between high school and college, to potentially reach his goal. In 1982 he enrolled, hopeful it would present him with a way to achieve his real goal. "There was a speaker who came to Bridgton and told us, 'You need to write down your goal where you'll see it every day.' So, I wrote that I would graduate from Babson in 1987. And I wrote it on every notebook I had."

Bridgton provided Dan with many firsts. That included his first "A" in any class he'd ever taken—it was in oceanography. His teacher, Peter Gately, also happened to be his Bridgton ski team coach. "BA is the type of school you don't want to be at, but you know it will be good for you," Dan said. "Slowly, over time, I could see that this place could and would sort me out, so I bought into it, and it worked."

One thing the coach couldn't get through to Dan on was his obstinacy over his ski equipment. "The coaches hated the fact that I was ski racing in rear-entry boots," Dan said. "Salomon was kind of the cool, new boot, but it wasn't a race boot. But, because the pros raced in it, John raced in it, too, because he was sponsored by Salomon. Plus, we sold them like hotcakes at Ski Market, so I had to have 'em. Of course I was defiant, but I'm sure the coaches, Gately and Bill Bearse, were right."

That same winter, John moved to Squaw Valley in Lake Tahoe, California, with his girlfriend Emily Hart. They were both great skiers. Just the winter before, they'd set the endurance record for skiing "The Mall" trail under the Valley Chairlift at Sugarbush. The Mall, situated next to Stein's Run, is a narrow mogul field with lift towers running down the middle. John did forty-two runs of Mallmania in a single day, and Emily, who was on a similar pace, was just a few laps behind. The combined feat has not been matched since.

While Dan was at Bridgton learning to study, John was learning what Squaw had to offer him as a skier. He'd filmed for Warren Miller at Sugarbush in 1979 and 1981, so images of him ripping the bumps in stretch pants and a flannel shirt became his calling card for the locals in Tahoe. Later that winter, he found himself skiing in the same stretch pants for Warren Miller, alongside new ski friends, Scot Schmidt and Tom Day. Dan received postcards from John: ". . . it's amazing out here bro, the places you can make tracks down and over cliffs will blow you away."

So, while Dan was attending Sunday-through-Thursday mandatory evening study halls at Bridgton, John was painting a picture of another way of life for him. "It was a constant tug-of-war inside me," Dan said. "John leading a wild and attractive life, while Bob and my folks were trying to get me to buckle down and focus on structure, college, and their version of success." Dan was succeeding on the soccer team; he was co-captain with roommate Mike Neff. The team went 14–2–1, regularly beating college JV teams in the area. On the slopes, Dan teamed up with Massachusetts state ski champion Brian Sawyer, from Bedford, along with other New England standouts. The team had the best season in Bridgton's history.

Academically, though, any ambivalence Dan might've had in terms of his grades suddenly withered in Maine. In fact, Dan was third in his class when Coach Rogers arranged yet another interview with the Babson dean of admissions. No student from Bridgton had ever gotten into Babson, and Dan's SAT scores had yet to budge from their previous unimpressive state, but Rogers saw grit in Dan's approach to soccer. His being a year older—and maybe with more structure around studying—might be enough to keep his dream alive. Bill Rogers booked him a forty-five minute appointment with the dean, with the admonition: "This is it. This is your final opportunity."

Dan talked his way in. "The dean point-blank asked me, 'Did I think I could pony up academically and survive Babson?' I said, 'Yes. Bridgton Academy has given me a new confidence as well as the discipline to make it.' So he said, right there and then, he'd give me a chance. There was also another admission officer, a former soccer player, and I think he spoke to the dean on my behalf, as well. Plus, all the BA coaches and teachers wrote recommendations, so it all came together."

In the end, Babson took a total of three Bridgton Academy students that year. Perhaps the most enduring lesson from Dan's time in prep school was about making his goal the primary focus: "'I will graduate from Babson in 1987.' I'd written it down every year I was at Babson," he said. "I had it on a mirror. I had it everywhere. I was going to graduate Babson in 1987, four years after I started. That promise never left me."

Dan's freshman year at Babson, beginning in 1983, was fairly normal from an athletic standpoint. The soccer team went 14–2–2, which made Dan immediately feel like he was part of a successful collegiate program. He was one of only two freshmen to make the varsity squad, along with Dan Caldicot, from Sherborn, Massachusetts, who was the leading goal scorer that season. Dan, however, could only observe from the bench. Coach Herget taught Dan how to play; Bridgton taught him how to succeed; now Babson was teaching him how to persevere.

"That was a tough lesson for me," Dan said. "I made the team, but only saw three total minutes of playing time. When we were playing at the Coast

Guard Academy, coach put me in at the tail end of the game. I touched the ball three times; the first was a two-touch pass down the line, and the ball was played back to me outside of the eighteen-yard line. My second touch was a shot that rang the far-left post. After the game, coach told me if I had scored, I might've had a chance of getting into another game. It was a new level of competition at Babson, so it was back to the bench for me. That style of coaching was totally new to me."

Of course, Dan brought his skis to the Babson campus in Wellesley, Massachusetts, and raced for the school in the winter, helping the team make it to the New England Championships. In the spring, Dan was awarded the Colin Chip Brown award for outstanding freshman athlete.

Babson was not known as a party school, and Wellesley was a dry town. But in the mid-eighties, cocaine was everywhere, even in sports. Sadly, most notable was Lenny Bias, who died of an overdose just two days after the Boston Celtics chose him with the second pick in the 1986 NBA draft. For Dan, even more turmoil was added to the mix when head coach Bill Rogers was passed over for the school's athletic director position. Rogers resigned in the fall of 1985, during the soccer preseason of Dan's junior year. "Which was extremely disappointing, because he was the guy who told us never to quit," Dan said. "And here he was quitting. The school passed him over because they were fed up with the soccer culture. We knew we were crazy."

Pete Ginnegar stepped in for a year, as interim coach, but the season was pretty much a disaster. Babson wound up with a 10–4–4 record, but, while they made it to the postseason tournament, it was not without plenty of personality and conduct issues. "We were a team with a partying problem, and we were going through a tough transition without Rogers," Dan said. "He'd recruited all of us and we were there to play for him. Without him, the wheels came off the bus. We were partying a lot. The interim coach had no influence on us. The senior captains stepped in and were running the show, which helped keep it together. We beat the number one school in the country and made it to the NCAA New England finals that year, so it never occurred to us the partying was something we shouldn't be doing."

Early in 1986, Babson replaced Ginnegar, hiring Jon Anderson, a member of Babson's 1975 national championship team. With Anderson on its roster, Babson went 56–5–4 and earned three NCAA tournament berths between 1972 and 1975. Anderson's new role, though, was not only to stabilize the soccer program, but also to get the off-field shenanigans under control. "It's actually been going on since I've been there," said Anderson, who has now held his position as head coach for thirty-five years. "Slowly, the tolerance for anything and everything has changed. Not acceptable. Right away, I had to talk to them about reigning in things that the school talked about. Especially when they went through an interim year where, I think, things really got crazy. Right away, I was told 'you've got to correct some things.' It was years of trying to figure out what traditions were good and what was not going to be acceptable anymore."

The mission to improve the perceptions of the Babson soccer team led to bonding between Dan and his new head coach. It was a few years before college institutions began widely cracking down on hazing rituals, but when Dan became a co-captain of the team the following year, they knew things had to change. "So, we came up with some tamer ideas, some of which were harmless and some that didn't work." As co-captain, Dan was ultimately held responsible for the team's behavior, on the field and off. He and his fellow co-captain were suspended by the athletic administration for a portion of the 1986 season, during which the team went only 7–9–1. It was the only losing season of Dan's collegiate soccer career.

"That season was a big-time struggle," Anderson said. "We had to deal with the turmoil right up front, coming in and trying to deal with the different problems. They'd spent a year going away from the bedrock of the program."

During his junior season, Brandeis University's soccer team was 15–0 and ranked number one in the country in Division III. Babson needed a win against its rival in order to remain in contention for the NCAA playoffs. Dan scored the winning goal against Brandeis in a 2–1 game, when Paul "Ozzi" Ostberg head-flicked the ball into the open space, giving Dan the break-away to score the winning goal. But Dan gave all credit to the senior defenders Babson relied on during that game.

"Alex Von Cram, Mark Sullivan, goalkeeper Bob Muscaro—it was those guys who really won the game," Dan said. "I had never seen such fierce intensity in anybody in my life. Once we went up by a goal, our guys were not going to allow another goal against us. They and the other seniors had fought hard to keep us going that season, on and off the field, and I just remember being on the field in awe of what they were willing to do to get that ball. It was an amazing display of the desire to win."

That moment stuck. Maybe not for the sense of passion and desire which would one day define Dan's own pursuits, but perhaps in reflecting on how they were lacking in the years leading up to that moment. Because, in the fall of his sophomore year, in 1984, Dan decided he was going to drop out. All that work. All that determination. All that defying the odds. He was ready to turn his back on it all.

"I was having too much fun," he said, but it was only the tip. "Emotionally, I was having a really hard time with school. I'd begun to realize soccer was more of an institution than a game. It had been hard, emotionally, to make the team, and harder still to stay on the team."

The Babson Beavers went 8–5–2 during the 1984 season, and Dan scored only one of Babson's seventeen goals over its course. He was having a hard time balancing everything at once. Maintaining his soccer prowess at a level where Rogers would still want him on the team was one thing, but his flailing academics in the face of the party culture that came with athletics was something else. Dan felt like sustaining it all was an impossibility. Better to cut sail than lose the boat. Surrendering and avoiding it all seemed to be the best plan.

Babson's dean of academics didn't exactly beg Dan to reconsider. "I sat in his office and he said, 'You know, Dan, I just want to tell you one thing. You can leave here, and nobody cares. Your parents are probably a little upset because they're paying the bill. Your friends don't care, your teachers don't care. The only person in this room who needs to care is you. Even if you tell me you're going to go wash dishes all winter and re-enroll in May for summer school, I won't believe it.' He really piled it on, and it was one of the most pivotal speeches an adult had ever made to me. And it reminded me of the speech I'd heard at Bridgton. So, I rewrote my graduation date and decided to take time off."

Dan saw the way out for him was to take a semester off. He saw his brother, John, living the life of a ski bum at Sugarbush, and wondered if that sort of carefree lifestyle wouldn't suit him, as well. Maybe that sort of respite would curtail the difficult decisions he was making about his college life, which seemed to be herding him down a path to unreliability.

"After Bridgton, I knew what I should be doing and what I shouldn't be doing," he said. "And I knew I wasn't doing what I should be doing. But I just didn't feel like I could get it together."

Marlen and Robert were less than thrilled that their son was taking a break on the education he'd professed so deeply was the most important achievement in his life. They were even more baffled by Dan's plan to join John in Vermont. He was in the kitchen of his parents' Milton home when he called John to ask if he could come sample his lifestyle. John didn't fully endorse the idea. "Dan, you're going to come up here to wash dishes?" John asked him. "Why are you doing this? You have to finish school." He wasn't exactly laying out the welcome mat, but Dan saw it another way: He didn't say 'Don't come.'

The birds can't believe Joe Powder is at such a high altitude as he preps his pole plant for the landing.

Photograph by Glenn Randall

Dan drops in on Mount Evans in Colorado during the summer of 1991.

Chapter Nine

SKIBUMOLOGY 101

THE WARNING SIGN THAT DAN was stepping into an atypical lifestyle came shortly after he pulled up to the Alpen Inn, where the owner, Robert Forenza, had told his friend John that he'd hook up his younger brother with a dish-washing job. Forenza, whose family moved to the area when Sugarbush opened in 1958, when Robert was three, pointed to a chalet at the rear of the property. Dan would be living there with a roommate named Tom. "But he doesn't like to be called Tom," Forenza warned. "Call him Gary."

. . . *Gary.*

Dan met "Gary" as he stepped into the chalet. There was a thumping sound, growing louder as he approached the front door. Upon inspection, he discovered the noise came from a man standing in the middle of the room—throwing a knife at the wall.

Ka-ting . . . Ka-ting.

Like Dan even had to ask, "Are you Gary?"

Forenza told Dan he shouldn't be fooled, by Gary's rough exterior, into thinking he was an ex-convict. That was hardly the case, especially because he was an *escaped* convict from Florida. "He carries a knife in his back pocket," Forenza told him. Except for when he was systematically tossing it into the wall, of course.

"He also has Dobermans," Forenza said.

Wonderful. Anything else?

"Oh, and he's a male stripper."

So, here's Dan stepping into the Alpen Inn with a roommate named Tom-Gary, who happens to be a male stripper on the lam from prison in Florida. This was already a bit different from college life, for sure.

There were plenty of other quirks about life at the Alpen Inn, including Dan's downstairs shower, which he discovered had a hole in the ceiling with droplets of water condensing at the edges, dripping into the drain in the floor.

"Hey, Tom, er—Gary," Dan asked his new roommate, whoever the hell he was, "there's a hole in the ceiling of the downstairs shower."

"Yeah, there was," Gary said with a sense of pride. "I fixed it."

Fixed it? Dan had just seen the damage. Gary fixed it? "You fixed what?" Dan asked.

"I fixed the shower," Gary said. "The upstairs shower wasn't draining, so I punched a hole in the floor so it drains into your shower."

Genius.

This is my fucking roommate, Dan thought to himself, as if trying to make the oddity of it sound more normal. "It was crazy at the Alpen Inn," Dan said. "Larry, the chef, would get so drunk by 8 p.m. at night, he couldn't finish the meals. So that's how I learned to cook. I would be washing dishes and Larry would go to the bar and never come back to the kitchen. I would pop over there and take over. Some nights, I would also be the waiter: take the order, cook it for Larry, and then wash the dishes."

Dan soon received help. A woman named Amelia moved into the chalet in order to take on waitressing duties at the inn. Amelia was an aspiring fashion designer, and immediately wanted to redesign the atmosphere of the lodge. "Amelia's Fashion Fantasy," she wrote in pink paint across the outer wall, immediately transforming the aura of the place.

"She made, like, 'George Jetson' stuff," Dan said. "It was some of the most insane stuff I'd ever seen."

"Dan didn't realize the transient work crew he was going to end up living with," John said. "One was actually a wanted man who got up and left before the cops came and got him. I think it might have been a rude awakening into a real-world situation."

The characters weren't all eccentric, though. A kid from Virginia, named John Woolard, also moved in. Hailing from the South, Woolard had never really skied, so Dan took him under his wing. They became fast friends. Woolard provided his own share of comedy. His novice approach to skiing was a challenge unto itself. Keeping up with the more experienced crew on the slopes of Sugarbush was something else entirely.

It was on those slopes where Dan found satisfaction in his move to Vermont, from the ability to ski the day away with his brother John and a group of fellow ski bums. In the ski-bum life, there weren't similar concerns to the life Dan had left behind. Instead of preparing for who you were to become, life was just about being, dictated by the morning snow report each day. It was a life preached to Woolard by a good friend and whitewater kayaking partner at North Carolina's Camp Mondamin. John Dockendorf grew up in Maryland, and every March his family traveled to Vermont for spring break skiing, the highlight of every year. "Vermont was as far away as I had ever gone to ski, and it was paradise," Dockendorf said.

During his senior year in high school, Dockendorf knew exactly where his heart wanted to go, so he began applying only to colleges in Vermont, where he could continue to enjoy the Green Mountains. He spent much of his time, over his first three years at the University of Vermont, skiing locales such as Smugglers' Notch and Mad River Glen. But, prior to his senior year, he and classmate, John Gallagher, co-presidents of the UVM Ski Club, were approached by representatives from Sugarbush. "It was a ski area local college kids wouldn't normally ski unless their parents owned a house there," Dockendorf said. Sugarbush had just purchased the neighboring ski area, Glen Ellen, which would become known as Sugarbush North with the college kids, and was looking to create a market for the spot. So Dockendorf helped them design and sell the resort's first collegiate season pass program.

After graduation, Dockendorf moved to Colorado with a host of other Vermonters, but missed the culture of the Green Mountain State. He came back and swapped the Sugarbush North college crowd for the other Sugarbush ski-bum crowd, which suited him. "I was a pretty darned good ski bum," Dockendorf said. "From my world, it was how to have a somewhat responsible job and not lose ground completely, career-wise. Work hard at whatever your job was, but rig it so you could get free food and have minimal expenses. In a perfect world, you would work five-to-midnight, five or six days a week, and make enough money to be sure you never got stuck with a mountain job where you'd have to work days, taking away from Ski Time."

It can be tricky sometimes, moving to a mountain town only to find yourself bogged down with work instead of knee-deep in powder. "So many people get there, get the job, and can only ski two days a week. Dan was not built to only ski two days a week," Dockendorf said. He was impressed by the morning process at the Alpen Inn, where they were very good at inspiring guests to enjoy an early breakfast and get out on the hill, so they might, in turn, have the dishes washed as early as possible and get out on the slopes, as well. Dan was washing dishes one day during February school vacation week at the Alpen Inn when Sugarbush's marketing director called. He had only one question for Dan: Did he own any ski clothes that weren't held together with duct tape?

Well, he could probably borrow some, he figured. The guy told him if he showed up at the lift the next morning at eight, sans duct tape, there would be a Warren Miller crew waiting for him.

Dan jumped at the opportunity, first calling John, who immediately took the next day off from his condo-building gig. The next day, they met Fletcher Manley, one of the earlier cameramen to work for Warren Miller, with whom John had shot some scenes before. Let's just say Manley wasn't too impressed with the first frames he shot of the Egan brothers. "We weren't having a good day," Dan said. "We kept falling all over the moguls, and Fletcher was getting frustrated."

Dan and John were skiing Upper FIS, a steep mogul run overlooking much of the terrain on the Sugarbush face. Below, it runs into an intermediate run that crosses the bottom of the pitch, where a large crowd of people gathered to watch the exploits.

Manley would give them one last shot. "I want the Egan brothers to ski, one behind the other, and don't crash this time," he told them. "If you fall, it could be the last time we ever shoot you." Then Manley yelled, "roll cameras," and John jumped in with Dan right behind him. They kept it together pretty well until about three-quarters of the way down, where John hit a mogul and caught some air. "I can tell it's not going too good from where I'm skiing," Dan said. "He's looking at me, arms up over his head, and he crashes. So, I hit that mogul and leap over him. He's got skis, poles, everything all over the slope."

Dan made it to the bottom, where the crowd, which included Robert and Marlen, were in hysterics. Manley, on the other hand, was simply holding his head over the situation he'd just wasted film on.

"Who the heck raised these two characters?" someone shouted from the crowd. Dan looked over and saw his mom, and could tell what she was thinking. He watched as she raised her ski pole and whacked the commenter across the shin. "They're my boys," she said. It wouldn't be the only time she would react in a similar way, both in pride and defense, after witnessing the exploits of her sons on snow.

Dan brought an impressive skiing presence to Sugarbush, but he didn't simply waltz right into the iconic status that his brother had at the mountain. "He didn't have the mileage of John at the time," Dockendorf said. "John had already earned legendary status. Dan was the younger brother who ripped. But he was still the younger brother." It wound up being Dockendorf who took Dan under his wing to teach him the proper ways to live the ski-bum life.

"Dockendorf was my favorite guy to ski with, because he went rain or shine," Dan said. "My brother was the best skier at Sugarbush, and John Dockendorf was like, 'You know, if you're going to get there, Dan, you've got to ski.' He mentored me on the ski-bum life. Showing up to work on time— getting that bit right so I didn't lose my pass. And skiing every day, all the time." The other advice John should have given was "don't get sick."

It was a normal occurrence for the chalet crew to break into the bar at the Alpen Inn. Most of the time, Forenza would be there with them, imbibing during off-hours and sharing talk of the day's adventures on the slopes. Dan was sick in bed on one such occasion during spring break, when Slattery, a Babson friend, paid him another visit. It was late, and as one does when it's late at the Alpen Inn, Slattery and Woolard broke into the bar. Without Dan. Without Forenza. And that's where they spent the rest of the night, drinking and playing pool into the morning.

Forenza's wife wasn't pleased when she discovered the mess, and Dan was her scapegoat. "I wasn't on the property," Dan said. "I was in the chalet, but I got fired the next day. She knew I would have been there, and the fact that I wasn't, and my buddy was, pushed her over the edge. And that was the end of it. I lost my pass." It seemed Dan's pursuit of the ski-bum life was over before it had really begun. He had no job, no pass, and now no reason to be in the Mad River Valley, where he'd figured some semblance of answers might come from the mountains. Instead, more questions piled on.

It was spring break, and even though there wasn't a semester of school for Dan to return to at the end of the week, he snatched the opportunity. His brother Ned, attending the University of Vermont, also had time off, so Dan convinced him to join him on a trip out West. They bought plane tickets to Oakland, California, aiming to ski the rest of the week at Squaw Valley. Dan had little more than $300 to his name, but there was a decent Sugarbush network at Squaw already, people who would look out for other ski bums who followed in their footsteps.

John had regaled Dan with tales of the greatness of the Lake Tahoe resort, from his days living there in the early '80s. The plan came together easily: Dan and Ned would fly to Oakland and stay with John's ex-girlfriend, Emily, when they reached Tahoe. "Which didn't make any sense," Dan said. "Because, by this point, Emily was John's ex-girlfriend and she wasn't very happy with him."

Ned purchased a round-trip ticket on People Express, a budget airline that operated in the continental U.S. during the mid-80s. Dan kept his options open and bought an open-ended ticket for seventy-five dollars. Everything was working out perfectly, except nobody had told the brothers that Lake Tahoe was four hours, by car, from Oakland. The best airport to fly into would have been Reno, Nevada, still a forty-eight-minute drive to Tahoe. Luckily, they met a guy on the flight who not only gave them this information, but also allowed them to crash overnight on his hotel room floor at an Econo Lodge in Oakland. They could buy bus tickets to South Lake Tahoe the next day, and they did.

But John hadn't told them that Squaw was in *North* Lake Tahoe. Unknowingly, they called Emily to announce their arrival and catch a ride. "You're a fucking hour away," she said. "You guys idiots, like your brother?" Things were off to a good start.

Emily did come for the Egans, and Dan and Ned did have their first encounter with Squaw Valley, nicknamed "Squallywood" by the ever-increasing population of talented skiers who swarmed into Lake Tahoe each year. Squaw was a hot spot for filmmakers, such as Warren Miller, seeking out new athletes for films. John considered it one of the best resorts in all of North America, and, much like his home base, Sugarbush, also a training ground for skiers looking to expand their portfolios. "If you can ski Squaw and you can ski Sugarbush, then you can ski anywhere in the world," he said.

Dan and Ned explored Squaw. "We practically ran right up to the Palisades and started poking around," Dan said. "Here we were, at the place John had told us about, and we had seen in the Warren Miller movies with Schmidt and Day jumping these cliffs, and it was like, wow! Let's go!

"I saw a guy up there line up and fly off one of the cliffs and I said, 'That is where I must go.' So I followed him and crashed so hard on the landing. Ned had to pick up my gear as I tumbled down. We went right back up and did it again and again. I think I crashed every time." Ned stayed for a week and then flew back to Vermont to finish his semester at UVM. Dan managed to stay on and ski for the next few weeks.

"It was mind-blowing," he said. "I got introduced to Scot Schmidt and tried to ski with him, but he lost me on the first few turns as he ducked down through the trees. Then I met up with some other Vermonters who showed me around. The place was huge, steep around every turn, terrain that made me stop and think about my next move. I loved it."

Soon enough, though, Emily got tired of him sleeping on her floor and finally kicked him out. "She was nice to me and went beyond what any ex-girlfriend of a guy's brother would do, but it was just time to move on and explore the next spot," Dan said. "So I did. She lived on the main road in Tahoe City, so I just walked outside, stuck out my thumb, and hitched a ride to Reno. That city was amazing to me. I had never seen a gambling town before. I hit the tables, won a few bucks, crashed the buffets at Circus Circus, then headed toward the train station. I figured I could sleep on the train to Salt Lake City and look up some friends from Sugarbush at Snowbird. On my way to the station, I struck up a conversation with a homeless guy. He was asking me for money and said he had a train ticket he would sell me. The ticket looked legit, had 'SLC' on it, so I gave him ten bucks for a fifteen-dollar ticket and waited for the train."

The overnight train to Salt Lake City was packed, but Dan's ticket had a seat number, so he was comfortable, had a full belly from the buffet, and slept through the desert to Salt Lake City. The train pulled in on a Sunday morning. Once outside the station, not knowing where to go, Dan followed the crowd of people walking down the sidewalk, skis hanging over his shoulder. "It was a big crowd and they were going somewhere, but I didn't know where. Maybe it was a sporting event or a walk-a-thon, I didn't know. It was a warm spring morning and the crowd had energy, so I figured, let's see where they're going. All of a sudden, we came to these gates and we went through and walked into this big cathedral. I got to the top of the stairs and somebody asked me if I wanted them to hold my luggage. And they took my skis and my backpack, and I went in and I sat down. It was beautiful inside this church. I was lonely from traveling and hadn't been to church in a while, so it was nice to be there. The place was full, but I squeezed into a pew and sat next to a large family.

"And all of a sudden this chorus started singing. I had never heard anything like it. It was beautiful, so I leaned over to the lady next to me between songs and said, 'These people are really good. Who are they?'" As it turned out, they happened to be a little group called The Mormon Tabernacle Choir. "I had no idea. I had heard of them, but now I was like, they're really good. Like I'm discovering something new. After the concert I walked out of the church, gathered my pack and skis, and marched down those cathedral stairs like I owned the world. I had no idea where Snowbird was, but I knew to go to a neighborhood at the base of the canyon, called Sandy, where my Sugarbush buddies lived."

On December 25, 1958, Damon and Sara Gadd, and their partner, Jack Murphy, opened Sugarbush, along with Lixi Fortna, who helped run the mountain with Damon, Sara, and Jack. From ticket-selling to tending bar, the four worked long hours by candlelight. Lift tickets were just $5.50. Dan was on his way to catch up with Jack Murphy's daughter, Kelly, who worked in the marketing department at Snowbird. There were free lift tickets awaiting him, plus a host of John's friends waiting to show him around.

"Snowbird in the spring was amazing," Dan said. "The resort is so different from the East Coast resorts I'd grown up skiing. This was more like a mall than a base lodge, and the plaza with the tram was right there—it was a game changer for me. The atmosphere and the attitude of the skiers was so open. They were excited to show me around. The Sugarbush tribe is strong. They'd already heard about my Alpen Inn story and said, 'She did you a favor, firing you.' It was like I belonged there with this crew and could see how the West held possibilities for me. They gave me a place to crash, slipped me lift tickets, got me high, and we ripped for a week. It was heaven." But a week was all they could spare in both time and treasure, so for Dan it was off to thumb a ride to Colorado, eventually ending up at Steamboat. Where he knew absolutely no one.

"I was walking around town and saw the Nordic ski jumps," he said. "The place looked empty and I'd never stood on top of a jump before—so I climbed the stairs to the top of the jump. It's scary up there; that takeoff is steep. At the top there was a small starting shack. Nobody was around, so I decided to make it my crash pad for a few days. I lived in the hut at the top of the stairs for a week. I would scam lift tickets in the parking lot from skiers leaving midday. A few days, I snuck onto the lift and skied just the top of the mountain, where they didn't check tickets. I caught a run with famed skier and gold medalist Billy Kidd. He skis with the public every day. That was fun. At night I would go to two-for-one happy hours to eat and drink, and meet people. No one actually believed me, that I was living in the starting shack at the top of the Nordic jumps. That story entertained a few people at the bar, for sure."

That lasted for a week, until the Red Sox started their season with baseball in full swing on Opening Day. "That became a thing for me," Dan said. "Every time the opener would come, I knew I had to be getting back to Boston and eventually school. The summer semester started in early May, so if I got back by the Boston Marathon, I could run in the race and hang with my Babson friends during their last few weeks of school—and then I'd be ready for summer school."

But he wasn't having much luck thumbing his way out of Steamboat, ride after ride passed by the kid with nothing but a backpack and a pair of skis who'd lived in a hut for the last fortnight. It seemed nobody wanted to pick him up. But after a while, somebody did. The driver said he was just going to the top of Rabbit Ears Pass, not any further. "I was like, 'I don't know what that is, but I'll go.' It's desolate up there. I think he went Nordic skiing, but I don't know, because I never saw him again." Abandoned, and with it getting dark, Dan figured if he spent a week and a half in a hut, he could spend the night in a snowbank.

"Finally, a guy picked me up. His kid was out thumbing around the country and he liked to pick up kids the same age, to talk to." Dan got all the way back to Denver through a series of rides, and got dropped off at a hotel near Stapleton Airport. He knew he could sneak onto the hotel shuttle once he sorted out his open-ended airline ticket, a seventy-five dollar fare with People Express. He ended up being the only person on the shuttle, which was reserved for hotel guests. And Dan, who'd hitchhiked his way across the state, didn't exactly look like he'd just emerged from a hot shower.

"The driver said, 'you didn't stay here,' and started asking me questions," Dan said. So he told the story of his first venture into the ski-bumming lifestyle, a tale filled with hitching rides, scavenging food, and scamming lift tickets. The story ended as most ski bum accounts normally do. He was broke. It likely wasn't an unusual story to the driver's ears, particularly shuttling passengers back and forth to one of the country's most popular winter sports destinations. Instead of chalking Dan's story up to another scam artist trying to get by, he took pity on him and gave him the twelve dollars from his tip jar, so Dan could at least grab a decent meal before hopping his flight back to Boston.

Instead, Dan sparked a conversation in the terminal with a curious fellow dressed in an orange robe with a funny haircut. He was selling books. Dan bought one for six dollars and learned all about the Hare Krishnas on the flight home.

Chapter Ten

EUROPEAN HANGOVER

IT WAS A LESSON JOHN preached to Dan: Work all summer, ski all winter. Dan was sixteen when he first witnessed John's offseason focus. He was visiting Oswego, New York, where his brother had been recruited by a fellow ski bum he'd met on a lift at Sugarbush in 1976. His name was Dennis Ouellette, he owned an apple orchard in Oswego, and he'd hired John to drive his eighteen-wheeled produce truck. Dennis knew John would never make enough money on his own to take the entire winter off and ski with him. His solution: hire John to work for him.

"When my brother was driving eighteen-wheel trucks, he would swing by Milton," Dan said. "I'd get in and we would deliver to the Stop & Shop in Hyde Park. I'd unload the whole load of lettuce, just to be with him."

It was 1980 when Dan hit the road to check out what was keeping John so busy in Oswego. John had been spending the summers working for Dennis before returning to Vermont and Sugarbush to spend the winter skiing. Those were the years when Marlen hesitated every time Dan professed how much he wanted to visit John at Sugarbush. Dan was only a teenager, after all, and Lord knows what he might witness or end up getting involved with around twenty-two-year-old John and his friends. Fifteen seemed far too young to expose him to the extracurricular drugs and alcohol that helped define the other sector of the ski-bum scene.

However, she relented when Dan came up with the idea of riding his bike with his friend, Jimmy Lynch, from Milton to Oswego. "I thought, if I deny this, he'll hate me for the rest of his life," she said. Besides, Lynch's hobby at the time was reading maps, so Marlen figured the two wouldn't get lost, especially since she didn't figure they'd get very far. Dan's father even said he would pick the boys up in any nearby Massachusetts town if they decided to call it quits.

But, over the next seven days, Dan and Lynch made the entire 375-mile journey, stopping only periodically at backyard swimming pools, gazing at them long enough for the owners to invite them in for a swim. Their pockets were empty by the time they arrived, leaving the two without enough money to even replace the flat tires on their bikes. So they went right to work. Ouellette gave them clippers and told them to go prune the apple orchard. The job lasted a month. Eventually, Marlen sent Dan's brother Bob to New York to pick up the two teenagers. "She didn't think I'd ever come back," Dan said.

In Squaw Valley, John found more like-minded people who shared his work ethic and passion for skiing. Tom Day, a native of Montpelier, Vermont, moved to Squaw in 1982 and immediately fell in love with his new environment, captivated by the powerful presence of the Sierra Nevada mountains surrounding Lake Tahoe—Vermont had had a similar effect on him, growing up. Day understood then, as he does now, the art of being a ski bum. His resume in the late '70s and early '80s was heavily weighted with carpentry and roadwork-flagger jobs, each May through October. During the winter months, he tuned skis in the evenings. Tom was hyper-focused and willing to work hard, long hours all summer because he lived to ski. That determination, combined with his friendly and humble nature, his remarkable, friendly face, and his ability to ski in all conditions, day in and day out, placed him high up in the ski bum echelon.

"Tom's personality, boyish looks, and skiing style made his persona," Dan said. "People just liked Tom Day. The industry, the locals, the guests, and the camera lens, all got along with him. Then and now."

Toward the end of his first season at Squaw, Day began frequenting the slopes with a skier named Scot Schmidt, a Montana native whose racing coach at Bridger Bowl told him he was too talented to remain in his home state. He needed a bigger program in order to try out for, and make, the U.S. Ski Team. So, in 1978, Schmidt moved to Squaw Valley and quickly realized he didn't have enough money to survive on talent alone. He ended up working five days a week in a local ski shop, leaving the weekends to train under Squaw coach Warren Gibson.

The breaking point for Schmidt came when Gibson gave scholarship money to a racer named David Kong rather than him, which signaled to Schmidt that he simply wasn't going to have the backing he needed to fulfill his dream of going for Olympic gold. "I didn't get along with a lot of the ski team kids, and just ended up freeskiing the mountain with the long-haired speed skiers," Schmidt said.

Foregoing the gates, Schmidt instead spent his days skiing the legendary Palisades, a formidable series of rocky chutes and steep spines at Squaw Valley. He was in awe, watching speed skiers, like Steve McKinney and Paul Bushman, snap into their 220s and tuck the tube in Siberia Bowl, going as fast as they could.

By the time Tom Day arrived at Squaw, Schmidt was already making tracks. "Once we started hitting those cliffs, it was just this rat pack of guys going around the hill pushing each other," Schmidt said. Day and Schmidt had a lot in common, from their low-key approaches to a love of skiing. The pair hit it off and started skiing together for fun and in films. Over the next decade, both would carve out diverging and parallel careers.

"I kind of spotted Tom as a talent when he first arrived," Schmidt said. "I hand-picked him for a couple projects. We were looking for skiers to go places and do things with. He was always a great candidate—he had the right attitude, and he's fun to travel with. Just a good fit."

It was sometime in the midst of Schmidt's third season at Squaw when Warren Miller cameraman Gary Nate arrived with the anticipation of filming a segment for Squaw Valley marketing, focusing on the ski school. But once Nate spotted the tracks laid down through the chutes and off the cliffs in the Palisades, he got other ideas. He didn't want to film just another corporate segment for that fall's upcoming Warren Miller production. Instead, he could sense something new going on with those tracks, and sought out the person responsible.

A few days later, Schmidt received a call, out of the blue. "I hear you're the guy who left the track through the Chimney Chute," Nate said, and asked if he wanted to become a part of the latest Warren Miller film. The segment, which also included skiers Kent Smith, Dan Herby, and Robbie Huntoon, was set on the cliff-littered Kitchen Wall and the famed Palisades at Squaw. Featured in 1983's *Ski Time*, the opening shot features Schmidt dropping in on Eagles Cliff, a rock face at the top of the KT-22 chairlift. As Schmidt stands on top of the snow-covered rock face and begins his descent, Warren's opening narration (backed by the sound of a ticking clock) goes, "Time, there is all kinds of it. Time is the only thing in life we own, no one can give you any, but people can take it away from you. You can waste it or you can invest it in . . . Ski Time."

The film set a generational shift in motion, as far as the mentality of what could be skied and how those "ski bums" should be spending their time.

Schmidt left the most memorable impression on the audience, leaping off a 67-degree, hundred-foot line with a compact tuck of his knees and a leap that would become his signature. Warren Miller fans devoured the new-wave extreme skiing, and flocked to watch it in movie theaters nationwide.

"That scene was happening at Squaw, just nobody had showcased it before," Schmidt said. "The *Ski Time* segment was the first to showcase that stuff, and of course, it blew up."

Also featured in that film was a segment from Sugarbush, where a ski bum from Boston named John Egan ripped bumps, jumped over other skiers, and pushed the limits of what the scene could look like on the opposite coast of America.

Schmidt's reputation was blowing up as the '80s rolled on, and Warren Miller featured him in film after film with names like *Steep and Deep* and *Beyond the Edge*. Day was also busy filming for Miller, and his reputation grew through his yearly appearances in the films, as well. But Schmidt's busy schedule left Day looking for another skiing partner by the mid-1980s.

Day had heard stories about John Egan back in Vermont and watched his exploits both in person and in theaters. Day recalled, as a college student, seeing Egan ski at Sugarbush. "I was riding the Summit Lift at Sugarbush North and saw this guy rip down the narrow mogul trail below, as someone said, 'Hey, that's John Egan.' I had heard of him, but that was the first time I saw him ski and it was like . . . yeah, he rips."

But the two did not meet until years later, when both Tom and John moved to Squaw. It was John's first year in Squaw. "I just went up and introduced myself," Day said. "I just wanted to ski with him. I was just blown away by John's skiing." That introduction would lead to decades of moments together on the mountains, both on- and off-camera. John figures he hasn't been on any mountain or expeditions with anyone more than he has with Tom Day, a partnership that began when Day recruited John for a European venture.

It was 1987 when John received a call to go to Verbier, Switzerland, to film with Warren Miller. He hadn't skied for Miller in a handful of years, but Tom, who was scheduled to appear in the film, insisted that John be the other featured skier. By this point, Tom was starting to transfer his Warren Miller on-camera persona to one behind the lens, which helped lead John out of his so-called retirement.

Just don't call it that. "I don't know if you could ever really retire from letting Warren Miller call you and ask you to go on a film trip," John said.

John and Tom were always very complementary skiers, but had yet to work professionally together. To start things off right on familiar turf, they trained at Squaw, getting equipment in line for traveling overseas. Tom and John were doing a photo shoot in Squaw prior to their trip, and Dan, who had swung in to meet his big brother during a break from college, watched in awe—not his brother's skiing prowess, but something else for which he needed no introduction.

The last time Dan had seen his brother, John had played the part of the rebel, flashing his no-care attitude in front of the photographers on hand, essentially spitting in the face of their dressed-up propriety. Dan and John would snicker at the professionalism and poise of the subjects, sticking to their East Coast-hardened mentalities of dissent and nonconformity. Yet, here was John wearing nice clothes in front of the very same photographers the two of them used to make fun of. That left Dan in a sort of ski mentality purgatory: prim and proper, or sticking to his rebel roots? "I was like, wow. Look at him."

John would wind up in that year's film, *White Winter Heat*, in a segment during which he skied with John Falkiner, a Swiss guide known mostly for being a stuntman in a number of James Bond films, including the famous skiing scene that opens 1984's *A View to a Kill*.

The Warren Miller movie gave Dan more than just the delight of watching his big brother on screen, but also that of observing how importantly John was treated. "I'm thinking, 'let's go,'" Dan said. "The door is open here."

Gary Nate didn't know anything about John Egan before making his way to Verbier to film him for *White Winter Heat*. All the cameraman knew was that Tom Day had recommended him, and Nate, acceding to Day's eye and knowledge when it came to skiing, went along with the idea. Once he met John, he realized that enforcing any semblance of control or authority on the shoot was going to be a challenge.

"There was no controlling John Egan, that's for sure," Nate said. "It was impossible to figure out what would happen next with him. He had a charisma about him that I just could not explain. There are a few people you run into in your lifetime who just blow you away, and John Egan is one of them."

Verbier probably brought out an even more impressive aspect of John's skiing. This was, after all, home to the skiing and big-mountain cultures in which he'd started to immerse himself in upon arriving at Sugarbush in 1976, when he first got out of high school and became a ski bum. "Ski magazines always had little articles on Vallençant skiing the Matterhorn and other sorts of things like that," John said. "That always stuck in my mind more than Phil Mahre winning a medal or something. Then, when I was lucky enough to go to Europe to ski there, I was in a great crowd."

That crowd was called "The Clambin Kids," and included photographers Ace Kvale and Marko Shapiro, and mountain guide and adventurer John Falkiner. The Clambin Kids defined the small region within Verbier, when it came to skiing, when skiing as a sport was primarily thought to have its apex in World Cup or Olympic racing competition. The trio created a new lifestyle in the mountains of Verbier, beginning in the late '70s, "that came to symbolize the free, wild spirit of pursuing the good life in the mountains," as *Powder Magazine* once categorized them. Through photographs of their skiing exploits, the Clambin Kids (or "Team Clambin") found success in documenting a form of skiing unbeknownst to an American audience at that time. When it arrived on American mountains, it would come to be known as extreme skiing.

Suddenly, John was soaking up behaviors he'd only read about or aspired to possess someday. Now he was in the thick of it, reveling in the possibilities that his ski bum career could actually realize. Once John made it to Chamonix and ran into his idol, Patrick Vallençant, the reality of it all started to hit him. This wasn't a lifestyle to just read about any longer. It was beckoning for his participation. He decided he wasn't going to do anything but follow it for a while. "I'm not leaving town," he said. "I'm sleeping in the rafters and climbing the mountains and watching [Vallençant] ski. And it was just like, OK, this stuff I can get into."

John and Tom followed Vallençant, any chance they got, around Chamonix, watching and studying his turns and trying to follow in his footsteps. It was in Chamonix, in 1982, when Vallençant founded Degré7 outdoor clothing, featuring "high-tech materials, the rigor of the construction, and daring style and colors." If the skier's signature moves weren't telling enough, the clothing line's boldness seemed to shout where Vallençant was at all times. John and Tom focused on how he handled himself in the gnarly terrain, using ropes to navigate the many crevasses that populate Chamonix's legendary routes. That was new to John and Tom, who figured crevasses were just as well navigated by jumping over them.

Eventually, John had to make a decision. He'd been offered a job on a boat in the Mediterranean in the south of France and would have to leave Chamonix in order to take it. With the snow season waning, finding himself penniless, it seemed just as good an opportunity to begin his offseason regimen as doing construction in the Boston area. He decided to take the opportunity and hitched his way out of town. Perhaps he'd get a sign along the way telling him whether or not he'd made the right call.

That's when Vallençant picked him up on the side of the road. No way John was leaving now. John was in awe, and blurted out, "I've been following you," admitting that he'd been watching the Frenchman's every move, studying the smooth nature of his skiing, trying to mimic his style.

"I know," Vallençant said. "We think it's funny."

Funny? Funny how?

Vallençant told him he found it hysterical that John elected to cross crevasses without a rope. Neither of the skiers knew it at the time, but there was an eerie foreshadowing in the exchange. In 1989, just seven years hence, Vallençant would die in a climbing accident at La Beaume Rouge, in France. He didn't have a rope. Vallençant knew better than to climb without one. He even laughed at one young American for doing the same thing. About a month later, Vallençant's wife, Marie-Jo, would also die in a reverse bungee jumping accident. They left a son behind.

The fanboy in John, still alive today—now in his sixties—has posters of both Patricks, Vallençant and Sudan, hanging in his Vermont basement. That day, having been picked up and meeting Vallençant in person, John Egan, the skier, suddenly made a comeback.

Patrick Vallençant's death still doesn't sit well with John, a death he chalks up to what he calls "a numbers game," and his belief in the fact that time will come knocking at some point—eventually—on the door of those who live their lives on the edge without taking necessary precautions, is definite.

"At one point, you wouldn't have done that, but now you think it's the thing to do. So, what were you thinking?" John asked. "I can have that attitude because he wasn't my brother, my father, my mother, my son, I'm not *that* attached to this person, and I think it's part of the hero worship that screws a lot of people up, too: when it becomes hero worship instead of looking-up-to. Then you're dressing like Dennis Rodman and doing cocaine, yourself. You've got to see the limits within your heroes to understand how to be your own hero. You can't just say 'He does all that, so I'll do all that.' 'All that' might not work for you."

John said a sadness lingers around Vallençant's death, and wonders about his thought process. But there's a tinge of frustration when he discusses not-so-death-defying stunts, like Marie-Jo's. "There's anger in the stupid deaths," he said. "Jumping a hundred and sixty feet to prove a point, to have the highest score, to reverse-bungee-jump because *that's a good idea*. That just seems stupid."

John would end up staying in Chamonix for two months. The fun ended when Hertz came and took the rental car away. Warren Miller had rented the car in Switzerland for the shoot. "We were supposed to return it in Geneva, and instead drove it to France and kept sleeping in it until they found out where it was," John said. "That was the Boston boy in me." Without a place to sleep, John headed home, where he detailed the trip to Dan with a sense of awe.

"Dude, you won't believe what I've seen, where I've been, and what we did," John said. All of a sudden, there was a certain change in John's sense of off-season philosophy. He wasn't ready to work, and was more inclined to go windsurfing or sailing than pick up construction tools. Dan called it "The European Hangover." After spending two months in heaven, John was not eager to pound nails. Reality eventually set in though, and John went back to construction for the summer. Dan watched John head home to build condominiums along Massachusetts' Route 128 corridor, and would eventually find himself working similarly, along with other local ski bums—banging nails and hauling plywood. They worked weekends and the Fourth of July, whatever it took to make a paycheck.

Dan, meanwhile, landed a job as a sailing instructor at the Boston Sailing Center on Lewis Wharf, a marina situated in the city's North End. The job came with some unique benefits.

"I could drink. They're going to let me drink and teach sailing," Dan said. "I thought it was the best job in the world. I was a really good sailing instructor, but the best part was, we believed that if you were going to sail, you were probably going to drink, so you might as well learn drunk. Every Friday, we'd go out to the Boston Harbor Islands and have a picnic. All week we'd be telling the students, 'You've got to bring good beer. You've got to bring shrimp.' When we got to the island, we'd party our asses off."

All partying aside, the job paid off. The following summer, Dan was promoted to manager. In his spare time, when he wasn't navigating sailboats around the Boston Harbor Islands and partying with the center's clients, he was helping his brother on the construction front, every stroke of the hammer bringing them one step closer to another winter of skiing.

The career they would soon build together was finally on the horizon.

Photograph by Dave Roman

Joe Powder lands and hip checks on the only patch of snow on the face of the cliff.

The "hip check" is a technique used to both absorb the impact of a landing and to decelerate before the next turn. Here is Dan hip checking in Yugoslavia for Warren Miller's *Born to Ski*.

Chapter Eleven

NO FRIENDS ON A POWDER DAY

DAN HAD PROMISED JOHN HE would return to school, that taking these winters off in the mountains would produce something more than just another ski-bum mentality. Not that there was anything wrong with that, but Dan had already battled his way into admittance at Babson, where he was holding on for dear life. And John didn't want to be party to Dan's failure to graduate. "I skied all that winter, went to school in May, made up the semester I'd missed over the summer, played soccer that fall, and then took the next winter off," Dan said. "Every time I did that, he'd make me promise that I'd go back." Besides, the time off had motivated Dan. He was excited to get back to school. "I knew I would get to play soccer again, so I was training and playing in the summer league *and* going to school."

Mike Bisner, manager of St. Moritz Sports in Wellesley, gave him a summer job working for Ski Market. Dan filled a trailer with windsurf boards and went out to teach the sport in Quincy Bay, Wollaston Beach, and Lake Quabbin. "He was promoting a new sport that's not a lot of fun until you learn," Bisner said.

But, in 1986, the experiences he'd had in Squaw beckoned him to return. Knowing he'd made a strong connection with the network of Sugarbush refugees (Dockendorf and Woolard, among others, had made their moves permanent) in Tahoe, another trip out West seemed to be in the cards for the second semester of his junior year. Then, his former roommate at Bridgton, Mike Neff, announced he wasn't returning to school at the University of New Hampshire. Which was all the ammunition Dan needed.

Neff bought a Toyota Corolla for $400 and they beelined for California. This time, there would be no airport confusion or disgruntled former girlfriends coming to rescue them from their vehicular ineptitude. They would get jobs. They would ski. Dan would show Neff the life of a ski bum he'd dabbled in the previous winter, probably hoping to smooth some of the edges off his experiences this time around, as well.

John had his own first bite of success when he started competing on the World Pro Mogul and the World Pro Race Tours. He remains the only person to ever compete in both during the same year, an even more remarkable achievement due to the fact that he finished the campaign ranked ninth in moguls and in the top twenty in racing. Upon moving to Squaw Valley, he worked at the Clocktower Café, and the owner, remembering John, hired Dan to be a prep chef for breakfast. In pure ski-bum fashion, he also hired Mike to work at the restaurant, giving the pair the ability to drive to two jobs with one car. They lived in the "Ghetto in the Meadow," an inexpensive condo complex on the lake, that did its best to live up to its local reputation of a beer-soaked frat house. And they skied. A lot.

Dockendorf, who moved to Squaw in 1987, felt a sense of pride in how he'd tutored Dan to become a stellar ski bum, in those earlier years at Sugarbush. "How could you not be proud?" he said. "What I never wanted to be, and what I knew Dan never wanted to be, is that forty-year-old, now-almost-sixty-year-old ski bum with gray hair, hanging out at the bar with the twenty-five-year-olds, having the same conversations you'd had when you were twenty-five, and so never having grown."

Dan's professional career, born from the ski-bum lifestyle, was what Dockendorf had always hoped would happen. "He's done a far better job than me of keeping skiing first and foremost," said Dockendorf, who is also the founder and executive director of Adventure Treks, an outdoor activities adventure outlet for teenagers, with locations throughout the U.S. and Canada.

"Dockendorf and I skied every day," Dan said. "We knew the iconic lines. We knew the Palisades. We knew the Eagles Cliffs. We knew the finger chutes, and we were on a mission. We knew what we had seen in the movies, what Schmiddy and John, Tom Day, Robbie Huntoon, and the others had done." The Squaw Valley hijinks also made it to Hollywood, as in 1984's *Hot Dog . . . The Movie*. Not that there's anything brilliant about it—your typical rags-to-riches story about a farm boy who finds glory (and gets the girl) during a skiing competition at Squaw. There are plenty of drunken escapades, a wet T-shirt contest, racial stereotypes, drug use, and sexual encounters. Throughout, the rebellious band of skiers find themselves up against a finely depicted European nemesis—all in the name of having a good time and little else. It also featured some legitimate skiing sequences which still hold up, nearly forty years later, thanks to the presence of some veteran skiers.

Huntoon served as stunt double for main protagonist, Harkin Banks. Many of the key stunt skiers were coaches at Squaw's freestyle ski academy, or knew each other from the World Cup freestyle skiing circuit. *Hot Dog . . . The Movie* remains the highest grossing ski movie of all time, perhaps because the skiing is more legitimate than the plot itself, but also for the simple reason that the movie, in its entirety, was just a lot of fun.

"We wanted to be that," Dan said with a chuckle. His second winter at Squaw was already much different, because he'd set down some roots in town. Instead of sleeping on his brother's ex-girlfriend's floor, he had his own place.

He had a job and a ski pass. He had Dockendorf, with whom he'd learned the basics of life as a ski bum at Sugarbush. It all led to further exploration of the mountain. "I set a goal: once I started to ski a line, and once I could do it alone and make my own decisions, it became my line. Prior to that, Doc and I would work it out together—how to do it, where to go. I mean, straight skis, it's different. So I started to click off these lines by myself and gained some confidence."

Because he was a prep chef at the café, Dan got to know most of the instructors and the patrol who came in for their coffee in the morning. That familiarity bred bravery when it came to his ability on the mountain. He decided one day to ski the finger chutes of the KT-22, a portion of the mountain skied with some regularity today but not so much in the mid-1980s. Back then, it was a sign of the Alpine teeth you had. "I was skiing the looker's right. It's a very narrow chute and it's got a small cliff in the middle. I was skiing it on my own. I'd probably done it, maybe, with Doc, once. But I jumped in there and I fell, and I tumbled through it. My pole got stuck in the middle of the chute and I couldn't go back and get it. And that pole sat, in full view from the lift. In the morning, the ski patrol guy said, 'Hey, is that your pole, kid? You left your pole up there?' They razzed me, so I'd say, 'why don't you go get it for me? You're so good, why don't you go get it?' It was that Boston edge."

About a week later, Dan decided he was going to go get that damned pole. He went into the chute with two poles, skied down, and grabbed it on the way, skiing out with three poles. "The reaction from the patrol and the ski instructors the next day was amazing. It was like, 'You're all right.' They knew I had gone in and gotten my own pole, and that story went around the resort. It was a rite of passage at Squaw, for me. I wasn't just a curly-haired kid serving coffee, now. I was edging into their world a little bit."

There's an image of Dan from that winter, in a ripped one-piece suit with a shirt wrapped around his waist. "And I'm just hucking the biggest cornice I can find," he said. "That, to me, sums up what I was doing. I wasn't doing it for photos. I had one pair of skis, with broken edges. I was just a ski bum."

To the prim and proper crews at Squaw, where everyone is seeking the closest camera to capture their likeness in the name of possible sponsorship, Dan stuck out like a sore thumb, an East Coast Jerry skiing in a beat-up, one-piece blue suit held together with duct tape, who'd suddenly been transported to the West Coast world of Bogner and Oakley. "People would introduce me to the photographers of the day as John Egan's younger brother," he said. "But the photographers would look at me with that suit and say, 'We're never going to shoot you, kid. You need sponsors. You need equipment.' And I didn't care. I would purposely ski in front of them and flash it and mess up their shots. I kind of looked down on it, and them, at the time."

But Dan was already making a name for himself, in his rebellious fashion, particularly with some of John's friends, who began to include him in their ski gangs. That included Dennis Ouelette. It was Ouelette who'd first introduced John to the glories of skiing in the West. The truck-driving work helped support John in the winter, which included a heli-ski trip he and Ouellette decided to make an annual plan. Prior to the winter of '86, John picked up the phone to entice Dan to come, and plan accordingly. At the time, a week of heli-skiing with Canadian Mountain Holidays (CMH) would run around $2,500 (today, the cost is closer to $15,000). So Dan saved up with the trip in mind. He prepaid and was all set for the adventure with the crew. He had to tell his boss at the Clock Tower he'd be off for a week, which, in ski-bum land, was the equivalent of announcing you needed a coffee break once the picture had been laid out to one's superiors who understood how important the ultimate goal was in the first place.

The night before Dan left to meet his brother and friends in Seattle, they threw a rager at the Ghetto in the Meadow. There was plenty of drinking, bottles smashed against the walls, and a general sense of flippant revelry. As such parties tend to go, the beer ran dry. Neff took it upon himself to go get more, and went off into the night with a friend of his driving, while the rest of the party sat waiting for more brew. But they never came back. After a while, one might imagine the group would put the pieces together and begin making phone calls to make sure their friends were safe. Eventually, they learned through the grapevine that they were OK, but the driver had been arrested for drinking and driving, and Neff picked up by association.

This turn of events left Dan with a dilemma: He could put a few dollars together, make his way to the Tahoe jail where Neff was being held, bail him out, help make a plan for the aftermath, and try to soothe his nerves by getting him to the comfort of his own bed, rather than having to sleep in a cold, dark, metal cell . . . Or, as originally planned, he could just head out on his heli-skiing trip.

And so, Dan made a pivotal decision: it was off to Seattle. Neff was in jail, and Dan was in the air on the way to join his brother and crew. In John's eyes, it was the moment when Dan's career as a ski bum truly took its turn for the good. A ski bum has no friends on a powder day. Skiing, above all else.

The pupil was becoming a quick learner.

Chapter Twelve

HELI-SKIING

WHENEVER THEY WERE SUPPOSED TO meet up in some locale, wherever it may be, John and Dan never had a plan. Prior to immediate location services, incessant texting, and all the other contemporary means of communication at our fingertips, for John and Dan, reconvening with one another took a much simpler approach: find a bar.

"So, I flew to Seattle and went in the first bar I saw, then I went to every bar in the airport," Dan said. John had flown in with a pair of Vermonters, Karen Anderson and Stan Woliner. The trio had arrived around 10 a.m., Seattle time, and figured Dan would meet them at the gate. Except there was no Dan, of course. "We searched around a bit and decided the bar might be our best bet," Woliner said. "There was Dan on a bar stool, the only person in the place, chatting it up with the bartender. We said our hellos and laughed a lot. Then Dan pulled out a five-dollar bill, slapped it on the bar and said, 'Well, that's my last five bucks and it was well spent.' We tucked the little brother under our wings and off we went."

Well, in truth, his cash flow was a little more than that, but not by much.

Dan had left Reno with eighty dollars to his name—which would have to last for the entire trip to British Columbia. So, of course, the first thing he did upon their arrival at Sea-Tac International Airport was buy a round of drinks for the entire group. That cost him twenty bucks. The next day, when the crew went skiing at nearby Crystal Mountain, the lift ticket cost forty. One day in, and Dan was down to his last twenty-dollar bill, and hadn't yet crossed the border into Canada.

Anderson, the resident veterinarian at Sugarbush, was the only female in the group. Since it was Valentine's Day, she was adamant that it was her day; the men should do something special to help her celebrate. "This was pre-SUV, and I had rented a full-size boat for our journey north," Woliner said. "We sidled up to our four-door, red Chrysler Cordoba with Corinthian leather both inside and out, sporting it on the rooftop, as well." They decided to take Anderson to the aquarium in Vancouver after crossing the U.S.-Canadian border. But, as they were approaching the checkpoint, John asked a question Dan had never before considered: "Does anybody have drugs on them?"

Dan recalled the pills he'd been given at a house party the night before. He thought the guy called the stuff *ecstasy*. He had no idea how or when to take it, or how much, but figuring the border was closing in quickly, they needed to figure out what to do with it. "We snorted the stuff and . . . I don't know," Dan said. They got through the Canadian border without any issues and made their way to the aquarium. "We didn't see the exhibits," Dan said, "we were *in* the exhibits. We got in behind the tanks. We were in the water fountain. We were out of our minds on the ecstasy and we were having a ball. Karen thought it was awesome. A beautiful Valentine's Day." Hallmark-worthy? Maybe not. But beautiful all the same.

Kamloops is 225 miles from Vancouver—a four-hour-plus drive the Egans and friends had ahead of them after their aquarium adventure. John was driving, so that meant a good four more hours of partying in the back seat of the Cordoba for the rest of the crew, drinking to wash away the last effects of the ecstasy and to ride the buzz via a new elixir. They almost made it without being pulled over. They made quite the scene for the Mountie. "Someone was puking in a paper bag, there are empties in the car, and we are shattered," Dan said. The Mountie wasn't pleased, but when John told him they were all from the States, he was also exasperated. Arresting a whole carload of foreigners would be a lot more work than it might have been had he found locals partying in a car.

"If it wasn't so much damned paperwork I'd arrest every one of you," he said. "Get out of here." They did. The party continued at the hotel.

"I don't know what Kamloops is like now, but it was a sleepy little town back then, about ten years behind the times," Woliner said. "We had some dinner and headed for the hotel bar, which had a pseudo-disco. Upon arrival, things seemed to be pretty tame. I think there was a DJ and a rotating mirrored ball hanging from the ceiling and a fair amount of people, but no one was really dancing that much. We'd been drinking a bit and were feeling no pain. The next thing I know, Dan is jumping around, dancing à la Steven Tyler, and ramping things up about ten notches. We danced the night away with most of the men in attendance eyeing us wildly, but the women were all-in and having a ball. Dan was jumping up on the speakers and figuratively bouncing off the ceiling, but the party was on."

The most memorable intoxication of the trip, though, happened in the mountains. "That trip really changed skiing for me," Woliner said. "It was the first time I had skied untracked snow for endless days. You ski so fast in the trees, and it's steep. Something clicked in me up there. It was amazing. Valemount blew our minds. This was before CMH (Canadian Mountain Holidays) had built many of their lodges, and we were shacked up with about thirty friends from the Northeast at a budget motel in logging country. The heli-pad was just down the road. Valemount, at the time, was a pit stop for truckers doing long hauls across Canada. The motel had eighteen-wheelers stacked up outside and was filled to the brim with truckers and skiers. It was a dive, but who cared? We were raging, and skiing the best snow most of us had ever seen. Powder skiing with John and Dan was pretty damned epic."

"That trip transformed my skiing," said Dan. "The length of the runs, the amazing snow, and the terrain and inherent avalanche danger changed the way I would approach mountains forever."

At the end of the week, everybody was heading home. Dan had long since parted with the remainder of the eighty dollars he'd had in his pocket when he left California. And since he had only purchased a one-way ticket to Seattle, it left him wondering just how he would get back to Reno.

Dennis Ouelette, John's ski-bum pal who owned the apple orchard in upstate New York, met up with the group at the Dome Hotel in Valemount and told Dan he'd drive him back to Squaw Valley in his pickup truck. Trouble was, Dan would have to ride in the back with little more than a sleeping bag to keep him warm for the seventeen-hour drive from Kamloops to Tahoe, but Dan was out of options. He would also have to be patient, as Dennis wasn't planning on heading directly to Squaw. Their ski trip wasn't over just yet.

"We went to Whistler Blackcomb, back to Seattle. We went to Sun Valley, Jackson Hole, and Snowbird. We're on a road trip, and I'm in the back. You just sit in a bag and freeze your ass off," Dan said. "Just *freeze your ass off*. But I had all our equipment in the back with me. It was like I just knew we were going to another ski resort. Just going to another ski resort." In Dan's mind, they had something else to prove. "Dennis is a very loud guy. You knew when he was around, because he was always causing a ruckus. But he taught me a lot about life. Dennis is a big mentor of John's, and he mentored me, too, in just normal things and skiing. And the love. The passion to do it, to make it happen. His generosity was never lost on me. It was amazing. I'm a very generous guy, but I didn't know if I could ever be as generous as him. But in his spirit, I, too, am generous."

By the time they made it to Salt Lake City, Dennis had decided to break the news to Dan that he wasn't heading the entire way back to Squaw, after all. All told, it had been a month of bouncing from one place to another, and Dennis figured it was finally time to head back East. But, instead of leaving Dan stranded in Utah, he bought him a plane ticket back to Reno. "I said to him, 'Dennis, I could never repay you for everything you've done.' He paid for lift tickets, housed me, fed me all that whole month, and on top of that gave me airfare." Dennis grinned and replied, "Don't worry, someday I'm going to crash at your house and get my revenge."

This all left Dan in a good situation, finally heading back to Reno, where he'd started in February. But it had also been a month since he'd left his pal Mike Neff in jail, the night before heading to the airport. Never mind that he'd told his boss at the Clock Tower Café he would be back in a week from his heli-skiing trip. "I hadn't been at work for over a month. I hadn't paid rent. I didn't have any money to pay the rent. My roommates were pissed off because they weren't getting my share of the rent. Mikey was pissed because I left him in jail." His own tension probably should have given Dan a hint of the frustration he'd experience when he arrived at the Clock Tower. Fortunately, Jim might have witnessed such ski-bummery before. He just greeted Dan by asking how the trip had gone and how John was doing. "Dude, you must be dying to ski here at Squaw," he said. Then Jim gave Dan his ski pass and put him back on the work schedule for the following week.

And so, Dan kept skiing. Squaw had welcomed him back, and in order to take advantage of the final weeks, he wanted to share all the lessons he'd learned that winter. The lessons about passing it on. The lessons about sharing the wealth, with the mentality that whatever good will you can give to others, it will eventually come back to you. Countless people would recycle these lessons in their own karma over the course of Dan's career.

Certainly, Dan hadn't missed noticing the pivotal role Dennis played in launching the ski careers of the Egan brothers through his own generosity, both in making sure John had the means to ski with him at all times, as well as introducing Dan to the fact that penniless doesn't mean hopeless when it comes to becoming a ski bum. In turn, the same generosity Dennis showed John over the years got passed down to Dan. "John made a lot of money driving Dennis's truck," Dan said. "If it wasn't for John's work ethic, we probably couldn't have launched our career. He had the backing. He had money. What I mean when I say is, he had enough to get us lift tickets and keep gas in the car—way before I did. And John never asked me to pay him back. I paid John back by getting sponsorship deals. I paid John back by creating a career and managing that career. That was always part of my motivation: one, obviously to always get his approval, but two, paying John back. Never occurred to me not to do it. I knew he had invested in me, I knew why he had made me promise to finish school, and I felt obligated to him to honor my promise."

With those thoughts in mind, time was running out at Squaw Valley. On April 8, the Red Sox opened the season at Fenway Park in Boston with a 9–2 win over the New York Yankees. Baseball was signaling that it was time for Dan to head home. Babson and the Dean of Student Affairs were ready to welcome Dan back to begin his summer semester. The dean also told him it had better be his last. "You're on the edge here," he told Dan. "You're a standout athlete, you're a standout troublemaker, and your academics are only OK. We're not going to put up with this any longer." He gave Dan a year—twelve months—to finish his studies, which meant there would be no winter skiing sabbatical this time.

The message was clear: They said, if you're going to continue, we're not going to continue at this pace. *We want you out of here.* Dan heard the ultimatum and went wire-to-wire, from May until May.

May, 1987 was looming . . . *I will graduate from Babson in 1987.* "I'm a dreamer whose dreams come true," Dan said. "I have visions of things, and the vision comes into my life." The achievement of graduating from Babson College, and how that goal became his primary focus, would turn into a calling card for how Dan would experience events and milestones throughout his life.

Joe Powder "billy goats" off of a patch of snow, preparing for his next free fall.

John "billy goating" down a cliff in Val d'Isère.

Photograph by Dave Roman

Chapter Thirteen

WHY NOT TRY?

DAN'S FATHER HAD SOME SIMPLE words of advice and a book for his son at commencement, both inspired by watching him graduate college between stints as a ski bum. The book was *Catechism of the Catholic Church*, and Robert's advice was, "You can't meet every ski bunny and ski every mountain in the world." They were prescient words from a man who'd built his family and medical practice on his education, a neurologist whose attention to the tiniest detail was critical. Adventure has a limit. Youth has a limit. The whole course of life has a limit.

"My dad brought it all back to the Church," Dan said. "He believed I could find my way if I stayed anchored in faith. I know now he was right, but at that time I couldn't hear it."

And besides, Warren Miller saw life a little differently. "Warren told me that my skis were like a jet engine and could take me all around the world. So, I thought, Why not try?"

Why not?

"I was at a turning point in the tug-of-war between the structure of convention and unlimited freedom. My dad, Mom, and Bob were trying to get me to see things their way, which was reinforced by my experiences at Bridgton and Babson, but was in opposition to the taste of the ski-bum lifestyle I'd had with John, Neff, and Dockendorf. My stints at Sugarbush and Squaw had left me thirsting for more. I just figured there had to be a way to blend these two worlds together. There just had to be a way. So I packed away the Catechism for another day and started to pursue this free-spirited dream in my head to the nth degree. Warren and my dad, both role models—the two most influential men in my life. But they were very, very different individuals."

At the time, Dan was reading *Way of the Peaceful Warrior*, Dan Millman's semi-autobiographical book about a college student and world champion gymnast who is haunted by the feeling that something is missing from his life. The protagonist meets a sage warrior, an old man named Socrates, who would become his mentor.

"That search and unease was gnawing at me, as well," Dan said. "I had my diploma, had met the goal I'd set for myself at Bridgton, and while my friends were landing jobs at Pepsi and financial institutions, I was going to teach sailing and coach soccer with my Babson degree. It always made me chuckle that my employment was, at the time—and to some extent still is—based on what my parents had taught me to do athletically, by the age of ten."

During an interview with Stein Eriksen, recorded at the Boston Ski Show for Dan's television program, *Wild World of Winter*, in the late 1990s, the skiing legend told Dan that Warren Miller was to skiing what NBC was (and still is) to the Olympics. Meaning, its blanket of coverage brought many niche events to the TV-viewing masses. In his own right, Warren was one of the most influential people in bringing winter sports to an armchair audience, with his distinguished voice asking every viewer to participate. As Miller's most quoted maxim notes: "If you don't do it this year, you'll be one year older when you do."

Warren Miller embraced this sense of belonging. His films were an inclusive, rather than exclusive, look at sports and dreams that would never be pursued by most common viewers—but they would watch them on TV. "I spent my professional life taking pictures of people, observing what people did and what they said, and either took movies of them, or I drew cartoons," Miller said during a 2015 interview. "It was my take on the world." Miller documented, on film, the birth of the ski industry. He documented the change in fashion, the changes in technology and snowmaking. If there was a new lift, he shot it and portrayed it in a film. Another resort would see that lift and think they needed to get one of their own. In essence, that's how the entire business of trade surrounding winter sports was built—from watching one another, seeing what worked.

The Warren Miller formula—snarky jabs at the mundane and bits of humor, mixed with jaw-dropping footage—sounds simple, yet that very simplicity made it effective and lent it the ability to connect with people watching his films. This is the world in winter. Go live in it. "Because Warren Miller was always out in front of what was yet to be," Dan said, "resorts, manufacturers, and international destinations knew his films would reach and influence a worldwide audience. His films are the original social media."

But if Facebook had a specific beginning in a Harvard dorm room, then Miller's form of social landscape began in a very different fashion. In 1946, at the age of twenty-two, Warren bought an eight-millimeter movie camera with his separation pay when he mustered out of the Navy. He soon departed his Los Angeles home for Sun Valley, Idaho, where the zygote of his filmmaking empire would begin to coalesce.

Sun Valley was founded by Averell Harriman, chairman of the board of the Union Pacific Railroad, partner in Brown Brothers Harriman and Company on Wall Street, and a statesman. Harriman's European businessmen friends spent their winter vacations at resorts in the Alps. Whether they skied or not, they wanted to relax with mountain scenery, posh accommodations, first-class restaurants, and a friendly atmosphere among beautiful people. Harriman wanted his Idaho resort to be first-class in everything, and it was—except for the trailer in the parking lot, the winter of 1946–47.

Warren's trailer was a mainstay at resorts like Sun Valley, where he would shoot footage from the slopes and turn them into films upon his return to Los Angeles during the offseason. He often survived on rabbits he shot for dinner. He'd sneak into the resort's heated swimming pool to bathe. He tailed the likes of Ernest Hemingway and Gary Cooper on hiking trails which would one day welcome generations of skiers and riders who'd been inspired by his films documenting fun activities on the mountain.

You could argue that, until Warren Miller began presenting skiing as something visually interesting to watch at home, the sport was stuck in the elegant but superficial perception inspired by its European roots. Miller showed viewers that the discipline and precision of skiing, particularly when tied to slalom racing, could be learned. Skiing was not just for the professional. The sport could just as easily serve as a recreational activity for the family to enjoy; an enjoyable diversion, certainly with a learning curve, but not one that was insurmountable for the novice skier.

"When I ski, I often think about the beauty of the place—gliding, drifting over, on and through snow. These thoughts summon my inner Warren Miller and make the place prettier," Dan said. "Our job is to put the accent on the mountain, the track. And that's what I love to do." In Warren's brand of skiing there was no gold medal or trophy, but rather an appreciation of nature's beauty and a sense of fun that would attract everyone to the slopes, from the beginner to the experienced skier who might not have experienced a particular landscape in that year's film. Miller's fun, he once observed, came from the creative process: discovering something special and sharing it with his viewers. That could range from the sublime to the ridiculous—from experts skiing off cliffs to a beginner executing a "knee-drop stop." His dry humor was narrative accompaniment to the sights and sounds; really more of a crutch in the beginning, when he admittedly suggested that the photographs and videos he took weren't

115

very good. He had to massage them into something more useful somehow, someway.

The formula he evolved helped drive his brand. Skiers and locations changed, but there were few surprises from year to year in any Warren Miller production. "Our statistics show, a large percentage of our audience has seen a previous Warren Miller film," he said in a 1986 interview. "They know what to expect in a Warren Miller film. There is no sex or violence, only action and a little humor."

The overarching message in all Miller's films is one of freedom, visually self-evident. The films also became the basis for evening screening events in ski lodges around the country. A Warren Miller production was never released at a multiplex in a shopping mall, shown instead at smaller independent theaters for short runs. That remained true for how Miller presented his productions, narrating them in person to sellout crowds. In 1949, Miller presented his first film, *Deep and Light*, in an auditorium at John Marshall Junior High in Pasadena, California. Ski Club Alpine, which sponsored the event, took 60 percent of the revenue from ticket sales, leaving Warren with the remaining 40 percent. 836 people showed up, each paying $1 admission. Miller made $334.40 that first night.

"We make coming to the film an event," he said in 1986. "Our marketing approach is similar to that of a circus. For example, if you want to see a Warren Miller film in San Francisco, you have to go either October fifth, sixth, or seventh, to the one location. After that, you're out of luck. This single, four-wall concept approach has been very successful for us."

And it still is today. Warren's business model has prevailed for the past seventy-one years, with one slight adjustment—distribution for VHS. Admittedly, he hadn't foreseen how the advent of VHS technology would impact the way people watched his films. However, there was a certain puckish, red-haired graduate of Babson College searching for adventure, a mentor, and business opportunities, who did.

Chapter Fourteen

SPONSORED BY
YOMOMMA & MYMOMMA

DAN EGAN HAD A VISION. He just didn't have any clue what it was telling him, yet. Dan was out of school, with his marketing degree in hand. He'd watched John's connections take him to places they'd only dreamed of, and he figured it was time for him to take the next steps—whatever those steps were. The timing for getting his dreams to start paying dividends was coming up on his self-imposed schedule.

"We would always talk about the great winter of '88," Dan said. "We were going to break out. I would be out of school, and were going to get out of New England, head out West, and go do it. We didn't know what 'it' was, but we were going to go do it."

In fall of '87, however, Dan was juggling a number of jobs. He was the assistant soccer coach at Curry College, getting up at 3 a.m. to deliver *USA Today* newspapers, and substitute teaching in whatever class the Milton school system needed help with that day.

"I was terrible at it," he said. "Miss Britton, the art teacher, had hated me as a student. She came up to me one day and said, 'I hope you get everything you ever deserved.' Miss Siciliano, my Spanish teacher, warned me, 'You should get out while you're still alive. What are you doing here?'" Dan also drove a Pepperidge Farm bread truck—another job he wasn't great at. He could never get the route down properly, so inevitably spent the end of his shift giving away undelivered loaves of bread to the toll collectors on the Massachusetts Turnpike. His disparate responsibilities would not last for long. And the great winter of 1988 was beckoning.

By the time the winter season rolled around, Dan was back in Vermont where he landed a job as the night condo check-in guy at Sugarbush Village Real Estate. He wouldn't have that job long, either. His good friend, Stan Woliner, was heading back to Valemount, with a stop in Denver to watch the New England Patriots play the Broncos. The 1987 Patriots were two years removed from their first appearance in the Super Bowl, and some fourteen years away from becoming one of the NFL's greatest dynasties. With a record of 5–6 heading into the game against the Broncos, the Patriots were still in competition for the AFC East crown, a title that ultimately went to the Indianapolis Colts that year.

Woliner had recently been diagnosed with Stage 3 non-Hodgkin's lymphoma, with tumors all through his body, including one in his chest. Medicine has come a long way since then, but at the time, his prospects were not looking good. "Life was an emotional roller coaster," he said, "but one of my strongest recollections through it all was talking with Dan." Woliner, incredibly, responded well to chemotherapy, and after the eight-month regimen of assorted experimental medicinal cocktails, there were only traces left of the tumors.

"I'd stayed pretty active during treatments, so, physically, I was in pretty good shape. I'd sold my business and had a little money, so the plan evolved to ski around the West for four months." That all sounded great to Dan, except for the fact that Stan was flying into Denver. Without his skis. Or his car, which he'd need in order to keep heading west on I-70 into Colorado's Rocky Mountains. How could any dedicated skier not have skiing on their mind as an extracurricular activity in Colorado? Dan couldn't figure that out—but he had a solution.

He talked Stan into giving him the keys to his car, offering to bring all the gear and drive cross-country to meet him in Denver. From there, the two of them would take the highway into the mountains and see what sort of adventures they could find for themselves in the Rockies.

Stan went for it. "Considering Dan's track record with cars and his general 'balls to the wall' approach to life, it probably wasn't the most prudent decision on my part, but I offered up my Chevy Blazer," he said. "I'd meet him in Colorado for the start of the tour, hang with him and John for a bit, and then head north to British Columbia. It was always great to hang with those guys."

Dan promptly quit his gig at Sugarbush Village Real Estate and returned to John's house, where he'd been couch surfing, to pack for the trip. John was curious. Why, exactly, did Dan have Stan's car? "I quit my job and I'm going west," he said. Now, this might be where the older brother tries to talk some sense into the younger brother, or maybe the father's voice speaks up inside his head, saying, "Don't throw away your job on a whim. Think before you act. How are you going to get by?" Blah, blah, blah . . .

However, John Egan, professional ski bum, had a decidedly different reaction. In addition to his construction duties that winter, John worked at the Green Mountain Valley School, where he disagreed with the training. He was inevitably fired for taking his students hiking in the backcountry during a race. Call it a battle of Alpine philosophies.

"You can be a great racer and not a great skier," John said. "But the better skier you are, the better racer you'll be. They made the kids train, train, train and never took them off-piste. They didn't diversify and teach them the freedom of the sport. So they had the mindset of, 'Oh, I screwed up that gate—now I'm going to screw up all the others' instead of free-flowing it and pulling it back together. That's why you see Bode Miller kick everybody's butt when he gets in trouble, because he can free-flow it. Franz Klammer was always one of my heroes because he was such a wild man, just all over the place. He had this very free style and an independent leg action that dazzled people with what happened on the way down the hill, but he would get there first. At Green Mountain, I had to work with the older kids, but I really liked working with younger kids instead, because they're not so set in their ways."

So, the fact that Dan had just quit his job and was ready to bloom the winter into something bigger, left John with one reaction: "Let's get out of here."

John called the partner with whom he was building condos in Vermont that winter and told him he was quitting to hit the road with his little brother. Now, this might be where the building partner tries to talk some sense into his colleague: We've got jobs to handle. We can't just abandon what we started. How will we get by?

But, to his carpentering partner's credit, he had a decidedly different reaction. Figuring he couldn't build without John, he might as well pack his skis and hop in the Blazer with the brothers. One might assume there would be a foreman, livid over the sudden absence of four hands, but then again— this was Vermont, where the free culture translated well into the ski-bum life. Once the snow started to fall, one shouldn't expect everything to happen the way you think it should. Anybody in the right frame of mind living in a ski town probably understood such detours. It would be unrealistic to expect people to show up to work on time when it's a powder day.

The Egans were on the road to . . . something. Somewhere. They were broke by the time they reached the Rocky Mountains, and Stan's Blazer had a new dent from the storm they'd encountered in the Midwest. With little money for gas or food, John remembered a mogul contest that took place at Aspen Highlands every Friday, where the winner took home $500. "Let's go make some money," he said.

Dan had never competed on moguls, whether at Milton, Bridgton, or Babson. He arrived at Aspen with of one pair of 207 Rossignol giant slalom skis in his ski quiver—not exactly the preferred ski for handling bumps. Nevertheless, the opportunity to win some cash forced him to give it a go.

120

They entered the contest as "The Egan Brothers from Vermont, sponsored by YoMomma and MyMomma."

"And away we went," Dan said.

John won $300. Some of the other competitors recognized John from his time on the pro tour in the early '80s, so it probably didn't surprise anyone when he walked away with most of the prize money. "Are you guys here for the start of the World Pro Tour?" the brothers were asked. There was only one suitable response: "Yes, of course."

Of course.

"Where is it?"

It was scheduled to take place the next day, at Vail, a two-hour drive from Aspen. "We'll see you there," they said. Now able to fill the gas tank, they climbed into Stan's Blazer and made the hundred-mile trek to Vail, where they would take their $300 and lay it on the line. Once again, they entered as "The Egan Brothers from Vermont, sponsored by YoMomma and MyMomma." In all, there were sixty-four pros competing. Those who made it to the final thirty-two would, at the very least, make their money back.

"Once we'd done that, we thought we'd had a great day," Dan said. "Then we both skied into the round of sixteen. Once you start getting deep into the rounds, you're competing for the pros' money—their paycheck—so things start to heat up." Dan went up against a skier who entered the starting gate with more logos on his gear than a race car, which signaled just how deep into the competition the Egans had gotten. These were the racers with more to lose, especially against a pair of brothers who just rolled in from the East Coast. But if Dan felt any intimidation, he didn't show it. "I looked over and I winked at the guy," he said, "and beat him to the bottom. On my 207 GS skis."

The crowd was getting into the Cinderella story at this point. "*YoMomma*"— the fans chanted—"*MyMomma.*" John went out in the round of sixteen. Up next for Dan was Kirk Rawles. Feeling a little exposed without his older brother in the lineup, Dan asked him for advice as they headed up the lift for the upcoming round of eight. "What do you think, man, what should I do?"

he asked. John's straightforward reply was right out of Boston: "You're doing wicked good, dude. We need the money. Do it again and kick his ass."

Rawles would be an even stiffer challenge, one Dan probably couldn't wink away. Colorado's Rawles brothers had been legitimate pro mogul skiers for an extended period of time before the Egans came along. Scott Rawles, just a year younger than his brother Kirk, would one day be the U.S. moguls coach, tutoring Olympic gold medalist freestyle skiers Hannah Kearney and Johnny Moseley, among others. At the time of the pros, Kirk, Scott and Mike, were all in the top ten. But here was his competition in the starting gate, with his baseball cap on backward, sporting ridiculously long skis for the moguls laid out below. How had this East Coast punk made it to the round of eight?

"I waited till he was in the gate, I knew he would look over at me, and when he did, I asked him if he was ready to rumble," Dan said.

But, despite the seemingly out-of-nowhere appearance in the Round of 8, a whole two days into his mogul competition career, Dan's ski popped off as he hit the second jump. That would spell the end. There would be no grand prize for the Egan brothers at the World Pro Tour.

More importantly, "The Egan Brothers" had arrived. Inspired, the Babson marketing graduate started sifting through possibilities for himself and his brother.

Joe Powder pole plants to gain balance prior to launching off another cliff.

Dan pole plants to trigger the next turn on a steep face in Val d'Isère.

Chapter Fifteen

VHS AND THE EXTREME SKIING BOOM

THE EGAN BROTHERS. **IT HAD** the potential to be a captivating name in an industry always looking for new ways to market itself. The truth was, in the mid- to late-'80s, the skiing industry was desperately waiting for something to redefine it, like the Mahre brothers had done for nearly a decade.

Before the likes of Lindsey Vonn, Bode Miller, Mikaela Shiffrin, Tommy Moe, and Julia Mancuso helped define the contemporary American Alpine competitive scene, it seemed unlikely that any U.S. skier would manage to win a World Cup. Before 1984, no American man had ever won an Olympic gold medal in skiing, either (although Vermont native, Billy Kidd, won silver in the slalom at the 1964 Games in Innsbruck, Austria), a blight on the face of the country's skiing program that didn't figure to rectify itself anytime soon. Given the level of competition in Europe, where regimented training bred athletes for the sole purpose of producing precise racing techniques, American skiers were just not up to snuff.

Twins Phil and Steve Mahre, meanwhile, had grown up at the base of Washington state's White Pass Ski Area. They were two of nine children, and their Yakima Valley orchard didn't provide enough income for their large family. So, their resourceful father got himself promoted from his ski patrolman position to mountain manager at White Pass and moved the Mahre family the eighty miles to the ski area. Phil and Steve were only five at the time, and didn't really begin skiing until a year later. By the time they were thirteen, and skiing competitively, they were beating eighteen-year-olds. This would begin a career-long sponsorship partnership with the K2 ski company, located in nearby Seattle. When they were eighteen, they earned spots on the 1976 U.S. Olympic Ski Team.

In the introduction to the book, *No Hill Too Fast*, that noted ski writer John Fry co-authored with the Mahre brothers, Fry wrote: "In the early 1970s, therefore, it would have been laughable to predict that America's first Alpine World Cup would be won by a twenty-four-year-old with a profound indifference to programmed training, growing up with a twin brother who would be the second-best skier in the United States. It was an outrageous contradiction of two widely-heralded principles of how the United States should succeed: that the national ski team must be built on a wide-pyramidal base of athletes across the land, and that winning is the result of motivating individuals to perform in carefully-structured training programs."

Phil Mahre went on to win the overall World Cup title in 1981, then repeated the win the following two seasons. Ever since, no American male has managed to wrestle such a dynasty from the rest of the field. Bode Miller is the only other American male to win since then ('08), but both Lindsey Vonn ('08 and '10) and Mikaela Shiffrin ('17 and '19) have had stretches similar to Mahre's, on the women's circuit.

In the 1980 Olympic Games in Lake Placid, New York, Phil won a silver in the giant slalom, a precursor to the Games four years later in Sarajevo, where he won the slalom and became the first American man to win a gold medal in Alpine ski racing. Remarkably, Steve finished right behind him and took home the silver.

Billy Johnson, meanwhile, was fresh off a World Cup win in Wengen, Switzerland, on the famed Lauberhorn course, making him the first American to win a World Cup downhill. Johnson followed that victory up by shocking the world at the Olympics with a gold medal finish in the downhill.

"Phil and Steve Mahre were the faces of American skiing," Dan said. "Really, not since Billy Kidd had we had such success—and way more than Billy ever had. They were *the* brothers in the modern era of skiing, so K2 was actively promoting them. They were simply amazing." When both retired after the 1984 season, there was a void in American skiing that left the industry wondering who could become the new face(s) of marketing.

The free spirit that helped define the hotdog era of the early '70s was now structured and refined into something barely recognizable. The Mahre brothers moving into retirement didn't necessarily end their roles as ambassadors for the sport, but their penchant to shy away from public interaction meant they didn't exactly raise their role to the next level, as other more boisterous skiers would have done. Nor were they as genuinely marketable as they had once been, in particular not during the Olympic games.

After Phil Mahre and Johnson both won gold in 1984, it would be ten years before another American—Tommy Moe in the downhill at Lillehammer, Norway—would win Olympic gold in Alpine racing. Ski racing, by that point, had hit a nadir. It simply wasn't cool, at least according to *Sports Illustrated*'s E.M. Swift, who notably made headlines with his pre-Olympic takedown of the U.S. skiing program prior to the Lillehammer Olympics, promoting the dynamic allure of Italy's World Cup star Alberto Tomba to a level never seen by Americans. Swift wrote: "There has never been a charismatic, successful skier on the order of Tomba to attract young Americans to the sport. Phil Mahre, who had the talent, had the personality of soapstone. The attractive, articulate [Tamara] McKinney was never strongly promoted. And a generation of U.S. kids in ski country have ignored Alpine racing and, frankly, would rather be snowboarding."

In addition to Tommy Moe, American Diane Roffe won gold at the Games in the women's Super-G, an event in which Moe would take silver for the men's side. Moe made no secret about Swift's derision having been a factor in his success.

Swift's assertion that any skier without a certain amount of flair or charisma would fail to attract young Americans to the sport of Alpine racing was a thesis that had stood for years. The pure fun of freedogging didn't translate to the Alpine circuit, leaving the industry with the challenge of trying to market the European mentality of discipline to an American landscape where personal freedom and expression reigned above all.

In 1988, freestyle skiing made it to the Olympics in Calgary, Canada, as an exhibition sport, and was officially added in 1992, at Albertville, France, where American, Donna Weinbrecht, skiing out of Killington, Vermont, won the first gold medal in moguls. All in all, Americans have won twenty-five medals in freestyle events since then, tying with Canada.

Yet, aside from freestyle's success with joining more mainstream sports as an Olympic category, it had captured the interest of the extreme skiing scene when it burst onto American slopes twenty years earlier. "It was a long story to tell, from Wayne Wong, to the '92 Games, to what eventually happened to the sport of freestyle skiing," Dan said.

Because there remained a hole in the market looking to be filled, extreme skiing became the industry's next marketable wave. In fairness, the roots of what made freedogging popular still existed: doing things on skis that wouldn't necessarily be taught in ski school. But, it would not be enough to sustain the sport. What emerged was a growing interest in traveling to ski more exotic and often dangerous locales, clad in neon-bright colors, combined with extreme skiing's unique, scoffing attitude toward establishment ethos. The most interesting skiing, and skiers, were still nonconformists.

"We were the MTV of mountaineering," Dan said. "We wore neon-colored clothing and had new technology—the VCR—backing us. The market was looking for something new, and that was us."

It was this in-your-face cinematic appeal that filmmakers such as Warren Miller saw as ideal for their ski movies, which needed a shot of adrenaline from skiers with signature haircuts dressed in designer ski suits, jumping off cliffs. But, unlike the freestyle movement during the previous decade, extreme skiers came to the party with the ability to ski closer than ever to their audience, because of the advent of home entertainment. "I would say that extreme skiing actually emerged, not as a sport, but as a form of entertainment on VHS," said Mike Bisner, a former vice president of marketing at Salomon, where he inherited sponsorship of extreme skiers such as Scot Schmidt, the Egans, and the DesLauriers. "Extreme skiing would never have taken off without the VHS tape and the VCR. It was a 'once and done' with Warren Miller films. You saw it once, and that was it at the Warren Miller showing. Then, basically, once the VCR came on the market, you started selling tapes. Greg Stump followed in the steps of Warren Miller, and so did Eric Perlman. Later came filmmakers like the Jones brothers of Teton Gravity Research and Steve Winter, Murray Wais, and Scott Gaffney of Matchstick Productions—it went on and on. You had lots of great filmmakers with great ideas starting to make extreme and expanding beyond what Warren Miller did once a year."

So, it was that ability to replay the tape that made extreme skiing such a boon in the '80s. Ski shops would present the latest film on a TV beside the register while you got fitted with the latest clothing or equipment. In dorm rooms throughout the Northeast, college kids getting pumped for the next day's powder could watch extremists from their well-worn videotape collection. Skiers wandered the booths at their local ski expo, watched extreme skiers on TV for free, then bought the same videocassette for the cost of a pair of movie tickets, took it home, and watched it again and again.

"We went viral before viral existed," said filmmaker Greg Stump, who is most noted for the successful ski film, *Blizzard of Aahhh's*, which further launched the careers of Scot Schmidt and Mike Hattrup, as well as introduced the world to the unpredictability of Glen Plake and his signature Mohawk hairstyle. "The VHS tape to me is what YouTube is to kids today," Dan said. "It's the first time high technology was invited into homes. What I always loved about the VHS tapes was, they could live on your shelves for five to eight years, and probably even longer." Videotape was a luxury the freestyle movement never had, leaving the extreme skiers, a decade later, to run with it for marketing the wild side of the slopes. The fact that the VCR didn't exist for their predecessors seems to have left freedogging a forgotten sport—at the time perhaps most memorable for Wayne Wong's appearance in a Juicy Fruit gum commercial (*"The taste, the taste, the taste is gonna move ya"*) and Suzy Chaffee's role as "Suzy ChapStick" for the selfsame lip balm.

How might the freestyle era be remembered if the affordable home VCR had been around to support it? "I think it would have been a lot bigger, because you'd know the name Scotty Brooksbank," John said. "People didn't know who John Clendenin was—Jumping Jack Fleming—none of these people, who were the best skiers of their day in that genre, but never got the exposure. When the videotapes came out, you're at the ski show, everybody is seeing the movie, and they now have video stores where you can rent these things. So anybody can watch it. Freestyle didn't have those. They made documentaries and films and they're cool to look at and see nowadays. They did do a lot of filming back then, but they weren't in the era where everybody has a VHS tape deck in their living room, and they're all going to go out Friday night, and ski houses have them. The timing of everything was perfect for all of us in that era. We were all right there at a big time for that industry."

The extreme movement would take a combination of mountaineering and freestyle, add a ton of risk, popularize it, package it, and sell it. It seemed a natural fit for promoting and marketing The Egan Brothers.

Chapter Sixteen

THE GREAT WINTER OF '88

STAN ENDED UP GETTING HIS car back and the Egans recovered John's van from Vermont, then continued to Lake Tahoe and Squaw Valley where they made reservations to crash on Tom Day's floor.

It was time for a new scene, where their world of skiing wasn't as constricted as it had been on the East Coast. Besides, now that The Egan Brothers had made a little noise on the pro circuit in Colorado, Dan figured the next step would be to utilize John's Tahoe contacts in both sponsorship and film.

Athletes need to sell themselves to potential sponsors, trying to impress upon brands why they're a good fit for their clothing line or equipment. It can be a grueling procedure where, without an agent to serve as middleman, individuals find themselves constantly seeking sources willing to form partnerships with them. This can mean a lot of schmoozing over phone calls, dinner conversations, even tryouts for the gig. "It's really about relationships, as it always is in life," John said, "who you know and how you treat them and the respect you get in the industry. It's your reputation. I was already pretty well established, working for Warren Miller, and had connections at The North Face. I could get asked to go on film shoots and now I've got my brother. We're The Egan Brothers. We're here together. You get two-for-one. Let's go!"

Then, sometimes a sponsorship comes right to your door. Quite literally. Chris Davenport is a familiar face on the big-mountain film scene, having made more than thirty appearances over the years for Warren Miller and Matchstick Productions. A native of Salem, Massachusetts, Davenport won the World Extreme Skiing Championship in 1996, competed in the X Games, and in 2007 became the first person to ski all fifty-four of Colorado's fourteen-thousand-foot peaks in less than one year. He was inducted into the U.S. Ski and Snowboard Hall of Fame in 2014. These days, fifty-year-old Davenport is associated with brands like Scarpa, Black Diamond, and Cliff Bar—companies that were well-aware of Davenport's value before creating partnerships with him.

But it's a little different when a skier, as a professional, lands one of his first sponsors. Davenport had just won a Red Bull contest in Chamonix, taking home a pair of Salomon boots as one of his prizes. That led to Mike Bisner, in his role as vice president of marketing at Salomon, receiving an email from Salomon's headquarters in France, asking him to fulfill the boot prize to the winner, a fellow American. "It was this guy, Chris Davenport. They had never heard of him," Bisner said.

Bisner lives in Manchester-by-the-Sea, Massachusetts, and the Davenport's house was only about a thousand yards from his backyard. "So, basically I just called and said, 'Chris, I'm supposed to give you some boots for winning the contest. Why don't I just give you everything? Boots, bindings, whatever you need. OK?'" Davenport's sponsorship with Salomon lasted about twenty-five years, according to Bisner. Sponsorships are hard to hold on to. However, John Egan has maintained some of his original sponsors from the '70s and even landed a new one a few years ago. "Who thinks a sixty-year-old is going to get a new sponsor? That's the staying power of the Egans," Dan said.

Although the Egans were just in their twenties, they found immediate success in Squaw, doing a photo shoot for Volkl, an equipment manufacturer based in Germany, on their first day in the area. Tom Day introduced them to photographer Hank de Vré, and the brothers were outfitted in North Face clothing and Volkl skis. It wasn't just another day at the office. "We partied and shot photos all day," Dan said. Volkl representative O.J. Merrill knew John from their earlier years at Squaw, and was just thrilled to be partying with his old ski buddy. De Vré, meanwhile, saw the depth of talent in the brothers he was shooting.

"Hank was freaked out that we brothers were so close to each other, and doing all this crazy shit. So he started telling everybody about The Egan Brothers," Dan said. Word spread quickly throughout Lake Tahoe, and soon everybody was speaking double. The Egan Brothers were in town. One week later, they were invited to try out for The North Face Extreme Team at Tahoe's Alpine Meadows.

The North Face began as a retailer of high-performance climbing and backpacking equipment in San Francisco, in 1968. The company soon began sponsoring expeditions around the world, which launched their decades-long reputation for being one of the premier suppliers of outdoor equipment. In the '80s, The North Face added extreme skiwear to its product line. "These were the days of pastels, neons, hair dye, and Mohawks," it says on the company's website. "They laid the groundwork for today's free-spirited snow-sports athletes."

In most North Face stores today, there is an "innovation wall," a timeline featuring the brand's most notable shifts. As a promotional vehicle for its ski apparel, The North Face created The North Face Extreme Team, a group that would be filmed at various locales, skiing in the brand's clothing, and packaged into a series of action-packed VHS tapes produced by Eric Perlman. Listed in the '80s is The North Face Extreme Team logo and, next to it, The Egan Brothers' name. "When we showed up at Alpine Meadows, there were boxes of North Face clothing in the base lodge," Dan said. "They told us to put some on and go jump off cliffs."

The Egans did just that. They jumped off cliffs with skiers like Day, Robbie Huntoon, and Kevin Andrews. "This was all new to me," Dan said. "I had jumped off cliffs, but not for the camera. The only thing I knew was that I needed speed. I had to clear the rock. John and Tom were skiing together, and I was kind of on the outside. They had skied in the movies together, so I was just punching it on my own." This left Dan with an uncertainty as to how everybody saw him. On one chairlift ride up the mountain, he asked his brother how he thought he was doing.

"Has anybody asked you to leave?" John asked. "Just keep doing it." They both kept doing it. They both made the team. Their first payout? North Face clothing ("Biggest deal of our lives—" Dan once joked, "three jackets and four pairs of pants"). The first video, *Skiing Extreme*, was a twenty-minute venture featuring the Egan brothers, Andrews, Day, Trevor Petersen, and Schmidt leaping off out-of-bounds peaks at Mt. Robson in Canada, and Nevada's Ruby Mountains. The Extreme Team showed off their skills on resort terrain, such as Alpine Meadows's Idiot's Delight, Blackcomb's Teetering Rock, and Squaw Valley's Palisades, which "turned into an aerial three-ring circus" on trails that included Chimney, Schmidiots, and Extra Chute. The ski areas welcomed The Extreme Team to test their out-of-bounds terrain—after, of course, signing a four-page liability release.

"We were kind of lucky," said extreme film legend Rob DesLauriers, who moved to Tahoe in 1988 and hooked up with Day, who he'd gotten to know when Day's father was on the ski patrol at Bolton Valley, the ski area the DesLauriers family owned in northern Vermont. DesLauriers would eventually help produce five films as a member of The North Face Extreme Team. "We just kind of stumbled into it. These were the guys you wanted to ski with anyway, and then the camera was there."

The team made six videos over seven years, and the Egan brothers appeared in all of them. *Skiing Extreme* was available on VHS at local ski shops for $17.95. The film's producer held the rights; only REI and The North Face's retail outlet stores were allowed to sell the films. Beyond that, there wasn't much of a plan to push the movie further, despite mom-and-pop video stores popping up on every corner of the country, and Blockbuster Video having begun its franchise expansion, which would peak at about nine thousand stores. So, Dan asked the producer if he could be a sales rep for the videos—and he got a "Yes."

"He was making a movie. He didn't have reps to sell it," Dan said. "Here's some young kid saying, 'I'll sell it.' They had negotiated royalties for the skiers, so we were going to get royalties. Now, I had wholesale and retail. I thought, 'Yeah, for my next job I'll sell videos.'"

During the tryouts, *SKI Magazine* sent writer Laurel Hilde to produce an article about the "Wild Boys" of Squaw Valley. Hilde described the twenty-four-year-old Dan Egan as a skier "whose red hair mirrors his fiery desire for wild ski thrills." She crafted a chronicle of skiing the Poma Rocks at Alpine Meadows with Dan, John, Tom Day, and Robbie Huntoon. "Every cornice, bush, and mogul became a springboard for air," Hilde wrote. "From the first chairlift ride of the day until well after the last, they flew and laughed, entertaining themselves and everyone around them—especially me."

Through it all, Dan's brain started producing ideas that his marketing degree helped to hone. "We're in the magazine, we're with sponsors, we have our new Volkls, we have our new North Face outfits, we have our new Scott poles and goggles. We were creating exposure." The sudden wealth of opportunity pulled Dan right back to his business classes at Babson. "We're delivering on our promise here; these sponsors have to pay us for this shit," he said. "We are making these things happen. It's not something we're thinking about doing. It's happening, right now."

Realizing the situation, Dan made John call Warren Miller every day—(1-800-RAW-FILM)—to let the production company know about the brothers from Boston who were ripping up the scene at Squaw Valley. Perhaps out of curiosity—or exhaustion, due to hearing incessantly from the Egans—Miller's office sent an intern named Tom Grissom to get some footage of the brothers.

Grissom was fourteen the first time he saw a Warren Miller movie, and was instantly convinced shooting film was to be his life's work. That is, until a high school film teacher told him he could turn in any project, just as long as it wasn't a skiing movie set to the Beatles' "Here Comes the Sun." That sort of deflated Grissom's aspirations. A few years later, though, when he was a film student at the University of Southern California, fate came knocking. "My college roommate said, 'Hey, I've got a job with this guy you might know—*Warner* Miller?'" Despite mispronouncing Warren's name, Grissom knew exactly who he was talking about. The following year, after his roommate graduated, Grissom was able to latch on to the vacated position with Miller. He became a runner, taking film from Warren Miller's offices in Hermosa Beach to Hollywood, getting it processed, and bringing the processed film back every day. "I'd drive around LA and learn how to make films."

Grissom would go through every frame of footage with Don Brolin, Miller's director of photography. "He knew I wanted to be a cameraman," Grissom said. "We'd look through the footage—it would be all sixteen-millimeter film—on a flatbed film editor, and every time someone's head would pop up out of the screen, Don would stop, rewind it, and go right to that frame. He'd say, 'Does that look like the cover of *Powder Magazine* to you?' Because the benchmark was that every frame of footage was supposed to look like the cover of *Powder Magazine*. That was our job."

His first opportunity behind the camera came one day after picking up Tom Day and Robbie Huntoon at the airport, fresh off a shoot. "They knew that I wanted to be a cameraman, and told me to come up to Squaw and film them. I borrowed a camera from the camera locker, shot a few shots—some comedy, all the guys getting knocked over by the gondola—and some of them made it into the opening montage the following year."

Later that winter, Warren Miller sent another camera man, Billy Heath—a proper one, Dan pointed out—to capture the Egans skiing at Sugarbowl Resort. They made the cut later that year, in *Escape to Ski*. After producing thirty-nine films, it was the first Warren did not personally direct; he handed the reins to cinematographer Don Brolin, who took the helm for 1989's *White Magic* and 1991's *Born to Ski*.

Escape to Ski was the first of a dozen appearances Dan would make in Warren Miller films. "Squaw Valley was already becoming Squallywood," Grissom said. "There was a lot going on up there, and a few other film companies were just starting out. Snowboarding was really driving it." Squaw was ground zero for ski filmmaking, because it was where Gary Nate first caught Scot Schmidt on film, hucking himself off cliffs in the Palisades. It's where the stunt skiers tabbing for Hollywood movies—Huntoon included— could be found. It was also where Grissom and his ilk could find a special brand of skier who understood the work involved in making a ski movie. "There probably were skiers more skilled, but nobody wanted to put the work in to find them," he said. "It's a lot of hiking. There's a lot of logistics involved, there's a lot of standing around on a powder day. You really have to want to do it." The Egan Brothers passed that test. "We just had this amazing winter," Dan said. "We were in The North Face film, we were in *Powder Magazine*, we were in *SKI Magazine*, we were in *Skiing* magazine. We were working every day."

There was a "rat pack" mentality to the way the entire crew treated each day at Squaw Valley, like a daily reunion of rock-star skiers. John and Dan Egan were joined by fellow New Englanders, Rob and Eric DesLauriers, and Tom Day. There was Susan Lopez, who would make herself a Squaw legend for something other than skiing when she opened Wildflour Baking Company. The legend of KT Cheryl was beginning to bud, starting her daily ritual of getting first chair every powder day on the KT-22 lift, a habit that lasted for decades. There was Margaret Anne Fletcher, a native Australian who burrowed her way into Dan's heart by introducing herself as "Alexandria from Reykjavík" at a party one evening. The stunt won her a pair of Scott goggles from a friend who worked there, who'd bet her the ruse wouldn't last five minutes. Thirteen minutes into the prank, Fletcher came clean with Dan, and the two began dating. "He was out there. He was a pretty wild boy," she said. She became part of the group's "leap fest" in the confines of Squaw. "They got me to jump off some good stuff," she said.

136

Eventually, the great winter of '88 had to come to a close. Later that year, the Red Sox won the American League East division, spurred by a mid-season winning streak that coincided with third-base coach Joe Morgan's promotion to manager. "Morgan's Magic" would captivate Boston that summer, in what would become one of the more memorable seasons for the baseball-hungry city. But, on April 4, the team showed nary a glimpse of the drama to unfold. The Red Sox opened the 1988 season with a 5–3, extra-inning loss to the Detroit Tigers, despite nine innings of work from ace pitcher Roger Clemens, who struck out eleven Tigers that afternoon. Closer, Lee Smith, took the loss when he allowed a two-run homer to Baseball Hall of Famer Alan Trammell in the top of the tenth. And it was only Opening Day—the best was yet to come.

And it was time for the Egans to come home.

Kindred spirits, Joe Powder and a billy goat meet on the face of the cliff.

Photograph by Dave Roman

John high-fives Dan at the top of a couloir in Zermatt, Switzerland. This shot was the poster for the "Worldwide and Wild Tour."

EGAN BROTHERS

Chapter Seventeen

WHAT DID YA TELL 'EM?

DAVE FRANZELL WAS GETTING A little fed up with Dan Egan's exploits at the Boston Sailing Center. Dan began the summer of '88 as the sailing center's manager, and continued the combination of partying and lesson-giving he'd inaugurated the previous summer. But his boats were running aground—things weren't going as smoothly as Franzell had hoped.

"The Boston Sailing Center is an amazing place," Dan said. "It provides people with access to the harbor. You can learn to sail there. You have access to boats. I loved being on the water every day, teaching and keeping the place moving. It was non-stop adventures—some good, some not so good." Some incidents, though, were out of Dan's control.

One Sunday morning, somebody came into the sailing center's office to alert Dan that Franzell's plywood houseboat was sinking at the dock. Upon Dan's review, the boat was, indeed, taking on water, so he hopped on board to find the leak. "The thing was going down," he said. "Things were falling off the walls, and when I got out of there, it sank."

The boat would sit at the bottom of Boston Harbor for a few weeks before Franzell could make a decision on how to float the thing. In 1988, Boston Harbor was still a legendary pool of filth, only in the beginning stages of a cleanup project that would cost billions of dollars. And there was Franzell, swimming in epic pollution to get his boat back. He had his methods of disinfection: "His philosophy for not getting sick, diving in Boston Harbor in the '80s, was to slug down vodka," Dan said. "Come up, slug, go back down. *I'm the manager of this place?*"

Being "a resourceful guy," as Dan put it, Franzell figured out how to float the boat, but then had to devise a plan to get rid of the filthy thing. "Meet me at 3 a.m.," he told Dan. "We're going to tow the boat out and shoot it full of holes, and sink it where the water is deeper."

Dan, age twenty-four, admitted he didn't know too much. But he knew a little, and this stunt didn't sound legal. He casually mentioned the plan to his father, in search of his wise counsel. Robert was short and direct: "You might want to research Maritime Law," he suggested, "and look up the penalty for blocking shipping channels."

Dan managed to avoid the scuttling, but he still had a grotesque job ahead of him. "In the end, Franzell took it over to East Boston, put it on the mud flats, and patched the boat from the bottom at low tide," Dan said. "He eventually brought it back and wanted me to tell the crew to empty it. It was full of mud and Boston sludge. My conscience wouldn't let me make them do it . . . so I did it myself." Now the boat was back afloat and, thanks to Dan, cleansed from its trip to the bottom of a waterway teeming with raw sewage. Issue resolved.

It wouldn't end well for the boat, though. Later that fall, Hurricane Gloria hit New England. The storm put Franzell's houseboat up on the rocks, and it eventually sank to the bottom of the harbor anyway. Dan wasn't around to witness it; he'd already been fired from the gig "for various different reasons." He spent the fall as an assistant soccer coach, running Babson College's soccer camps, reporting to head coach Jon Anderson. Anderson had taken over the program during Dan's senior year. He'd dealt with Dan's antics and suspension early in the fall of 1986, but had also become Dan's mentor.

Coaching was a role Dan had tried once before, after graduation, taking an assistant position at Curry College, a Division III school in Milton, with little success. "I was way too young," he said. "I should never have been coaching at that age, because I could still have been playing, and I was just pissed off at being with a losing team. I could do everything better on the field than most of the team could do and I had no tolerance for them."

At Babson, Anderson was trying to pat the program down, so the soccer team wasn't in the same trouble it found itself during Dan's time as a player. He figured a more mature Egan could be a stabilizing addition to his coaching ranks. But there was, admittedly, still too much edge in Dan. He wasn't removed enough from the sport to have an authoritative view. Or maybe his mind was elsewhere, due to the change in seasons: leaves were falling and winter was in the forecast. It was time for him and John to head back out West and continue to build The Egan Brothers brand.

In the winter of 1988–89, Dan was back in Squaw Valley where he hustled his way into a Japanese ski movie that paid $300 per day. His days of slinging breakfast orders at the Clock Tower Café were over. He started the winter with enough money to not need a job, and he didn't have to work at the ski area for a pass. He had sponsors, such as The North Face and Scott, for equipment. John, meanwhile, began the winter building condos in the Boston area. Once he arrived at Squaw later in the season, it was somewhat of a new world for him, too, despite former relationships with brands that already sponsored The Egan Brothers.

The North Face Extreme Team was in production for its next film, *Skiing Extreme II*, which would feature the Egans, filmed at Alpine Meadows, Donner Summit, and Jackson Hole. At Squaw, photographers for *SKI*, *Skiing*, and *Powder* were calling daily, looking to book the Egans for photo shoots, not only at Squaw but other Lake Tahoe resorts, such as Alpine Meadows and Sugar Bowl, as well. Clearly, the Egans were making a name for themselves in due fashion. But it was when Warren Miller finally called that their game really began. Miller wanted to feature Dan, John, Robbie Huntoon, and Eric DesLauriers in a segment shot at Squaw Valley. Bill Heath, a cameraman from Canada, arrived at Squaw to capture the action.

It was a dream come true. "Filming for Warren at Squaw was big-time," Dan said. "It landed us squarely in the middle of the scene there. It was a ball. I had already filmed a little at Squaw, so, to jump off famous lines like the Fingers, rip down the Mainline Pocket, the Light Towers, Dead Tree, and the Palisades—I was in overload. Plus, I was with legend Robbie Huntoon, my bro, and Eric D. We had blue skies and all of Squaw to rip. I was in heaven."

It was a full winter with one more major stop, the annual Ski Industry of America trade show in Las Vegas. "Dan came out of school with his marketing degree," John said, "and all of a sudden, it's 'we're going to do this, we're going to do that.' I had this, what I would call little, mellow, really soulful career going. And all of a sudden, now it's full-on marketing with The Egan Brothers—branded clothing and videos and stickers. I was . . . whatever."

Whatever!?

But John also understood what was at stake with their sudden appearance on the skiing industry's map. With Dan at his side, turning themselves into a business seemed a reality more than ever before, which meant they'd have to begin seeking promotional and marketing opportunities. "You have to go shopping," John said. "You have to go to the Vegas ski show and all the right places. Having a sponsor? It was always easy to get another sponsor. Negotiating the right way to work the sponsorship, making sure your sponsor promotes you and puts you in their ads—now all your other sponsors are psyched because their clothing is in a sunglasses ad." With that in mind, John took Dan on a trip to Las Vegas to place a bet on their burgeoning brand.

Snowsports Industries of America is a non-profit trade association that has represented snow sports suppliers since 1954. At the centerpiece of SIA's events calendar was the annual Snow Show (rebranded as Snowbound, in Denver and Boston, in 2020), an expo that annually brought together thousands of retailers, brands, media, and athletes in Denver to get an insider's look at the newest gear, style, and accessories. It was, in essence, the place to be if you were anybody—or looking to speak with anybody—in the ski industry.

In the late '80s, the show was held at a convention center in Las Vegas. A number of ski companies from the Boston area were in attendance in 1988, including representatives from Fischer, Salomon, and Rossignol. Dan knew many of these representatives from his time at Ski Market with his brother Bob. Thus, John saw opportunities with Dan as his marketing arm. As Dan recalls, "John drove me to the trade show and said, 'You went to that fancy college. Get in there and make us some damned money.'" Ski companies and brands pitched projects for the season beginning in 1989. Orders were placed based on response at the trade shows, from which companies determined their marketing budgets.

The Egans had swagger coming into the trade show. They were in their second Warren Miller feature, The North Face Extreme Team was in full swing, and they were featured in both articles and images in all the most notable ski publications—so they had a lot to talk about. Dan landed a meeting with the marketing director of Fischer Skis and relayed the exciting opportunities The Egan Brothers might be able to provide that winter. It went well. "How'd you do?" John asked when Dan walked out of the meeting.

"Good," Dan said. "They're going to give us cash."

"Really? For what? What did you tell them?"

"I told them, 'We're the Egan Brothers, and we're going to go around the world and make ski movies.'" Simple enough. This all probably sounded tremendously easy to John's ears. "Tell the next guy that," he told Dan. "Just keep doing what you're doing."

Dan kept busy, setting up meetings with Leki Poles, Swany Gloves, Smith Goggles, Fisher, and Degré7—a new clothing brand started by extreme skier

Patrick Vallençant. The vendors he met with all promised cash and incentive deals for the 1989–90 season. Now, at least the Egans had financial support to produce a movie on their own and make plans for the upcoming season. They drove back to Tahoe to finish off the season before heading back East.

In late March, with spring temperatures setting in around the region, the brothers decided to raise additional funds before the drive back home. They began rolling into local ski area parking lots on busy Saturday and Sunday afternoons, opening the back doors of John's Dodge Ram van, and selling all the gear they'd collected during the season. "The spring sale was fun," Dan said. "We sold everything we could. Some of the gear still had hangtags on it. Other stuff, even beat-up skis with torn bases, still sold well." After two weekends of this rolling yard sale, the van had enough room in the back for a futon. The Egans headed east, taking turns behind the wheel and resting in the back. "We took the southern route through national parks," Dan said. "We started off by going to Yosemite, then off to the Redwoods, down to Joshua Tree, the Arches, the Painted Desert, and, eventually Nashville and Graceland. We would take random roads through the desert, stop at drive-thru beer stores in the middle of nowhere, and just go wherever the next turn led us. We were in no hurry."

Even at a leisurely pace, staying out of trouble remained a challenge. "We met the locals most everywhere we went, saw more than our share of blue lights flashing in our rear-view mirror, but managed to escape without any real damage," Dan said. "While a cop in Tennessee had me in his cruiser, John was making faces at me out the back window of the van. The cop looked at our Vermont plates and simply said, 'You're a long way from home, boy. If I were you, I'd drive sober and slower on your way up north.'"

Once home, John went back to banging nails and Dan went back to work at the Babson soccer camps. He also started distributing videos out of his attic office at the Egan home in Milton. He partnered with the video distribution company that had the toll-free telephone number 1-800-USA-TAPE, to provide the action sports titles. "The videotape business was taking off," Dan said. "I had worldwide sales rights to two North Face films, plus I'd picked up some instructional films to rep from 3M, and also *Ski Tips by Marty Heckelman*. So, all in all, I was shipping videos all over the U.S. and the UK, anywhere from a half-dozen to three or four dozen per order. I was also distributing videos to wholesalers who were supplying video stores around the country. Business was booming."

There were also appearances to book. Sponsors wanted the Egans on-site at the Warren Miller premieres. Bernie Weichsel booked the Egans again for his consumer ski shows, and interview requests started coming in from the *Boston Herald* and *Boston Globe*. Newspapers around the country were looking for quotes from these two Boston-based ski bums. "By now, we were The Egan Brothers," Dan said. "We had the magazines, we had the movies, we were on the hangtags in every North Face store and on all North Face clothing. We had business cards that said, 'Ski to double your exposure.' Extreme skiing was blowing up."

Wild Americans in neon suits were jumping off cliffs while European skiers held firm that their brand of mountain explorations and first descents was the true definition of "extreme." But the defining line was about to get blurrier.

Chapter Eighteen

EXTREME AMERICANIZED

GLEN PLAKE WASN'T SUPPOSED TO happen—not if *Blizzard of Aahhh's* director, Greg Stump, had anything to say about it. But Stump was left with few options in 1987, when he began filming his landmark ski rockumentary. Killington product, Lynne Wieland—no stranger to displaying her skiing prowess on film, as in the role of "Michelle Banana Pants," and as a member of Dan O'Callahan's rat pack in 1983's *Hot Dog . . . The Movie*—broke her back on the first day of filming in Chamonix. Stump had a role to fill with someone similarly qualified to match up with fellow skiers Scot Schmidt and Mike Hattrup.

Stump had met Schmidt several years before, while filming at a trade show, and began pursuing Schmidt to ski for him on film. But Schmidt had been less than impressed with Stump's earlier work, which included *Maltese Flamingo* and *Time Waits for Snowman*. "I thought his films were a little wacky and they weren't going far," Schmidt said. But Stump's rock soundtrack for *Blizzard* hinted at a new format and approach; Schmidt still wasn't optimistic, but he ultimately relented. "I didn't really have a whole lot of hope for the film," he said. "I thought it was going to be another one of those zany kinds of films. But when he said he was going to Chamonix for over a month, that was the hook for me. That was what got me interested in working with Greg."

With Wieland down, Stump and filming partner Bruce Benedict were in a bind—which brought Plake's name to the table. Stump and Benedict had filmed Plake, a Mohawk-wearing bad boy, earlier that season at Snowbird, Utah, and the experience didn't sit well with squeaky-clean Stump (who was, admittedly, "like Michael J. Fox in *Family Ties*" back then). "We're getting comped rooms, comped everything," said Stump, "and I smell pot when I walk into the lobby of the fucking hotel. I just say, 'Please don't let that be coming from the seventh floor.' Sure enough—I get off at the seventh floor, and Glen is just bonging away. He was just out of control on coke, pot, and booze. I just couldn't imagine bringing him to Europe."

Stump was particularly sensitive to the culture's "ugly American" image overseas, having spent a semester at school in England, and worried about risking his relationship with record producer Trevor Horn, who would prove vital in providing the soundtrack to the film. Stump didn't want to make his film with a loud, obnoxious California kid with hair sticking into the stratosphere, creating a scene in France. "Because he was an absolute fucking pain in the ass," Stump said. But he found himself alone in that mindset. Benedict and the other skiers pushed for bringing Plake on board; he would one day become one of the sport's most recognizable ambassadors. "He was out of control in Chamonix, no doubt," Stump said. "He was out all night, but he did his job on the hill. I didn't care what he did in his spare time. Obviously, hiring him was the right decision. But I wouldn't have made it on my own."

Blizzard of Aahhh's was released in 1988, and as one fan commented, "the eye- and ear-popping mélange of bad-ass music and rad skiing had much of the ski world talking." Schmidt, Plake, and Hattrup formed an exemplary trio on film, skiing to the sounds of emerging alternative rock bands, like

Frankie Goes to Hollywood and Nasty Rox, Inc. Stump received praise for his "unfettered creativity," which would've earned laurels in *any* filmmaking genre: mounting cameras for point-of-view shots; interviewing stars off-snow, in train compartments and hotel rooms; tossing in delightful outtakes; shooting candid chats with colorful locals, like Telluride's Rasta Stevie and Snowbird's Dick Bass.

"I'll never forget the first time I saw *Blizzard*," Dan said. "I was at the Hartford, Connecticut, ski show, hawking The North Face films, and on a big screen was *Blizzard*, and it gripped me instantly. The story and the skiing pushes you back, while the music pulls you forward. It's a magical story." The movie was seventy-five minutes of soaring freedom in Chamonix, and America took notice. Four months after releasing the VHS out of Stump's garage in Portland, Maine, Stump and Schmidt landed on *The Today Show*. "No non-competitive skier had ever been on *The Today Show*," Stump said.

Extreme skiing suddenly had its biggest exposure—on morning broadcast TV. Host, Greg Gumbel, could hardly hide his bewilderment over the sight of Plake, clad in red, white, and blue with a can or two of mousse in his spiked, blond hair, or the *extreme* exploits he and Schmidt displayed on film. Extreme skiing had a popular platform.

Except, where was the extreme skiing? "There's more bump skiing in that movie than there is cliff-jumping," Stump said. "When you look at that movie as a whole, only about 10 percent of it is extreme skiing. But the odyssey that it had, I guess, is more extreme." As mentioned earlier, there is a conflict in extreme skiing philosophy between American and European skiers. Some of it is born from different approaches to the World Cup circuit, how a skier like Phil Mahre had created his own dynasty in the face of more stringent preparation overseas. The antagonist character of Rudi Zink, in *Hot Dog . . . The Movie*, an overly-accented star German skiing competitor, may have been heavily stereotyped—but he was also a satirical portrayal of what some Americans saw as the arrogance of European skiers. There's even a two-page advertising spread in the 1990 *Skiing* issue, "Extreme Explained," that pokes fun at German regimentation.

"Here's one way to improve your performance on skis," it reads above the face of "Klaus," the ski instructor, who is shouting, "Bend ze knees, lean forward, straighten ze shoulders, chest out, feet together, are you listening?" The ad is for a line of Asics skiwear, a dazzling array of pink, black, teal, and purple presented in an image on the second page. The parkas and suits are worn by a group of relaxed, smiling skiers on a summit somewhere. They could even be considered a more genteel version of the "Hot Dog" rat pack, quietly laughing in the face of Klaus, their intense instructor.

Some of the argument stems from the fact that terrain in Europe is really more indicative of what extreme skiing should be. "What is extreme skiing?" Stump asked. "I think what Glen does in Chamonix, what those guys did in Chamonix—that's extreme skiing. But there's really nothing similar in North America . . . maybe British Columbia. For me, it was actually more of a marketing thing that I was actually making extreme skiing movies." What were American skiers like the Egans doing, performing as "extreme?" "*Play* extreme," as John Harlin, famed mountaineer, editor, and filmmaker told journalist Peter Oliver in "Extreme Explained." Yes, it's cinematically appealing, Harlin said, but it's also "often brainless, requiring no long-term planning or talent."

Ouch.

"I never considered myself an extreme skier," Schmidt said. "I was always uncomfortable with that. It was good for marketing and the industry. First descent, the record-breaking descents, that's what I always considered extreme. We're just showcasing a more explosive and dynamic aspect of skiing. Trying to go big and go fast and trying to make it look like fun. Pure extreme skiing is very slow and calculating. It's kind of boring to watch."

European extreme skiing was built from landmark descents by the likes of Sylvan Saudan, Heini Holzer, Patrick Vallençant, and Jean-Marc Boivin, each of whom began skiing routes in the Alps which nobody previously thought skiable. *You fall, you die.* Except, that's not the sort of thing that translates easily to film. In his *SKI Magazine* article, Oliver wrote about kinship with the mountains, as in the vision of extreme: "reveling in the physical, sharpening mind and strengthening body to the point of adapting to nature, like a chamois does to survive. Developing senses so as to feel the presence of a crevasse or unsafe snow, knowing all the while that humble man is but a fragile straw in this environment, to be broken in an instant by a slab of falling ice, an avalanche, or a sudden storm."

But if there's one thing Americans tend to do better than anybody else, it's sell and commercialize. And the American "in-your-face" films of extreme skiers jumping off cliffs in neon suits and Mohawks was a much easier sell to the general public than showing movies about daring but slow-moving French mountaineers ostensibly risking life and limb. American extreme skiing wasn't necessarily born from its mountaineering grandfathers, but rather those who'd created the freestyle movement in the late '60s and '70s. "We didn't know what freaking harnesses or ice axes were when we went to Chamonix," Dan said. "I laugh now, but I can't even remember if we had avalanche gear."

Kristen Ulmer, generally recognized as the first female big-mountain skier in the world, and a 2018 inductee into the U.S. Ski and Snowboard Hall of Fame, said that the word *extreme* quickly shifted away from meaning "the consequence of failure is death." "Next thing you knew, there are *extreme tacos, extreme banking, extreme meal deals*. The things we see as extreme . . . (the word) just sort of lost its verve. So we don't use that word anymore. Now we call it 'big-mountain skiing.' And big-mountain skiing is not necessarily risking your life. Like, jumping off a cliff doesn't necessarily mean you're risking your life."

Hers is an assessment Dan disagrees with, arguing that skiers of his generation pushed hard to get Madison Avenue to take notice of the genre. "Don't go and reinvent the brand. You're doing the same thing," he said. "People have been pushing their limits to see what and who they are forever, in the sport," John Egan said. "Nowadays, everything is extreme. There's extreme freaking Gatorade. Toyotas have extreme off-road driving packages, I mean, it's insane, it got overused and then it was almost frowned upon to be called extreme, because it was just too popular a word. But it was the fun

150

end of the sport that I've always looked at. I never wanted to be a racer or a mogul skier, I just liked the freedom of going down the hill. And the further away you got from the resort, the cooler that seemed to be."

The Americanized version of extreme was more in line with what Wayne Wong and friends hatched from their freestyle incubator. Stein Eriksen's front flips and the "Wong-banger" had more to do with what Warren Miller and Greg Stump documented in their extreme films. The best extreme skiers of the 1980s and '90s were really phenomenal mogul skiers before they were mountaineers. The marriage of freestyle acrobatics and radical terrain introduced a gymnastic element to the concept of extreme skiing, filmmaker Eric Perlman told Oliver.

The Europeans dismissed it all as little more than another short moment in a long line of American stunts. As Perlman saw it, "there weren't serious efforts to establish new standards of Alpine accomplishment." There was a survival technique lacking in the Americanized version: missing was the solitude of being one with the mountain. "It does nothing for the mountains," Eric Charamel, a Chamonix mountaineer and associate of Vallençant's, told Oliver. "Not in the way skiing a new route does something for the mountains."

Dan told Oliver, "Cliff-jumping isn't really extreme skiing. The risk comes and goes quickly. When there's a soft landing and a good runout, there isn't much to it."

Skiers like Saudan and Vallençant are stars overseas, but the fact is, in America they are difficult to compare. The mountains in the United States differ greatly from the Alps, where slopes can reach sixty degrees. The steepest trail at your average American ski resort is around the thirty to thirty-five degree range. The American style of extreme skiing might be described by some as a watered-down version of what the French claim to have invented: an untrodden downhill steep with plenty of risk, maybe even death, although most are not as intense as Chamonix. There was no particular necessity for the mountaineering skills of Europe in American extreme skiing, which was more focused on seeking the thrills of cliffs, forests, and straight-down chutes.

Chris Landry is an American extreme skier recognized for his pioneering descents, including Pyramid Peak near Aspen, Colorado, in 1978. *Sports Illustrated* ran a long feature on the mountaineer in 1981, in which Landry described the line he believes exists between mountaineering and skiing. "When you assess it realistically, extreme skiing is harder to do than climbing. If you make a mistake, there's almost nothing you can do to recover. In climbing, you can build up to a tough solo rock climb by practicing a lot in places where you can't get hurt. There are degrees of difficulty in climbing, degrees of risk that you can predict and, to some extent, control. With extreme skiing, you take a quantum leap. It's all or nothing. There's no safe middle ground when you're skiing on a thousand-foot slope over forty-five degrees. So there just aren't many people able—or willing—to get into it."

The 2007 skiing documentary, *Steep*, explores the history of extreme and big-mountain skiing in the United States, and suggests its roots stem from Europe. But it also unwittingly further blurs the line between mountaineering and extreme skiing. It lauds Bill Briggs, the first person to ever ski Wyoming's Grand Teton, as the godfather of extreme skiing, and compares the steep powder lines of Valdez, Alaska, with the jagged mountains of Chamonix.

Dan doesn't see it. "There's no connection for me there. Valdez is hardly an American Chamonix, and the early ski pioneers of the Tetons have more in common with European Alpinists than just jumping into Corbet's Couloir. But the extreme sports movement comes out of Squaw Valley. Nobody can deny that. Snowboarding videos and extreme sports videos were out of California. That's where the industry was in the '70s, '80s, and '90s. The dire consequences that impact skiing in Chamonix simply aren't as present in Valdez," Dan said. Instead of considering the Alaska destination an "American Chamonix," he's more inclined to refer to it as "the mini-golf of Chamonix." "I've seen big-mountain ski film stars in tears in Chamonix," Dan said. "They can't straight-run it. Of course, you can't straight-run any mountain in Europe. You'd die."

The true pioneer of what most Americans characterize as extreme skiing might just be Rick Sylvester, who joined the Squaw ski patrol in 1967 with some mountaineering background, eyeing the Palisades for the possibility of descent. He also went on to become a Hollywood stunt man, most notable for his BASE jump in the 1976 James Bond film, *The Spy Who Loved Me*. As Oliver wrote, by the mid-1960s, only one of the Squaw chutes had been skied. The National Chute, which he described as the easiest of the bunch, was once under consideration to be part of an FIS downhill course. Once that idea was abandoned, sometime after 1959, the idea of the Palisades as a playground was left alone until Sylvester and partner Bob Carter "belayed themselves on ropes over the chute-top cornices and laid their tracks." It wasn't pretty, Sylvester conceded, but it did help open the door for Squaw's future. Soon, a new generation of skiers was tackling the terrain in the Palisades. Sylvester noted that, in the late '60s, there were no more than a dozen people in a single season who would have tackled Chute 75. Soon, moguls started appearing. Extreme skiing all of a sudden appeared to have a new mantra: "You fall . . . you might get hurt, break a bone or two, whatever . . . but die? Nah."

"Not to say, if you did it really, horribly wrong—you could die for sure,"Tom Day said. "But the consequences weren't as final as for the original extreme mountaineers." Yet, here was something people wanted to watch. There's a reason not many knew names like Chris Landry or Bill Briggs, and it had nothing to do with their prowess in mountaineering or their willingness to push their limits on skis. Viewing and following such exploits were equivalent to watching paint dry. But put a bunch of talented skiers in brightly colored clothing and ask them to jump off cliffs in front of the camera—well, that was how Squaw Valley earned the nickname "Squallywood."

"John and I have first descents all over the world," Dan said. "Turkey, Slovenia, Baffin Island, the Arctic, Greenland, Kamchatka, and South America. They were steep, dangerous lines for sure. Did we ski where we could not be rescued? Yes. Did we ski where, if we fell, we could have died? Yes. Was the avalanche danger real? Absolutely. But, compared to Vallençant and Jean-Marc Boivin, and what they were skiing in Europe in the early days, it really wasn't the same. However, we did sell the story—the dream of what it was like to be in faraway mountain ranges, because that was what the market wanted. We're watching Schmidt and Plake, and they're blowing up, and we start blowing up. It was like what people wanted was to feel involved." Glitz and glamour. Flair and flash. It all led to a generational shift for extreme. Promoters like Red Bull and the X Games kept pushing the boundaries of what was extreme, in the interest of catching eyeballs more than with personal achievement alone. "We just continued to evolve," Rob DesLauriers said. "Kids who were eight and ten, watching us jump off cliffs, went out and jumped off cliffs—at that age. It became so normal for them, and then they were going to the skate park and it evolved into tricks."

Whatever the definition of extreme skiing, it was the Americans who were now having a worldwide impact, at least commercially, more than the Europeans had ever managed with their version.

The billy goat can't believe his eyes as Joe Powder flies by.

Photograph by Dave Nagel

John dazzles onlookers as he "billy goats" his way down this cliff in Squaw Valley, CA.

Chapter Nineteen

EGAN BROTHERS TOO UGLY

THERE WAS, REALLY, NO INTENTION of coming home for the Egan brothers once they hit Europe in January of 1990. The same Japanese film crew Dan had skied for the previous year—the one that paid him to the handsome tune of $300 per day—recruited the brothers to ski for them again, this time in Val d'Isère.

By now, the sponsorships were rolling in: Fischer, The North Face, Leki, Smith, and PowerBar. "Some of the payout was based on incentives," Dan said. "We had to get their logos in the magazines, but we could do that. There was an estimate, a figure we had to hit—to get in so many magazines and so many movies—then they'd give us the base. And there would be a bonus if we hit more than that. For that fee, we'd give them so many promotional days, let them use our images, all that sort of stuff." The sponsorships complemented how the Egans were able to control the logo appearances, a matter made all the easier with Dan's creation of Egan Entertainment Network, a home for the adventure footage they were able to curate from around the world. By creating its own reels, Egan Entertainment was able to monetize the product by selling the scenes back to Warren Miller, then take further advantage by managing—and charging for—the distribution rights.

The Egan Brothers were becoming a marketing commodity and Egan Entertainment a full-time business for Dan. Which was a good thing for him to be doing when he returned home to spend his off-seasons in the Milton family house. "My mom's attitude was like, 'you can't live in the house for free. If you're going to have a ski business, that business needs to rent the office and pay for food.' Everything was billable and billed. My mom said, 'You can do this, Dan, as long as you can afford it.' I had always said to myself I would run the business as long as it got better every year. My parents' support for that idea was that it had to work. It couldn't just be a lark."

To be sure, there was a tiny level of guilt bred into Dan and John's parents, who'd always hoped their children would enjoy skiing. But making a living out of it? That seemed a bit far-fetched. "I gained my parents' confidence pretty early in life, where I would follow through," Dan said. "So, when I told them that it was going to be a business, they had some confidence that it really would be a business, that this 'ski bum' thing John and I were doing was going somewhere. They did believe, as I think John did, it would become something. Somehow."

Dan's eye for how people were spending their time away from the mountain became an integral building block for the growth of their business. Warren Miller, admittedly, hadn't yet gotten the scope of VHS, despite the amount of revenue video was providing his company by 1986. "I can't say I really understand the videocassette market," he said in a 1986 interview, "but I know it gave me the opportunity to take my first vacation in thirty-five years." He continued, "The growth in [video]cassettes has been phenomenal. We have a product that fits well into that market, because our films don't have a pronounced beginning, middle, and end. You can just as easily watch a part of the film as the entire film."

By the mid-'80s, Warren Miller Entertainment (WME) had landed a distribution agreement with a Los Angeles-based subsidiary of Lorimar Telepictures, Inc. Once they had that agreement, Miller needed an East Coast sales rep, and Dan Egan landed the job. WME was in transition at the time. Warren's son, Kurt, was purchasing the company from his father, bringing opportunities for growth. The Lorimar Telepictures agreement led to the Tri-Star Pictures agreement with WME. In that agreement, there would be two VHS releases each season: the feature film, and a shorter film focused on the extreme movement. This led to a number of secondary videos in which the Egans would be featured along with Schmidt, the DesLauriers, and newcomers such as Paul Ruff, John Treman, and Brad Vancour, among others. This created a whole new division at WME, and the person with the newly-created job title—director of VHS sales—quickly hired Dan to be WME's East Coast distribution arm.

"I had convinced Kurt and the director of sales that I should be the East Coast VHS rep," Dan said. "They ended up giving me east of the Mississippi as my territory. There was a video store on every corner in America, and now I had the names, phone numbers, and addresses for all those stores. And I called them all. I had the titles from the largest name in winter action sports, plus The North Face, our own films, and other titles needing sales support. I had the distribution outlets, the sales rights to the films, and the incentive contracts, all coming together." This all provided Egan Entertainment with its business model, and Dan with the income he needed to create not only a full-time job, but also the opportunity to funnel his own films, as well as those of other producers, into the company's distribution pipeline, giving Dan a slice of what was estimated to be about a $5 million business, based on attendance figures at the showings, plus cassette sales. The VCR's popularity was booming, and the cost to own one was steadily decreasing. When introduced in 1975, the average price for a VCR ran between $1,000 and $4,000. Ten years later, a wide selection of VCRs cost between $200 and $400. Those lower prices gave consumers the ability to purchase more than one device, say, for both the living room and a bedroom or, more importantly for marketing purposes, a dedicated VCR in a college dorm or ski shop.

In addition to his sales territory for Warren Miller Entertainment, Dan also made a deal for the international sales rights to The North Face films, which meant he was shipping hundreds of videocassettes a month from his parents' attic, while simultaneously providing exposure for The Egan Brothers by boosting sponsorship logos in the movies they both starred in and produced, as well as giving them a piece of the action on the actual film sales.

So, things were going well when they arrived in Val d'Isère to work for the Japanese. Tom Day was on the crew; he had skied for the company the year before and was the direct connection for Dan and John. On this trip, accompanied by his wife, Lizzie, and infant son, Danny, Tom was the action producer, a major step forward in his blooming career as cameraman.

"John and I left Vermont in our typical fashion—packing in the driveway at the last minute, which resulted in me forgetting the pack with my street clothing. Plus, John was pissed off because I made him cut his hair, as I knew the Japanese were conservative and didn't want long hair in their film. Let's just say he was so mad that I've never made that request ever again." Not that it was all of a sudden a situation of style and glamour for the two Boston kids. "We went for the paycheck, to ski in Europe, and to shoot with Tom," Dan said. "It was a fashion shoot for a clothing company. We were the action guys, and then there were models for still photos, from England. So, every time the still cameraman wanted to take our photo the Japanese director would shout, 'No, no, no. Egan Brothers too ugly!' So they wouldn't show our faces."

Maybe two scruffy kids from Boston didn't exactly fit the portrait the Japanese were aiming for in a glitzy resort like Val d'Isère, but when the Japanese left town, the Egans and the Days settled in for some exploring, photography, and video work. It was a bit of a coming-of-age story in, and for, Europe, where the Alpinists had become a bit weary of the bright, loud, self-promoting brothers. "We knew some of the established locals, like Marty Heckelman and my old high school ski racing rival, and now friend, Henry Schniewind, who eventually established the relationships we were seeking with the mountain guides," Dan said. "Both Marty and Henry were members of the Ski Market/Bernie extended family. So, slowly, over the next several weeks, we were able to access the chutes, steeps, and powder slopes that make Val legendary."

And over the next month, the Egans began to make an impression on that classic European resort. They'd penetrated the hard-core inner circle of local ski bums and guides.

"John had skied in Europe in 1986, but hadn't been back since," Dan said. "It was my first trip, and Val d'Isère changed me. The lengths and steepness of the chutes were so much greater than Squaw. Add to that the avalanche danger, and it was a transforming experience. Every day, we explored new slopes, skied deep powder, and over time I stepped into this new level of the sport."

The industry knew the Egans were in town, too. Being sponsored by Degré7 clothing certainly aided their notoriety. The brand, born in Chamonix, being endorsed by these Americans broadened the scope of attention their exploits received during their stay. They were invited to Salomon headquarters for the press conference announcing their new skis for the 1990–91 season, and to the presentation of The North Face video featuring them.

They also made a name for themselves in the legendary nightlife at Val d'Isère. Schniewind was running weekly avalanche talks at the famed Dick's T-Bar, an après-ski and late-night disco hangout near the center of town. Dick, the owner, had taken a liking to "Henry's wild friends," and agreed to host a ski movie night, featuring The North Face films, with Dan and John. "The nightlife in Val d'Isère is a full-time job, and we fit right in," Dan said. "We would ski all day, network on upcoming conditions and routes during happy hour with the ski locals, and then charge into the bars at night for 'frozen T-shirt' contests, bands, and discos where the vacationing Brits were tearing it up."

By mid-February, the French and English holiday season was upon them and the resort was shifting to high season, which meant the small, one-bedroom apartment where they were squatting was packed, with John, Dan, Tom, Lizzie, and three-year-old Danny all calling the place home. But, soon it was going to be rented for more than the Egans and Days could afford. The North Face wanted them in Zermatt, Switzerland, in a few weeks to shoot for the latest Skiing Extreme production. So, with no place to live, some time to kill, and with all of Europe in front of them, the situation screamed "Road Trip!"

But there was a problem. The crew had no wheels. Getting transportation turned out to be easier than expected, though, particularly after the Egans became friendly with Ewing Guinness, grandson of the Guinness beer empire. Ewing had become a late-night friend of the Egans, and one evening, while partying in an all-night club, he mentioned that his van was for sale due to some legal issues he was having. Over the loud music, John said to Dan, "Ewing is selling his funky old English van. You think we should buy it? Or maybe test-drive it first?" The plan sounded good to Dan, so John went to talk to Ewing and came back with the keys. Ewing had given him the OK to test-drive the van.

The next morning, they moved out of the apartment at the end of the box canyon in Val d'Isère, just steps away from the Fornet Tram, and loaded the van with the Day family, the Egan brothers, and a few new friends. Joining them was Lotta, a Swedish mogul champion who'd become friendly with John, and a fellow by the name of Andy Stockford, who'd gained a reputation as the best extreme skier in Britain—which is to say, a bar not set too high, considering the history of English skiers. Dave Roman, a Canadian photographer, also agreed to come along on the trip, in exchange for access to all of the images he shot. All in all, there were seven adults and one three-year-old, still in diapers. They hopped in the van, two adults in the front and the rest sitting on a mattress in the back with no windows, all the skis, boots, luggage, and camera gear, and pondered the road ahead.

"Where should we go?" John asked. Dan remembered what he'd told Warren Miller at his office in Los Angeles a few months earlier. It had been his first meeting with the filmmaker, and they'd talked about the art of narration. Dan told him the vision he had for his adventure on skis; it was more than finding deep powder and gnarly steeps that drove his ideas. He told Warren he wanted to go wherever CNN was, that The Egan Brothers should follow the changing landscape of the early '90s, and document a world in transition, as portrayed through the eyes of skiers and the power and unity skiing brought about.

"And he loved it," Dan said. "That brought me closer to Warren, and it solidified our career. One of my main business strategies is to attach yourself to something bigger than you. Warren was bigger than us, and CNN was bigger than Warren. That was a natural tie for us." With that all in mind, only one place seemed to make sense for the crew's destination: "The Berlin Wall," Dan said.

Dan had been right—Warren Miller would often repeat what noted ski school organizer Hannes Schneider said after training Austrian ski troops post-World War I: "If everyone skied, there would be no wars."

"Man's fundamental drive is his search for freedom," Miller once wrote. "For no reason that I can explain, some people—especially skiers—answer to that instinctive search for freedom more than others. My skis have taken me to many corners of the world in my own search for freedom." What better way, then, Dan figured, to represent this sense of freedom than by jumping off the Berlin Wall with skis?

The images from the previous November were fresh in the group's minds: Germans, no longer labeled as "East" or "West," using hammers and picks to chip away at the Wall's cold concrete—one of the most imposing images of the Cold War. The fall of the U.S.S.R. spelled a new beginning in Berlin, reuniting the German city and sparking a new vision of peace around the world. "There was no place bigger for us to be than the Berlin Wall," Dan said. "I didn't even know if it snowed there. I had no idea. We just beelined it for the Berlin Wall."

Guinness's van had no registration and no insurance, and was not exactly the most dependable form of transportation to be bringing into the Eastern Bloc. Yet, off they went. They pointed the van toward East Germany and took turns at the wheel, driving through a pounding rain as they began the nine-hundred-kilometer trip. "We first went to Chamonix to touch base with some of John and Tom's friends, and to set up a future film shoot there with the office of tourism," Dan said. Leaving Chamonix at night, heading to Italy via the Mont Blanc Tunnel, driving an English van with a right-sided steering wheel, was a new experience for Dan, who struggled to judge both the center line of the road in the dark tunnel and the distance of the oncoming traffic. *Smack!* came the sound of the left-side mirror colliding with an oncoming truck. "It was like, shit, I hit something," Dan said. "And then I swerved back into the center of my lane. 'That truck clipped us!' I yelled back into the van. I think Lizzie was mad that it woke up Danny. John and Lotta didn't notice, Dave was disappointed he missed the shot, and Andy, in the passenger seat, calmly said, 'Stay off the center line, mate.'" The adventure had begun. The route took them across multiple borders: France, Italy, Germany, and, eventually, East Germany. "Each time we crossed a western border, the border patrols would comment on the number of nationalities in the van," Dan said. "They were always fascinated by the amount of gear, people, and child in the car as they looked over our passports. But they never asked for insurance or registration."

That all changed at the East German border. When the guard began asking for papers, they all got a little nervous. "None of us spoke German, and had no proof we owned this van. The East Germans were slightly more contentious with this oddball group from the Alps. One guard turned into two. Then, three, four, and more. They started asking lots of questions. It was tense. 'Papers, papers,' the guard kept saying. So I reached for my wallet and pulled out some money," Dan said. "Deutschmarks? Francs? It was dark, I don't know what we held out to him, but he leaned in and stared at me, then grabbed the money, handed me the passports, and waved us through."

"I remember cracking the back door and filming some of that transaction from a stealthy position," Day said. The van made it through. After arriving in East Germany, they had to shell out a little more money—it seemed the border guard had called all his colleagues. Every ten miles or so, the van would get pulled over, with guards and police looking for the same sort of payout. With good reason, most likely. It had been, after all, a place of despair for so many decades, that despair now instantly abandoned in favor of freedom.

Which was also probably one reason why the Egans and friends were having a hard time finding any sense of civilization. "We're in East Berlin. There's no food. There's nothing on the shelves. Places are empty," Dan said. At the Brandenburg Gate, an East German guard suggested they make their way to West Berlin to find something to eat. "We, of course, had never even thought about whether there would be snow in Berlin," Dan said. "We were there for snow, and as it turned out, it did occasionally snow but rarely ever accumulated." Once through Checkpoint Charlie, they were in West Berlin, near the once-dividing wall. "We climbed up the wall and jumped off it. We landed in a mud puddle, and those photos went around the world." It was February 28, 1990; the Wall had fallen only a few months earlier. Day was shooting video of the proceedings for Eric Perlman's *Skiing Extreme III*. "In the people all around us, there was just this energy, a freedom of life all of a sudden," Day said.

There were two Berlin Walls, one on the east and one on the west. What lay in between was known as "the death strip," a dangerous battleground for those from the east seeking freedom in the west. All told, over one hundred forty people lost their lives scrambling across this narrow strip of land covered in barbed wire. "I always joked that we skied the east and the west faces of the Berlin Wall," said Dan. "But I'll never forget jumping off the western wall, which was about twelve feet high, landing in the no-man's-land and thinking how crazy it was to be there, a place where many had died longing for freedom. As a Cold War kid, all that had happened in this place was hard to imagine. Then this patrol of East German guards pulled up and surrounded us."

Some unarmed East German guards had arrived to watch, probably wondering what in the world they were witnessing: a bunch of kids dressed in neon winter suits covered in dirt, jumping off the Berlin Wall on skis. It was, rightfully, hailed as the first-ever descent of the landmark most notable for dividing a city and its people. "The guards looked at us as if we were from Mars," Dan said. "They also seemed uncomfortable not knowing what to do, as just four months earlier they would have shot and killed people here. That interaction is what I remember most."

With the Berlin Wall stunt captured on film, it was time to get back to the Alps. In a second nonstop driving marathon, the band of ski bums found its way to Zermatt. This meant they could move out of the van and become guests of the town's tourism office. Now back in action with free lift tickets, lodging, and food, Eric Perlman's *Skiing Extreme III* filming ventured onto the steep, powder-covered glacier at the base of the Matterhorn.

"When I think back on 1989–90, that was the foundation for The Egan Brothers' entire career," Dan said. "The Berlin Wall, Japanese film, real money. Living in hotel rooms all over the world. We didn't have a care."

There was yet one more video still to come—one which would cement Dan and John's legacy in extreme skiing. If the Egan brothers hadn't already felt they'd left their footprints in the skiing industry, they were about to become a whole lot more definitive. For, soon after the return trip to Switzerland, the Egan brothers got a call. Warren Miller wanted them back stateside to shoot at Grand Targhee, Wyoming. The Days were off to Verbier to continue their family filming adventure, and the Val d'Isère locals were headed back to the French Alps to return the van to Guinness with the message that, on second thought, they'd decided not to buy it after all. Alas, they'd had to install a new exhaust, put new tires on the beast, and clean it up a bit before returning it, so, if and when Guinness ever retrieved his license, he'd have wheels. On the way, they dropped the Egans off in Frankfurt to catch a flight. The brothers sensed they were on their way to something special, but little did they know what Grand Targhee would have in store for them and their careers.

Chapter Twenty

YOU BETTER SKI LIKE A BADASS

WARREN MILLER VIDEOGRAPHER GARY NATE, and skier Tom Levitt, arrived for the shoot at Grand Targhee to encounter some surprising news: the Egan brothers had things pretty much wrapped up for the movie.

Wrapped up?

"What the hell do you mean?" Nate asked.

The Egans had arrived at Grand Targhee a week early, unbeknownst to Nate. The idea was to scam an extra week of lodging for themselves and their "cameraman," who happened to be their old friend, Dennis Ouelette, shooting things with a technologically advanced wind-up, cardboard camera. This had become a tried-and-true method of securing lodging and lift tickets for Dan and John. Now, at Grand Targhee, they were continuing to build their business from the parking lot of the resort, not by selling movies but various pieces of their equipment, instead. "They were in a North Face van, they were supposed to be on Rossignol skis, and were selling Volkl skis and Degré7 clothing in the parking lot," Nate said. Anything for a buck. They even managed to sell a pair of Volkls and a one-piece Day-Glo suit to

Grand Targhee's owner, Carol Bergmeyer, who, as it turned out, was from Boston.

It was the beginning of what would be a long relationship with Grand Targhee, but no one—not the Boston-based owners, not the famous Warren Miller cameraman, not the ski bums just off the plane from a multi-country trip across Europe—could have foreseen what would happen when high winds, four-plus feet of new snow, and the luck of the Irish got mixed together on a mountain named Mary's Nipple. The weather at Grand Targhee appeared to be straight out of a ski bum's dream. It had snowed for seven straight days, leaving a blanket of deep powder on the ground and bright, sunny skies overhead, when they finally decided to shoot scenes for Miller's latest film. John and Dan wore their bright, one-piece suits from Degré7, and off they went. So, too, it seemed, did the warning bells.

"We were like pent-up animals, wanting to get out there and rip," Dan said. "The storm was wild for several days. We'd only been skiing from the mid-station down while it raged, and now the snow was off-the-chart deep. So, we could only imagine what it could be like, snowcat-skiing off of Peaked Mountain."

"It was one of those days when all sorts of weird things were happening anyway," Nate said, recalling how a snowcat driver had bailed on the way up the mountain, apparently the result of an argument his wife had with Targhee management. "About half a mile up, toward the target area, the guy quit and left." Later in the day, in an unrelated yet totally related incident, one of the ticket booths at the resort just happened to burn down. There was some trouble at the higher elevations, as well.

"One skier watching the Egans do these hundred-foot jumps decided to get camera-courageous," Nate said. "He jumped off a cliff and put his teeth through his lip." Dan, John, and Levitt, meanwhile, were skiing along a cornice line earlier in the day, when it broke. Levitt was flushed down the cliff face in a small avalanche. Warren Miller wouldn't end up using that shot, because the next one was even more death-defying, and would become one of the most memorable moments in the history of all ski films.

John and Dan went up to ski Mary's Nipple, a summit of Peaked Mountain that boasts some of the most delicious powder skiing in all of the Northern Rockies, giving way to the imposing presence of Grand Teton looming in the background. The brothers had no ski patrol with them; the patrol was with Nate, across the valley at the top of the chair, where he was shooting with the long lens. The idea was to capture John skiing behind Dan down the ridgeline of Mary's. Nate and the patrollers were joined by still photographer Wade McKoy, who knew the terrain well, as he regularly shot for the resort.

"I first shot Dan Egan the year before, during the filming in Jackson Hole. He was the first pro skier I had ever shot," McKoy said. "I had shot great skiers, but not pro skiers. There were a couple of big differences: first was how hard Dan worked; second was how much more dynamic his turns were; and third was how he charged every run. Shooting both Dan and John together amplified all of that to another level." Earlier in the day, the brothers had boosted big air off the front side of Peaked Mountain, where the cliff drops range from twenty to sixty-plus feet. The lines captured in the movie, of the Egans launching off the top cornice, then flowing down the cliff face between the trees and over the huge rock faces, are considered by some as the best action sequences ever shot. "The Grand Targhee segment really showcased how we ski on many levels. That footage showed how agile and sure-footed we were when skiing and jumping sight-unseen cliffs," Dan said.

With no locals or patrol around on Mary's ridge, it just looked like a ridgeline below where the Egans stood looking down, preparing for their run. It looked like one piece to the naked eye, but it wasn't. "Nobody said that," Dan said.

"It was an aggressive line, in that the other side of the ridge is a huge cliff," McKoy said. "They were dancing on the edge all day, off of the cornices and cliffs. This properly looked tame compared to what they had skied during the day."

Dan said, "We were on fire and felt fearless and untouchable. That might have been what saved our lives that day: the adrenaline pumping in our veins." Gary Nate, meanwhile, had set up with his camera across the canyon and was looking into it. "No particular reason for doing that, except it was just a fantastic-looking shot from my perspective," he said. Or, as Warren Miller would say in the narration of *Extreme Winter*, "Looks dangerous, but it's going to be fun."

John and Dan took off down the face, in the distance from Nate's perspective across the canyon. Dan was in the lead, clad in a neon green suit from Degré7 with black, pink, and blue striping over the shoulders. John followed in an all-pink number personally sent to him by company founder Patrick Vallençant. It was an item for which John never got to thank his mentor; the suit was stuck in customs when Vallençant died in his climbing accident. "Back in the day, pink was not a big color for guys," John once told *Sugarbush Magazine*. "One-piece pink suits *really* were not. So, to wear that, you better ski like a badass. Patrick's magical powers went with it, I guess. I felt like the suit was a good omen." That day on Mary's, it took maybe a dozen turns before the suit would work its magic.

"As I was skiing along the ridge, I saw a big hole right on the edge of the mountain and I jumped over it," Dan said. "So, when I landed off that little jump, the whole cornice broke. The cornice, without exaggerating, was the size of two semi-trailers. I didn't realize the snow was breaking from under me when I landed. It just felt like a big wind drift. I sort of did a double pole plant to pull myself up and out of it. The momentum carried me back to safety, and John got, for better or worse, a better view of it because had it broken right before him. As I was skiing that ridge, I saw daylight. And I jumped over the daylight, thinking, 'that was a good move.' But when I landed, I kicked the cornice. I was skiing off the piece as it broke off over a five-hundred-foot cliff. And John is skiing right at that same piece."

As Warren Miller narrated in the film, "And now I want you to watch closely, because a cornice as big as a three-story apartment house is going to break off." So, when John realized that the cornice had broken off, he thought for a moment that he might stop before it, so he stemmed. But he immediately realized he wouldn't be able to stop in time and was destined for a one-way ticket down below, along with the enormous chunk of ice. So instead, he pushed. "That push is what saved his life," Dan said.

"That hundred-ton block of ice and snow fell a thousand feet before it hit the first time," Miller said during his narration. "Fortunately, without either of the Egan brothers."

Dan said he'd been totally unaware of what had happened. "I was unaware that John was turning in midair, unaware that the snow fell away," he said.

Nate's shot captured John turning back to safety, skiing on nothing but the air below him. He caught snow long enough to make a second turn and then, as Miller put it, "makes turns as if nothing had happened."

"It was just one of those things that you might say was total luck," Nate said. "But it happened to be one of the most fantastic shots that I ever shot. That someone got himself into that position and still made it out alive is amazing."

It would turn into the most-viewed segment for Warren Miller films, appearing in a number of releases and viewed over and over again online and on video, including in Warren Miller's 71st release, 2020's *Future Retro*. "I'm not one of those who always said 'Gee, there's a hundred-foot cliff over there, Schmidt, jump off it,'" Nate said. "It was always Schmidt or Egan scoping it out. I had total trust that they knew what they were doing—minus the possibilities of Mother Nature thrown in the middle. I had complete trust that these guys were the best in the world at what they were doing. I always felt like they had it under control, if there ever is that sort of thing in that type of filming."

John and Dan, somewhat remarkably, kept skiing, and the camera kept rolling, catching them bursting through the snow-covered forest, John exploding off an eighty-foot cliff. Fear wasn't driving John, despite the close call with death—but the residual energy from that fear was. "The fear of what could go wrong has always been a driving force for me," John said. "People say 'you're fearless,' but I don't think so. I think I decipher and dissect what's going on. Fear is healthy. It's good for you. It's not good for you not to be afraid. It's good to be confident and understand what could happen. Living in fear is not good, and letting fear run your body and your body language is not good. But understanding why you would be fearful of that avalanche—too narrow, too steep, too icy—those things will let you solve the problem so that you've solved the fear issue and you're not backing away from it."

It's also easy to forget just how much more of a challenge the entire sequence was, considering the Egans were at that time skiing on straight skis, not the curved wonders that made the sport easier, beginning in the mid-'90s. At Targhee, John and Dan were skiing on the Rossignol Quantum, a ski with a plastic, see-through tip. "It was a noodle of a ski," Dan said. "It was really soft. It was a crazy bad ski, and we were hucking those cliffs. We called them the 'Rossi No Want-ems'."

If that shot were reproduced today with modern skiing equipment, who's to say how it might turn out? The skier would probably straight-line it down the ridge and might have enough speed to beat the cornice breaking before them. Or, without that inherent instinct to turn, which was how John, Dan, and other extreme skiers of their era defined their approach, perhaps the less experienced skier would have been in the pile of ice rubble far below. "It really highlights the difference between the straight ski and the wide ski," Dan said, "because when the wide ski came out, the athletes could go straight. They could be up *on* the snow. We skied *in* the snow. When we would approach the edge of a cliff, we had to make a lot of calculations: 'If I'm going to be knee-deep in that snow, how much speed do I need to clear what's below it? When do I stop turning?' And then you're free-falling and have to decide, 'Well, am I going to posthole when I land?' Or, 'how do I ski out of this?' That's why you always saw us landing on our hips. We would take the impact on the side of the body, bounce back to our feet, and continue skiing. Sometimes it went right and sometimes it didn't. But with the wider skis, you land on the snow and you don't punch through."

As far as the Egans punching through into the mindset of the average ski movie attendee, Targhee turned out to be a hit. *Extreme Winter* was the forty-first film from Warren Miller, and was shown in some two hundred cities that winter. Watching the Egans alone was "worth the price of admission," according to *Snow Country* magazine in its November, 1990, issue.

Nate's shot was "one in a million," according to Miller's narration, which the cameraman attributed to the unpredictable madness that often occurred while working with The Egan Brothers. "The things they do and the things they pull off are so unexpected," Nate said, "not something you think is going to happen. Then, out of nowhere, comes some adventure, whether it's skiing or being on location. It just seems like the Egans are always amazing me. I don't know what's coming out of them next."

A hawk frees a rabbit from its grip as Joe Powder lands in a couloir.

Photograph by Dave Roman

When a rope was too short repelling into a glacial couloir in Zermatt, Switzerland, the Egans had to untie from the repel and jump the glacial ice into this chute.

Chapter Twenty-one

YOUNG MEN SEEKING ADVENTURE

YOUNG MEN SEEKING ADVENTURE DON'T always seek financial reward. This has been true throughout history. When Ernest Shackleton announced his intention to cross Antarctica on foot, he received more than five thousand applications from volunteers wanting to join the explorer on his journey. "The Shackleton story has always amazed me," Dan said. "It's a story of leadership, faith, and perseverance, where giving up was not an option." Almost without exception, the volunteers were motivated solely by the spirit of adventure; the salaries offered were little more than token payments for services expected, and ranged from 289£ ($240) a year for an able seaman to 860£ ($750) a year for the most experienced scientists.

Twenty-seven men joined Shackleton on *Endurance*, a ship that set sail from England in August of 1914. Passing through the iceberg-filled Weddell Sea in the Antarctic Peninsula, the travelers had come within eighty-five miles of their destination when the ship became trapped in ice pack. It had been nearly a year since the explorers had any contact with the civilized world, and the ship drifted until it was finally crushed under the pressure of ten million tons of ice. Shackleton and his men were left stranded on an epic ordeal that would last twenty months, crossing a jigsaw puzzle of ice through 850 miles of the South Atlantic's heaviest seas, a trip that "defined heroism." They were alone in another world, one that had yet to be charted by any human being.

Dan said he kept Alfred Lansing's book about the expedition, *Endurance: Shackleton's Incredible Voyage*, with him on his travels around the world, "because there are so many scenes that show how man can remain calm under the most extreme situations." Lansing described the calmness with which the men proceeded to abandon ship. Dog-team drivers took forty-nine huskies from their kennels on board and slid each to men waiting on the icy surface below the ship's deck. There was no excitement among the dogs, almost as if they realized something extraordinary was happening. Not a single fight broke out. Not a single animal attempted to run away. Lansing credits this to the attitude of the men, who worked with a deliberate urgency, hardly speaking. "There was no display of alarm," he wrote.

Under Shackleton's leadership, the men were compelled to become self-reliant. Alexander Macklin, a "stocky young physician," was one member of the crew who realized a deeper understanding of himself throughout the ordeal. After spending four hours sewing a patch on his pants, he wrote in his diary: "What an ingrate I have been for such jobs when done for me at home." In a world of emptiness, the men had found a sense of enlightenment, a kind of contentment. "They had been tested and found not wanting," wrote Lansing.

"The quote about being tested and found not wanting is a standard that I find impossible to reach," Dan said. "I know I have been tested, but rarely have I found myself not wanting." Adventures rarely result in financial rewards but abound in feelings of personal accomplishment and satisfaction for reaching an external goal. The internal goal is a discovery of one's inner self from exploring the external, physical world and everything about it. Adventurists commonly push their limits, with the knowledge that there is an uncertain monetary return on investment. "What surprises me now is that we were willing to risk our lives for very little money," Dan told *Skiing* magazine in 1990. Author Peter Oliver even noted, "Only a handful of U.S. extreme skiers—Plake, Schmidt, Andrews, Hattrup, the Egans, perhaps a few others—earn more in a year than the average burger-flipper at McDonald's."

In 1990, the minimum wage earned by many fast-food workers was only $3.80 per hour. But there is a vast difference between making a scant amount of money doing a job in order to put food on the table or one that sends someone on an encounter with adventure. The "undisciplined freedom," as Warren Miller described it, of traveling the world, exploring and creating landmarks of discovery, is something that pays in its own way to those who have accepted it as their calling and a way they define the meaning of life. "It's a self-discovery sport," skier Scot Schmidt said. "You learn what you're made of."

The phrase "No friends on a powder day" speaks to more than just ditching camaraderie for first tracks. It also whittles down skiing's social characteristics to their core. "You could be with a whole group of people, but once you push off, it's an individual sport," John said, which he came to understand at a young age during weekend trips to New Hampshire ski areas. "We would go up as a whole family, but the second you push off, you're on your own. You're controlling everything, and it just felt like freedom to me. Always has been, and it still is." But there's also a sense of belonging, as Dan sees it, that can drive us to do something bigger than ourselves. That has always included his time with John on all the mountains they've descended together.

"Skiing behind John through a mogul field, ripping toward a cliff, I came to know his movements," Dan said. "I relied on his pole plants. I knew what the head bob meant. I knew when he was going to accelerate. I knew when he'd go left, right, or just air it out over a cliff. And I always just followed."

Shackleton once said, of his adventure in Antarctica, "I had grown bigger in the bigness of the whole." It is a cherished phrase still used by many explorers in the modern era, whether in mountaineering, deep-sea diving, or attempting to break other barriers yet to be tackled by humankind. That sense of self-purpose is why athletes are willing to risk themselves in the face of fear, the driving force that pulls others away from such ventures. How they translate or understand that fear is a different matter.

Long after her extreme skiing days concluded, Kristen Ulmer became a specialist in fear. Her book, *The Art of Fear*, aimed to sharpen abilities in all aspects of life, from sports to relationships to the anxiety of networking. "What I saw was that a lot of professional athletes have a paradox in regard to fear," Ulmer said. "There are a lot of things going on, but just when it comes to fear, the paradox is usually that they have a love-hate relationship with it. Anybody who is going to be a downhill racer is going to be having a love affair with fear. But if they also repress it, it causes problems. I had a rabid addiction to fear and I also repressed it to the extreme. Part of me loved it because it made me a world-class athlete. But part of me resisted it and that caused a lot of problems."

It's this sense of fear that John refers to when talking about understanding problems in order to figure out solutions without simply running from them. It was this healthy form of fear that drove Shackleton and his crew on their journey for survival.

Fear is part of the equation when it comes to extreme skiing—being afraid is something else entirely. "I pause every day up on the mountain," Schmidt said. "What are the consequences? I look at every line with that same thought. *I've lost friends, it's so dangerous. What are my escape routes here?* If something goes wrong it's usually the variable, the thing that surprises you, the thing that ends up getting you. I'm pretty comfortable with my ability and my control, but the things you can't control are the things that freak the shit out of you."

There is also a great difference between managing one's fear versus smothering it. Part of what kept the European approach to extreme skiing from being of interest to the public was its inability to commercialize itself. Stories of the mountaineering exploits of men and women rarely extended beyond their respective communities.

There is plenty to be said and admired about first ascents and descents, but it's not as eye-catching as, say, skiing on air over a falling cornice in Grand Targhee, Wyoming, or cliff-jumping skiers in neon one-piece suits. But maybe Dan misunderstood the allure, too. Maybe that misunderstanding was what left him on the brink of dying in a snow cave in Russia, only weeks after his and John's other brush with death at Targhee. Maybe he was attempting a higher level of what was considered extreme, yet wasn't necessarily consistent with what The Egan Brothers and their on-snow colleagues were trying to convey in their marketing approach.

The expedition to Mount Elbrus arose as a way for Degré7 to honor the memory of its founder, Patrick Vallençant. John had his relationship with Vallençant, and by this time, both the Egans were sponsored by the brand and clad in its clothing. By 1990, Janet and John Markman were planning on importing Degré7 skiwear from Europe to America. Although already sponsored by The North Face, Dan saw a marketing opportunity with Degré7 for The Egan Brothers. "We went right up to them and said we could get their clothing in the movies," Dan said. "They did not ask us to drop The North Face, and The North Face gave us permission to ski in their suits." One of the negotiation points with The North Face was, if they weren't going to increase the Egans' contractual residuals, the brothers wouldn't have to give them appearances in the Warren Miller films. Still, the well-known brothers were wanted in The North Face Extreme Team films. Thus, Dan and John sold a portion of their Warren Miller exposure to Degré7.

It was his connection with Vallençant that John always treasured, but he looks back now in wonderment. How had their misapprehension and failure to properly consider fear and common sense, for the first time in their skiing career, led them to agree to the trip to Russia in the first place? In John's mind, having fear and ignoring fear were two differing facets. One can lead to safety. One can lead to death. Or, they can combine so both can be managed. When the opportunity of Elbrus arose, the Egans latched on to that idea and committed to climbing 18,500 feet to the summit and skiing down. In the name of . . . well, Dan still isn't quite sure.

But, like Shackleton's, seventy-five years before, Dan's quest in Russia was about to turn into something else entirely, where his translation of the spirit of adventure would ultimately be tested; where his ability to face and harness his fear would mean the difference between life and death. Not to mention how some sort of divinity would guide him through the event . . . the same sort of presence Shackleton had written about and called Providence. He and his men, Worsley and Crean, endured a "racking march of thirty-six hours" across South Georgia Island. Both men confided in their leader that they had heard "the dearth of human words, the roughness of mortal speech," of another, intangible being. Shackleton wrote, "it seemed to me often that we were four, not three."

As it reads in Deuteronomy 31:8, "He will never leave you nor forsake you. Do not be afraid; do not be discouraged." Mortal fear was about to inject itself into Dan's life as it never had before. How he reacted and fought against it would always be because of the way he was led by his higher power.

Chapter Twenty-two

SIBLING RIVALRY

ROBERT EGAN AWOKE, UNSETTLED, IN a holy place. As a neurologist at Cardinal Cushing Hospital in Brockton, Massachusetts, Robert volunteered to go on pilgrimages in Lourdes, France—an annual mission to dedicate medical resources to handicapped children. Marlen was with him on this particular pilgrimage. In this southwestern French town, in 1858, fourteen-year-old Bernadette Soubirous was said to have had her first vision of the Virgin Mary. Bernadette told her mother that a lady had spoken to her in a cave at Massabielle while she was collecting firewood. After repeated apparitions, Mary asked Bernadette to dig a hole in the ground and drink the water. This hole would eventually become a stream purported to have miraculous healing powers. Water from the province of Lourdes would become a symbol of remedy from affliction and spiritual faith for believers around the world.

Nearly one hundred years after Bernadette's encounters with the Virgin

Mary, Richard J. Cushing, the Archbishop of the Boston Diocese, led a group of more than five hundred Americans to Lourdes to witness the site of the miracles, a trip that inspired him to create the Lourdes Center in Boston, in 1950. The Lourdes Center is the official distributor of Lourdes Water in the United States and Canada, and helps spread the devotion of the Lady of Lourdes. The Lourdes Center's website explains, "The Lourdes Center emphasizes that, in itself, Lourdes Water is simply water from the spring at Lourdes, France. It has no curative or miraculous ingredients, but it is known that due to one's faith and God's mercy, Lourdes Water has been miraculous for many who have used it. The Church has officially recognized sixty-eight miracles resulting from individuals who used Lourdes Water or journeyed to Lourdes on a pilgrimage. Thousands more claim to have had physical healings but have chosen not to go through the long process of official verification by a team of medical professionals."

Since 1868, there have been sixty-seven recognized healings and four recorded miraculous cures, and Robert is the doctor on record for three cures that occurred during his time in Lourdes.

Sometimes, he brought his own children to participate in caring for the children. Dan went for the first time when he was sixteen, and was given full responsibility for the care of a twelve-year-old boy with cerebral palsy. He fed the boy, cleaned him, even administered enemas, a dose of care and realism that powerfully affected Dan's teenage soul, a soul which often self-centeredly considered the world to be his for the taking. "I had never done anything like that in my life," Dan said. "It was an eye-opening and spiritual experience for me, and I got to see my dad in a different light, as well."

In this same place of the soul, where healing and optimism for life reside, Robert awoke with a start in May of 1990. He'd had a dream that would not give hope to the sick and suffering, the very aura that characterized Lourdes, but instead suggested that pain and loss were coming. He'd dreamt his son had died. On a mountain peak. In Russia. It was John.

The elements we meet will give us reality and God will deliver our destiny.
— Dan Egan's Elbrus diary, April 27, 1990

As far as the degree of difficulty for each of the world's Seven Summits is concerned, the challenge awaiting seasoned mountaineers climbing Mount Elbrus is low on the list. A rock peak in the middle of the steaming rainforest of Indonesia is why Carstensz Pyramid/Puncak Jaya is considered the most technical of the mountains on the list. Mount Everest's aura of danger and death has fascinated and attracted thousands of people each year to attempt its rocky spines. But Elbrus? It's not the walk in the park one might expect, as when scaling Australia's 2,228-meter Mount Kosciusko. Nor is it as easy as Kilimanjaro, described by some as a straightforward stroll to the summit. Elbrus is noted for the danger of its sudden weather changes which kill hundreds of climbers annually. On average, each year fifteen to thirty people die on Elbrus, including a high total of forty-eight in 2004. Compare that to the number who died on Everest in 2018—five—and it can be surmised that Elbrus might actually be the deadliest peak of the Seven Summits.

Warren Miller cameraman Gary Nate grew up in Utah with Jeff and Greg Lowe, famed Alpinists who recorded first ascents in the U.S., Canadian Rockies, Alps, and Himalayas. So when he informed his old friends that he'd been asked to film a journey to Elbrus sponsored by Degré7, they were quick to describe the unwelcome experiences they'd had on the mountain. Nate also turned to his friend, Frank Wells, for an opinion.

Wells is best known today for his role as president of the Walt Disney Company, from 1984–94 (when the sixty-two year old died in a helicopter crash while returning from a ski trip in Nevada), but he was also an avid mountain climber whose bid to become the first person to climb all Seven Summits came just short, at Mount Everest. His partner in the Seven Summits pursuit was Dick Bass, the sole proprietor of Snowbird Mountain Ski Resort from its inception in 1971 until he sold his stake in 2014. Bass would complete the goal of all seven mountains in 1985, conquering Everest on his third try, along with David Breashears, who simultaneously became the first American to summit the mountain more than once. Wells had had a bad experience on Elbrus himself—it was the first mountain he and Bass attempted to summit in their Seven Summits bid in 1981. Altitude sickness put an end to Wells's climb, fifteen hundred vertical feet behind Bass, who was at the top. Wells was concerned a similar fate could impact Nate.

"Every one of them said 'this is not a good situation that you're getting yourself into'," Nate said. "Going from almost sea level up in British Columbia to this trip—talking with Dick Bass, and Frank Wells, and the Lowes—not one of them thought it was well planned out, or a good project."

After Wells's failed attempt on Elbrus, the team descended via the mountain tram and made its way back to Moscow. Rather than being disappointed, Wells was elated because he now knew what it took to turn around on an expedition. He felt good about this self-realization—that it was the easiest thing in the world for him to turn back. Two years later, in better physical condition, Wells would make it to the top of Elbrus, the fifth summit in his attempt at all seven. It was the story of his failure, though, that might have saved Nate's life.

Skiing Mount Elbrus was, from start to finish, intended for Degré7 promotional purposes, beginning with a hangtag contest. Cameraman Tom Day would accompany the Egans to shoot the trip for an upcoming ski film from Egan Entertainment. The trip kicked off when the twenty-two participants met at Charles de Gaulle airport in Paris. There were friendly greetings and cautious smiles, but Dan noted confusion right away in the eyes of many of his new acquaintances, particularly with the difficulty of communicating with each other. While some obviously had experience—the luggage, food, tents, sleeping bags, climbing equipment, radios, and transceivers they brought indicated as much—others were clearly novices. He wondered about their overall ability to stay focused and perform their duties under difficult conditions. Suddenly, this Elbrus event didn't seem like the best place to host the winners of a hangtag contest.

Degré7 welcomed nine winners on the excursion to Mount Elbrus in honor of its late owner, Patrick Vallençant, and provided mountain guides from Chamonix, Vallençant's home town, to lead the expedition. Alfred Jimenez-Segarra was among the prizewinners. The twenty-seven-year-old was living and working in Brussels one year earlier, when he purchased a Degré7 beanie in a sports store and was given a postcard to enter the sweepstakes. There was a disclaimer on the card, basically explaining that participants should have some level of ski-mountaineering ability and be physically fit enough for the hike. Segarra had spent some time living in Lleida, Spain, close to the Pyrenees, so he at least had some experience in ski-mountaineering and rock-climbing. He'd climbed both Mont Blanc and Monte Rosa in the Alps and felt confident that Mount Elbrus would be feasible. So he mailed the postcard.

But even Dan, with moderate mountaineering skills, was unsure of his ability to climb to 18,500 feet. And that was only one of the concerns heading into a trip that carried with it a number of insane factors. "They offered this to people from nine different countries and didn't vet any of them," John said. "Nobody knows anybody else. Nobody knows if they speak the same language. Nobody knows anything." The first sign foreshadowing trouble should have been the fact that the tram that took visitors from the village of Terskol to a height of eleven thousand feet didn't have a door. Dan was already experiencing anxiety from the language barrier, and felt self-conscious in his inability to communicate with everybody. There was an awkwardness to listening to conversations and being unsure what prompted the laughter that followed. But there was another anxiety as well. This one existed between Dan and John.

The contrast between the Egans was in constant flux. The six-year age span and differences in their childhood experiences were signs of demarcation: John had run with a rough and tough crowd, while Dan had found his place in the varsity flock. Their fitness routines were different, as well. Dan was a runner and soccer player, known for running players who were defending him into the ground. John, who had always relied on skiing himself into shape, was lean, strong, and known for his cat-like balance and energy. But he also had asthma, and wasn't necessarily an endurance guy. Their life experiences were different. Their personalities were different. The combination of similarities as well as differences made for amazing feats on camera but, behind the scenes, Irish tempers mixed with pride and ego often made sparks fly.

There were also the barriers of corporate prejudice to overcome. When Vallençant died in 1989, those in charge of Degré7 were left reeling, trying to figure out the company's future, especially as it made an attempt to expand into the United States. Degré7's U.S. distribution company was a family-run firm from L.A. which had few connections with the ski industry, but did, however, see the authenticity and exposure the Egans brought to the table. Still, the company didn't send a representative on the trip, leaving the Americans at the mercy of their European colleagues.

Those on the trip included Ingrid Buchner, Vallençant's original business partner and clothing designer; Eric Charamel, a personal friend of Vallençant, mountain guide, and the connection between the brand and the Chamonix guides; Volodia Shahshahani, a French journalist; and Michel Petit Perrin, the lawyer who was CEO of Degré7.

Buchner was the Egans' main contact with the European brand and a big supporter of their activities and marketing. The Elbrus expedition was Charamel's brainchild, and he was in charge on the ground. He and his fellow guides chose Elbrus over other contenders, such as Mount Kilimanjaro in Tanzania and Mont Blanc (the highest mountain in the Alps), because it was easier to ski and summit.

The problem with the contest was that Charamel and the others didn't know what to expect from their fellow climbers. The primary skills needed to tackle Elbrus—the abilities to ski and acclimate oneself to the elevation—weren't universal traits throughout the group. Case in point: the British winner of the Degré7 contest was skinning along with the rest of the group, except this was a new experience for him, being that it was his first time skiing on natural snow. His only previous experience had been skiing at an indoor snowdome in his home country. Clearly, he would not attempt to summit the mountain.

"It's better to know that in the beginning rather than have it dropped on the mountain," Charamel said. "'Welcome to Russia. Have a good time in the hut.' So, we brought more beer for him."

Overall, the guides didn't prove to be much help. While the Americans tried to plan their movements with great detail, the French climbers would grunt indifference through a stream of cigarette smoke. These were the same guides tasked with providing food for the venture, but Dan's recollection of what had been available made the raisins he'd brought a more viable nutritional option. Presumably, they'd relied on local suppliers for food options, which, in the poor surroundings of the Soviet Union, wasn't the best plan.

John and Dan were downhill skiers by nature, so they didn't have much experience in Alpine touring. It was only on their stop through Chamonix, on the way to the Berlin Wall, when they'd purchased backcountry ski boots and heavy trekkers that fit in their bindings, allowing them to skin. The Secura-Fix binding plate was heavy and crude compared to modern styles, so to lighten their gear they purchased Dynafit Tourlite boots and chose to stay with their Alpine bindings and Fischer skis. They brought North Face packs, tents, and sleeping bags. Their Degré7 clothing—burly snowsuits—would prove essential for the warmth they provided. They had ice axes and shovels. Each brother seemed well-equipped to face any misfortune on the mountain. That is, so long as he had his pack.

But the brothers had had a long winter of travel, and with that came the occasional spat or disagreement on schedules, sponsorship obligations, and gear. There were also personal relationship issues; there was drama between John and Lotta, and Dan's longtime girlfriend, Laurie, had split with him over his drinking, his newfound career, and the lifestyle that came with it. They were still in touch, but the realities of his choices were front and center in his mind, and even written in his journal: "I miss Laurie, it's been over a year, but I still miss her. She would like it here."

All this while, Tom Day's wife and family had been traveling with the Egans. The dynamics of blending work with family life on the road with a three-year-old child made for some unaccommodating adjustments to the ski-bum lifestyle. John's longtime relationship with Day sometimes left Dan feeling like the odd man out. Tom and John were peers, had traveled together, ski-bummed together, and had the perspective of years on the mountain. After all, they were five and six years older, respectively, than Dan, the twenty-six-year-old college graduate. They saw the world differently, as brothers often do. "In the early years, John was a business owner with an amazing ski reputation and Dan was young and wild, not very responsible," longtime Sugarbush local Karen Anderson said. "Over time, Dan came of age and then things shifted a bit. Elbrus was a turning point in their dynamic."

Part of the riff on Elbrus was about John not remembering all his gear. He'd managed to leave behind in the States the critical Secura-Fix bindings that made skiing in Alpine conditions possible. That was OK during the set-up shots for the film, during which they shared one binding plate each, but for the long slog to the summit of Mt. Elbrus, that would not be possible.

Dan had his gear and his ambition. But he was frustrated that he wouldn't have his most-trusted family member, John, with him for the summit attempt. And it was soon apparent that John was unwilling to go, anyway. The morning of the summit bid was actually quite clear of the storms that had threatened the attempt over the course of the past few days. It was, from some accounts, a beautiful day, a gift from the heavens, made-to-order for tackling Elbrus. The Chamonix guides were prepared for summiting. The Russian guides, assisting in the ascent, were much less certain. There were lots of clouds below and the climbers couldn't see the valley, only some mountain peaks sticking up here and there.

Much like any venture of its kind at the time in Russia, mountaineers would hire a native handler or a liaison with similar experience to keep an eye on the expedition. It was this person's duty to analyze conditions and recommend procedures based on prevailing winds, snow depths, rainstorms, or anything that might be important regarding the history of the snowpack. The French guides had little use for this liaison, though, indignantly rebuffing any advice he might share with the clients. But John felt it was wisest to listen to the liaison, who might be better informed about the Caucuses. "I'm going to listen to the local guide about his local mountain and utilize that to my benefit, to come out alive," he said. It was the Russians who, after all, had relayed an ominous message while climbing in a storm on the previous day.

"The Russians were like, 'Yeah, this is a bad one,'" John said. "'It's Ramadan.

It's May. Allah is mad. Doesn't like what's going on. It's bad.'" According to one Russian handler, the pristine conditions were because they were in the eye of the storm, not its periphery. Charamel voiced his own concern and instructed everyone to begin their descents by 2 p.m., regardless of how high they'd gotten. So, while a handful prepared to reach the top, John balked and conferred with Day about the situation—but not Dan. John had what he called "Spidey sense," developed on the streets of Boston—an intuition when danger lurks. Having that perception in a seedy back alley of the Combat Zone, the notorious Boston neighborhood where adult entertainment, crime, and prostitution reigned for decades, was the sort of city-bred trait that John said kept him alive on the rough streets. "If you don't lose that, it'll keep you alive in the mountains," he said.

It was making a mutually shared decision that put Day at ease. "I was really tired," Day said. "I was suffering from jet lag more than I ever had. When we were at the door of the refuge, looking out, we both didn't say anything right away. So, when John said that he was tired and wasn't going to go, I was kind of relieved. I wouldn't want to go up there anyway, and I certainly didn't want to drag a camera up there." Their conclusion was to trust the local guide, who understood more about the geography and climatology of the present situation. The climbers were on a mountain, situated between the Black and Caspian Seas, rising to eighteen thousand feet, and surrounded by fourteen-thousand-foot peaks. If there was a man who lived here and had been in this kind of situation before, and he was certain this was merely a break in the storm, there was little reason to argue with his logic.

There was gloom in the air surrounding the camp that morning. John remembers climbing the night before and running into some Japanese climbers going the wrong way. He tried to convince them to come back in the direction from which he'd come, but instead, the climbers hung out and built an igloo. "That night, the igloo blew away and those guys died, sleeping in the igloo," John said. "The Russians hid the bodies from us. There was so much fishy stuff going on that morning that wasn't clean, that just wasn't right. Tom and I didn't think it was worth it."

Claudio Abate, a mountaineer and journalist from Italy on assignment for *Alp Magazine*, an Austrian publication similar to *Outside Magazine* in the United States, agreed and decided to stay put as well. He joined Tom and John in the discussion to simply try and get the film done by enacting some climbing and skiing, securing a bunch of short shots within sight of the refuge, so everybody could see what was going on with the weather—as well as the circus of human antics. That, again, left Dan as the odd man out, a familiar position when he was with Day and his older brother, and he didn't like it.

While John was turned off by his intuition of danger, Dan wanted to go for the prize, just as he'd gone for the varsity letter John had so minimized. Surrendering the ascent wasn't an option in Dan's mind—not with the peak in sight and the opportunity to ski this mountain and get the film—that was the goal of this entire trip, and it was within reach. He'd spent the past few days internalizing the meaning of the mission, seeking isolation in the mountains, experiencing the peaceful, solitary freedom he'd found both on skis and in a sailboat. He needed to feel the vastness of the mountains surrounding him, to exorcize the negative thoughts that filled his head and replace them with all the good surrounding his physical presence. But now, Dan found it hard to remind himself of the good when so much bad stared back at him, a realization he chose to set out and change in his attempt on Elbrus. He felt like he was coming closer to himself in those mountains, where he didn't feel so alienated. "It is going to take everything I have to make it," Dan wrote in his journal the day before the summit. "I must remember my limitations and my inexperience. I have heart and will. I will rely on these two things. God will help me. I know he will not leave me on the mountain, no matter what."

So, give up? Now? That wasn't an option for Dan Egan, especially not when his brother told him these weren't the right conditions and refused to go. He'd listened to his big brother enough, lived in his shadow enough, and tried to accomplish what John had enough. This was too important for Dan, especially when the opportunity was right there. Certainly, he was upset that John wasn't coming along. He berated him, calling him lazy and forgetful for leaving some of his gear behind, and accused him of being in these situations only for the good time, not the landmark moments they could be.

"It was not pretty," John said. But he still wasn't going up. And his brother still wasn't quitting.

"Dan's last words to me were 'Fuck you,'" John said. "And he walked away."

Dan ripping powder for Warren Miller's *Vertical Reality* at
Waterville Valley Resort, NH, 1994

Photograph by Wade McKoy

John dropping in for Warren Miller's *Steeper and Deeper*
in Cappadocia, Turkey, in 1992

Dan skiing in Central Anatolia, Turkey, 1992

Marlen Egan on the skimobile at Cranmore Mountain, NH, circa 1970

John (R), Bobby (M), Mary-Ellen (L) skiing at Cranmore Mountain, NH, circa 1970

Family Ski Trip to Sugarbush, VT, to visit John, 1980
From left to right: Ned, Suzanne, Mike, Mary-Ellen, Marlen, Dan

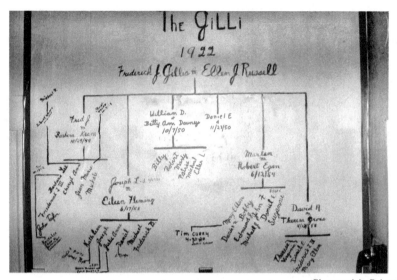

The Gillis Family Tree on the kitchen wall in Grandpa & Grandma's house
in West Roxbury, MA

Daniel E. Gillis, son of Joe Gillis, Marlen's nephew, and Dan and John's cousin, 1975

Marlen's twin brother, Uncle Daniel E. Gillis, training for the Korean War in Florida, 1950

196

Dan and Frederick J. Gillis at the highest point in Boston, MA, at
the West Roxbury Water Tower, 1975

Dan, age 10, in the Blizzard Ski Club Annual Race at Mount Sunapee, NH, 1974

SUGARBUSH

Photograph by Sugarbush Resort

John in the Ski Bum Race at Sugarbush, VT, circa 1981

Dan racing for Babson College at Waterville Valley, NH, at NE Ski Championships, 1987

Dan during his ski bum days launching a Granite Chief cornice in Squaw Valley, CA, 1985

199

Dan and John celebrate Dan's graduation from Babson College, 1987

John and Dan on the Degré7 and Fischer Skis photo shoot in Val d'Isère, France, 1990

Dan and John launch a cliff for the North Face video *Skiing Extreme III*, 1990

Dan and John's promotional post card for Fischer Skis, 1990

Cameraman Tom Day in Chamonix, France, shooting the North Face video
Skiing Extreme IV in 1991

Cameraman Tom Grissom in Turkey shooting Egan Entertainment's *Extreme Dream*, 1992

John during his interview for the documentary *Ski Bum: The Warren Miller Story*, 2018

John jumps off of the Berlin Wall, 1990

Dan jumps off of the Berlin Wall, 1990

Dan with Warren Miller at the Yellow Stone Club, Montana, 2016

Photograph by Jeff Proehl

Dan skiing with his Dad, Robert, at Cannon Mountain, NH, 2003

Photograph by Mike McPhee

Dan filming for his television show *Dan Egan's Wild World of Winter* at
Kicking Horse in Golden, British Columbia, 2009

Photograph by Jim Cole

Dan and Dean Decas jumping out of the tram at Cannon Mountain, NH,
for Warren Miller's *Vertical Reality*, 1994

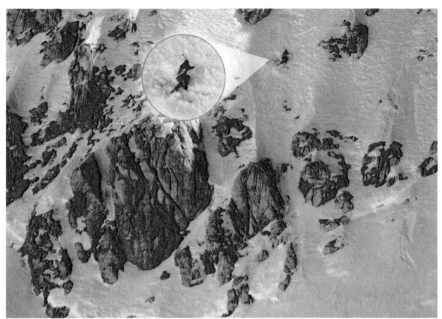

Dan skiing in Yugoslavia for Warren Miller's *Born to Ski, 1991*

Dan drops in on the Apple Core Chute in Big Sky, MT, 2020

Cameraman Eric Scharmer capturing Dan, filming for
Great American Freeride video in Valle d' Aosta, Italy, 1999.

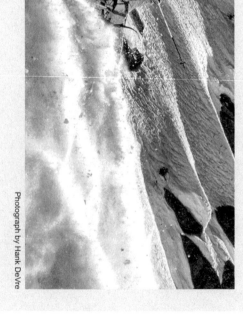

Joe Powder is airborne again at the bottom of the couloir and the rabbit celebrates a potentially safe landing.

Photograph by Hank DeVre

John defies gravity skiing down this rock face in Squaw Valley for *Skiing Extreme IV*.

Chapter Twenty-three

LOST IN A WHITE HAZE

THE PHONE RANG IN THE Egans' Moscow hotel room at midnight. It was April 27, 1990, the day the expedition had arrived in Moscow, the day after everyone met in Paris.

"Are you OK?" was all the voice said. Then the line disconnected. Everyone on the trip received the same call, with the same question in their native languages. There were nine western nationalities—the Russians were letting them know they were being checked on.

The group departed the hotel at 5:30 a.m. for a two-hour flight, followed by a five-hour bus ride in the rain. "The bus ride was unreal. The windows leaked and my seat was soaked," Dan wrote in his journal. "The roads were rough, there were mudslides everywhere, and lots of traffic." The May Day holiday is an important public celebration in Russia, known as the Day of the International Solidarity of Workers. Begun in 1918, it was celebrated in most Soviet cities with parades and obligatory workers' marches until 1990. From Dan's journal: "The whole country looks so poor and dirty, no new buildings. Everything is run down, lots of farms, and animals in the street. We are a long way from home."

Bad weather greeted the group, leaving four-and-half feet of snow on Mount Elbrus. It was still snowing late on the afternoon of April 28, when they arrived in the village base camp. It is told in Russian folklore that Allah doesn't like the national holidays, especially May Day, when it always rains. The group free-skied on April 29, in deep snow, during the rainstorm. The next day, they moved into the Priyut refuge at 13,780 feet, to begin acclimatizing for the summit attempt. The expedition climbed from the top of the gondola at eleven thousand feet. Skinning the next 3,700 feet with packs weighing more than sixty pounds took a toll on everyone; some members were sick from the altitude right from the very beginning.

The skin was even harder for Dan and John, who shared a Secura-Fix binding set. Dan wrote in his journal: "John is excited, and his attitude is great. This is a good trip for us. However, we are one mountain binding short. He expects me to have everything. It never occurred to him that he should pack his own bindings. So now we share one set, and this is making climbing tough! If he wasn't my brother, I'd let him walk."

The way John saw it, his deciding not to summit wasn't necessarily an abandonment of his brother, or due to the lack of equipment. It was because the weather conditions were worsening. The opportunity to try still could have arisen while they were on the mountain, if it weren't for the storm forcing the guides to make other decisions. "We were in for the long haul with plenty of days to get up there," John said. "The goal was to go home on these trips, not to go to the summit. That's always been my philosophy and I've always come home."

The guides told the group that, given the current weather, outside the chance of it clearing on May 1, they'd have to vacate the mountain the next day. This left only a small window of opportunity for the summit attempt. With the elevation and varying levels of skills on hand, Charamel figured that gave them five hours to reach the summit, then two hours to ski down. Or thirty minutes for Dan and John to navigate the descent on skis, Charamel said. Dan didn't want to miss this weather window, so started for the top, securing his pack and the one set of Secura-Fix binding plates. The friction between John and Dan detached them at the soul of their once-shared purpose for being at Elbrus. The elder Egan was choosing to live to fight another day; the younger was looking for a brawl with no concern for tomorrow.

Dan climbed. The weather stayed clear. In fact, so clear that Abate, who'd initially heeded the Russian guide's warnings that this was merely the eye of the storm, now had second thoughts. About an hour and a half after the initial group had left, he told John, "You know, I think I'm going to try and catch them. I think it really is a clear day." With a deep understanding of mountaineering, Abate prepared himself and set off for the top. John and Tom would be the last people to see him alive; later, Charamel found him in a snow cave.

Dot Helling, who hailed from Vermont, was the American winner of the Degré7 trip. She was climbing with her husband, John Peterson, a physician who'd been asked to join the trip as the expedition's doctor, only twenty-four hours before departing the United States. "We were at the base of the icefield at 15,749 feet when it started to snow," Helling wrote after the fact. "We were looming around the 2 p.m. turnaround time, and we decided to turn around there." It was actually 12:30 p.m. Above, on the face, the Chamonix guides had trekked pretty far, but ended up turning around after 2 p.m. themselves, abandoning their pursuit of the stony, snow-covered peak. That left Dan, Alfred, Michel, and the French journalist Volodia Shahshahani climbing, as well as Abate, approximately ninety minutes behind.

"The guides got spread out on how to manage this diverse group of people," Day said. "The only way they could really make it as safe as they could was to have a turnaround time. No matter where you were, turn around. That's safe protocol in the mountains, to manage the clock a little bit. But a lot of people disregarded that request and went on to the summit anyway."

From even a novice mountain climbing mindset, it might seem foolish to remain in pursuit of the goal after a group of experienced, albeit standoffish, guides from one of the most physically challenging mountains on earth decided to retreat. But the low opinions the guides seemed to have for their clients were also mirrored within the group itself. Of course they want to turn around now, Dan remembers thinking—his blind, young ambition now in control. *They want to go smoke and were never really going to go to the top.* "They didn't give a shit," Dan said. "They weren't there to summit. They weren't there for the film. They had no ambitions of going to the summit. I was like, this is my last chance, this is my last day, so I'm going to be known for going to the top."

In reality, there was probably no chance in hell the twenty-six-year-old Dan Egan was going to listen to a group of guides who didn't share the same goal. "I was so set on going up, I didn't listen to John, I didn't listen to the guides. It's easy to say that at fifty-six, but looking back, it was just . . . fuck, I'm going to the top." So he moved forward, and soon, much to Dan's surprise, Alfred, the undaunted sweepstakes winner, had caught up with him. The two of them hadn't even been together at the point where the guides had turned around. Yet, they pushed on—the pair of them slogging it out, counting twenty steps at a time, eventually arriving at a spot both surmised was probably near the top of the mountain. In between the two summits of Elbrus was a saddle with footsteps marking the obvious trek up. But, instead of taking the route that led to the saddle, the duo decided to attack the summit. It seemed only about a two-hundred-foot trek to reach their goal, but it led to what would become an extremely drastic mistake. They would leave their bulky packs behind to ease the climb, and pick them up again on the way down. "You make decisions along the way. Dan made a couple of bad ones," Day said.

"That decision was a twenty-six-year-old's decision," Dan said. "Alfred, having no experience, and me just saying, 'Oh, we'll go up and come back, it's only two hundred feet, whatever.'" But the short distance would prove to be an unforeseen knot in the safety of the excursion, making the next thirty-six hours a living hell. The wind was increasing and the storm getting worse by the moment. But they ignored common sense and the turnaround time, and pushed on. Segarra had never been this high on a mountain in his whole life, and what he classified as the "devil" half of his brain pushed him to continue. He'd even encountered one of the chief guides earlier on the climb, who advised him to turn back, but it didn't prohibit Segarra from continuing. He was on his own, decisions and fate in his own hands.

As they were taking the final steps, they spotted Michel, the lawyer, making his way down from the top. Michel, with his pack in tow, had a message: "You're close. You're going to make it." The words buoyed Dan and Alfred, gasping for every breath in the thin air, pushing and laboring for twenty steps at a time before pausing to recover.

Twenty steps.

Pause. Recover.

Twenty steps.

Meanwhile, John and Tom were about four thousand feet below, climbing and skiing to get shots on film. On their final climb, hyper-focused and concentrating on making the correct maneuvers, they failed to notice the storm lurking below, a disturbance that hit the two just as they managed to film a final shot. The two of them figured they were probably about a hundred feet from each other when the whiteout hit. Neither could see a thing. It took forty-five minutes for them to find each other. They were paying attention to corralling the climbers and guides who'd been left up above—those who'd decided to climb and were subsequently abandoned by the Chamonix guides. John and Tom were able to find three of them, who eventually made their way back to the refuge, where they ran into more bad news. The Russians would not let them in.

A fight broke out between the Americans and the Russians, an altercation that released all the negative energy that had been percolating since the trip's advent. The Russians knew the kind of weather they were in for, and were hunkering down, taking cover. In this instance, nobody else mattered, especially not some obnoxious group of French mountain guides, a couple of show-off upstarts from America, or the handful of novice climbers who probably didn't belong up here in the first place. This was *their* refuge. There were too many people who would be stuck on this mountain overnight, and they needed every bed. After all, it was only midday. There was plenty of time for John and Tom to make it to the base, they said.

The confrontation exhausted John, who finally, after some ferocious convincing, got the Russians to at least open the door long enough for them to grab their things. After all, this had been their home, too, their living quarters for the past three days. The Russians stated the terms: only John could enter. The rest of the group was forced to sit and wait outside while he gathered up their belongings, hoping there would be time to make the journey down—straight into the storm. They would have to ski down—over 3,700 feet—to the tram station, but there was no other option. "The ski down was hard," Helling said. "Visibility was less than ten feet, there were fierce winds, and the snow drifts were four to five feet. We barely made the last tram."

There was also Dan's return to worry about. Hopefully the Russians would allow him to enter the refuge out of absolute need. Hopefully they would have a different idea of mercy, should John's brother come knocking. But he didn't panic about what might happen if they didn't.

"We've been in a lot of shitty situations where we don't freak out," John said. "That's what we gotta do. I know it sucks, but we're going to do it." He tried to contact Dan by radio before making the trek to the tram, but there was no answer. In a storm like the one enveloping them, the odds of reaching him were probably slim anyway. Besides, even if he had made contact, the roaring wind would have prevented him from hearing Dan's response.

Four thousand feet above, Dan's radio wasn't receiving anything. The battery had died and the unit had gone dark. Had it not, and under more ideal circumstances, Dan probably would have used it to contact his brother and deliver the news that he'd made it. He had summited Mount Elbrus.

Chapter Twenty-four

APPARITIONS AND TWINKIES

THERE WAS ONE HULKING PRESENCE in the midst of the chaos who probably couldn't believe what he was seeing. Had two people just reached the top of the mountain where he stood? And were they celebrating? *In this?*

In any normal situation, the Soviet guide would probably have nodded in their direction with welcoming congratulations. But these two didn't seem to understand the gravity of the situation on this mountain: the fact that a storm like the one currently raging on Mount Elbrus had been known in the past to take a great number of lives. This pair, they did not seem like they understood. Confused, exhausted, and desperately trying to eke out whatever drips of water remained in their frozen canteens, Dan and Alfred certainly did not grasp the gravity of the situation. They probably hadn't turned around often enough to witness the storm's progress, climbing up from below. The thin air had its hypoxic effects on their brains, while the whiteout conditions made it impossible to see very far.

When their celebration was over, the Soviet had a simple message for the men. Wasting no time with salutations, he simply said, in English: "Come with me." He told them his name was Sasha, that he was a guide assigned to an expedition from Italy, a group he'd lost in the storm just before he happened upon Dan and Alfred. He insisted the two of them had to hurry so they could make it off the peak in time to rejoin the others who were stranded atop Mount Elbrus. That sounded like a plan to Dan. He and Alfred just had to make a quick trek back to where they'd left their packs before joining the group. According to Sasha, that was a suicidal idea. "Come with me," he said. "Or go look for your packs and die."

Dan and Alfred had to face the possibility that going back for their packs meant the group would not wait for them. Sasha said as much. And without a guide, trying to navigate through a whiteout blizzard, even if they could find their packs—which was doubtful—they might not make it back to the refuge.

So, they had to choose whether to go on their own or follow the advice of a robust Soviet who was explicit in saying that searching for their packs would mean certain death. They chose Sasha, confident they'd be able to find the refuge, some four thousand feet below, where Dan presumed John and the rest of their party would be spending the evening. The prospect of reuniting with his brother and Tom seemed a lot brighter if they stuck with someone who knew the mountain a lot better than he and Alfred did.

"Sasha was yelling to his Russian friends," Dan said in an interview in the days that followed. "We couldn't see them, but we could hear them. There was a group of people we would go join. We would all go down together."

Sasha helped gather everyone they could find into one group on the saddle. Among the other climbers Sasha's Russian compadres rounded up was Michel, the French lawyer in charge of Degré7. In all, Dan said his memory will always tell him there were fourteen people, but also maintains the number is irrelevant. It's a similar stance that head Everest guide, Anatoli Boukreev, took in his personal account of the worst disaster in Everest's history.

It was 1996, when things went terribly wrong for a pair of Everest expeditions. Eight climbers were killed in a storm that created the utmost confusion and poor decisions. Journalist Jon Krakauer chronicled the event in a famous piece for *Outside Magazine*, and a year later published a book about his experience with the same title as the magazine article, *Into Thin Air*. Krakauer was critical of some of the procedures taken by the guides, criticizing them—and Boukreev in particular—for their roles in contributing to the miscommunication and delay. The guide addressed many of these criticisms in his own rebuttal, *The Climb*, published not long after Krakauer's bestseller arrived in bookstores. Boukreev's book includes a lengthy letter he wrote to *Outside* editor, Mark Bryant, voicing his concerns over how Krakauer had misrepresented him. He also admitted that he felt "fairly well-maligned by the few voices that had captured the imagination of the American press."

So, does it really matter if Dan can't remember the exact number of men who stood in the saddle of Elbrus on that May afternoon, particularly in the midst of the oncoming storm's blinding conditions? "This has always been my knock on Krakauer, because he is very critical of people who don't remember those facts in *Into Thin Air*," Dan said. "But at the time, you're not taking head counts. That's the last fucking thing you're doing. It wasn't relevant to survival how many of us were there. What was relevant to survival was, We're here. What are we going to do to get out of here? Particularly when you're with strangers, it wasn't my job to count heads."

Dan, Alfred, and Michel were the lone members from the Degré7 expedition, and the Russians who they'd suddenly teamed up with were less than friendly, seemingly unwilling to have more members join the group. But they at least had an inkling of what was going on, and so all gathered and began the descent, Dan and Alfred both without the additional clothes, food, and water in their rucksacks—not too far away, yet too much of a distance to risk losing their new Soviet alliance. "It wasn't a conscious thing, to find the pack," Dan said. "We were going down. At the time, my mindset was more in line with, Let's get the hell out of here. Plus, with the wind and the clouds, you couldn't see a foot beyond your feet."

As they fought to push against a wall of bitterly cold wind, the group came upon a pile of rocks with a metal pyramid, which was clearly a marker leading to a path normally marked by red flags. But the storm had either buried or blown the flags over, and the path wasn't as clear as the men had hoped. "We find this pyramid and the Russians are talking to somebody on the radio, arguing, trying to explain where we are in Russian," Dan said. "Every time that happened, we would go in an opposite direction. So, clearly, whoever was on the other end of the radio knew we were up there, knew we were lost, and was trying to get us to go somewhere else." Dan figured the group had lost the track due to walking into the sixty-mile-an-hour headwind. They slowly turned their backs to the wind more than once, which forced them to reconfigure themselves. After a few different turns, it became clear they were lost.

They arrived at the middle of a glacier, hoping the glacial ice, blue and as hard as granite, would provide the safest passage. But Dan also knew the problem with a glacier was crevasses—major cracks in the ice—so he was checking every step with his ski pole to see how solid the snow was in front of him. He hung close to Sasha at the front of the line, figuring he'd established a good rapport with the Soviet, and that he'd be able to get information, if there was any, about what the team on the radio was doing and why.

At one point, Dan felt his pole hit a soft spot of snow, forcing him to jump over the questionable area. He was safe, but a heavier climber behind him fell through. Sasha didn't hesitate—he grabbed a rope, threw one end over the crevasse, and tied the other around his waist. Dan lowered him into the hole, where Sasha retied the rope to the fallen hiker. With the two now able to begin climbing out, the others pulled Sasha through the mouth of the hole, then managed to pull the first man out, miraculously unhurt. The incident was proof to the group that they couldn't travel along the glacier at night without risking another crevasse mishap. The sky was already beginning to darken and the late hour would certainly make another rescue impossible.

So, the Russians stopped. There was no announcement, no discussion about what to do, considering the situation. There was just a seemingly immediate need to stop. They spread out along the hill and started to dig snow caves. Evidently, they were all going to spend the night there. Then everybody started digging. "I think we summited at five, and it was getting dark now," Dan said. "Everybody turned and faced the hill and just burrowed in."

Dan was at the end of the line, with a group next to him who made it clear he was not welcome in their cave, and that it wasn't supposed to connect with his cave. The Russians hit him on the back, just in case he didn't understand their barking, and ordered him to dig. That left Dan with his snow pick and his ski boots to dig a hole. Alfred and Michel had nothing. Alfred was tired. He was in the snow, laying down. "He's a rich man, he doesn't dig ditches," Michel said before abandoning the two of them, heading down the line. It never occurred to Dan to see what the other caves looked like, so he just continued to dig his own snow cave, large enough for three people, assuming that Alfred and Michel would join him.

He used his pick, then kicked at, then scooped the loosened snow. Pick, kick, scoop. After a bit, Alfred tried to help, but Dan said it was agonizing to watch his lame attempt. Dan started to work on a rotation of digging every twenty to thirty minutes, but nobody else offered to help. Frustrated and frozen, he abandoned the ice axe and started to kick at the snow with his ski boots. The process turned out to be faster, allowing him to use both feet, kicking deep and wide. Slowly, the cave began to take form. The hardest part was removing the snow from of the hole without a shovel. He'd extend his arms down deep into the pit and spring backward, pulling the snow out like a human plow. Despite it all, though, he was still lucid. Panicked, but somewhat confident.

In the end, the cave wasn't bad. In fact, thirty years later, Dan even seems to reflect on it with pride. "It was a pretty nice cave," he said. It was big enough that he, Alfred, and Michel could sit in it and hopefully survive the night. But when he looked up from his task, neither of the other two were anywhere to be found. They were gone. Either they'd abandoned Dan, or something had happened to them. Either way, it could not be Dan's concern.

"Was my reaction that I should go out in the storm and look for them?" Dan asked. "No, it didn't even occur to me. I had the cave, and I also still thought I might not make it. When you see those Everest pictures, of people coming down the ridge, dead bodies hanging over it, everybody in survival mode, that state of mind—you might think you should stop and help some guy, but . . . nobody else was thinking about me. Clearly. So, I was just in survival mode." Dan made a decision: Survival was all about himself from that point on. If the other two members of his expedition had not taken notice of his efforts to build them shelter, it was going to be for himself and himself only. Their only presence that evening had been standing in front of the snow cave entrance anyway, obstructing Dan's ability to remove snow.

Hours passed, and while he was sweating on the inside, a ferocious wind chilled him from the outside. Dan lay in a heap on the floor of his snow cave, realizing now that, outside, the entire group had disappeared, presumably having turned in for the night. He was alone with his thoughts. There was no time to wrestle with what might be. He had to prepare himself for the conditions and hope he was still alive when light broke in the morning. The first thing he did for comfort was adjust his mountaineering boots. They were set up for Alpine skiing, and he removed all the extra pads from the outer shell. This gave his feet more room to keep warm. He laced and buckled his boots loosely, and pulled his ski pants down over the boot tops to keep the snow out. His hands froze during the process, and he quickly put his gloves back on.

After regaining some energy, and feeling in his hands, Dan adjusted his hood and hat, which looked like a snowball due to the construction of the cave. He shook the snow from it, from inside and out, broke the ice away from his hair, and donned a headband he had in his pocket. His hands, too frozen to carry out these tasks, had to be replaced by his teeth. Dan's last bit of preparation was to take a piss, understanding that if he didn't go he would only get colder. So, he emerged from the cave and went out, within sight of his crampons and ice axe where he'd left them at the mouth of the cave. He suddenly felt the strong presence of his grandfather, and simultaneously saw the moon and thought maybe it could be a break in the storm, albeit a very brief one. It was during this pause in conditions that Dan noticed he was able to see down the line to some of the other caves, and they were glowing. It occurred to him that they had stoves and were melting water, and he made note in case he made it until morning.

Back in his own cave, he lay back to relax. He survived the moment and then he survived another moment, in order to survive another. This was how he would have to live in order to survive. By moments. By seconds. The question hit him during one of those intermittent flashes of time: Did I just dig my own grave?

There is a scene in *The Shack*, the 2017 film adaptation of William P. Young's 2007 novel of spiritual fulfillment, during which protagonist MacKenzie Phillips sees the light. He's strolling along a lush, green field manicured to a perfection any elite eighteenth-hole green would envy, with massive pine trees dwarfing him and his small group as they come to the top of a hill. The dusk sky then transforms into a starry canvas and the field turns dark, illuminated by hundreds of glowing apparitions lining the horizon from one end to the other. They are hundreds of personalities the group sees as "color and light." And from the shimmering lights emerges MacKenzie's late father, yearning to deliver forgiveness for incidents committed in the past.

There's a warmth of colors, a peaceful glow emerging from the individuals in the field. This passage brought Dan back to Elbrus when he later read the book—back to his encounter with what he now calls his guardian angels, spirit-type figures that beckoned him to follow. Dan resisted, while his physical self was shivering, coughing, and spitting up blood. It wasn't that he was afraid of the destination—he was content, and not necessarily afraid of dying. In fact, the memory lingers as among the happiest of his life, which is difficult to comprehend given the situation. Instead, Dan describes the encounter as something having been settled, an acceptance of what might be inevitable. He would be OK with dying. But it would be really hard on John, he thought.

That wasn't the only apparition that evening. Once the spirits understood that Dan wasn't willing to follow, they returned a short while later, delivering Twinkies and other convenience store foods, like what you'd find in your average 7-Eleven.

Were they enticing him, now, to surrender and follow? With Hostess products? Dan had never been this close to freezing to death, so the symptoms were unclear, but the visions—those were distinct. His understanding, over the years, of what the apparitions were has changed, but the clarity he experienced that night never has. There was a defined presence in the cave with him, accompanying him as he was hypothermic, groggy, and fading.

He was losing consciousness.

He was letting go.

The rabbit is left hanging as Joe Powder
prepares for landing.

Photograph by Wade McKoy

Dan skis through sluff in Yugoslavia.

Chapter Twenty-five

COILING ROPE

FROZEN PELLETS OF SNOW HIT Dan in the face like shrapnel, waking him from his out-of-body experience. A burly, bearded man had shown up to deliver a present in his time of need, a gift that might very well have been another heavenly event. The imposing figure slid right down the icy chimney that Dan had created to either protect or entomb himself.

"I was having a white-light experience and it got interrupted by a six-foot-four Russian," Dan said.

The man positioned himself in back of Dan, wrapping his arms around Dan's freezing body to share warmth. They huddled against the elements as best they could.

"Tonight, we sleep like brothers," Sasha said.

The Sportiva Hotel in Georgia was where Dan remembers first seeing the face of the man who ultimately saved him. There'd been a meeting with the guides and the Russians early on in the trip, before the expedition headed up Elbrus. Dan could remember seeing the man in the group, who he describes as "a big stud with long, blonde hair and blue eyes." His presence had been commanding; think Alexander Godunov, the Russian ballet dancer who defected to the United States while with the Bolshoi, and went on to an acting career in films such as *Die Hard, Witness,* and *The Money Pit.* The man was strong, not the sort you'd want to mess with in a time of strife, but maybe, just perhaps, the sort of security you could depend on in a time of great need. But Dan hadn't seen the man in the refuge, where the expedition had spent three nights. In fact, after that meeting in Georgia, Dan didn't remember seeing his sturdy face until he least expected it—on top of Elbrus.

The theory that the Soviet Union would have some sort of watchdog on an expedition comprised mostly of Americans really wasn't that far-fetched, particularly in light of the Cold War. Sasha clearly had the best interests of his fellow climbers in mind, and he certainly wasn't blowing them off. Upon meeting up in the saddle, Dan found Sasha open to communicating with him. "I had built a relationship with him," Dan said. "I had zeroed in on him because I could get information from him. But he wasn't, like, chatting me up." Nor did Sasha ever ask where anyone was from. "He was communicating with the other Russians up to the point where he showed he had some pull with them. But he wasn't calling the shots."

In hindsight, it was a mistake Dan made that probably led to Sasha finding him in the cave and cradling him. He'd left his crampons and ice axe at the entrance, where they could have been lost in the storm. Maybe that's how Sasha knew somebody was in the snow, perhaps alone. Dan didn't know if the man took a head count, or had seen Michel and Alfred and was trying to add the missing person to the roster. He wondered whether Sasha's intrusion that night was only partly about rescuing him, and partly doing his job as watchdog for the KGB. There was only comfort that night, questions to follow, and answers that would never materialize. They didn't talk, only huddled and waited for the light of a new day to serve as some semblance of a compass to get out of the mess they were in.

Meanwhile, far below, it had taken John and Tom hours to descend. After leaving the refuge to catch the last tram, fighting huge snowdrifts and snow-blindness, they arrived at the hotel with the others. John still had no idea what happened to Dan. But he knew the worst hadn't occurred. He just knew.

"It's your brother, you can tell. He's alive. I know he's alive. But it must suck for him." With the storm still raging above, there was little anybody at the lodge could do in terms of forming a search party. The local guides were making preparations for a search, but couldn't push forward until the storm subsided. Then, they would go back up to look for people—either dead or alive.

"We were being ushered out of there," Day said. "They wanted to send us back to Moscow. At the time they were making these orders to us, Dan was still lost on the mountain." John was adamant—he was not going to leave without finding Dan first, and Day decided to stay with him. "There was a lot of tension and unknowing that was going on," Day said. "It was hard for us to fathom their rescue approach. We weren't getting a lot of information on how the rescue party was going to work, and the storm was still happening, so we couldn't expect much to happen until it cleared. It was mayhem." So, they stayed and hoped, and prayed.

When morning came, Dan remembered the glow from the other caves the night before. He figured the other climbers had made fires and melted snow to make enough water to share. He grabbed his water bottle, went down the line, and asked a group of Russians to fill it for him. He dropped it into a cave and waited to re-hydrate himself after the long night in the cold. The bottle came back up. It was empty.

At this point, others began to emerge from their snow caves, including Michel. "I'm surprised to see you alive," he said to Dan. "You dug a terrible cave." They waited for the others to break camp. The weather was still fierce, with five feet of new snow to grind through and a constant wind creating drifts everywhere. They continued along the glacier, on which it was not possible to walk without crampons. Luckily, everybody had their except

Michel, who made his way on skis, an annoyance for the rest of the crew, as it slowed their progress. "Nobody was really ever thinking about everybody else's safety," Dan said. "I didn't know where I was. They supposedly knew where we were. There was some urgency to move on, but not a coordinated effort, either. We were supposedly together, but in truth we really were not."

They continued walking down the steep ice, until a guy from the rear of the line fell. He came sliding past the group on the blue ice, whipping past a crevasse in front of them. He landed on the other side, his feet dangling over the edge, but the snow let go and dropped him into the hole. Once again, Sasha put the rope around his waist and went in. The man's face was bleeding, broken in multiple places. It looked like hamburger, pocked with wounds and scratches. But he could still walk, which was of utmost importance.

When a third person fell into a crevasse, things turned dire. The group tried to get him out, using the same system as with the previous two emergencies, except this time the rope sawed its way into the snow. "Every time we went to pull him out, he would hit his head," Dan said. "We had to lay him back down and the only way we could think of to get him out was to lay a ski pole on the edge and run the rope over it. At that point, I was kind of like, 'You know, I'm kind of done here. I don't really give a shit about this.' I stepped back and went to the end of the line. Sasha was in the crevasse with the other climber. The other Russians forced Michel to take the pole and go out to the edge. They didn't really like him that much. When he crawled by me, he was scared. I wouldn't have done it."

Michel sat down, holding the pole underneath the rope, and they were able to pull the man out of the hole. He'd broken his leg. This was, obviously, a problem. "Now, there's a real issue on how to best keep this guy moving," Dan said. They took one of their sleeping pads, had him sit in it, and rigged the rope through the pad to create a sled. The problem was, the pad was wider than the path, pulling snow from the sides of the trough and burying him as they pulled. That meant stopping periodically to dig him out before moving on again. Dan was trying to get the others to use a ski pole to create more structure in the pad, but they didn't want to. It took hours to cover very little distance. "We wasted the better part of the day on this," Dan said. "Very frustrating and very slow."

Also frustrating was the fact that the group wasn't descending. It seemed, instead, the Russians were looking for a place out of the wind to put the stove up and melt some water. It was late in the afternoon when Dan finally figured this out and realized that it might mean another night on the mountain. That became an even more evident possibility when the Russians finally found a windswept rock in a site that looked good for camping. They lit the stove. But again, they weren't sharing any water. Dan, however, was ready to share, no matter how much the other party had proven to be a nuisance. "During all this time of dragging this fucker through the snow, I had a PowerBar with me, but they are basically inedible when they're cold. I kept it close to my body; meanwhile, Michel was flailing, dehydrated and suffering." Dan broke the bar in half once it became pliable and gave some to Michel, the same man who'd criticized his cave-making ability that morning. "He later accused me of stealing it from him," Dan said.

By then, it had become clear the Russians were planning on staying the night. That's when Dan decided he'd had enough. "The serenity is gone," he said. "I was not dying, I was alive, and we were somewhat further down. Just not far enough. And I wanted to get down." That's when he decided he was leaving the group. He was making a move for himself. Nobody else mattered. He was frustrated and anxious and couldn't face the prospect of spending another night in that frigid hell. The calm of the previous night had turned into irritability.

Sasha encouraged Dan to re-think his decision, to not head in a direction that might result in the rest of the party discovering him frozen to death the next day. But Dan had his route planned. He knew they were near the tongue of the glacier, so he would go down around the edge. He explained this to Sasha, who immediately rebuffed the plan, explaining that the cracks in the glacier are the biggest at the edge. Walking directly down the center of the glacier would be the smartest move, where cracks are the smallest.

Once again, Dan's mountaineering skills were up for debate and it was clear he would be much better off waiting for a guide like Sasha to bring him to safety. But another night? He couldn't handle that. The risk was worth it. Dan did his best to convince Sasha this was their best way out. "Had John been with me, it's very likely we would have made the wrong decisions. We would've made our own plan and would have already left."

But Sasha relented and decided to go with Dan, leaving the Russians, who were clearly in survival mode, to fend for themselves. They would take Alfred, Michel, and Hamburger Face, and try to navigate the glacier. Sasha didn't seem pleased, but probably would have felt an inevitable guilt should he just allow them to make their way on their own. So, he would go. On one condition. He told Dan to go get the rope. Simply grabbing a pivotal piece of equipment from the Russians, who weren't willing to even share water, wasn't an easy task. Maybe Sasha was afraid of the havoc it might cause. It was the only time he exhibited some semblance of fear during the entire ordeal. Dan didn't want to have the encounter either, but his desperation to get out of there weighed more heavily than any fear of confrontation. He agreed to get the rope.

The rope was a disheveled mess. Dan found it at the camp where the Russians were already preparing for the night. It was laying in the snow, unwrapped and frozen. It had never been coiled, and there were pockets of ice along its length. Dan picked it up and tried to untangle it before coiling it, just like his father had taught him at the South Boston Yacht Club, thousands of miles away. He could even hear his father's voice in his head as he worked with the rope. *Because, if you don't untangle it, you can't make a good loop.* "My dad was irritating about that," he said. The Russians noticed what Dan was doing, and a group of nine or ten formed a circle around him. It was clear he was planning to take the rope. One of them pulled out a knife, possibly hoping to get the American to back off. Something else happened, instead. "The moment I saw the knife, I slugged the guy," Dan said. "I just hit him. I wrestled with him for the knife and got it. I think they were shocked that I did that, and the other guys didn't pile on."

231

Dan waved the knife as he grabbed the rope. An idea occurred to him which might appease both parties. Coiling a climbing rope is different from a sailing rope. You don't coil from the beginning, but instead put the halves together. He'd already managed this stage before the encounter with the knife-wielding Russian, so he simply took the hunting blade and slid it through the center of the rope. He threw one half to the Russians, like meat to a pack of wolves, who immediately understood. "The minute they saw I had cut the rope, they chilled," Dan said. "They probably thought, 'This kid is crazy.' But after that, the mood changed. It was almost like, 'Oh. Why didn't you just say you wanted some rope?'" This left Dan feeling pretty good, so he decided to wave the knife and see what else he could procure. "Where's the water?" he demanded. But the Russians, now probably over the excitement, shrugged their shoulders and went back to preparing to turn in. There would be no water. But it had been worth a shot.

Dan figured Sasha would be impressed. He was running on adrenaline from the encounter and came back to the group with the trophy rope. Surely, they would all want to hear how such an event had gone down and how the youngster from the States had secured what they needed. Instead, Sasha just sort of nodded. "Oh, you got the rope. Good job."

Their lack of astonishment wasn't particularly deflating. The five of them were now on their way. Off the mountain. Away from Elbrus, for good.

Chapter Twenty-six

A LOT OF CONFUSION

DAN'S GROUP TIED THEMSELVES TOGETHER with the half-rope for the trek down the middle of the glacier. The snow was waist deep, and Sasha and Dan would leapfrog down through it, creating a route for the other three climbers. None of the others offered to help. For all intents and purposes, this was the Dan and Sasha show now.

"It was slow going," said Dan. "Sasha and I were breaking trail, Alfred had his head down and was slogging along, Michel was spent, and the guy with no face was just following the group. I'm not sure where my energy was coming from. I was just focused on getting the hell off that mountain."

Eventually, the cracks in the ice began disappearing, signaling they were at the tongue of the glacier. They had no idea exactly where they were in the dark of night, but their confidence was high enough that they removed the rope and continued to break trail. The storm had mercifully come to an end, and the night was clear, allowing them some guiding light to see their surroundings and get an understanding of what was in front of them as they made their way down. Most importantly, they saw the glow of a campfire several ridges from where they were standing, still a bit of a traverse away.

May Day was being celebrated in Russia, a public holiday in honor of the International Solidarity of Workers. A group of Russians were camping out in observance, with no idea people were dying above them on the higher elevations of Mount Elbrus. In their world, it was merely a bad weekend, weather-wise, to camp in an old, small tent, one that Dan compared to something out of a Sears and Roebuck catalog from the '70s. "It was one shitty-looking tent," he said. Sasha explained their situation to the campers, who made tea for them. They provided Hamburger Face with some medicinal tablets. "They recommended the guy take one and he instead chugged the entire bottle," Dan said. They cleared out of their tent and let the newcomers regroup in it. It was a hospitality and relief that the exhausted climbers found hard to imagine after what they'd endured over the past thirty-six hours. But it was also clear: they couldn't stay. There was no room in the tent for five more people, and in any case, they weren't far from the bottom of Elbrus at that point. That was some good news at least. Not far from what, though? "They were welcoming, up to a point, but very clear that we could not stay the night," Dan said.

So, back into the wild they went. By this point, after conferring with the campers about their location, Sasha seemed confident that he knew where they were. So, too, did Hamburger Face, who simply wandered away from the group. Dan told Sasha they should go get him, but the guide simply brushed off his concern. "No. He is a strong man. Leave him alone," he said. Dan would never see Hamburger Face again. Now there were only four of them remaining: Sasha, and Dan, Alfred, and Michel—the three remaining members of the Degré7 expedition.

After making it to the snow line, they found themselves in ankle-deep mud. The four had been cascading down on snow, but now found themselves in a field with a farm and, mercifully, a stream. They were thirsty and raced to the river, each lapping as much water as he could. It was only then that it became clear to Dan that Sasha hadn't had any water either. Even though the other Russians were making water, they hadn't given him any. "In hindsight, the fact that he didn't have water and didn't get the rope, those things are related," Dan said. "He didn't sleep in the same cave as the other Russians. If only one of those things had happened it'd be weird, but they all happened."

Dan wasn't sure what these observations added up to, and ultimately wouldn't have a chance to ask Sasha if his presence had another purpose. They came upon a shed where Sasha said he was going to spend the night. He told the rest of the group to go find the road. "In the morning, I go back up for the others," he said. Sasha assured them they were only about five kilometers from the hotel. He declined Dan's offer to go back up with him, but did accept a pair of snow goggles and Dan's water bottle. Dan hugged the man who he would soon come to understand had saved his life. His memory of Sasha would play a pivotal role in his life from that point forward, but Dan would never have an opportunity to either thank or repay the Russian for his wise decisions and leadership on Elbrus.

Now, it was only the three from Degré7 remaining. Michel, who apparently thought the situation was ripe for celebration, suggested the three of them discuss dinner plans. That was the breaking point for Dan. He had to get away. He started running down the road as fast he could in his Alpine boots. Alfred figured it must have been an adrenaline boost. It was that—coupled with mental exhaustion.

"I just left those guys," Dan said. "I just peeled off. I didn't care about Michel or Alfred. Sasha and I had said goodbye and I could leave. I said, 'I've got 5K to go, and I'm doing it.' I had done everything for them. I dug the snow cave; I broke a trail. And they still were not thanking or helping. I ditched them and got myself to the hotel." He arrived alone at the lodge in Terskol around midnight and climbed to his room on the fifth floor. He passed out in the hall, where one of the Chamonix guides eventually found him. The guide immediately went to find John and Tom. Of course, he knew where they were—with everybody else, in the bar. "I guess what you do when you don't have anything else to do, you go to the bar," Dan said.

It didn't look good, John admits as much. But there was nothing else they could have done. They'd been on lock-down at the hotel, due to the storm, and were hoping the weather would permit them to form a proper search the next day. "We were eating and drinking and waiting to go up. It wasn't like we went to a party. We were with a bunch of athletes, a bunch of people that live in that environment. Storms happen. People get stuck on mountains all the time. People die up there all the time. We'll deal with it tomorrow. Here, we're going to make dinner. I'm sure it looked worse than it was, but if you're stuck in a snow cave and somebody else is warm and cozy, it's not going to go over well. But I don't think I was inappropriate or not sympathetic to what he was going through. Barring me going off on my own, trying to climb that mountain by myself, there was really nothing I could have done, and that would have been silly for me—for my own life. That would have left one more person who they would have to go rescue."

Before John could get to see his brother, he ran into Michel, who told him the whole story—embellished with a litany of fictional twists. Michel told him he'd been responsible for saving Dan's life, that he was the one who ultimately had been able to guide the remaining members of the team back to the hotel. So, when an emotional John found Dan and embraced him, he started asking questions based on what Michel had told him. "He was saying things to me that weren't true," Dan said. "It was very confusing. And I was out of it, so I couldn't have a real conversation with him. His story was not matching my experience." People can experience shock very differently. Some are quiet and don't say anything. Others rant and rave and nothing really makes any sense to them or others to whom they're trying to explain things. Dan was a combination of the two, quiet and in awe of the stories he was hearing, knowing, for one, that they were not true.

The Russians on hand were handing Dan a shot of vodka to calm his nerves. He'd tried not to drink all winter, but surely this situation called for it. One flick of the wrist, and the inner radiance returned, eliciting a rush of warmth through the entirety of his yet-frozen body. He immediately wanted more. His craving triggered amidst the chatter that didn't make any sense. "It was all confusion," Dan said. "Michel was pretty adamant about having saved our lives. So, from John's point of view there was a lot of that. He wasn't being difficult; he was just trying to get information."

They left the next day on a bus without any word of what had happened to Claudio Abate, the Italian journalist who'd made the late decision to pursue the climbers to the summit. They had no way of knowing if he was dead or alive. Abate was close to Degré7, a friend of the brand, who was writing about the expedition. Eventually, they would learn that the recovery efforts found Abate alive on the mountain. "Claudio had dug a snow cave, but he was alone," Dan said. "They found him because he had one hand out, above the snow at the entrance." On one of his searches, Charamel noticed a set of bindings on a pair of skis that he understood were Abate's. The journalist was, indeed, alive, but in bad shape. He was not brought down by helicopter, but stacked on a sled with other bodies. He wouldn't survive the trip and died before the recovery effort arrived back at the base. Among the dead, on what turned out to be one of the most gruesome days in Elbrus's mountaineering history, were some members of a group of Japanese climbers. They'd died somewhere within four or five hundred feet of the refuge. The Japanese wore down jackets; the Russians did not. The story goes, the two parties fought over the jackets. And every one who lost got kicked out of the cave. In the end, only one remained—a man named Sojiro Makino. There were eight frozen bodies with him when Charamel encountered Makino. They found Sojiro wearing all the coats. Dan said he met the guy in the Moscow airport and asked him how he survived. "He told me he wanted to be the last one to die."

Lower on the mountain, Joe Powder lands in a snowfield and heads towards the forest.

Dan drops in on a chute in Yugoslavia. This image became a poster in *Powder Magazine*.

Photograph by Wade McKoy

Chapter Twenty-seven

GETTING OUT OF THE U.S.S.R.

GETTING OUT OF RUSSIA IN 1990 wasn't as easy as heading to the airport and catching the next flight. What's more, it was even more difficult if you wanted to leave the country outside the day of your visa. "Because of the inflexibility of the Russian authority, our visas could not be changed. Our scheduled departure was May sixth, and that was that," Dot Helling told us.

Dan and Alfred both needed medical attention. Helling's husband, John Peterson, was the group's doctor. He thought it best not to seek out physicians in Russia, where poor conditions and political barriers could prove costly, if not risky. The best option, he said, was to get both of them to France, where they could rely on more modern medicine. The rest of the group would have to stay in Moscow while he worked to secure special medical visas for Dan and Alfred. "His joining of the expedition last-minute was a godsend," Dan said. "He really knew how to ease our feet and hands back from the frostbite, and he advocated for us with the Russian authorities. I really don't know what we would have done without him."

John. The film crew. The expedition—Dan left everything behind, save Alfred . . . and Michel. "We still had to finish the trip, go to Moscow and finish it the way our permit and visa said we would do," John said. "There were a lot of logistics to get those two out early. It's pretty remote. Travel probably still isn't much better out there today." It turned out, Michel was conveniently able to get permission from the authorities to leave Russia early. His brother was a doctor in France, he said, and he would be sure to get Dan and Alfred the medical attention they needed. "He spilled this story that his brother was a high-altitude specialist and was going to get a doctor to look at us once we got out," Dan said. Before the three of them left, Michel gifted both Dan and Alfred a can of caviar, which they both found rather odd, but at this stage in the aftermath of what they'd experienced, everything seemed a bit off. But that was only the beginning of the chicanery.

On the plane, Michel started hitting on the stewardess, asking her which hospital was best to bring his fellow passengers to upon landing in Paris. It was only then that Dan started to recognize how the facts didn't add up. Why would Michel need to know the location of the best hospital if his brother was, in fact, a high-altitude specialist? "This is a fuck job," Dan said to himself. The proof came when they landed in Paris and Michel put Alfred and Dan in a taxi to the nearest hospital. Dan had to be restrained from Michel, infuriated, in disbelief that the lawyer was not coming with them. He'd brought them to Paris for the expressed mission of getting them both the medical help they needed, and here he was, abandoning them upon his first steps back on his native soil. What about his brother, the guy he'd told Russian authorities would be able to give them proper treatment? It was clear now. There was no brother. Michel had been lying, in order to get out. That night, though, would get even worse.

"The mistake was not going to a U.S. military base," Dan said. "We should have gone to Germany. We never thought of it, because who would have thought that the French hospital was going to be a disaster?" A disaster it was, as Dan and Alfred would find out, because French doctors didn't work on weekends. It was a fact that nobody knew—except, well, Michel. Dan and Alfred only discovered this after arriving at the Raymond Poincaré University Hospital. It was Friday night, which meant a doctor probably wouldn't be seeing them until Monday morning. That reality was hard to accept. Dan was trying to explain to the nurse what they were doing there. *Russia? What? Mountain? What?* "To some extent, they thought I was nuts," Dan said.

Once again, Dan had to be subdued, fueled by anger over the situation he found himself in. "He was like a tiger in a cage," Alfred said. "He even wanted to escape from the room, jumping down to the garden." Alfred, meanwhile, was more subdued, just going along with whatever happened. He desperately needed medical attention for his bandage-wrapped hands and feet. He couldn't walk with the frostbite he'd suffered, and yet—no doctors. Nobody would come to check their pulse, take blood, nothing. Well, they did have a visitor Saturday morning—the TV repairman. Later in the day, they had another. It was Michel.

The lawyer had his teenage son with him and was going on about introducing the young man to the two climbers whose lives he'd saved in Russia. By now, Dan was boiling. He was at a breaking point, furious that he couldn't get any medical help, and as if doubling down on the situation, here comes this French caricature bragging about events on Elbrus which never happened. It was because of Michel that he and Alfred were here in the first place, in this hospital, without any money, denied desperately needed medical care because it was a weekend. And Michel was spinning this story of how he'd saved them, despite a reality that was anything but. But Michel had arrived with a request. You see, he said, when departing Russia, there is only so much caviar a person can take out of the country. So, he was here to ask Dan and Alfred if they wouldn't mind giving him back their cans. This was the tipping point. After making sure the lawyer's son was out of the room, Dan took a glass Coke bottle and broke it against a table. He threatened Michel, demanding he turn over his wallet. He emptied the Francs from it and kicked him out of the hospital room.

Now, at least, he had some money. And Alfred's girlfriend, Gabi, was on her way from Belgium to rescue them. Upon her arrival, Dan and Alfred signed a document releasing the hospital of responsibility. Dan caught a ride from Gabi to the hotel in Paris where he was supposed to rendezvous with John, who would not be departing from Russia for several days. Dan still hadn't had medical attention. He was alone. In France. Sitting with nothing but his thoughts about what had happened and how to escape the nightmare. "That time in the hotel room was hard," he said. "I was alone for days. I wasn't going to go drink or anything. Just sitting there. Waiting."

He thought about trying to visit his parents in Lourdes. But it was more than five hundred miles from Paris, and he didn't know how to get there. He called a friend, John Schiffman, who told Dan he was rambling nonsensically. He called Laurie Magoon, a quasi-girlfriend at the time. She'd been waiting for his call. She, too, had a dream that John had died, just like his father had. So that was that.

Three days later, John and Tom arrived at the hotel to reunite with Dan. He told them the story of how Michel screwed them over regarding the doctors and the hospital, clearly still agitated over the circumstances. "The fucking asshole lawyer," John said. "That guy was a dirtbag."

The three of them thought talking through everything that had happened would be therapeutic, so they set the camera up in the hotel room's bathroom ("Nice backdrop, huh?" John said) and conducted interviews with John and Dan. Tom and John were still in production mode, and still hadn't heard the entire story from Dan's point of view.

"It is a learning experience about how fragile life can be," Day said. "How you can foresee things and react sooner. Lessons are how we all get by."

In the clip, which would make it into the Egan Entertainment production *The Extreme Dream*, Dan's face looks tired. His lips are swollen and he speaks lethargically as he tells the story. His eyelids appear lazy, and he's reclining against the bathroom wall, a pair of Oakleys dangling from his neck, atop his white T-shirt. It clearly frightens him to retell the story. His eyes dart around the room, punctuating his feelings and memories of what turned out to be a Russian roulette of survival. It is moving to see and hear on camera. Off-camera, though, Dan felt like John and Tom had a slightly different point of view about his life-altering experience.

"They were like, 'Hey, OK, you're all right. You didn't die, all those other fuckers did, you know."

What's your problem? You lived. What's the issue?

Dan knew he was lucky. But he did not feel so brazen about his survival.

Dan, Tom, and John had reunited, but soon it was time to split up. Tom was staying in Europe, awaiting his wife Lizzie's arrival. John had other endeavors to pursue, namely Lotta, the Swedish moguls champ the crew had met in Val d'Isère earlier that winter. "John took our last two hundred bucks and went to Sweden," Dan said. "He asked me to carry all his shit back to Boston." John's memory of the incident is a little foggier, saying he thought they all flew back to the United States at that point. But when he's reminded about visiting Lotta, his itinerary comes back more clearly. "She came to the U.S. for the second half of the winter, and broke her leg," he said. "I might have gone to visit her to see how she was healing up. I got there and she dumped me."

Dan borrowed money from Tom to get a taxi to Charles de Gaulle airport. He was finally escaping the trauma that would continue to shape him. It would take him some time to put together the incidents and focus on what had truly occurred, but he knew he'd had an encounter with something life-changing. The clarity he sought from the experience wasn't quite with him yet. There would be confusion and anger, and a variety of hurdles Dan would find becoming potholes on his road to recovery.

"My spiritual journey started there," he said, suggesting that he's among the many extreme athletes who drank the wrong Kool-Aid in their attempt to define just what it was they were doing. Like, what the hell was he doing trying to summit one of the world's tallest peaks in the first place? He wasn't a mountaineer. He was a skier. A skier looking for some attention which might lead to some financial windfall. It was a trap.

"What powers American media is the power of sponsorship," Dan said. "The power of what makes America great is our ability to market things.

Our ability to market and go to market and to sell ideas. The revolution of the sport we ushered in was the modern day of extreme sport contracts and sponsorships. That changed things all the way to the X Games. We *did* take it from the mountains to Madison Avenue. Did people go on to ski great descents and other wild stuff? Yeah. Were they in danger of avalanches and cliff falls? Yeah. Just look at the number of people who've died trying to do what we did. But I would argue that the people who died misunderstood what we were doing. I put myself in that category. 'If I take this risk, there is some kind of economic reward. I'm going to be famous if I summit.' I fell into that, for sure. I was not above believing any of that.

"Quite honestly, that's crazy. I don't think I had skinned, or backcountry skied, more than a handful of times. I was not a mountaineer and it almost killed me. The mistakes I made were my own. There was a lot of ignorance, youthfulness, and thinking that, somehow, this trip was part of our contribution to the sport and what we would end up being known for. All of that is true."

It wasn't jumping off a cliff that almost killed Dan Egan. It was following the lure of sponsorship into unfamiliar territory that, ultimately, nearly finished him.

Chapter Twenty-eight

ROADBLOCK AND THE KGB

IT WAS AFTER MIDNIGHT AND Dan was driving his van along the Jamaicaway, a roadway in the Jamaica Plain neighborhood of Boston, when he came upon a roadblock. His partying ways had returned since his horrific ordeal in Russia. He'd arrived home in confusion and despair.

A bit wired from a long night, he was experiencing the common aftereffects: edginess, cravings, intense paranoia. Police lights were flashing ahead, and Dan's hands started shaking. His heart started pounding. He checked in the rear-view mirror and noticed his pupils were still dilated. Panic filtered through his body, the fear of being caught. The police were stopping every car, soon to include his blue 4x4 Toyota, a vehicle he'd customized with wooden panels to cover the back windows and carpeting on the floor, darkening the rear space where he had a mattress. He was, essentially, living in the van, with only the two passenger seats up front intact. This left things a little cramped, particularly when he had the responsibility of driving his two nephews to the Babson soccer camp where he'd worked one summer. A grown man in his twenties driving five- and seven-year-olds in a van with only two front seats and a mattress in the back definitely would not fly a generation later.

But now, Dan's operating under the influence was in the crosshairs. He waited and stared at the cops up ahead as they diligently checked each vehicle, his turn creeping closer with every tap of the brake. "I'm fucked," he thought. He could try to explain to the cops why he looked and acted how he knew they would see him, but it's not like anyone really understood the dramatic impact his experience on Mount Elbrus had had on him. Instead of a homecoming in Milton, Dan ricocheted for months, after realizing nobody could ever understand what he'd overcome in Russia. "It's not that they didn't believe me, but they just didn't know," he said. To make matters more confusing for his friends and family, John's version of events essentially boiled down to, *Well, Dan got lost and then he was found. What next?* Dan had no idea what was going to happen next.

He'd finally left the hotel in France, flew back to Boston, and made it home to Milton. His younger brother, Mike, twenty years old at the time, and the only family member home, was entertaining some friends. Dan walked in the door disheveled, black and blue, and frostbitten, insisting Mike's party had to end. Dan was "weirded out," as Mike put it, by a welcoming committee that was anything but the serenity he needed. He needed comfort and peace, and had instead found a party. His parents were still overseas in Lourdes. Mike told Dan that their oldest brother, Bob, was skiing at Tuckerman Ravine with some friends.

Dan ended up spending the night in the back of his Toyota, then headed north the next morning. It was a cloudy day with mixed precipitation when he arrived in Pinkham Notch. He left his gear in the van, humped his ass up into Tuckerman's bowl and almost immediately found Bob, along with his friend Dave Casey. It was bizarrely easy. Dan had skied the Ravine with the two of them when he was twelve years old. Casey had given Dan his first beer when he'd visited him and Bob at Norwich University. He'd spent countless hours with Bob at Ski Market and was as close to him as he was with any of his siblings. Bob was surprised—to see him, of course, since Dan was supposed to be halfway around the world at the time, but also at the recuperative skill he showed, hucking up the Tuckerman trail in clearly less-than-ideal physical condition. Consider that it had taken Bob and his friends two and a half hours to hike into the bowl, whereas it took Dan forty-five minutes. "Right out the hospital," Bob said.

Dan hoped Bob could understand the hardships he was going through, although he admittedly was still trying to figure them out himself. But the Mount Washington weather was unnerving him, prompting more panic, reminding Dan of the Mount Elbrus snowstorm—the one he almost didn't escape. As he tried to tell his story, he was rambling because he had yet to come to grips with it himself. Why was he there in the first place? Why was he *here*? "The clouds parted, and he said it was bringing back bad memories," Bob said. "Then, he just took off." Dan didn't want to be in a storm anymore. He darted back down the trail to the safety of his van. Later in the week, when Robert and Marlen returned from France and heard Dan's story, Robert's dream came back to him, the one he'd dreamt in Lourdes, in which John had died, an eerie coincidence, even more so considering how similar it was to the dream Dan's girlfriend Laurie had told Dan about. But there were even more oddities to come.

A few weeks later, Dan's father came home with a story about a Russian woman who'd come to his office as a patient at Milton Hospital. The neurologist recounted to her what Dan had experienced in her country, expressing relief in the outcome for both of his sons. But instead of politely nodding, the woman asked Robert to describe what Dan had told him about the man who'd essentially rescued him. She pointedly asked about Sasha's appearance, commenting that his blonde hair and blue eyes didn't exactly match the ethnic characteristics of a native Russian. Indeed, she said, Sasha was probably from Moscow, in itself a good indication as to why he didn't get along with more rural fellow countrymen. There was also a good chance that Sasha was KGB, she said. Dan was eager for more information, additional confirmation about his run-in with a possible KGB agent. He asked his father to contact the woman, but the phone number she'd left wasn't a good number, and the address didn't exist. Both fake. "It did make it seem like they were checking up on me, and that he could have been KGB," Dan said. No doubt, the woman knew Robert was Dan's father. No doubt she'd been sent to be sure Dan was all right.

"Sasha's being KGB might explain why he was denied water or food, or didn't sleep with the other Russians, and wouldn't get the rope himself," Dan said. "There's some thread connecting all those incidents. But the twist to the story is that no Americans died. He was in the background and then he was on the summit, following us the whole time. I think that's what his job was. He was assigned to the Americans. It's not out of the realm of possibility. Nothing to do with espionage, obviously, but any number of other reasons."

Dan met a photographer some four years later who'd just returned from Russia. He'd met a man who said he knew only one American, and that he was the strongest man he'd ever met. The man said that American's name was Dan Egan. It was the only information Dan would ever hear about the man he'd called Sasha. He did learn, through Degré7 some years later, that Sasha had died, but then he heard elsewhere that wasn't the case at all. It was just more bafflement on top of intrigue.

Getting the story published wasn't easy either. Degré7's communication with Dan had gone silent, both in Europe and the U.S. "They never wanted to talk about the trip," Dan said. The ski publications used portions of it in compilation stories of danger and extreme skiing, but never the entire story or Dan's version.

Dan eventually found a buyer, though, even if the publication wasn't ideal. The story went to the *National Enquirer*, the American tabloid newspaper known for bold headlines mostly focused on sensationalism and celebrity gossip. The publication originally offered Dan $2,500 for his account of the misadventure, then backed away. "How many dead bodies did you see?" an editor asked Dan. Apparently, the fact that no American had died meant the story wasn't juicy enough. The dead men were all foreigners, and Dan, the tabloid's one American connection to the disaster, hadn't seen one of them. A dramatic and dangerous tale, to be sure, but one morbid enough to spark outrage among *Enquirer*'s readers? Not likely. "We can't write the story," the editor told Dan. Later that year, Dan would include a segment about the Russia experience in what would be Egan Entertainment's first true stab at a ski movie, *The Extreme Dream*, featuring the film shot in front of John and Tom Day, just days after Dan's ordeal, in the Paris hotel's bathroom.

John and Janet Markman, Degré7's American distributors, came to one of *The Extreme Dream*'s showings the following fall, at an REI retail store in Los Angeles, and sat in the front row. They apparently didn't like what they heard, or how they were ultimately portrayed as bearing some blame, and walked out in the middle of the film. The next day, they officially canceled the Egans' contract with Degré7.

To this day, Dan and John have yet to sit down and talk with one another about the Elbrus trip. They'd each had a different experience in Russia, to the point where it's difficult for one to even comprehend the other's logic about what exactly happened. "But, looking at it from his point of view, he did everything he could for me," Dan said. "He got me what he thought at the time was the best medical care. He had organized a rescue. He did everything but climb up Elbrus to find me." But Dan has always felt like John could never understand why this has continued to be such a big deal in his life. "And that's just kind of how John is. He's like, 'What's the big deal?' I'm not angry at him about those things, but I was alone with my experience, and over the years, it made me think I was crazy. Did these things really happen to me? I had nobody to confirm or deny what was truly true. It sounds crazy, right? The KGB. Stealing a climbing rope from some rogue Russians. A caricature French lawyer trying to smuggle caviar out of Russia. Apparitions. Who believes this shit?" Dan asked. "But it happened to me. All of it."

Over the years, Dan would find some comfort in reading books about near-death experiences, feeling like he was part of that special group. One book in particular, *The Boldest Dream* by Rick Ridgeway, would give some confirmation that what he'd experienced on Elbrus was real: Two brothers were members of the Mount Everest bicentennial expedition, but only one summited—a similar story to the brothers Egan, except that brother was lost while the other remained in base camp. "Reading Ridgeway's book made me really understand that I wasn't crazy," Dan said, "because the way he described freezing to death was the same as I'd experienced. It's like drowning, and then you go to sleep. I had not had that explained to me, but in Ridgeway's book, I was like, 'This is exactly what had almost happened to me.' His story really settled it for me."

But there was little settling in the immediate aftermath. Just over a month after his return, Dan took to partying, living out of his Toyota van, and expecting he would continue this way for the foreseeable future. And he wasn't in good shape when he came upon the roadblock on the Jamaicaway. Dan had had his share of brushes with the law, all related to late-night antics, but this seemed like it could be a lot worse. He was still traumatized by the trip. His girlfriend wanted nothing to do with him. Partying was becoming a way to get by, not a social treat and not the escape he needed. But nothing was going to help him escape this roadblock. It was finally his time of reckoning.

Dan rolled down the window and the officer poked his head inside. He saw the mattress in the back, a few pairs of skis, boots, a bag of soccer balls, and assorted clothing. It probably looked like the typical belongings any other college kid at the time in Boston would have tossed in his car for the summer's drive home.

"Moving day?" he asked Dan.

"Y-y-y-y-eah," Dan said. "Moving day."

The officer looked at Dan, who was clearly in an agitated state, the smell of alcohol probably emanating straight into the officer's face. He could have asked Dan to get out of the van. But he didn't. "You should *keep moving* then," he said. Call it rock bottom, a wake-up call, or whatever, but the roadblock served to point out a few truths to Dan. He was clearly abusing to the point where it probably should have landed him in jail. He had a movie to produce that summer for the Egan Entertainment brand and couldn't take a chance on not delivering. A few times over the past several years, when Dan was at least a little curious about living sober, a friend's mother had brought him to "some of those meetings." He called her then, for advice. She recommended going back to those meetings, which he began attending that summer.

"He was a frightened boy," Marlen said. "Afraid of everything. When he was on the mountain, he said, that night he saw the light. I think that just brought him closer to God." That late-night stop on the Jamaicaway wouldn't be the only roadblock Dan would have to face. But the message had, at least, been clearly delivered and just as clearly heard: *Keep moving.*

Joe Powder, a major powder hound, heads into the trees.

Photograph by Wiliam R. Sallaz

Ned Egan joined the crew for cat skiing in Fernie, British Columbia. He drops into the deep snow for the film *Extreme Dream*.

Chapter Twenty-nine

SAINT MARLEN

IN ADDITION TO CORNERING THE local market on skiing equipment in the early '90s, Massachusetts-based Ski Market also launched itself into the upper echelons of bicycle retailers in the Boston area. Much of that was due to a side business Dan's older brother Bob established from the back door of his Braintree location. Alternative Recreation Unlimited was a way for Bob and co-founders Dave Casey and Mike Sheehan to stay active in the outdoor sports retailing world on the weekends.

"It turned out to be a great way to be the number-one bike store for Ski Market, too," Bob said, "because my customers were buying bikes, joining the club, learning how to ride them, and then upgrading."

Dan enjoyed the weekend cycling trips with his older brother. "We would meet at various locations around New England and take long bike tours around Acadia National Park up in Maine, or ride a hundred miles down to Cape Cod," he said. "I met a lot of people on those rides. There was a group of regulars; some were employees at Ski Market and some were just looking for fun people to have adventures with. Long rides on my bike had inspired me as a teenager. I still love cycling, even now." ARU also focused on a number of other adventure outings, including camping, whitewater rafting trips in the summer, and cross-country skiing tours in the winter. Eventually, though, Ski Market would consider ARU a conflict of its business interest and cease operations, leaving its stock folder gathering dust on the third floor of the Egan house in Milton.

But ARU provided the foundation for Dan's company, Skiclinics.com, and the clinics he runs around the world today. In the mid-'80s, Dan was drawn to the name of the company and would occasionally take a glance at the ARU documents. "It had stock issues, and it was like a real company," he said. Dan figured the name alone deserved more value than sitting under a bed. "It was a great name, and John and I were definitely doing alternative recreation." So Dan offered to take the company off of his brother's hands. The transfer of ownership cost him one dollar.

Rather than stick to the formula ARU had focused on—being a brand for outdoor sports enthusiasts—Dan decided to turn the volume up a bit. It was a period, after all, of a vibrant music scene in Boston. Rock musicians were performing every night at clubs which became legendary throughout the city. "That period of time, in the late '80s and early '90s, was the birth of alternative music, and people who loved it had a chance to see bands they loved and champion them in small, intimate settings," veteran Boston disc jockey and photographer Julie Kramer said. "It was a lifestyle. It was a time and place that seemed more carefree and easygoing." Among the heavyweight settings in Boston were the Rathskeller ("The Rat") in Kenmore Square and The Channel in what is now the Fort Point neighborhood, two clubs that helped define the grittiness of the Boston music scene. Kramer's sister worked at The Rat in the '70s, and pointed out that their mother just happened to see The Police perform there one night as she was picking up her daughter. Local bands, such as Tribe; O+; The Stompers; Pixies; Throwing Muses; the Mighty, Mighty Bosstones; and The Lemonheads all got their start at the tiny confines around the corner from Lansdowne Street, which was, in itself, a nightclub haven for the city.

"The Rat was *the* place," said Kramer, who in 1988 joined WFNX. The station was, perhaps, the greatest influence on the local music scene at the time, a launching pad for indie, progressive, and punk acts. "I just think it was one of those hangs where you wanted to be, and so did everybody else." The Channel, however, boasted a bigger venue than The Rat, and free parking. "I think The Channel had bands coming around for the second time, or bigger bands. If you missed them at The Rat the first time around, you might have caught them at The Channel the second time." That included the likes of The Red Hot Chili Peppers, Iggy Pop, Echo and the Bunnymen, The Ramones, Social Distortion, and Alice In Chains. "You made friends with concert-goers, bartenders, and doormen," Kramer said. "You didn't walk through metal detectors or get patted down before entering. You could dress any way you wanted and not be judged. You were all there to see a band or musician you loved. It was a community. The people booking those clubs were on the pulse of what was happening in music at the time, and local bands were championed, revered, and sold out many nights."

Dan's younger brother, Ned, had a few friends who formed a band called The Stingers, named after a fictitious high school gang, who were seeking just a small slice of what was one of the strongest music scenes in the country. With ARU now his, and a hot music scene ready for the taking, Dan figured the next step for the company's business plan should be creating another form of alternative recreation. "We were hanging out at The Rat, we were going to The Channel," Dan said. "We loved the Boston music scene, so we had this idea. Let's do our own booze cruises." Dan had spent some time in his senior year in high school as a deckhand on Boston Harbor party cruises, mostly scrubbing the decks, and had witnessed first-hand the allure of a night out, drinking on the harbor. He'd watched people rent boats and throw parties on the harbor, and saw the ease with which a buck could be made. So they rented Boston Harbor cruise boats and ARU delivered its own musical nights out on the water. They weren't afraid to introduce themselves to bands at the clubs, a bravado that would also pay off when they were looking for soundtracks to provide backdrops in Egan Brother productions. As a precursor to the way many live acts handle their post-show merchandising today, everyone on their cruises received a cassette tape recording of the band's performance that night, as well as a button featuring a guy hanging over a railing, urging guests not to puke.

Ned needed a summer job while attending college at the University of Vermont, so it seemed natural to expand the business to a second location, on Lake Champlain, in Burlington, Vermont. But, sometimes things didn't go as smoothly as they did in Boston. One particularly rowdy ARU-sponsored cruise on Lake Champlain lasted only forty-five minutes before the captain decided he'd seen enough. He turned the boat around and headed back to shore. "It was a good move on his part," Dan said. The passengers were drunk and their excessive partying had prompted the early return. Something within Dan told him that what he and his brothers were doing wasn't right after that. For starters, Alternative Recreation Unlimited now found it impossible to rent a boat for booze cruises on Lake Champlain. But the darkness of the scene also convinced Dan that his imbibing might have been encouraging others, as well. "I decided I should stop drinking, but I didn't know how to not drink," he said. It was around this time that Dan's friend's mother took him to "some of those meetings."

It was a good season for snow at Sugarbush, in 1987—there was skiing into May—and John and Dan were still on the slopes when they were supposed to be further north, up Vermont's I-89 in Burlington, where they were scheduled to be helping their brother Ned pack for the trip home after a semester at UVM. As can be the case in perfect spring-skiing circumstances, it was party time—drinking and smoking while harvesting the corn snow—all of which led the brothers to arrive late at Ned's apartment that evening. By the time they showed up, Ned had already arranged his living room furniture on the front lawn and was throwing a party of his own for neighbors and anyone passing by. The outdoor living room was complete with a keg of beer. Ned had been waiting for John and Dan to show up, anticipating their late arrival, knowing what the skiing conditions were like. John and Dan rolled up with John's van and Marlen's station wagon, so Ned could get his things back to Milton for the summer—the furniture certainly wouldn't fit in Ned's tiny Renault Le Car (nicknamed 'Le Can' by the Egan clan). They packed up. They kept partying. "We were all pretty hammered," Dan said.

It was getting dark by the time the brothers decided to point the cars south on I-89 and head home to Massachusetts. Dan, in either a moment of generosity or acquiescence, gave Ned the keys to their mom's station wagon. Dan would take the Le Can, without radio or air conditioning, and John drove his van.

The three of them eventually made it back to Milton, but Ned arrived a bit later, sometime after John and Dan had already passed out in bed. The next morning, Ned showed his brothers their mother's car, wrecked in an accident on the way home and tucked out of view in the garage, waiting until a plan could be devised for what to tell their parents. "I was always so thankful that we switched cars, because the little Le Can wouldn't have survived whatever he hit," Dan said. "He didn't want to tell Mom. John didn't want to tell Mom. So, I told Mom I crashed her car. The other two were nowhere to be found for that conversation."

It was Mother's Day. Marlen was furious. "You've lost hold of everything I've tried to instill in you," she told him. It was hard to argue.

"It was really the beginning of the end for my drinking," Dan said. "That comment had its impact on me."

There was reason for Marlen to fear the effects of alcoholism in her children, and not only because of their Irish-Scots heritage. Her brother, Joe, had made it his hobby to get drunk and pass out at his country club. This was such a common occurrence, the staff would just leave him there until he woke up from his bender. But one of those evenings, Joe had a heart attack and died in his sleep, right there at the bar. "Mom told me, that Mother's Day, 'I'm afraid you're going to end up like Uncle Joe,'" Dan said. Joe's son, Danny, was a good enough hockey goalie to earn a full scholarship to Boston College. One night, he and his brother, Joe, Jr., were partying at a local dive bar called Mary Ann's, in Cleveland Circle. The celebration was a precursor to Danny's death in a car accident later that evening. It's a scar that Joe, Jr., will forever live with.

"So, my mom was acutely aware of alcoholism and the effects of it," Dan said. "She worried for all of us. My parents didn't completely understand all of our activity. They were both very conservative people and didn't want to know 'what we were really up to.' When I started to get sober, it was a reality for them they hadn't considered—what that meant. Why did I need to get sober? And what would it be like to have a son in recovery?

"Mom was quiet until she wasn't, and then she was very direct. In most cases, this was when she had hit the wall and you could see the pain in her eyes. At those moments, her intervention was powerful. This time, it stopped me cold in my tracks and rocked my soul. It would always be the one thing that started something positive in me." Her intervention was an overriding theme, preparing the Egan children for the world. "My parents had no interest in pleasing us. I don't remember either parent ever asking me if I was happy. That was not their purpose. Their purpose was to provide. They pleased us through gatherings and at meals. There was an inherent happiness, but it wasn't like, 'Are you OK? Are you happy? What can I do for you?' No, it was like, 'I've provided for you, why aren't you happy?'" Providing versus pleasing became a necessity for Robert and Marlen, who ran what could have been considered a stricter environment for the Egan children to thrive in. "It was hard to frustrate my mom, but there were times when she would say, 'I've had enough. I'm leaving.' And the hush would be unbelievable because none of us could fathom anything working without her. Those few times when she was at her wit's end was such a staunch slap in the face. It was like, 'Oh shit. We'd better get it together, because this can't happen.'"

Marlen said, "I know there's lots that Dan has done that I don't know about." Marlen had used the same "Don't tell me" approach when Dan and John hit the road to film for Warren Miller. Ever since Dan got in front of the Warren camera for that first time during the FIS run at Sugarbush, Marlen pleaded for a hush blanket where their activities were concerned. She could recall her heart in her mouth after witnessing that scene, something she later would leave for the theater. "I never knew what they did until the movie came out," she said. When their movies did come out, Marlen played the role of a minor celebrity in the audience. Her daughter, Sue, recalled one such instance when she and her mother were waiting for the film to start during a showing on the Boston University campus, chatting about what they might potentially see from Dan and John. A woman in the row behind them tapped Marlen on the shoulder. "Are you talking about the Egan brothers?" she asked. "You *know* The Egan Brothers?"

"Know them?" said Marlen. "I'm their mother."

"My God," the woman said. "You're a saint." As if that wasn't something Marlen, who had raised seven Egan children, didn't know already. She nodded in response, and said, "Yup."

But there were some moments that were too much for her to re-live—namely, Dan's experience in Russia. When somebody would pop *The Extreme Dream* into the VCR at the Milton family home, Marlen would actually relocate to the other end of the house to avoid watching the sequence, as if trying to avoid the inevitable downfall that might happen to yet another Danny on the Gillis/Egan family tree. "Here is my mom, mourning the losses of her brother, son, and nephew, and I choose a career jumping off cliffs," Dan said. "I was in transference with her emotion, because I was causing it. My mom would never drop us off at Logan Airport, but she would always pick us up. She couldn't stand to see us leave on a ski trip or a film trip."

In 1989, Warren Miller came calling for Dan to take part on one of those film trips, arranging for him to fly to South America that summer. By this point, most everybody knew he wasn't drinking, including the camera crew he joined on the plane. But there was a shot of booze in the middle of them, and when Dan picked it up, one member of the crew reminded him that he didn't drink. Dan looked at the guy, examined the shot, and shrugged his shoulders. Down the hatch.

"There are parts of the Portillio segment I love," recalls Dan. "I was skiing with Kevin Andrews and we were having a ball, partying and heading up the crazy "Rocka Jack" Poma lift, which fit five people in a row; ripping up the Primavera and Kilometro Lanzado runs; climbing and skiing the Super C Couloir. There is one shot with Kevin and I making seventy-five powdery figure-eight turns down a huge slope and jumping over the train tracks at the bottom of the slope. So classic."

However, while in Portillo, because of his drinking, Dan would get kicked out of the world's only hotel at an altitude above ten thousand feet, and would never work for that particular cameraman again. "We had a ball, but he wasn't very happy," Dan said. It was also another sign. On the way home, Dan decided to revisit "not drinking." This time, he made it. Three decades later, his sobriety remains one of the foundations of his life.

Chapter Thirty

PHOTOGRAPHERS AND CINEMATOGRAPHERS

DAN WAS FINDING LIFE ON the road an isolating experience. During the winter of 1990–91, he faced a transition—his first real winter traveling sober. Drinking and partying was the lifestyle of his fellow travelers—including John, Tom Day, and Tom's wife Lizzie—one that followed them regardless of the culture of their foreign or domestic destinations.

The struggle came to the forefront at the family home of fellow North Face Extreme Team member, Alenka Vrecek. Alenka's family had agreed to host the Egans and Days while they filmed another unique ski trip for their videos. When the group arrived at the Vrecek residence in Yugoslavia, there were traditional meet-and-greet shots of homemade pear schnapps waiting for them. Dan attempted to pass on the alcohol, telling Alenka's father, Zvoni, that he'd prefer water.

"Water?" Zvoni asked. "Water is for bathing. Drink." With that, he handed the schnapps to Dan. It was John who immediately snatched the glass out of his brother's hands. "His insides are dirty," he told Zvoni. "Give him as much water as he wants." John's presence was a blessing for Dan in moments like these, particularly in places where the party never really stopped.

"His personal transformation to being drug- and alcohol-free is an incredibly strong and powerful statement that was very hard in the pressures of the life we were living back then," fellow North Face Extreme Team member Rob DesLauriers said. "I always admired him for that." But even though it was Dan who faced the hardships imposed by sobriety, neither was it always easy on the crews he traveled with. "Those years of him quitting drinking were really hard, because nobody else stopped," John said. "Weed is one thing I've found in every country. It's everywhere. It's not like it's a bad city-kid thing to do. We'd be in some remote part of the world, and a guy in Yugoslavia would have hash, and that would piss [Dan] off to no end." Dan's internal struggle was also showing outwardly, John said. At times, it became a distraction, as when John felt Dan was overly worried about the extracurricular activities of the others and how it would affect the filming.

"Tommy and I had just smoked hash and were raring to go," John said. "We filmed for another three hours and that stuff ends up being the best stuff in the film. The interruptions that take place, that screw up projects, are hard to avoid. That distraction of him being so worried that the cameraman is smoking weed or I'm smoking weed, tended to distract from how well we could perform. We'd be polite, and not do it in front of him. But we didn't feel like we were struggling and had to stop doing what we were doing."

At times, DesLauriers said, it would lead to Dan becoming a bit righteous about his sobriety. "But he had a right to be," DesLauriers said. "I've seen other friends who have slipped down that slope because they couldn't get any traction. A lot of other people were just a decade behind him." It wasn't until he reached his thirties, DesLauriers said, when he finally understood that his days were much more valuable than his nights. Dan was learning that at the still-prime partying age of twenty-six.

Once John and Dan strapped on their skis and jumped off the Berlin Wall, then watched those images travel across the world, they began to understand what sort of power a feat like that could have. Their personal travel agent, Steve Kassin, whom John met through the Sugarbush network, was really into remote spots around the globe, especially where there was snow. The Elbrus trip had proven to be an epic adventure and forced the Egans to face the reality of venturing into mountaineering in remote regions of the world. Individually, it forced each of them into some soul-searching. As brothers, it created new fault lines in an already dynamic relationship. Professionally, it lined up perfectly with their worldwide tour to newsworthy locations.

The Iron Curtain was collapsing. They'd been photographed and filmed at the iconic Berlin Wall just after it had fallen. They'd witnessed massive demonstrations in Red Square, in the spring of 1990, just months before the fall of the U.S.S.R. The world was changing, and they found themselves capturing that perspective through the lens of skiing, visiting mountain cultures as the Cold War was ending. "The common thread in both Berlin and in Russia was how curious people were about American culture," Dan said. "What they knew about the U.S. was MTV, President Reagan, and Hollywood movies. The conversations with people we interviewed were all centered around the common ground that unites people, family, work, and a desire to explore. The paradigms I had grown up with—like nuclear war and communism versus capitalism—rarely came up. Rather, it was more like them saying 'you were both there, I was born here, and we are alike.' We were dealing in the currency of mountains—snow and fun. And it made for great videos that the American audience was eating up."

When Iraq invaded Kuwait in 1990, sparking the beginning of the United States' involvement in Operation Desert Shield (which would lead into Operation Desert Storm four months later), it triggered a desire in the Egans to ski more off-the-beaten-path locales. They put the sport in the midst of scenes of turmoil that were shaping the world, rather than just presenting their extreme skiing as a form of escapism. The decision to visit Yugoslavia was no different. The country was only months away from a civil war, and the brothers had connections there, with Alenka's family.

The Egans and Days were at Chamonix, shooting for The North Face's *Skiing Extreme III.* The legendary terrain of the French Alps was the proving ground for extreme skiing. The Elbrus trip and the fallout from the canceled Degré7 contract had led to a lot of interesting conversations with mountain guides in the Chamonix Valley. "I had guides coming up to me who had heard one version of the expedition and wanted to hear my side of the story," Dan said. "They had questions about the Vallençant guides who'd been on the trip; how they behaved and what went wrong. The younger guides seemed to be more open to the fact that the guides who'd gone to Elbrus were past their prime, chain-smokers, and had hated the idea of the trip from the start. That was validating to me, for sure."

The production crew for Yugoslavia included John and his new girlfriend, Lilly, Tom and Lizzie, Danny Day, and Dan. They boarded a train in Chamonix and headed toward Zurich, Switzerland, where photographer Wade McKoy joined the traveling band of ski bums. The trip to Yugoslavia would take just over twenty-two hours and pass through France; Switzerland; Italy; Austria; eventually, Ljubljana, the capital of Yugoslavia; and Bled, in the republic of Slovenia. "We had loads of luggage and gear, and in the middle of the night, somewhere in Italy, the train crew woke us up because only the front half of the train's cars were continuing on to Ljubljana," Dan said. "So, we not only had to change cars, we had to scramble to find a cabin to crash in and move a mountain of luggage, skis, and camera gear. Once all the gear was in the passageway of the train, outside the new cabin, John, Lilly, and the Day family all scrambled to the seats and the bunks to crash for the night. Wade and I moved all the stuff into another cabin. It was stacked most of the way to the ceiling. Wade and I slept on top of the pile.

"This was all fine and good until we hit the Yugoslavian border at around sunrise. The border guards wanted to see our passports and search every bag. I knew what they really wanted was American dollars, so I broke out a wad of cash and we haggled over the amount of the bribe for them to leave us alone. All the while this was going on, there was a grandmotherly-looking lady sticking her head out of her cabin and ducking back in. She did this several times while I was greasing the guards with twenty-dollar bills. When the guards finally left the train and we started to move down the tracks, this woman ran out of her cabin and started to hug me and kiss me on the cheek, over and over. I couldn't make out what she was after, but eventually a passerby interpreted for me that she wanted to thank me for smuggling her goods into the country. I was stunned because I didn't know what she was talking about. As it turned out, the woman had hidden a bunch of items in our luggage while we were moving them from car to car in the middle of the night: silverware, pots, pans, and household goods that weren't available to her in Yugoslavia."

In 1991, Slovenia boasted about 75 percent of Yugoslavia's total wealth. With rumors of a civil war, as Serbian nationalism grew in other regions of the crumbling Yugoslav state, the northern republic of Slovenia had the economic means to pave its own path. So, it seemed a pretty safe place to visit. Civil war would break out in Yugoslavia in May of 1991. During the Ten Day War, Slovenia deployed troops to their borders and won its independence, just two and a half months after the Egans' trip. Alas, the first place the conflict escalated was atop a Slovenian ski resort. Attackers wanted the communications towers. The Egans had visited the site just months earlier. It was a spot where McKoy and Day had shot film and photos of Dan and John skiing a steep couloir, an image that would eventually become a poster in *Powder Magazine*. These were still the days when Day was transitioning in his role, switching from on-camera skier to behind-the-lens cameraman. He was, admittedly, not very skilled in his new role, but in his early stages, Dan and John gave him space to learn, helping him become the cameraman he is today, generally regarded as one of the most respected in the adventure sports business.

"Their willingness to put up with my pace, knowing I wasn't nearly as skilled as some of the expert cameramen at the time, but still they spent their time with me," Day said, "I think that's what made our shots so good, in the years to come, was that chemistry. That we learned together, approaching the combination of a skier-cameraman. It's a collaborative effort and the communication is so key on how to orchestrate one shot. We didn't want to miss shots on either end. We both had to be on at the same time to get the one shot. That time together over several years was fantastic."

For McKoy, it was his first big trip overseas with a film crew. "I learned so much from the entire crew," he said. "But overall, it's amazing how hard we all worked. We loved it, so it wasn't a big deal, but it was hard work. The Egans hiked a lot. They would repeat shot after shot, and then do it again if either Tom or I asked them to."

Among the scenes Day captured in Yugoslavia, a few stand out as definitively telling the story: John and Dan sword-fighting atop the ruins of a church that was hundreds of years old. The brothers milling about through old-town Serbia, clad in their orange and yellow one-pieces, displaying their ski culture in an old-world atmosphere. At Vogel, the lift attendant at the resort's single chair, drinking draft beer ("Chairs come by about once every mouthful of beer," Warren says during the narration in *Born to Ski*). The liftie even offers a swig to Dan, who graciously passes. "I love skiing so very much, and that's what I try to capture," Day said. "I try to capture what it is about skiing that is so beautiful, so that other people can maybe understand it through the shot."

In Slovenia, it was easy to find such beauty. The Vogel Ski Resort is located in the Triglav National Park, Slovenia's only national park, all wrapped around Lake Bohinj. Here, the scenes were perfect for the crew to capture the location, the people, and the skiing. "In Vogel, they say the people have lived in the valley so long they don't have necks," Dan said. "But it's true. Check out the footage. The lifties had really short necks."

The Egans also skied at Kranjska Gora, a Slovenian resort town in the foothills of the Julian Alps, where the World Cup is held each year. Then it was on to Kanin Resort, the highest resort in the country, overlooking the Alps and the Adriatic Sea. Surrounding the lifts are huge rock walls that tower above the lifts. "It took well over an hour to hike up along the ridge, and the snow was firm," Dan said. "Picking our way through and over the rocks made for great footage and images."

Alenka's brother was on the Slovenian national demo team and had taken on the role of their guide. One of the stops he arranged was a meeting with the folks at Elan Skis, the Slovenian ski company located in Begunje na Gorenjskem. The brand was famous for sponsoring Ingemar Stenmark, the greatest slalom and giant slalom skier of all time. However, on this trip, Elan wanted to show off its latest creation to the westerners—its "shaped ski," the Elan SCX (SideCut eXtreme). "The ski was crazy-looking," Dan said. "It had the widest tip I'd ever seen." McKoy remembers, "They didn't even want us to touch it or shoot it. It was so top secret. They were really edgy about the whole visit."

Compared to the seventy-four-millimeter-wide skis Dan was skiing, the concept was crazy. The cocky American came out in him: *Yeah, good luck with that.* Of course, shaped skis would revolutionize the skiing industry, proving to Dan that sometimes, when you're on one cutting edge, you can't see the next one. "I don't know if that tip was eighty millimeters wide, or whatever the first SCX was, but it was the beginning for the SCX. We laughed at it. We just thought, maybe in Yugoslavia that thing will catch on."

Dan *had* seen the edge elsewhere, at least in terms of building his business relationship with Warren Miller, particularly after watching what Willie Vogel was managing in Canada. Vogel, a former pro skier, effectively ran the Canadian office for Warren Miller, which led to him always ending up in the movies, in some form or another. Vogel would make deals to get himself and Canadian tourism companies in the films each year, promoting the country. Seeing this, Dan noted how The Egan Brothers' sponsors—Head, Salomon, and The North Face—were aligned with Warren Miller, as well. Head's chief of ad agency, John Creole, was also looking for innovative ways to promote the Egans. With Egan Entertainment doing the heavy work, securing locations and getting the filming done, those were steps Miller could skip each year when making his movies. By having that agreement, the Egans would definitely be in the film, allowing for a variety of synergies.

"This was great for our sponsors, but Creole sweetened the deal, creating advertising campaigns around the segments, and putting posters of us in *Powder Magazine*," Dan said.

With Tom Day behind the lens, the Egans also knew they had a direct connection to The North Face films, as well, sweetening the pot for how far the distribution of footage from any one location could go. Day was also an approved Warren Miller guy. "So they would take his footage," Dan said. "Warren wanted to vet the cameramen we worked with, to ensure the footage was worthy of his films." When it came time to travel to another unexpected skiing destination a year later—this time Turkey—Day was tied up with a different project, which left the door open for someone else. That lead to the inclusion of Tom Grissom, who'd shot the Egans at Squaw Valley. The former intern was starting to transform himself into a more full-time cameraman for Warren Miller. He'd also shot some for The North Face, and would wind up shooting a fair amount of footage for the Egans' forthcoming *The Extreme Dream*. "I usually call that my favorite shoot," Grissom said. "Dan produced it, he got us over there, and everyone who was on that trip just put out maximum effort. Everybody chipped in."

Again, the crew captured iconic ski and historical images. The Warren Miller segment opens up in the ruins of Ephesus, one of the Seven Wonders of the Ancient World. They shot in the Grand Bazaar and outside the Blue Mosque, and made a stop in Uludag, outside the city of Bursa, just south of Istanbul. After that, they took an all-night bus ride to the classical region of Anatolia (Asia Minor) and skied during a rare snowstorm in Cappadocia, where early Christians had hidden from Attila the Hun in underground cities. The images of the Egans skiing among the sandstone spires of Cappadocia flooded magazine and ski video jackets for years after the trip.

"Wade was freaking out over the uniqueness of the area," Dan said, "and we had just enough snow on the smooth rock faces that we could ski without catching an edge. It was magic." Their lodging was a hotel carved into the rock; the crew slept on rock bunks with mattresses on them. "Dan understands the work it takes," Grissom said. "He is such a good producer, he can get me right where I need to be and he understands the work that is involved. When I worked with Dan in the movies, it was very much a partnership, where he took a lot of the work off my back, and, hopefully, I took a lot of the headache off his back, too."

Just as they had in Yugoslavia, the Egans sold the story to a publication, this time *Skiing* magazine, which sent writer Josh Lerman and McKoy (who'd also joined the Egans in Slovenia) to cover the trip. Lerman's story, "Skiing to Byzantium," leads with the trip's tensest moment, which doesn't have anything to do with tackling dangerous mountain terrain. He wrote about how, after spending two hours trying to find someone to take them up Mount Erciyas, in Kayseri (where the Egans, dressed in brightly-colored suits in a society where "there were no clothing colors brighter than a kind of dull rust," looked as if they'd come from another planet), they finally found a driver with a van. He looked benign enough, Lerman wrote, but that was before he pulled the gun on them.

After "skidding, sliding, and swerving" their way up a one-and-a-half-lane cobbled road on "the flanks of the treeless Erciyas Dagi massif in central Turkey," the passengers figured it was just a matter of *when* they would get stuck. Not *if*. When it finally happened, the driver pulled the gun on them, pointing it at each of them while shouting incoherently. They figured that could only mean "get out and push."

"Dan was fast losing his patience with the driver," Lerman wrote, "and was expressing this with increasingly internationally recognizable gestures of disgust and disdain. At least twice, using our hands and avalanche shovels, we dug the bus entirely free of the bank, only to have the driver spin us right back in again." It took two hours of struggling before they were finally rescued, when a truck came along and pushed them free.

Don't let that incident portray how the travelers felt about their experience in Turkey, though. "When people ask me, where's my favorite place to ski, I always say my favorite place we traveled to was Turkey," Dan said. "The Turks are beautiful people—very kind, very open, and it's a totally different culture. They're just so open, the cultural differences were a little eased." Unlike some of the other European destinations they visited, there was no begging in the streets of Turkey. "There were street people, but they wouldn't beg," Dan said. "They would offer to shine your sneakers, but it wasn't begging." Grissom caught one such instance on film, a segment that made it into Warren Miller's 1991 production, *Steeper and Deeper*. A street vendor put a shine to Dan's San Marco ski boots, squeezing fresh juice from an orange to polish things up. This was after filming John and Dan, fully decked out in their colorful ski garb, taking a ride on a rickshaw through the streets of Cappadocia. "You just try to shoot as many interesting shots as you can," Grissom said. "Whether it's the knife-sharpening guy or the meat hanging on the rack, or the carpet stores."

They also had Hakan Cakar to thank for much of the ease the crew discovered in Turkey. Their old friend, John Dockendorf, had a friend, Carolyn, who was doing a semester abroad in Turkey, and she recommended Hakan, a fellow university student, to be their liaison. "He wasn't a mountain man," Dan said. "He was a Turkish interpreter. He would sort out all the things you see in the movie: the cart with the horse, the Turkish bath, the shining of the boots with orange stuff. He was a college kid who understood what we were after and he wasn't afraid to push the limits and bribe people. If we couldn't solve a problem, we would just try and fix it with money." Perhaps the most enduring scene that Grissom caught was the defining shot of John and Dan hiking up a ridge past a helicopter that had crashed into the chairlift. As they made their way past, Warren Miller narrated: "Dan and John are from Boston, using skis made in Austria, Italian ski boots, wearing Japanese goggles, underwear made in Georgia, at a ski resort in Turkey, trying to ride a ski lift that was made in France and had been broken by a helicopter made in Russia. Which proves that skiing really is a way of life that knows no international or economical boundaries."

"We literally hiked out of bounds, came over a ridge, and saw the heli there," Dan said. "Crashed. You couldn't buy a lift ticket because there was no real resort. The hotels owned chairlifts, but it wasn't like anything was laid out or interconnected. So when we hiked out of bounds and came over this ridge, which we didn't know went to another small town, it was where the lift had come out of. That was the lift that was out of operation because the heli had run into it." There was never any real explanation for why the helicopter was laying on the mountain, or whether anybody had been injured. Nobody even really knew, despite Miller's narrating script, if it truly was a Russian helicopter. "A lot of that stuff is lore made up by Warren," Grissom said. "But we just tried to use it as part of our story. We would shoot as much skiing as we could, but what Warren really liked was to have the travel parts and the exotic parts. So when we came across that helicopter, it was kind of obvious what had happened. It had hit the cable on the chairlift, so we just built a story around that. I was hiking up and kind of checking it out, getting wide, medium, and tight shots, enough for the editor to work with. That gave the story time to breathe and it gave Dan or Warren time to talk. And it made it interesting and exciting."

So, too, did Grissom's capture of John and Dan skiing, making first descents on some gnarly Turkish chutes. "You would really want to be able to set up everything," Grissom said. "The framing—if you wanted it to be slow motion, you needed a variation between wide shots and tight shots. Then, some running footage shots that we would get with a 5.9-millimeter lens, so we could ski with the camera beside the guys. That was an early version of the GoPro, even though it was a full-size camera."

Indeed, had there been a GoPro in 1991, the filming process would have been a whole lot easier. Even so, getting the film, even without the luxury of digital equipment, was the easy part. It was what came next that proved to be the real hassle.

Joe Powder skis neck-deep pow,
savoring every turn towards the
bottom of the run.

Photograph by Mike McPhee

While shooting *Dan
Egan's Wild World
of Winter* TV show in
Kicking Horse, British
Columbia, Dan soaks
up some fresh snow.

Chapter Thirty-one

EXTREME DREAM

DELIVERING THE FOOTAGE WASN'T THE hardest part of making a ski film, Dan said. The real challenge was in processing the story that went along with it. "We kind of left the shooting up to the cameramen we hired," Dan said. "Tom Grissom, Tom Day, Eric Scharmer and others, we trusted them and knew their ability to compose shots, and that they knew how to tell a story visually."

But when it came time to deliver the finished product, Dan found himself in completely new territory. In addition to finding space in Warren Miller's *Steeper and Deeper*, the footage from Turkey, as well as from Yugoslavia and Mount Elbrus, would create the heart of *The Extreme Dream*, the follow-up project to the *World Wide and Wild* slideshow, and Egan Entertainment's first run at making a real ski movie. This was the task Dan faced during the summer of 1992, at Warren Miller's studio in Ketchum, Idaho. "Because I had hung around Warren's office in Hermosa Beach a few times and traveled each year to host premieres of the annual film, I was becoming part of the inner circle of Warren Miller Entertainment," Dan said. "I met Kim Schneider, the editor of the movie that past winter, when I came to town to shoot a segment with Sun Valley Heli-Ski. Grissom shot it and introduced us. Kim took an interest in the project and invited me out to edit the *The Extreme Dream* in his studio outside Sun Valley. I was eager to escape Boston and break away to the west, so over the Fourth of July, I packed up my van and drove out to Idaho. I had just read *Blue Highways, A Journey into America*, a book about traveling through towns and places off the major highways around the country, so I drove all the back roads, from Boston to Sun Valley, during the week of the Fourth. It was amazing."

It was a different world, Dan noticed, as he was closing in on Iowa. "On the local AM radio station, the DJ kept saying, 'Up next is the Farm Report.' Then he would play a song and plug the farm report again. 'Don't go away, the Farm Report is at the top of the hour.' Then, when the top of the hour arrived, he said, 'Welcome to the Farm Report, your source for the people, process, and policies that produce America's food. It's the Fourth of July. Celebrate safely. There is no Farm Report today.' I just about died laughing. Here I was alone, driving through who knows where, focused on hearing my first-ever farm report, getting excited by the hype the DJ had created, and *bang!* he lets me down, wrapped in red, white, and blue."

It would be a trip where Dan could find solace in his newfound sobriety, free of the inherent struggles staying sober had wrought upon him over the winter in Boston. He parked along the Mississippi, showered in a Kansas thunderstorm, and ate at diners, all while discovering the gems described in his new traveling bible, *Blue Highways*.

"I knew Kim would guide me through my first video edit ever, and I'd also learned I could source and find what I needed to know about the things I didn't know about," Dan said. "I had confidence we could create the movie." That bravado waned, though, as Dan got deeper into the editing process.

"There was pressure once I got to Idaho, because I had limited funds, and *The Extreme Dream*'s narration was not really mixed right. There's a hollowed-ness to it, and the music was just OK. It was a little disjointed. I remember calling John, basically in tears because I thought the film wasn't going to get done." Dan ended up recording the narration and creating the music mix in Steve Miller's Ketchum studio, which the famous rock star lent him the use of—Sun Valley was such a small community.

It still didn't go well. "There were too many pieces. It wasn't coming together, and the editor and I had been up too long and weren't seeing eye-to-eye," Dan said. "John did what he normally would do at that point—got really focused on what the main problem was and directed me to fix it. He just sort of said, 'Work it out, bit by bit. Do this. Call me.' John didn't know how to make a movie. But John knows how to build a home, so he understands process. Any time I'd panic and call him, he'd go into the mode where he would give clear instruction for me. He was always very helpful."

Even with its flaws, *The Extreme Dream* was well-received by *Skiing* magazine in 1992. "It's almost impossible not to like John and Dan Egan," *Skiing*'s Mike Finkel wrote. "Watching their first feature-length film, you get the feeling that they love skiing so much, they'd do it just as often even if it weren't their occupation. This passion comes through loud and clear—perhaps even too loud—in *The Extreme Dream*."

According to the magazine, it was worth the price of admission to see the Egans jumping off the Berlin Wall, bouncing through ruins in Turkey, and threading chutes in Yugoslavia. "All told, there's more exciting footage in this movie than in most others; for their first try, it's an exceptional film," Finkel wrote. "If you're a pessimist, *Dream* ain't for you—the brothers' sickly-sweet sentiments may have you running to the dentist. But, if you're like Dan and John—hopelessly addicted ski bums—then you may have just found your two new heroes." As for how Dan pulled it off, it was a matter of learning on the fly with the lingo used by the Warren Miller editors. "I just watched," he said. "I asked questions. I tried to stay out of the way. A lot of the struggles of the early movies was, I didn't understand what they were talking about or what could be done. So, a lot of times, I didn't understand what it would take to make a change, or wouldn't understand why the guy was grabbing three tapes. You had all these different playback tape decks and you had one 'record' deck. So, you could preview the edit before you recorded it, but that was like, set in time. It wasn't like it is now, when you can preview the whole five minutes."

Graphics were impossible, Dan said, and the edit was built frame-by-frame, a factor that today's filmmakers probably couldn't even fathom, with the digital tools at their fingertips. "To go back and change a frame or a shot, because it was a linear build, you had to reshuffle every shot," Dan said. "You couldn't just replace it. The whole thing was built—from the first frame to the last frame. The kids today don't understand that, because they can basically go in and insert anything they want and it doesn't destroy the timeline. We couldn't even look at the timeline. I couldn't say, 'at three minutes, twenty-five seconds, and fifty-two frames—that shot . . .' I couldn't see that laid out in front of me. I would have to scroll back to look at it. I couldn't have multiple screens open. I couldn't layer it. I had to narrate while watching the movie to get the timing of the track. And editing the narration isn't what it is today. I couldn't plug it in.

"Then we had to reassemble to edit. So, once the edit was on a master tape, you had to reassemble, because you had to go back and get the color corrections, which was expensive—you only wanted to color-correct the shots you were going to use. So you had to go back and color-correct and reassemble the edit. And you didn't dare do that with your master tapes— so you had these work tapes. And the timecode became the master edit from which you reassembled, with the master tapes."

Got it?

"It took me all summer," Dan said.

It wasn't until Dan began his stint at the New England Sports Network, nearly a decade later, that he came in contact with the latest digital technologies for creating video content. The seeds for what would become Egan Entertainment's *Wild World of Winter* TV show began in 1989, when

Dan hired an accountant, Michelle Moreau, who also happened to work at the regional sports network whose studio was located right at Fenway Park, in Boston. Moreau thought her new client would be perfect for NESN's *Front Row*, a nightly sports magazine program. Dan was "the ski guy," of course. "*Front Row* was my introduction to television," Dan said. "How it got made and how it had changed from what I'd done. It upped the ante as far as standards, because it was broadcast-quality." Dan's presence on *Front Row* impressed NESN personnel, including producer Steve Garabedian, which led to Dan's own monthly ski show. *Wild World of Winter* ran on NESN and other outlets through 2011. NESN producer, Steve Sera, a musician on the side, wrote the theme song.

The soundtrack is imperative in any action sports footage, to evoke emotion and enhance the adventure for the viewer. Dan also had his own inside track for music to feature in his films and television show, thanks to the booze cruises he'd ran, years earlier, with Alternative Recreation Unlimited. The first local band he chased down was one he'd seen more than a few times at The Channel. Face to Face was a new-wave outfit, originally formed in Manchester, New Hampshire, that played together from 1979 until 1988. Dan particularly liked a track of theirs called "Out of My Hands," which has a ripping opening that builds for more than a minute before vocalist, Laurie Sargent, starts belting out the lyrics. "The problem with most songs is, they usually only have a thirty-second open before the singer," Dan said. "But this one had a long open and it built like a storm, which I used in my slide shows."

Face to Face had broken up by the time Dan was creating his own content, but drummer Billy Beard had taken a part-time job as chef at Harvard University, and Dan tracked him down. "I wasn't afraid to approach people," Dan said. "I wasn't afraid to find Face to Face. If I heard a song I liked, I'd go after it, but for the musicians who could write music, I'd tell them I was looking for a song 'that sounds like this,' and would give them a pop song to basically create an original song from."

Music was something Dan felt comfortable pulling together. Through the

Boston Film and Video Foundation, a regional art center whose mission was "to encourage and facilitate access to and understanding of film, video, and electronic media as a means of creative expression," Dan made contact with Paul Geary, the drummer of popular rock band, Extreme. Geary left the band in 1994, a few years after their hit single, "More Than Words," rocketed up the pop charts, to become an artist manager. In addition to his former band, his credits included such heavyweights as Smashing Pumpkins, Godsmack, Creed, and Fuel. Through Geary, Dan hooked up with some of Boston's more notable bands, including the Del Fuegos. There was a grittiness about the Boston music scene in the late '80s and early '90s that reflected the hardened edge of its residents. Much like grunge would define Seattle, the new-wave, alt scene was happening in the Hub, a nightly orchestration of rock and roll and the quaint environments that became home for the music and its fans. For Dan, there were few places that boasted this identity better than The Rat, in Kenmore Square.

"Hanging at The Rat was probably one of the coolest things I ever did in Boston," he said. "As a suburb kid at The Rat, you felt like you were in it. The Rat had sticky floors that would fill up and swell. And as crazy as that place was, it was pretty mellow. It was OK to hang out there. It wasn't a crowd that was going to fight or cause problems. There was a belonging. You knew you were part of the scene. The Rat said you're a Boston kid. And these were Boston bands. That piece of it, that belonging to the music scene was important. When you went to The Channel, you were likely going to get into a fight. The Rat wasn't really like that."

By inserting local music into their skiing productions, the Egans were more easily able to characterize themselves: East Coast skiers with a Boston edge they were promoting around the globe. "It tied into my Boston roots," Dan said. "I loved the Boston sound. I loved the Boston scene." The list of artists contributing music to Dan's next film, 1993's *Return of the Shred-I*, included local heavyweights such as Buffalo Tom, Drivin N Cryin, and Mike Hurley, who penned the catchy title track. It wouldn't be the music, though, that would wind up becoming the most noteworthy item to emerge from the film.

And it would be a trip to Romania that helped dictate the path—and derailment—of Dan's life over the next decade.

Chapter Thirty-two

SKI 93

THERE'S A SCENE IN WARREN Miller's 1994 production, *Vertical Reality*, that depicts Dan in a different light than his normal on-film persona. Skiers Alison Gannett and Dean Decas were suited up and ready to head out for a day on the slopes in New Hampshire, but not before making a pit stop at the executive offices of Ski 93. A marketing arm of the White Mountains 93 Association, Ski 93 promoted a handful of Granite State ski areas: Cannon Mountain, Waterville Valley, Loon Mountain Resort, and Bretton Woods Resort—all an easy two-hour drive up I-93 from Boston, a city that boasted more skiers and snowboard riders per capita than most others in the country. Gannett and Decas were there to wrangle Ski 93's executive director from his desk job and get him to join them for some turns.

"Check this out," Decas said, pointing to a closed door with a placard featuring the Ski 93 logo and Dan Egan's name. "Dan Egan's got a job. Executive director. Let's go get him." Despite the half-hearted protest of an office assistant ("No, no, he's in the middle of a major project"), Gannett and Decas pushed past her into Dan's office, where he was seated at a desk cluttered with dozens of folders, talking on the phone. Gannett ripped the phone from his grip and told whomever was on the other end, "Dan is going skiing."

Dan put up a fight—sort of—based on the workload he likely had to complete. But within seconds, he was on his way out the door with Decas and Gannett, slipping into a black jacket as he exited the office. The back of the coat read, "Real skiers don't have real jobs." Except, it seemed, for Dan Egan. A year earlier, Dan might've been feeling a need to hit rewind, based on how the first few months of the year had gone. Things had been in motion that should have clinched a memorable year.

Since the middle of 1992, Dan was the engine behind a "Ski for Peace" event in Lebanon. The nonprofit expedition would have led twenty representatives of Middle Eastern countries up 8,625-foot-high Mount Sannine, one of the highest peaks in Lebanon, overlooking Beirut. As part of the Middle East Peace Ski, Dan invited skiers from around the globe, including Israelis, Jordanians, and other Middle Easterners, to climb and ski the mountain together. Dan hoped to prove that, despite the world's troubles and differences, there was truth to one of Warren Miller's most famous mantras: "If everybody skied, there would be no war."

"We wanted to prove that mountaineering people from all over the world could ski together and get along," Dan told *Ski Country* magazine. He'd already established sponsorship from a Middle Eastern airline and endorsement from the American Arab League. The United Nations was sponsoring the trip, and there would be a spread about the Peace Ski in *Powder Magazine*. Everybody would be outfitted, with uniforms bearing the U.N. logo and Ski for Peace T-shirts. "We had all these different people ready to go to Lebanon," Dan said.

But then, on the morning of February 26, terrorists drove a Ryder truck into the parking garage between the North Tower of the World Trade Center and a New York City hotel. The truck contained a twelve-hundred-pound homemade bomb that would go off at 12:17 that afternoon. Six people died. More than a thousand others were injured in the precursor—test run, if you will—to Al Qaeda's destroying the towers eight years later with a pair of jet airliners. Peace Ski might have been a worthwhile effort, perhaps even particularly more so in the face of such brazen terrorism, but the trickle-down effect was that nobody wanted to take their chances in the Middle East at such a volatile time. The Peace Ski was off.

Dan had traveled to Beirut late in the winter of 1992 to set up logistics for the trip. In '92, it was illegal for Americans to travel to Lebanon. Dan had sneaked into the country at a time when Western hostages were still being held by the Lebanese Hezbollah, an Islamic political party and paramilitary organization. The Peace Ski was supported by the League of American Arab States, based in Washington D.C., who connected Dan with Middle Eastern Airlines. The trip had the elements of a James Bond film, and the plan was simple. Kind of. Middle Eastern Airlines didn't have flights from the U.S. to Lebanon, so the company set up a ticket on an American Airlines flight to London's Heathrow. Once there, Dan was to transfer to a Middle Eastern flight to Damascus, Syria. But there was a twist.

"They told me to go to the Damascus gate, tell them I was there for the Damascus flight, then wink twice and they would put me on the Beirut flight," Dan said. "So, I went to the gate, showed them my ticket and winked twice. They ushered me off in the opposite direction and on to the Beirut flight. Once I was on board, I saw I was the only American male. There were some American women who'd married Lebanese men—they all told me the same thing: 'get off, go home, it's not safe.' One woman came up to me before the flight took off and said, 'If you were my brother, I would never let you on this flight. It's really not safe.'" Dan went anyway.

"Getting off the plane was surreal," Dan said. "The Beirut airport in 1992 was torn up, having been shelled for fifteen years during the war. There were bombed-out planes beside the runway. Most of the buildings were empty. We went into one building, which was, effectively, a chain-link fence cage. I'd learned that the key to getting home without a $10,000 fine was to not have my passport stamped. I gave the guard behind the desk my passport. He looked at it, looked up at me, and said, 'Mr. Egan, we've been expecting you. Welcome to Lebanon.'

"I think the experience of traveling to the Cedar Mountains of Lebanon—making all of the connections to pull that dangerous trip off, getting the Middle East Peace Ski logistics, fundraising, and planning—figuring all of it out—moved me in another direction. That trip would have been a game-changer had it not been for the World Trade Center bombing. But it also showed me there was an even more important horizon beyond The Egan Brothers."

While tensions between Dan and John had bubbled over into a standstill of brotherly angst, John had his eyes on his own horizon, as well. He'd been planning an expedition, without involving Dan. John had been asked, by a Russian general with a passion for skiing, to visit Kamchatka, the Russian peninsula that juts out into the Siberian Pacific Ocean. The area boasts 122 volcanoes—the most active ring in the world—and had been closed to all but Soviet military personnel for years, because of its top-secret military installations. So this was not like hopping the next flight to Sun Valley for the weekend. "That was a new place," John said. "Nobody had been there from the U.S., since Communism. It was a big coup to get to go there." For help, he turned to his old friend, Steve Kassin, who'd run travel arrangements for the Egans over the past decade.

Kassin had been a self-described punk from the Brooklyn streets, forced into growing up quickly at a young age, after the death of his father. When he was eighteen, he moved to Sugarbush to become a ski bum. There, he met John and established a friendship that lasted through Kassin's moving back to New York. He wound up returning to school to study tourism and hospitality, and eventually launched a company focused on ski touring. Naturally, the

Egans became clients, leaving Kassin to handle the arrangements for "all their crazy ski movies." In those days, before internet, a travel agent was a necessary component. "We had to use different methodologies to get the deals, communicate, and send money," Kassin said. "All these things we take for granted now were much harder. I also had other clients who were outside the ski world and did some pretty crazy stuff, which allowed me to know all the consulates . . . and the international airlines also kind of knew me."

Among Kassin's clientele was the National Lawyers Guild, which traveled to South Africa to monitor the first re-elections after apartheid fell apart. He also handled United Methodist Church global missionaries' travel in Russia. John's trip to Kamchatka, though, proved quite the challenge, even for Kassin's well-connected network. "They arranged for this Russian ex-general to make all the arrangements for the trip," Kassin said. "I was just arranging plane tickets. Three days before the trip, they called and said, 'Steve, we've got a problem.' Well, the Russian guy hadn't come through and things were falling apart. Nobody had visas." The only way to get visas in 1993 was to fill out an application after you'd received an invitation from a Russian entity. The process involved visiting the consulate with passports, filling out all the forms, and taking three passport pictures. The former general had done none of this. Now, Kassin was being asked to do it all in the blink of an eye. Nearly a dozen travelers were scheduled to go on the trip, coming from a variety of spots across the U.S., including Jackson Hole, Telluride, and Boston. It would not be an easy fix.

Kassin had everyone send him their passports via Federal Express, while he completed their applications "to the best of my knowledge." He literally created an invitation from a Russian company that didn't exist, and "because I only had a few pictures, I actually had to make Canon color laser copies of passport pictures and cut them to size." Next, he was off to the Russian consulate in New York to present the papers he'd feverishly doctored. Their response: "Nah, this is no good." Kassin pleaded, "Listen, these are good people. They're going to shoot a ski movie and it's going to be great for your country." That worked. Kassin managed to get everything expedited and they all got their visas in time. The trip was on. "I don't think that would be possible today," Kassin said. "But the embassy guy was proud of his country, and knowing an American film crew was coming to feature it in a video made him feel good about issuing the visas."

Dan's passport was not among those Kassin FedExed back to their owners. In fact, he had no knowledge of the trip—until John and his fellow travelers realized they needed distribution for the scenes they were planning to film in Russia. And since Dan happened to be working on Egan Entertainment's latest film, *Return of the Shred-I*, would it not make sense to have him in the footage they planned to bring home? "They're all figuring it's going into *Return of the Shred-I*, because they're promising the Russians this distribution, which they would not have without my company," Dan said. "But they're not including me. They didn't invite me. They're getting visas, and I don't know a thing about it. All of a sudden, they realize the movie has got to go somewhere and they'd better get permission to put it in my film. So they finally ask, 'Can we get it in? Want to come?' And I said, 'No, thanks.'"

The way Dan recalls it, he was likely not invited because he and John's current girlfriend didn't speak to one another. Determined to play the role of John's manager, her viewpoint was that Dan was cheating John out of the limelight. But once Dan's invitation was finally made and turned down, John realized there might be a different reason for him passing on the trip: it would have been his first time back in Russia since the experience at Elbrus. John only had to look back to the previous summer to understand why Dan might not have been ready to make a return to the country where he'd nearly lost his life.

"I'm sure I wanted him to get over it. I think we had a pretty good relationship back then, so we probably talked about it more often. He didn't want any part of the trip to Kamchatka. He didn't want anything to do with it. That was probably part of the resentment, 'How can you go back to Russia after what the Russians did to us? How can you go on another trip without me? How can you make a film without me?' I'm sure there was all that," said John. Instead, Dan focused on another project he had lined up with Warren Miller, shooting for the director as a still photographer at the freestyle championships at Breckenridge, Colorado, that spring. That gave Dan another way to escape the headache of his brother's Russian trip, but he'd have more on his mind when he ended up blowing out his knee at the Breckenridge event. So, he returned to Denver, celebrating the inaugural season of its first Major League Baseball franchise. Dan was one of 80,277 in attendance to see the Colorado Rockies earn their first win, 11–4 over the Montreal Expos, on April 9, 1993. After the game, he got into his van and pointed the headlights east. Back to Boston. The journey gave him plenty of time to reflect. "I have to drive all the way home with a blown-out knee. My Peace Ski in Lebanon had been cancelled. My brother and those guys were in Kamchatka. I had to make this movie, which we'd promised to sponsor. I would have to have knee surgery again—for the third time in as many years. It was all a bummer."

Dan would continue work on *Shred-I* following knee surgery. This time, he worked with Blake Miller, a young filmmaker from Fort Collins, Colorado. Blake had made a series of films on his own; the two had met via the Resorts Sports Network, a television network of local cable stations in ski resorts around the country. "For *Shred-I*, I wanted and needed a more polished film," Dan said. "Blake's movies were really creative and fun, and I knew he would add a lightness and soulful feeling to the movie. *The Extreme Dream* was too dramatic. *Shred-I* needed to be more of a music video and adventure, less about The Egan Brothers."

After his surgery, Dan drove the van back out West, again following the blue highways. "The trips west to edit were always rejuvenating for me," Dan said. "I knew the journey would produce a transformation that would present itself in the movie-making process. And I needed a transformation. I was coming up on three years sober and I could feel a shift coming."

Shred-I hit the mark. Blake's influence, mixed with ripping footage of Eastern bump skiing from Sugarbush and Jay Peak, powder skiing in Crested Butte, the cliffs of Squaw Valley, the mysteriousness of skiing in Romania, and John's trip to Kamchatka made the film a vast improvement over Dan's first attempt. But, back at his parents' home in Milton by late summer, depression was following Dan around. The icy relationship between him and his brother continued. John and his girlfriend had planned other expeditions in his absence. In the midst of it all, though, Marlen planted a seed.

One morning, there was an ad from the Help Wanted section of that day's *Boston Globe*, cut out and waiting for him on the kitchen table. Ski 93 was looking for an executive director. "My mom was never one to interfere," Dan said, "but if anything in the newspaper ever said 'ski,' she'd cut it out. I'm sure this had a little more meaning than the normal ski article. There was a lot of turmoil, so, when I saw that ad, I wrote Ski 93 a letter." Joe Barossa, who was the marketing director at Loon at the time, called Dan upon receiving his application. "Dan, we have two hundred and fifty applicants for this job. Are you serious?"

Dan drove up in his Toyota van, which he'd been living in, for an interview. In 1994, New Hampshire was set to host the North American Ski Journalists Association's (NASJA) convention, and Ski 93's executive director had just quit, leaving the organization in need of raising $150,000 in sponsorship funds. They asked Dan if he could organize and sell the sponsorships for them, a process he was well-equipped to handle. It was right up his ski trail. So, out of 251 applicants, Dan's application the last to arrive, he got the job. Not that it didn't lead to some sly negotiating, on his part. In addition to a yearly salary, Dan asked for twenty-five percent of all the sponsorship money he raised, as well as sixteen weeks a year off to ski. Paid. They agreed to it all. A few months later, a Warren Miller crew showed up, with Decas and Gannett knocking on his door, to film Dan Egan in his new role.

Dan Egan has a job?

Any sense that Dan had settled down and succumbed to a mundane life behind a desk was whittled away immediately in the scenes he shot with Decas and Gannett. The Warren Miller people on location in New Hampshire suggested that the crew ride the famed Cannon Mountain tramway (the first of its kind to open in North America, in 1938) and jump from a suitable point, en route to the top of the mountain. But the weather was not cooperating and had left the tram enveloped in clouds, which was the norm at the Franconia Notch ski area in the White Mountains, but certainly not conducive to getting the shot. When the clouds finally did part that day, Ski 93's office manager, Jan Kotok, was left hanging out at trailside, wondering where everybody was. They were going to miss their window of opportunity to get the shot. "I called them up and said, 'Get your asses up here right now,'" she said.

In what would become one of the most iconic images in New England skiing history, Dan and Decas hopped a ride on the tramway's red car, nicknamed Ketchup. About halfway up the line, they pointed their skis out Ketchup's side door and leapt to the snow below. In the remainder of the segment, Dan, Decas, and Gannett took laps under bluebird skies until they were transformed by the white haze following them, all as Warren Miller narrates: "It makes no difference how long an icy-death Friday-night drive from the city is. When you get to Ski 93 and the snow is falling and there are no people, the reality of it is that you, too, can quit your job in the city and move to a ski resort. Nobody is stopping you but you."

That influenced a monumental shift in Dan's career. "I'm moving out of my van, into my first apartment in ten years," he said. "I hadn't lived in one town for more than twelve months in a long time. And now I've taken a desk job."

Breaking the news to John came with its own set of concerns, particularly in terms of who was going to handle The Egan Brothers' contracts and filming segments, a role which had been Dan's, with Egan Entertainment. It also required a semblance of humility on Dan's part. "Walking away, moving to Lincoln, New Hampshire, to help market Bretton Woods, Cannon, Waterville Valley, and Loon, when I'd been spending my career in Chamonix, was such a contrast," he said. Dan's own vertical reality, as it were, had planted new, unexpected roots.

The snow is never too deep for Joe Powder.

Photograph by Jen Bennett

Sometimes the snow is so deep you can't even see, like in this shot of Dan in Big Sky, Montana.

Chapter Thirty-three

PROMOTIONAL IDEA

A FEW MONTHS INTO HIS new gig with Ski 93, Dan's team wondered what they could do in terms of running promotions around the upcoming Olympic Games in Lillehammer, Norway. Bode Miller, the Franconia Notch native who'd grown up skiing at Cannon Mountain before attending Maine's Carrabassett Valley Academy, was only sixteen at the time. He wouldn't appear in the Winter Olympics for another four years, when they were held in Nagano, Japan. The U.S. Ski Team, meanwhile, was regarded as a lower-class citizen among the rest of the world's athletes. *Sports Illustrated*'s E.M. Swift famously characterized the U.S. team members as "soft as grapes" by comparison with their competitors. Then, Tommy Moe and Diann Roffe won gold in the men's downhill and women's super-G, respectively. Moe would add a silver in the men's super-G, and a twenty-two-year-old named Picabo Street would claim silver in the women's downhill, becoming the face of women's ski racing in the United States and paving the way for the likes of Lindsey Vonn and Mikaela Shiffrin. For the U.S. Ski Team, it didn't get much better in terms of proving critics wrong.

But, aside from Stoneham, Massachusetts, native Nancy Kerrigan, the figure skater at the center of the Tonya Harding fiasco, the 1994 Olympics was lean with talent from New England, which left Ski 93 and the state of New Hampshire trying to think outside their comfortable box in order to do something unique. Which led Dan's mind back to Romania.

He'd spent some time there the previous winter with John, Dean Decas, and Eric and Rob DesLauriers, shooting footage that would end up in both *Return of the Shred-I* and Warren Miller's 1993 film, *Black Diamond Rush*. This being Transylvania and all, the scenes naturally featured the likeness of Dracula (convincingly played by Decas) wandering through a snowy graveyard, as well as glimpses into life in the southeastern European nation, only four years after the execution of its Communist Party General Secretary Nicolae Ceaușescu. The civil unrest from the violent Romanian Revolution (more than a thousand people had died) led to economic reform and political changes which were only in their infancy when the Egans' cameras arrived. Of all the many locales John and Dan can include on their resumes, though, none was perhaps as life-altering as that trip to Romania—not for the rewards initially reaped, but for the seeds planted. Dan's initial thought, thinking back to Romania, was of running into an attractive Olympic skier who just might be what Ski 93 was looking for.

At that point, Mihaela Fera had already been to a pair of Olympic Games: in 1988 in Calgary, Canada, when she was only seventeen years old; and again, four years later, in Albertville, France. Her best finish was twenty-first in the women's combined at Calgary, which was to be expected based on the differences between Romanian Olympic training and the rest of the world's. She was the lone representative for her country on the Romanian Ski Team in both instances. "There were not many competing," Fera said. "We had a handful of kids and, for some reason, they always picked me to go." Fera's parents were both Romanian physical education teachers who encouraged their children to participate in their country's state-sponsored sports programs. Fera remembers the first time she went to the offices in her native town of Sibiu and told them she wanted to learn to ski. She received a pair of yellow skis with old bindings and leather boots.

Fera's parents didn't ski, but that didn't stop them from somehow teaching their children to handle skiing on little moguls—a skill that stuck with Mihaela, all the way to the Olympics. "She was a legend for all of us," said Radu Nan, a young Romanian ski racer who, within a few years, would train with Fera in the United States. "I didn't know any other name in skiing, international or local, besides Miki. She was it. I didn't care about anybody else."

The winter of 1993 was a low snow year in Romania. In fact, the crew almost didn't go on the trip, due to the lack of snow. However, with plane tickets booked, the Warren Miller contract in place, and time open in the schedule, the Egans and DesLauriers headed to Bucharest. Their first stop was Poina Brasov, the most popular ski area in Romania, one of its tram cars painted pink at the time.

When the Egans and DesLauriers arrived in Miki's neck of the woods, it wasn't as if Warren Miller's name was synonymous with skiing, in Romania. Thus, the brothers' exploits with a camera might not have been seen as anything notable. But, when Fera saw the small group of skiers dipping into the woods one afternoon in the Postavaru Mountains, she knew she had to follow. "I just saw these people having fun in the woods, which was like, wow," she said. "And then I just joined them." Despite a strictly-disciplined racing background, Fera was no stranger to the woods at Poina Brasov. "But they found different glades I didn't even know existed in my ski resort," she said. "I love tree skiing. Me and my friends, we would rip it up in the woods, bumps, and everything. But it was just a new group of people that were just really good skiers. I was probably one of the best skiers at the resort, and so having other people do the same, it was fun." It was also an eye-opening experience for the crew, many of whom later noticed Fera's training slope had gates made of tree branches. "We did have some racing gates," Fera told *Sports Illustrated* in 1994, "but we had to save them for races."

Fera, then a senior at Transylvania University, was skiing in hand-me-down boots, and owned only one pair of skis. Her pay for being the Romanian national ski champion was equivalent to forty U.S. dollars per month. In post-communist Romania, the level of training for the country's only winter Olympian didn't seem to be much of a concern. Fera's skills, on the other hand, did fall upon eyes that wondered what her ceiling might be, were she put into a proper training program. Fera might have cut her teeth on homemade gates, but she fired through them with impressive speed. After watching her prowess on the comp slope, the crew filmed her and later featured her in a segment in the movie. Her segment was edited to the sounds of the New England band, Buffalo Tom. The haunting lyrics, for example "I take one more breath it's worse than death," "I, I'm borderline almost every time," and "In my frozen mind I'm stuck in time," would foreshadow a turbulent time ahead for Dan.

"The segment was so good in the movie. Audiences at the ski shows were glued to it," Dan said. "The prospect of having Miki come to New Hampshire to train was addictive. I knew she would benefit from the training and the press would eat up her story." In 1994, Dan told *Sports Illustrated*, "I'll admit, I asked myself, Is this unpatriotic? But we all agreed that this is a country of opportunity, so we decided to bring her over here to train." Said Kathe Dillmann, then a spokesperson for Waterville Valley, "We thought this case unique, and her need very great. Putting her with our coaches was the least we could do."

Sponsoring Fera was a promotional idea for the Ski 93 Association of New Hampshire. "Waterville [Valley] said she could train there," Dan said. "We had the money from *Shred-I*, and Ski 93 put up the money for plane tickets and other stuff. She came over and trained for the Games and then left for the Olympics."

When Dan hit up his old friend, Mike Bisner, to ask if Salomon might want to sponsor an unknown Olympian, it didn't go without being questioned overseas. "The people from France were like, 'Who the fuck is this person and why are you sponsoring her?' And I did it only because of my relationship with Dan," Bisner said.

So, Dan secured a visa. "It was hard to travel on a Romanian visa," Fera said, "not as open to get a visa back then. Close to impossible." But Fera boarded a flight to Boston on Dec. 17, 1993, less than three months before the Winter Games were to begin in Lillehammer.

"All of this happened before we even knew how to track her down to tell her about the opportunity," Dan said. "Her athletic club was sponsored by the local police department, so eventually I got a phone number to the guard shack and they tracked her down in the barracks. We hadn't spoken to her since we'd filmed her. She remembered us, but was shocked at the opportunity."

Upon descending in Boston, Fera was struck by the lights stretching across the landscape ("a wonderful Disneyland"), the first real sign that she wasn't in Romania anymore. As for her first taste of the White Mountains, Fera said there wasn't much that felt out of place. It was definitely colder in New Hampshire, but other than that, "it was just mountains."

Dan told the *Boston Globe* that he believed Fera was "a rose in the woods which deserves attention."

Fera got right to work the day after she arrived, entering a North American Trophy Series Race, finishing eighteenth on new Salomon skis provided by Bisner. It was one of seven North American Ski Championship races she would compete in during her stay. "It was definitely something different," she said. "With the national team, we had a limited budget, nothing like the U.S. Ski Team, and we'd been training in other countries, including Italy. When Dan offered me this opportunity, I thought it was great. I was excited. In Romania, we were better gymnasts than we were skiers."

The weather didn't necessarily cooperate; Fera said it rained for the entire month she was in New Hampshire. In early January, the United States Pro Ski Tour agreed to let Fera enter a race at Wachusett Mountain, with the condition that, if she won any prize money, it would be donated to a nonprofit cause. Fera came in second after Roswitha Raudschl of Austria, a three-time world professional women's champion, earning $450 which she donated to the New Hampshire charity Nobody's Children, which supported orphans in Eastern Europe. "Nobody knew where she had come from," Kerry Metivier, spokesman for the Pro Ski Tour, told the *Globe*. "It was like a fairy tale."

On Jan. 25, 1994, Fera packed up and returned to Romania, then traveled to Lillehammer for the Games in February. "Our time together had been amazing," Dan said. "And then it was over and she was heading back to Romania. She joined me for a trip to Targhee for an X-Team Clinic with

John and the DesLauriers brothers before she left. Our conversation turned to what if she came back later in the year, and about a future together. Looking back, it seems crazy, but we were young and falling in love." It was something that slowly happened, Fera said. "We spent a lot of time together. I just felt like everything was new and exciting and a new chapter in my life. How things happen, it's always a mystery, right?"

The training in New Hampshire did little to make her a serious contender, but it was not expected to. Fera finished thirty-sixth in the Olympic women's downhill—thirty-four slots behind Picabo Street, and thirty-ninth in the super-G. But she was twentieth in the combined, her best finish in thirteen career Olympic races. "It was exciting and intimidating at the same time," she said. "Great opportunities for me, but I just took each one as another race. It was never my goal to make it to the Olympics. Little kids, sometimes they go, 'Oh, I want to make it to the Olympics.' I always wanted to beat the next person in front of me, or somebody that was . . . mean to me—I wanted to beat that person."

Later that spring, Dan headed back to Romania and returned a month later with Miki. In October, 1994, Dan and Mihaela were married. "Everything happens for a reason," Dan told *Skiing for Women* magazine. "The reason we both became skiers was to have a way to find each other. We're each other's gold medal."

For a while they were, at least. But some gold medals have a way of tarnishing.

Chapter Thirty-four

X-TEAM AND EXTREME COMPS

READE BAILEY WAS AT GRAND Targhee, staring down at the Toilet Bowl chute, envisioning himself as the "smartly dressed gent in his rowboat being repeatedly sucked down a watery vortex to meet his unknown fate," as he described in his story for *SKI Magazine*.

Luckily, Dan was by the writer's side with some advice: "If you fall, get your goggles off your face so they don't fill up with snow and blind you. Then get your feet below you. Know your options. Where are the rocks? Where are the trees?" Bailey made his descent, grunting loudly with each turn, swiveling his skis a dozen times or more. He encountered a five-foot drop-off, where the rock-lined chute narrowed to less than a ski's width before opening up again. "It's OK," Dan called, recognizing his apprehension. "Just pick your line and ski it." Bailey, noticing there was no turning back at this stage, flung himself off the ledge. He got twisted sideways as he landed, but managed to hang on. He didn't fall. Several more hop-turns, and he was at the bottom, where Dean Decas had videotaped the whole affair.

"Throughout my run, I remembered the most important thing I'd learned during this clinic," Bailey wrote, "the one skill crucial for any extreme skiing movie star or wannabe: I smiled the entire time." This was, ultimately, the goal of the Extreme Team Advanced Clinics, an idea Rob DesLauriers came up with in order to create a little bit of Vermont style and camaraderie between him, his brother Eric, and John and Dan Egan.

The brothers had started their pursuits together after meeting at Squaw Valley in 1989. "We really had a good, symbiotic relationship, all four of us, for quite a long time," John said. Rob had been studying hotel management at Cornell University, and was planning to take over the family business at Vermont's Bolton Valley ski resort after his graduation in 1987. Except, he ended up going out to Squaw Valley in the classic New Englander's "one winter" scenario, and quickly discovered he didn't want to come back so soon, after all. He and Eric quickly became known as The DesLauriers Brothers, which would become a marketing feature for The North Face Extreme Team, along with The Egan Brothers. After skiing in their first Warren Miller film, in 1990, Rob made the move back East to become Bolton Valley's director of marketing, because, as he put it, "What the hell, right? I was like, how can we get people to come to Bolton Valley because we skied in a Warren Miller movie?" Rob applied his skills and experience, gleaned from running tennis camps as a teenager at Bolton Valley, to running multi-day ski clinics for guests in the winter of 1991. He used his and his brother's Warren Miller fame to create an extreme skills camp at Bolton Valley; and seeing as John Egan was so close by, over at Sugarbush, concluded—why not run them together, with the DesLauriers and Egans? "People loved it," Rob said. The X-Team Advanced Ski Clinics expanded from their humble beginnings at Bolton Valley and were soon offered around the world, including locales such as Chile; Big Sky, Montana; Chamonix; Squaw Valley; and Jay Peak, Vermont.

John recalled the days when he was a tractor-trailer-driving ski bum for inspiration for his instruction. Back then, he'd had to deal with a whole variety of personalities, from the Newark docks to the back-country farms of

Pennsylvania and everything in between—that "navigating life" thing, as he put it. It didn't hurt that the Egan brothers were descendants of Grandfather Frederick Gillis's teaching mind—his lessons on how to teach and really listen helped John form an instructional bond on the slopes. "Almost every skier is going to walk up and tell you what they suck at," he said. "It's really a simple sport that is made so difficult by the intricacies of how to teach and the mechanics of it."

Dan agrees. "I'm always amazed by how skiers always tell me what they did wrong during a run. I immediately ask them, what did you do right, because that is what I saw."

Only occasionally would the clinics attract true "expert" skiers. More often, they were populated by spirited low- or aggressive-intermediates. "We really evolved our teaching techniques," Rob said. "We could transform anybody, but they ideally had to get off the groomed snow. It was a lot more about the spirit. Some people would show up with a little too much ego, and we would just chomp them down so quickly. It was beneficial because we had a platform beyond being a ski instructor. We would get super-wealthy guys and we'd treat them like dirtbag buddies and totally give them crap like they'd never gotten before. We had a great rapport with the people."

By 2001, the cost for their clinics had climbed to $985 per person. An instructor would earn somewhere between $1,500–2,000 a weekend. "Everyone's got a freak-out point," Dan boasted in a *Skiing* magazine advertisement for the clinics that November, kicking off what would be its eleventh season. "It's that point where fear takes over and you can no longer turn. And you bail out and stop." The X-Team clinics were designed to help skiers learn to identify their freak-out point and develop the skills necessary to reach beyond their fears, so they could make their next turns with confidence. As Rob once put it, the clinics were aimed at getting people to "push the fun-button they forgot existed." Skiers of all ages and abilities were welcome to join the fun, taking on steeps, powder, crud, bumps, couloirs, trees, and air. All coaching was done by the Egan and DesLauriers brothers, with rotating groups giving participants the chance to ski with each coach for at least half a day. Decas's videos would show the skills mastered and re-hash the sessions in which skiers might improve. To be clear, though, the clinics were not designed for participants to huck themselves off a cliff. Not until they were ready, that is.

"It was such a great concept and people loved it," Rob said. "And we were just having fun. It was just a raging party. We were so grateful for the opportunity, because it made no sense to think we could make a living skiing. Because nobody else was able to do that back then. We kept re-inventing ourselves to keep it going." At the center of the clinics' philosophy was a method of coaching that didn't hold back for fear of students becoming better than their teachers. That was not the point.

"We were really different in the ski world, in that we weren't hoarding information," John said. The combination was magical—a proper blend of technical instruction and Zen influence. "Each one of us could figure out a way to get to all forty of those people who showed up to learn that weekend," John said. "So maybe we didn't get to everyone, but we all got to at least one of them. So they all got this fulfilling experience. And it just worked." Several of the X-Team's clients ended up in movies, won contests, and became great world-class skiers and guides. "We could transfer the knowledge of how to ski to others in many different ways, so the combination of how we taught was really fantastic," John said.

The clinics were hailed as the first off-piste instruction of their kind in the world, introducing feelings of ease and non-competitiveness. *Skiing* magazine became a sponsor, giving the Extreme Team dedicated ad space and sending staff members to attend without charge, in exchange for the publicity. "The first clinic we ever had, we invited a bunch of writers," John said. "We had, like, two paying clients, and the rest were writers. We told the writers to be quiet. 'Don't tell anybody you're writing; we just want everybody to act natural.' They probably all knew each other anyway. Who were we fooling?"

But, with the Egan and DesLauriers names firmly ensconced in the minds of the general ski movie audience, the clinics quickly caught on. The crew promoted during their sixty film stops per year, at ski shows all over the country. "Our names were out there," John said. "We were in most major magazines, at least one magazine per month, for years on end. It was really a no-brainer. It would have been silly not to take advantage of our name recognition."

When personalities work together—athletes, musicians, mathematicians, what have you—with no egos getting in the way, it creates a flow state of ideas and inspiration. "Landing Apollo, none of those mathematicians could have done it on their own, but they worked at a higher level together, with no egos," John said. It was this combination of training and playing together that made the X-Team so successful in teaching. "We invited other ski guys to come in and coach, but we realized that it was a rare talent to be able to deal with clients," Rob said. "Both John and Dan have it. They're entertainers, they're funny, they're smart. They love skiing. We had a bunch of other people come in and guest-coach, but there's no way they could be at the same level that we were with people."

All told, the DesLauriers, Egans, and Decas combined to star in some hundred movies, and claimed two hundred first descents around the globe. Using their influence within The North Face camp would also create new destinations for the X-Team's clinics.

"We would tell Eric Perlman (the filmmaker in charge of The North Face's series of *Extreme Skiing* films) 'We want to go film in New Zealand.' So, we put together a clinic in New Zealand," Rob said. "We'd bring a photographer and cinematographer, go down and coach a camp for a week and stay for three or four more, filming a segment, doing stills. Anywhere we wanted to go, we started putting that together. We had a formula we could repeat anywhere."

Perhaps the coolest perk of all, according to Rob, was having season passes in Chamonix three years in a row. "Because we would just put the show together and show up with this group of clients who would infuse some money into the place," he said. "Then we'd stick around and film with writers and photographers in tow from different magazines. It was great." *Skiing* magazine writer Allen St. John detailed his experience at the clinic (as well as at another camp, Extreme Adventures, run by Scot Schmidt and partner Kim Reichhelm, at Crested Butte) in 1995, at Squaw Valley, describing the experience as "a guided tour. Squaw is the kind of place where, if you make a wrong turn, you can become a very funny story for the ski patroller who finds your body, say, in June. We would embark on these endless traverses that begged the question, 'Are we in Nevada yet?'"

As Dan once noted, mountaineering world legends aren't born, they're self-created. But being legendary didn't always mean going to the extreme. "What people need to learn is that, to get the rush that we got, you don't have to put yourself in a life-or-death situation every time," Decas said during an X-Team forum on ESPN2, in the mid-1990s. "That's just not the way it is. The rush is not just skiing something that's maybe dangerous or exposed. It's also just being in a different country."

Dan's first lesson with St. John was Terrain Recognition 101. "Look at the tree," Dan told his group, pointing to a small stand of trees at the bottom of a steep bowl. "It's a nice tree. It's a dead tree. It's kind of a lonely dead tree, sitting there among all the live trees." Dan's assignment for the students was to simply keep their eyes on the dead tree while making their turns down, letting gravity handle the rest.

"Lo and behold, I bounced, absorbed, and skied the damn thing," St. John wrote. "By the time I got up close and personal with the tree's decaying bark, I realized that my feet knew more about skiing than my PSIA-addled brain did."

According to John, the whole thing worked thanks to the eclectic mix of talents and approaches. "Eric, being so technical, and me on the other end, being Zen. Then with Dan and Rob mixing both of those in, the combination was magic," he said. "Each one of us could figure out a way to get to each of those people who showed up that weekend. So, they all got this fulfilling experience. And it just worked. It snowballed."

The X-Team Clinics came during a pivotal period for the extreme movement. ESPN's X Games were still a few years away, as was Red Bull's association with extreme sports. But, in 1991, the same year the clinics began, the World Extreme Skiing Championship made its debut in Valdez, Alaska. The idea came from Alaskan lodge owner Mike Cozad, a native of Colorado who first arrived in Valdez back in 1984, for commercial fishing. Cozad needed to do something big for the skiing world to take notice of Valdez and the heli-ski operation he'd built at his refurbished Tsaina Lodge. Up until that point, Valdez was known for little more, worldwide, than the Exxon oil spill in 1989. So Mike hosted an extreme skiing competition.

Glen Plake, Scot Schmidt, and Mike Hattrup, stars of Greg Stump's *Blizzard of Aahhh's*, served as judges the first year. "We knew it was Alaska and that it was insane up there, so [Cozad] had to work pretty hard at it," Scot Schmidt said. "He hammered me pretty good to get me up there." Ask many an extreme skier and they'll likely tell you the same thing: extreme skiing has never been about competition. It should never be about who's the best. Extreme skiing is creativity. It's about the expression of mountaineering and of skiing, and the mix of the two.

"I wasn't too interested in the contest," Schmidt said. "I don't really think contests are a great thing, because you're pushing people to do things on maybe the wrong day. I was really uncomfortable with the concept of competitions. It's dangerous enough. Then you start getting that Kodak courage, trying to get on the podium, pushing it too hard."

Dan was among those who was not a fan of the idea. "The promoters had been calling me for up to six months, asking me to compete. They were willing to cover our expenses and put us up if we entered. But I thought it was an assault on my career," he said. "There are limited sponsorship dollars in the industry, and we had a lot of them. Getting judged didn't seem like a good career move. Besides, if Plake and Schmidt weren't going to compete, why should I? The things we were doing and the places we were going were way crazier than Alaska—of a much higher consequence from a cultural point of view and a skiing point of view. We'd been skiing 'you fall, you die' locations in Baffin Island, the Arctic, the Alps, Russia, South America, Kamchatka, and Greenland. And none of that had anything to do with contests."

Of the thirty-seven skiers who competed that first year, the competition was won by Bedford, Massachusetts, native Doug Coombs, a thirty-three-year-old who was a fixture in the extreme scene in Jackson Hole, Wyoming. But the contest took away what should have been at the center of the extreme skiing mindset: the relationship between person and mountain, an interaction with nature that is built on respect, not prestige.

"Extreme is you and the mountain, me and the mountain; it's a personal thing," John said. "If you make it a contest, first of all it's really not extreme, seeing as there are safety people there. There are helicopters to bring you up. That's not some remote mountain that you climbed and scaled and figured out how to get down safely. That's not extreme. That's a contest to see who's the best skier."

Schmidt's fear that somebody was going to get hurt didn't happen over the first two years of the competition, but in 1993, Steamboat Springs skier Wilbur Madsen would become the World Extreme Skiing Championship's first casualty, when the twenty-eight-year-old wandered too close to a roped-off area and fell to his death when the cornice broke away.

"A body started bouncing off jagged rocks, and just tumbling down the hill," John Woodbury, owner of Alaska Adventure Media and *Coast* magazine, told the *Anchorage Press*. "After about six hundred feet of rocks and tumbling, the body started sliding head first, leaving a red stain of blood in its wake. It slid perhaps another five hundred feet before coming to a halt." Madsen had a peak near Valdez named in his honor.

"The contest in Alaska has pushed the sport to absurdity," Warren Miller told the *New York Times* in 1993. "They've taken something that's very much a free-form, totally individual experience and turned it into a competition of one-upmanship. That's not what it's all about."

Another competition, the U.S. Extreme Freeskiing Championships, began at Crested Butte in 1993, and organizers asked John to be one of the judges. They wanted big names for the judging, so skiers would feel they were being judged by those who understood the process. While John was impressed with the skiing he watched, he was left wondering about the participants' true purpose. "I would never want one of these guys on my team in Russia or climbing in Romania," he said.

That version of extreme sometimes had a difficult time translating to a younger generation, who attempted to be extreme in everything. The '90s brought a new wave of extreme athletes, each trying to one-up the other in terms of jaw-dropping feats. Shane McConkey was chief among them, a product of Burke Mountain Academy who went on to a professional skiing career that included death-defying BASE jumps. McConkey finished second at the World Extreme Skiing Championships in 1994, and took top honors at the U.S. National Freeskiing Championships the next year. He was one of the winners who ended up coaching with the Extreme Team, giving instruction at a level of extreme likely not in the same handbook as the founders of the clinic. Soon, McConkey's stunts were no longer death-defying: he died in 2009 while attempting a ski-BASE jump in the Italian Dolomites. During the jump, one of McConkey's skis failed to release, sending him into a spin. Once corrected, it was too late to deploy his parachute.

"It took my whole life to hone the skills I have on the hill," John said. "I didn't have time to learn how to BASE jump, or kayak, or any of that stuff. Some would say that, now, they can train at a heightened level all year, which is good for your athleticism and root-finding and staying calm in tough situations. But you can do that mentally, without putting yourself in a new danger."

That was the scene on March 29, 1993, when twenty-eight-year-old Paul Ruff, a former cliff-jumping record-holder who'd fallen short to Coombs in the 1991 competition at Valdez, seemed intent on making a statement. He invited a group of friends—including Gary Nate and Robby Huntoon—and photographers to a backcountry butte near Kirkwood Ski Resort in California, where he planned to find two hundred feet of air—the largest cliff jump anyone had ever attempted.

As Alex Markels recounted in the *Los Angeles Times*, "At a little after 11 a.m., the sun poked through the clouds scudding over Thimble Peak and Ruff gave the signal, pointed his tips downhill, and skied for the drop-off. But just before he reached the edge, he turned suddenly to his right—perhaps a line readjustment, maybe a too-late premonition—then shot into space. By the time he was halfway down, he was moving so fast that the photographers watching through their viewfinders had lost sight of him. Their cameras, however, caught the sequence. One, equipped with a motor drive that could reel off four photos per second, captured sixteen frames from the edge of the cliff to the bottom. In the first five, Ruff was in fine form—a loose, cannonball tuck. But by the sixth, he began to lose it. He waved his arms in wide swoops, trying to keep himself in balance. Two frames later, he was falling back-first. In the twelfth shot, he slammed into the rocky outcropping and bounced thirty feet in the air, his skis exploding off his heels and his limbs flailing. His momentum carried him down the hill, where he landed on his back, sliding head-first another hundred feet." Ruff crashed on his back on solid rock. He died an hour later.

"That kid just didn't have that in him," John said. "He'd be like, 'Well, I'm going to climb five feet higher and jump further.' That was his attitude. And I never had that attitude, like, I'm going to beat that guy. That's why I didn't like racing. I'm going to go faster than you, jump higher, it was always like what can I do, not how can I beat that last kid who might get in a movie if I don't jump bigger. I think that's what kept me alive for all those years, for sure. There are a lot in that category with Paul Ruff and you see it with McConkey and half of that whole crew there. It's just something you know. I don't know how you know it. I know people can feel it when you're around. If you play on the edge, you're going to slip off of it a few times. One or two of those are going to be really bad. One could be the end. So, how long do you play at that level?"

The basis for deciding winners has further blurred the actual modern equivalent of winter sports. "If you look at the competitions now, kids aren't extreme skiing," Dan said. "They're extreme flipping, they're extreme traversing, but they're not skiing the fall line. It's just radical stuff. So, trying to figure out who's best is more for publicity and marketing reasons, rather than for the pureness of the sport."

It was the beginning of what John classified as "too much extreme." But it wasn't like the X-Team clinics discounted the Extreme Championships in Valdez. The winner of each year's competition would have the opportunity to be a guest coach the following year with the Egans and DesLauriers. But it wasn't always a success. "We've got all these young kids who look up to us and want to be working with us," John said. "Hardly any of them could transfer the knowledge of skiing to someone else. All they could do was show off. Some of the biggest names out there just sucked at sharing it with other people. They didn't like teaching it, or they thought they liked it but they weren't good at it. The clients were like, 'All they do is show . . . we can't ski like that. We want to know how to get there.' So, that program didn't work out well."

The World Extreme Championships were held in Valdez through 2000. They were relaunched for one year in 2011, but interest never really caught back on. Similar events continue in one form or another all over the skiing map today, though, whether it be X Games, Red Bull, or some other sponsorship competition. John's son, Johnny, is a regular on the circuit, and even his father, one of the most renowned extreme skiers of his generation, is in awe of what accounts for competition. "Unless you're throwing double back flips off of sixty-footers, you're not even competing," John said. "And no one in their right mind in an extreme situation would throw a backflip in the middle of a remote area and think, 'this is a good idea.'"

The Extreme Team clinic was more known for teaching how to control the extreme nature of the sport. They taught skiers how to have fun on the mountain without ever really putting themselves into the jaws of risk-taking. Dan's nephew, Steve Curry, took part in the clinics at Big Sky, Montana, and Jay Peak, Vermont. "Those things were packed, and it was the most fun you could have on skis," Steve, the thirty-seven-year-old son of Dan's oldest sibling, Mary-Ellen, said. "I think they would have had just as much fun sitting in a hotel lobby talking for eight hours instead of skiing, because they were comedians and world-class personalities. It was so infectious to be around them."

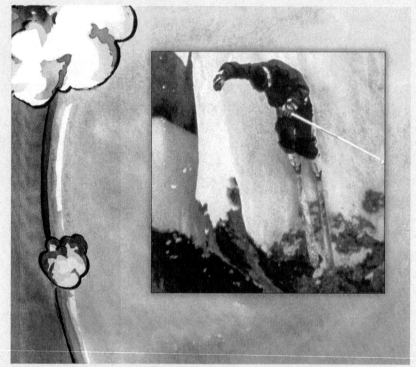

Photograph by Wade McKoy

In our minds eye,
we can relive our best runs
and ignite our inner Joe Powder.

Chapter Thirty-five

THE END OF NEVERLAND

SKI MAGAZINE'S READE BAILEY RECOUNTED an afternoon bump session with Dan during his 1992 visit to Targhee. Up to that point, Dan had already led the group through a series of "tough and sometimes bizarre drills on groomed trails."

Dan hadn't finished with the offbeat instruction, yet was telling the clients to unbuckle their boots and surrender their poles. "Skiing with your boots unbuckled will help you find a balance point," he said.

Bailey wrote that he felt naked. "I make three turns and a stop, feeling awkward and sloppy. I realize how dependent I am on my poles for balance and my snug-fitting boots for precise control. By the end of the run I'm feeling more comfortable and I stop cursing Dan under my breath."

The real breakthrough came a few runs later, when Dan handed the poles back and allowed everybody to re-buckle their boots. As a result, Bailey's turns now felt "staccato-quick," and he noted that, now it would "take an NFL linebacker" to knock him off-balance.

"The hard part of being a coach was thinking about your own skiing and then trying to teach it," Rob DesLauriers said, "because it does mess with your skiing to think about it and to try and analyze it. It was hard for (the contest winners) to sort of check their egos at the door and yuk it up with these guys and give them good information. We needed a balance of our humor and structure."

It wasn't just the ski instruction that resonated from the lessons. It was about learning an approach to problem-solving and how you approach your life. The clinics would sometimes "lose their balance," not necessarily due to lack of interest from paying customers, but from the organizers themselves. Teaching group after group, week after week, would become grueling and tiring. "It was complicated to put it all together and have it flow smoothly, but that's like any hospitality art," Rob said. "You go and have a meal in a restaurant, you don't realize what it takes to get that meal on the table."

It became harder for the group to travel together as life took over their off-snow agendas. John would sacrifice the clinics for other gigs that paid better. Rob became busy developing a hotel in Jackson Hole. Eric found other sources of revenue in Squaw Valley. It all led to a great deal of frustration for Dan, trying to make sure the clinics stayed relevant. "Dan felt like he was putting in a lot of work that we weren't showing up to for," John said. "And we weren't. We'd maybe show up to one this year, two the next, so we all kind of maybe outgrew them." Which left Dan trying to pick up the pieces.

"I sensed that everything came very easy for John, and that Dan had to work really hard to get the same recognition," Dan's wife, Miki, said. "But I think Dan worked a lot harder. He did more for that Extreme Team that nobody knew. He was the man behind everything. I always felt like he was the mastermind behind everything—the trips, organizing people. He just created stuff out of nothing."

Despite re-inventing themselves each year in order to keep the clinics fresh, things eventually fizzled out. Dean Decas embraced the teaching lifestyle, leading to a lifetime of coaching work which he continues today in Chamonix. But John said he saw a different opportunity in the world to parlay his ski bum career into . . . well, a career. "Seeing the possibility of ski-bum jobs, and being an old ski bum, the writing was on the wall," he said.

"Things were moving and shaking and it was time to move on from that. You can't stay in it too long."

Of course, the clinics kept Dan on the road for long stretches of time, often without his wife, Miki, who was doing her own training. "He really wanted to see her career progress," Ski 93's office manager, Jan Kotok, said. "But they were apart a lot in winter." Those frequent separations would lead to their union beginning to crumble.

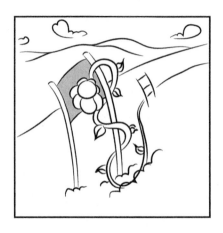

Chapter Thirty-six

MY FLOWER WILTED

DAN EGAN IS NOT A good golfer. At least, that's according to his nephew, Steve Curry, who noted that Dan will step up, take a full rip at the ball, then watch as his shot winds up as a dribbler that only manages to travel about twenty yards from the tee. It's the sort of scene where one might expect a violent reaction, like launching the offending driver into the woods. But such a response is not part of Dan's golf game. "Instead of reacting frustrated or poorly, he'll say, 'Well, it went forward,'" Curry said. "'It's closer to the hole than it was before.' He has a level of optimism that most people don't have. He's tenacious, and that's what made him a world-class skier. I don't think he's a world-class athlete. But I think he willed himself into that due to his mental strength."

That demeanor, however, was about to go through its most turbulent phase, a period during which his commitments would be tested and, in some instances, would end up shredded or broken.

Being married hit all the things Dan needed in life. He felt like he'd won the lottery. He started thinking ahead and was more grounded. It also kept him busier than he was used to. In addition to his participation in the X-Team Advanced Clinics, Dan was busy with his work for Ski 93, putting together an international marketing program for the state of New Hampshire, and running TV's *Wild World of Winter*. Married life brought the ensuing chaos to a boil.

"Being busy was fine," Miki said. "In between was hard, not knowing what to do." On the rare occasions when she traveled with the X-Team Clinics, Miki didn't do any coaching. However, there was still a role she and Dan had begun, hosting a variety of couples-only clinics throughout the years. "That was fun," she said. "I liked that project. I believed what Dan believed. Couples can teach each other how to ski. We split them and then brought them together."

"Dan and Miki might ski like gods, but they're not hardcore or pushy" according to Nathaniel Reade, who, along with his wife, Michaela, took part in the clinic in 1999, at Big Sky Resort in Montana. The *SKI Magazine* writer was left impressed by how his skiing-weary wife went from, in Dan's words, "Oh, no," to "Oh, yeah." Reade also ran into Mike "the Pipe" Nelson, a veteran of fifteen previous Egan clinics, who explained why he was a repeat customer. "At the end of the week, the muscles that hurt the most are the ones you use to laugh," he said. There was plenty of laughter in Miki and Dan's off-snow relationship, for a long stretch.

And while Dan was busy with clinics, running Egan Entertainment, and promoting Ski 93, Miki's racing career continued. She won the 1998 Women's Pro Tour GS World Championship and was coaching at the New England Mountain School, a refuge for young Romanian skiers Dan helped fund.

"I learned Romanian so I could speak with her parents, relatives, and all the visitors to our home," Dan said. "Miki had a lot of friends who wanted to come to America. We brought over twelve Romanian kids, over the course of three to four years. That was, effectively, the Junior Romanian Olympic team. One by one, we placed those kids with families. Those kids got to go to school—Northampton, Holderness, Plymouth State, Keene, New England College. They were rock-star kids, great athletes, super-smart, and committed. The community thought it was a great program and really stepped up. Everybody went to bat for these kids. Hosts were covering day-to-day costs and schools were giving them full scholarships."

New England Mountain School wasn't the only place where international relations was taking place in the New Hampshire skiing community. In England, Dan had noticed a ripe market for promoting the sport of skiing stateside. Rather than skiing in the Eastern Bloc, Bulgaria, and Romania, Dan figured it was worth showing them what sorts of inexpensive vacations they could discover on the other side of the pond. "Killington and Stowe really started the program," Dan said. "Then it spread throughout New England, so New Hampshire got involved, then Sunday River. The regional associations were hugely successful with it and, at Ski 93, we had the beds, and the ski areas were close. It was one of the most successful international marketing programs the state had ever done. Bernie Weichsel had organized SKI USA, a marketing group that attended the biggest ski shows in the UK, Germany, and the Netherlands. The New England resorts, represented by the regional associations, featured their hotels, attractions, and resorts—and that, combined with easy access and proximity to Boston's Logan International Airport, made New England a popular destination for both youth and adult groups from overseas. We had these roots in England, so we started training British racers. We funneled them into the New England Mountain School, and focused on international kids, mainly Romanian and English."

Miki's sister, Roxanne, was living in New Hampshire, as well. She came over for the wedding and didn't want to return home. "Roxy lived with us right from the beginning, and we got her enrolled in a community college, then, eventually, Keene State University in New Hampshire," Dan said. "That was an expense I hadn't anticipated. But for Miki to be with family, I didn't think twice about it." The Egan's house in New Hampshire was a lively spot. "Our home was busy," Dan said. "We had the Romanian Junior Ski Team coming and going, Miki's sister, as well as their cousin. My brother Mike was a liftie at Loon Mountain and living with us. We had a roommate to help with the mortgage, Miki was on the World Pro Tour, I was traveling the world and holding down a full-time job."

And there were Miki's parents to consider. "For my parents to come here, that was like traveling to the moon," Miki said of the overwhelming transition. "For them, it was like I was going to die somewhere far away."

"We would head to Romania each spring," Dan said. "We'd spend three or four weeks there, and eventually started to bring the folks back with us for the summer. They were great around the house; we had an amazing garden and the meals were over the top. But we also had a lot of personal dynamics bubbling up." Certainly, living in America was a transition difficult to explain to Romanians who were just experiencing their first steps in life out from behind the Iron Curtain of the U.S.S.R. But the change was also hard on Miki, who didn't easily mesh with her new life in America.

"I think it was very hard to adapt to life here," Miki said, "because I felt like, [in Romania] I lived in the city, but here I felt like I had cut my roots and it was really, really hard for me to have no friends, no one to talk to. I was very social in my other life, in Romania. I liked having different relationships with different people. And I didn't have anything like that here. It was really hard."

Dan used the example of a trip to the grocery store as an illustration of her being overwhelmed and confused about the complexity of it all, especially for somebody who'd never had so many options, back in her country. "If I said, 'Go grab some olive oil,' well, there are twenty choices and prices," Dan said. "She would buy a little bit at a time and not know what anything cost. Embarrassed by that, she'd go sit in the parking lot for a bit, and then go back in and buy some more stuff. I could never figure out why she spent half a day shopping. She probably didn't have a voice in how to express that. When she first came to ski here she didn't even know what an ATM was."

There was always the intention of having children and raising a family together. They even had names picked out, but they never got to use them. "Miki was having success on the tour," Dan said. "She was sponsored, they were giving us cars, she was winning prize money and learning how to live in this county. But, in hindsight, she probably didn't give a shit about the career. We probably would've had kids right off the bat, but I was thinking economically: let's build a career now, so we can bank on it moving forward." That plan got sidetracked in 1998 after the World Pro Tour went bankrupt, leaving Miki without a professional platform for her skiing career. To make matters more difficult, Ski 93 let Dan go after a five-year stint, leaving the couple without the steady incomes which had carried them through the first four years of their marriage. "I did the only thing I knew how to do, which was create something," Dan said. "I had the television show, I had the clinics. I started consulting to resorts on international marketing and I published my first book, *All-Terrain Skiing*, with Miki. I was pretty busy. In my mind, busy providing. I think somehow that got misunderstood. I think she just thought I was too busy. Miki never knew what it was like to go to work. She never had to work, because she was a state-sponsored athlete in Romania. The winnings from the tour came easy. But going to work, getting a job? That was a different deal."

It was difficult for Miki to find her place in her new American life. "I know Dan encouraged me," she said. "I always had him up there on the pedestal. He was this person who was always creating something. And I felt like I could never keep up. It was always a change. For me, I needed more stability. I think that kept me unsettled. We did buy a house together, but I had no idea if I would have an income. I never worked, because I was racing. I could never get a job. I was, maybe, too dependent on him."

In Dan's mind, he and Miki had it all, including the farm in Romania where her parents lived, where they visited every spring. They had community in the U.S., she had Romanian friends and her sister. "We had a full American life, but it became a culture clash, I think," Dan said.

Slowly, Miki and Dan each started to see the future differently. "I think that's how we kind of separated," she said. "We didn't have common things." Her focus shifted from athlete to coach, and the New England Mountain School was picking up steam. Miki, the World Pro Ski tour champion and Olympian was the face of the school, Dan was the money and the motivation, and then there was Gus DeMaggio, a former college racer who ran ski clubs at the local mountains. He'd coached Miki over the last few years on the tour and was a partner in their ski academy. He had the knowledge and the connections at the ski areas, and had run summer camps at Oregon's Mount Hood and in Europe. His wife was the USSA race official and ski club administrator.

Dan said it was hard to figure out when the shenanigans between Miki and Gus DeMaggio began. "His wife and I were the last ones to know, to be honest," Dan said. DeMaggio and Miki were running the New England Mountain School together, and their relationship soon morphed from coach-athlete into a romance that split up both of their marriages. Dan remembered noticing a few things that weren't adding up, but assumed Miki was having a hard time trying to manage everything. She wouldn't answer the phone while she was in Europe, and there were other telltale signs that things were not right. "I'd started to check the voicemails on her phone," Dan said. That snooping led to a message from DeMaggio that sealed the deal: An "I love you" which explained everything.

"The gig was up," Dan said. "I was the one who told Sharon, Gus's wife. She was in complete denial. 'Dan, you're always causing problems.' Gus and Miki pitted Sharon and me against each other. Gus always talked to his wife about me being a pain in the ass and over-controlling, and Miki always told me Sharon was a bitch. So, there was no relationship between me and Sharon." The fury Dan felt was like nothing he'd ever experienced. "It would have killed a mere mortal. It's a miracle I'm not in jail. Jealousy made me do a lot of things I'm not proud of. I was gutted and not ready to give up—I loved her, I had geared my life around her and was at a loss as to how we'd ended up here," stated Dan. But, for all the frustration and anger Dan was left to sift through, one thing he didn't turn back to was drugs and alcohol, a true example of the uncommon mental strength Curry had said was one of his uncle's most endearing traits.

"How'd I get through it? I don't know if I ever really did," Dan said. "It took years to get over that. I stayed close with my sobriety and my sober friends. My friends and the community wrapped their arms around me. There was the wife of another ski coach who lived nearby—I'd see her at church; she started sitting a pew behind me, and would smile and embrace me each Sunday and tell me things would be OK. I guess that's how you get through hard times when you don't know what to do. You let other people hold you up."

Dan's parents would get in the car and make the trip north to New Hampshire, just to make sure their son was all right. "It was painful, because it was so painful for him," Marlen said. "We loved the girl. She had found another skier. And she just left Dan cold. I think it's in him to be busy all the time. He'd have been a great father if he were around. I feel bad that he's not married with kids. He looks at the rest of the family, with their kids, and maybe he is jealous, I'm sure. But he doesn't say much."

The Romanians at New England Mountain School found themselves stuck in the middle, between what one student had once called "the ideal skiing family." "To see them unravel, you start to question why these things come apart," student, Radu Nan, said. "It was confusing to understand why it didn't work, but I wouldn't inform myself—I stayed away from the stories. You don't want to hear those things. You want your ideal image to continue to work in your mind. You do not question it. You say, well, it's not that bad. It's just confusing."

Dan's brother, John, called him every day for a year to give his support, even though he'd never truly understood Dan's marriage. "It seemed like Miki had been his new project," John said. "I don't know if he thought that whole marriage thing through. At all. I just don't think they had a deep enough relationship that warranted a marriage. I think they thought that would show up at some point. Maybe she saw a ticket out of Romania to America. And I think she probably wanted a simple life, skiing a lot. I don't think anybody was surprised that it didn't work out. Nobody was happy about it. We all wanted the best for him and they seemed like a great couple together. Both loved skiing and whatever, but I think they got different things out of it, perhaps."

According to his friend, and Warren Miller cameraman, Tom Grissom, Dan could definitely get down in a funk in the years that followed the divorce. "I'd always just try to lift him up," Grissom said. "I really felt that was something I was uniquely qualified to do, just because of our relationship. And I don't feel like I'm a great motivational speaker, like Dan is, but if I could just be there for him and let him complain to me, then hopefully we were able to move through it together. During that time, he would always put on the best face, for skiing and for the show. John, myself, and people who were traveling with him would see him at some low points. But when showtime came, he was always right there and ready to go."

Miki had always figured she and Dan would be long-term, and kids were part of the plan. There was no way she thought that was not going to happen. "Looking back, I do believe things happen for a reason," Miki said. "I'm just sorry that I had to hurt a person. Not had to, but I did. I pretty much ran away because I couldn't deal with the guilt to begin with. It wasn't easy to make the break from Dan. That's for sure."

Today, Miki and Gus are married with children of their own. Both work in the racing program at Bretton Woods Resort, in northern New Hampshire. Those are about the only particulars Dan knows about their lives. That's enough for him. "People always want to tell me about Miki and Gus," he said. "I don't really care. I know what I know. I'm happy Miki has a family, whatever that is. I'm sad I was never able to do that myself, but I have nothing to be ashamed of. I made it through that time without killing anybody." Through it all, Dan has said he still has compassion for Miki, convinced that she was manipulated in her new relationship and didn't know how to break free. But that has been left in hiding ever since. "I think, possibly, that the mistake I made was that I gave her choice," Dan said. "I always said, 'You choose. You pick. You can do whatever you want.' She didn't know how to do that. She'd been told her whole life—since the fifth grade—what to do. She was born and bred to be a ski racer. Gus stepped in. He's controlling and told her what to do. I think that felt familiar to her. Because of the commitments of the ski academy we ran with him, I would unknowingly put her back in situations she didn't know how to control."

Nearly twenty years have passed now, and Miki says she has never stopped feeling guilty over her affair. "I would probably find peace only if I knew that he forgave me," she said. "I was too immature and I caused him deep pain. I am still sorry for it."

From Dan's perspective, meanwhile, the focus is on the dream he lost, the one of creating his own family, which he's realized he had to let go of. That's not easy for someone who envisions certain steps in life and then works feverishly to make them come true.

"Miki was my wife. I never wanted her to leave. I don't think she understood the 'til death do us part' bit," Dan said. "The frustration of that dream not coming true has haunted me. Because I am almost always able to achieve it. The last years of our marriage were like watching a beautiful flower wilt. She was so consumed with the guilt that she couldn't be present. She would put her fingers on her forearm and pluck at the little hairs for hours. I could never figure out what was wrong with her. She just wilted. When people ask me today what happened to my marriage, I just say, 'My beautiful flower wilted.'"

Chapter Thirty-seven

10E

IT TAKES ANYWHERE BETWEEN FOURTEEN and fifteen minutes to ride the Eclipse double chairlift to the summit of Tenney Mountain in New Hampshire. As Dan once promoted it, it was the longest, slowest lift in the Northeast. That, mind you, was a positive attribute. Because, for all the complaining visitors might do about the lift, there were very few grumblings upon reaching the top of the mountain, where skiers and riders were greeted by a roaring fire and served hot chocolate with marshmallows. "They were transported and transformed, from the bottom to the top," Dan said. The same sort of dramatic transformation rang true for Dan, as well, during his two-year stint as Tenney's general manager.

In trying to save his marriage, which, by this point, was crumbling, Dan pursued a full-time job with Tenney Mountain, a ski area close to home, which hadn't had the most stable history. Sam Hall, a veteran of the 10th Mountain Division, the famous infantry formed to handle extreme mountainous conditions during World War II, had returned from the war to expand Tenney's trail system beyond its lone Edelweiss Trail, which had been developed in the 1930s. The Plymouth ski area opened in 1960, just as a handful of other resorts were starting to pop up in the White Mountains. The '80s brought periods of instability during various expansions of the ski area, and in 1989 Tenney was forced into bankruptcy and closed. It reopened under new ownership in 1991, was rebranded in 1992, and ultimately shuttered again until 1996. It was placed on the market again in the year 2000, and failed to open for the 2001–02 season.

In the fall of 2002, another new owner took over. In an effort to promote its unique snowmaking technology, dubbed SnowMagic, a Pennsylvania-based company purchased Tenney, promising to make significant investments, including snow independent of temperature, making ritual snow dances a possibility no matter what time of the year. SnowMagic's president, Albert Bronander, first saw warm-weather snowmakers while working as a consultant in Japan in the '80s. Skier Yoshio Hirokane came up with a way to make snow in warmer temperatures, and called the process Infinite Crystal Snowmaking. Whereas typical snowmakers require twenty-eight degrees Fahrenheit (because sprayed water droplets must freeze before hitting the ground), the ICS system reversed that process. Water was instead frozen into thin sheets inside an ice house, then crushed into tiny pieces and shot onto the mountain. The system cost between $400,000 and $1 million, but promised to deliver up to fifty tons of snow every day—enough to withstand even summer heat.

Dan needed a place to "auger in," as he put it, and hoped the steady job might help save his marriage. He signed on to become Tenney's new general manager during its time of ownership transition in September of 2002. SnowMagic's promise to make snow was the dawn of a new technology, and it needed a front man to handle what it figured would be a big draw to New Hampshire skiing. Dan's hope was that he could take on that role while Miki took over the ski school operations, giving the couple another way to work together and heal the wounds which had surfaced in their relationship. At the time, there were only two other employees on staff: an office manager, and a guy called Moyt, Tenney's longtime head of operations.

Dan met Moyt during his first day on the job, as he sought to learn how to handle certain functions at the ski area. Moyt introduced himself and pointed to his hand, where his name was spelled out in tattoo. Just so he wouldn't forget it. Realizing Dan's seeming lack of knowledge after showing him how to turn on the lights and how the pump ran, Moyt asked, "Have you ever done anything like this before?"

"No," Dan said.

"Huh," Moyt replied. "Sure would be nice if you knew more." Despite Dan's newness, in only four months he helped the ski area, which had been closed for two years, add snowmaking (using "the world's smallest snowmaking pond"), fixed the lifts and electricals, and managed to open for business on Dec. 12, 2002—the earliest opening in the history of Tenney Mountain.

Moyt, for one, couldn't believe it. It also struck him as odd when the general manager came to him and asked to be taken to the top of the hill on a snowmobile. Dan wanted to take a run before the mountain's official opening, to sample what he and the crew had accomplished. "By yourself?" Moyt asked with an air of incredibility. Dan assured him he'd be fine taking a stab at Tenney's fourteen-hundred-foot vertical drop. "Oh, right," Moyt said, "you skied the *Him-a-lie-ays*."

It ended up taking a whopping thirty days to make enough snow for top-to-bottom skiing with Tenney's limited snowmaking system. At other resorts today, in the right temperatures, that can be accomplished in less than a week. "I was so green, I didn't know anything," Dan said. Tenney had never run more than sixteen snow guns at any one time, and Dan quickly learned that, in order to open the mountain from the summit, it would take nearly double that number.

It was through a marketing connection at Wachusett Mountain, which sponsored *Wild World of Winter* on NESN, that Dan hired Rich Satagaj, a veteran employee of a handful of New England ski areas, including Sugarbush and Connecticut's Mount Southington, to help teach him the snowmaking process (he hired the whole family, actually: Satagaj's daughter to work in marketing and his wife to run the ski area's food and beverage operations). Satagaj had been the general manager at Powder Ridge Ski Resort, in Middletown, Connecticut, where snowmaking posed its own share of complications in the fickle winter temperatures of southern New England. "He didn't want to be in charge," Dan said. "He wanted to be a ski area guy and get this thing done." Satagaj helped Dan lay the groundwork for the snowmaking Tenney needed to become a serious player on the local skiing map. That meant getting the right crew in place—a challenge in itself.

"To get a good snowmaking guy—a chief who can run a crew at night and keep them together, keep them happy—it's a miserable job," Satagaj said. "You've got to have some kind of love for skiing."

The pursuit of better snowmaking also meant the need to secure snowmobiles and snowcats for grooming purposes. No problem, Dan thought, placing a call to Bombardier, a Canadian corporation known, in part, for its line of winter-terrain vehicles. "How much do those groomers cost?" Dan asked. "I'm going to need a couple. Oh, and I need about six or seven snowmobiles, too." The Bombardier rep on the other end of the line was a bit taken aback by Dan's hyperactive ordering.

"Tenney Mountain?" he asked. "Are you guys even open?"

"Yeah, we're going to open," an over-exuberant Dan told him, still hoping to figure out how much this order was going to cost. Instead, the rep led Dan through the process of how ski areas normally lease these sorts of vehicles. "People don't just buy stuff like that," he told him. He offered to get Tenney a couple of used cats and see where things went from there, allowing Dan and the mountain to ease into securing equipment instead of purchasing a new fleet, which could have put them in a financial hole. It was another step in the learning curve the new general manager had to figure out. "I was like, where's the menu, you know?" Dan said.

Beyond the snowmaking, Dan was instrumental in handling other aspects of the business with which he was more familiar, namely, securing sponsorship. He landed a huge one with Coca-Cola, as well as with a local Subaru dealer, which netted vehicles for the mountain's use. The mountain also gave Dan an outlet to share the sport, once again, with his family. His father joined a crew of fellow retirees helping out in the parking lot, while his siblings would come visit to check out what Dan had managed to accomplish. Dan's sister, Mary-Ellen, a staunch defender of her rear-entry boots and non-shaped skis, made one such visit during that winter's February break. "Don't bring anything," Dan told her. "I'm going to set you up with new boots, new skis, the works." With that, Dan was off to put out some fires, such as the lift that had broken down, leaving a line of frustrated skiers. In the midst of it all, he got a call on his radio. It was Mary-Ellen. "The equipment sucks. I fell down. I hate shaped skis . . ."

"And she's yelling at me," Dan said. "I'm the fucking general manager getting yelled at by my own sister. Whoever gave her the radio is fired," he quipped. There was more than a minor jab in that last threat, as Dan was seen as a walking grim reaper for most workers at Tenney, laying people off with the ease of snapping his fingers. He admitted it was a place where he felt he could displace a lot of the aggravation he was feeling from his failing marriage. "It was a place for me to work out a lot of anger," he said. "I fired a lot of people. I was so pissed. Rich Satagaj was really the magic, because he would just absorb my rants. On a Saturday morning, they'd call over to see if I was going into the base lodge. They'd get on the radio and say, 'Dan's coming over.' Everyone was so scared they were about to get fired, they'd run and hide."

Beyond the tension within the staff, though, business was good. Bronander was happy about all the positive press the mountain was getting with Dan as its front man, and the winter turned out to be a windfall in terms of natural snow. Then, in advance of summer 2003, the SnowMagic ice machine showed up.

Dan had originally hoped that SnowMagic, by using Tenney as a showcase for its groundbreaking technology, would deliver enough power to cover a slope to be opened for snow tubing during seasons normally reserved for mountain biking. He started focusing on climate in southern New Hampshire, where the year-round, average daily temperature was right around sixty degrees. From there, he started making calculations about how much ice the ski area could make and how much it would lose at a temperature of roughly fifty to fifty-five degrees. The ICS could potentially create 150 tons of snow in twenty-four hours in temperatures up to sixty degrees.

The system was supposed to show up in May, but was delayed for more than a month because of a longshoremen's strike in New Jersey. Weighing in at more than a few tons, the SnowMagic machine gave folks at Tenney even more concerns, namely, how to get it off the flatbed. "We didn't have a backhoe or anything to lift it up and off," Dan said. "It almost tipped over as we tried to get it off. Then we had to figure out how to get it up the hill, so it could blow snow down the hill."

"The bizarreness really happened when the machine came in," Satagaj said. It didn't turn out to be the wealth of firepower Dan expected. SnowMagic wound up sending only one used machine. And it was a rat trap. The unit worked with a cylinder; water dripped down inside and was frozen, then a scraper went around every three minutes, making a circle around the cylinder. Water would freeze and the scraper would scrape it out, the frozen cone would then fall onto a conveyor belt that would take it to be crushed into ice crystals. The SnowMagic technology could adjust the crystal-crushing. "So, we could adjust the flake," Dan said. "We could make big chunks of slush or little chunks, and we would do that based on temperature." The slush went into a huge blower and came out a four-inch pipe. "We would have enough pressure coming out the pipe to propel the snow only about 250 feet, so you couldn't cover all that much ground."

The system did, however, come with instructions—they just happened to be written in Japanese, so they had to figure out on their own how to handle drainage. They created a track made out of hay and PVC piping, so the melt would drain into a puddle below. They formed the sides of the tubing track out of hay, creating a course where people could ride down on a tube into the big puddle below, likely covering themselves with mud. It wasn't perfect. But snowmaking during the summer hardly ever is.

Dan now needed a way to put Tenney on the summertime map, to convince customers there was a legitimate tourist attraction in Plymouth, born from wintertime activity. That's where the idea for the Fourth of July Big Air Contest began, a celebration that involved fireworks, a concert, and, most improbably, a swath of snow developed for a mini-terrain park. It would become known as the "Mount Tenney Glacier."

Tenney's workers were immediately put in a bind with the delay of the SnowMagic equipment. Instead of getting used to it for weeks leading up to the holiday, it showed up with only days to spare, a project that predictably required learning on the fly. For instance, it didn't occur to anybody that the workers shouldn't have been using heat-conducting metal shovels to transfer snow from one spot to the next. Still, they worked endlessly in the days leading up to the Fourth, making Hershey's Kisses-shaped piles of snow down to the jump, then just pushing them down the hill repeatedly. By the wee hours of the morning of July 4, Dan's crew had created a jump. They covered the landing in hay, along with a four-foot-wide stretch of slush off the jump. "The landing was hay, mud, and rocks," Dan said. "And not small rocks. These were like boulders." It wasn't much, but Dan still stayed up all night grooming it before finally falling asleep on the porch of the Tenney lodge. He was still there when competitors started arriving around 7 a.m. They weren't impressed.

"I could hear the chatter," he said. "The kids were going, 'I thought it would be bigger.'" Among those showing up was sixteen-year-old Simon Dumont, the future professional skier who had driven two hours from his home in Bethel, Maine, to check out "the glacier."

"Don't even tell me that is the jump," he was quoted as saying in the *Hartford Courant*.

"I am not sure it's worth it," Deanna Bartlett, fourteen, of Laconia, NH, told the paper.

Nearly ninety skiers and riders showed up for the event, many of whom actually ended up understanding and appreciating the novelty of skiing on Independence Day. "I'd gone out on a limb, spending a ton of money to make this shit," Dan said. "We had a great day. People loved it. I still think, every Fourth of July, what could have been. That would have been a huge event today, had we been able to continue it."

The "Tenney Glacier" got a lot of press, and found itself the focus of various media outlets. It made the front page of the *Miami Herald*. The *Boston Globe* ran a feature story on it. One day, the phone rang in Dan's office. It was the marketing director at Mount Hood Meadows ski resort in Oregon, the only ski area in the lower forty-eight with a legit glacier to its credit. He wanted to know why Tenney's "glacier" kept growing while Mount Hood's was retreating. In this day and age, to have a glacier growing was really something. Dan's reaction? "You're out of your mind, right?"

"It just went to show, the effect we had," Dan said. "People were paying attention. Some knew it was an ice machine, and some actually thought it was a glacier." Tenney welcomed some three thousand tubers during the summer of 2003 before being forced to close down due to huge issues with the machine. It kept breaking down and, in the summer heat, the runoff turned out to be more than the ski area could handle. Besides, Dan had another feat ahead to pull off: becoming the first ski area to open in the Northeast that fall, which the mountain accomplished on October 12, even beating Sunday River and Killington—annual competitors for that distinction. They beat everybody.

Granted, it was little more than a football field-worth of snow, but it was enough to run some gates and attract some local teams to come train at the mountain. It was also, admittedly, a bit of a joke, but Dan still managed to get others to take the bait. He invited U.S. Ski Team members Cody and Tucker Marshall, brothers from Killington whose styles, he said, reminded him of John's and his own, to train at Tenney. They both showed up and he gave them passes. Bob Fisher, a local ski racing icon and father of former Olympian, Abbi Fisher, also took a taste.

Whatever Tenney was lacking in its quest to be first to open, it still led to another good winter, no doubt in part to offering its season pass for only $199. For the second year in a row, Tenney would boast seventy-five thousand skiers—not too shabby for a ski area that had never done more than thirty-five thousand in any prior season.

"People were excited, really excited that the place had opened," Satagaj said. "We had so much Boston traffic, it was fantastic. I was just thrilled. It was a great year. Season passes were being sold; we had some good racing going on. It was a great winter. It really was."

Then, cracks started to show in the foundation. Dan discovered somebody had dipped into a line of Tenney's credit for $30,000. It wasn't until he received a phone call from SnowMagic's president, and owner of Tenney Mountain, Albert Bronander, later in the day that he started putting the pieces together. Bronander was heading to see the Super Bowl duel between the Patriots and Carolina Panthers, and was calling Dan from Las Vegas, where he was placing a few bets before heading to the game in Houston. As it happened, he needed some cash in order to do so. $30,000 cash, in fact. Dan was furious. "Don't ever call me from fucking Vegas again," he said before hanging up. In Dan's mind, Bronander was stealing from the families who depended on Tenney for their well-being. A payroll of $22,000 per week went toward taking care of his staff, including the school programs, ski patrollers, and instructors. "I was so insulted by that," Dan said. "I realized I was working for a crook. He never paid his bills, and by this time, in the second winter, I'm spending every day calling vendors we're not paying. I'm realizing this is my face, this is my name—I'm the guy people are pissed at. They don't know this Albert Bronander guy. People thought I owned Tenney."

As Dan was watching the investor's checks roll in, he realized that none of them actually had Bronander's name on them. They were coming from a childhood friend who was footing the bill, floating Bronander's dream of running SnowMagic. "I started reaching out to him and told him money is not getting to us," Dan said. "'Your buddy is in Vegas betting on the Super Bowl. I've got families to feed here, and trying to make payroll. And we're not paying our vendors. People are pissed. Things are not good.'" The situation became even more inflamed when Bronander got kicked out of his house in the following months and wound up moving to Tenney. With little to do, he had eyes on the general manager job. He fired Dan. Well, he tried to fire him. Dan refused to leave. He showed up the next day for work. And the next day, and so on.

"I don't blame Dan for being upset," Satagaj said. "His eyeballs were spinning many times." About two and a half weeks later, Bronander realized his attempts to get rid of Dan were futile, so he sent him on the road with the hopes of selling the SnowMagic product to other ski areas and attractions. Dan took one of Tenney's Subarus and hit the road, visiting every ski area south of Washington, D.C., trying to sell them on the technological concept of creating snow in moderate temperatures. He set up a meeting at Dollywood, country singer Dolly Parton's theme park in Knoxville, Tennessee. There was a meeting with baseball Hall of Famer Hank Aaron, who was interested in using the product to create a winter wonderland, complete with big ramp tubing and snowmen, at Hank Aaron Stadium in Mobile, Alabama. A project at Stone Mountain Park came to fruition—the Atlanta theme park still uses SnowMagic each winter for tubing purposes.

When Dan returned from his road trip, his office had undergone a transformation. Bronander had set up shop like he was running the resort, which pretty much, finally, spelled the end of Dan's tenure at Tenney. "It took him a few more times to fire me," he said. "For a while, I was sweeping the floors." The ski area would last one more winter before shuttering the lifts again. It was a brief passage in time that sticks in Dan's memory for the sense of balance it gave him, even in the midst of the hectic lifestyle the job entailed. "Tenney was a good place for me, because it was like an island," Dan said. "Running a ski area is twenty-four/seven chaos. And I love chaos. It was a perfect job for me." It came just at the right time, too, as Dan was trying to get through his divorce. Tenney Mountain gave him something to really occupy himself with, a laundry list of the sort of nonstop problems he loved to solve.

"My goal with Tenney was to have a place that brought back the real essence of skiing," Dan said. "It was a huge success for me, personally. And we achieved a lot. We reopened and rebuilt a ski area that is now destroyed."

Dan was on the Eclipse double, alone on that "longest, slowest lift" in skiing, on Dec. 27, 2003, when he found out that Tenney's founder, Sam Hall, had passed away. It was a fitting place to learn of the news, just prior to disembarking the lift and skiing some of the trails Hall had cut by hand, decades before. It was a lift that could transport and transform. Just when Dan desperately needed it most.

Joe Powder reminds us to always soak in the moments of your life and reach for the next.

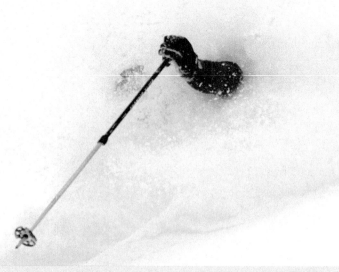

Photograph by Mike McPhee

Dan finds deep snow in Kicking Horse, British Columbia, shooting for *Dan Egan's Wild World of Winter*.

332

Chapter Thirty-eight

SHIFTING GEARS

PETE HAMELIN, AT TWENTY-TWO YEARS old, was seemingly going nowhere with his life. He'd dropped out of high school in his hometown of Spencer, Massachusetts, and spent more time in probation offices and jail cells than he did at the odd jobs he took at local factories, doing the same occupations that had consumed both his father and uncle: stuffing paper into cardboard boxes and preparing them for shipment. Perhaps, Hamelin figured, he was destined for the same sort of mundane life.

But there was also the troubled young man's need to get sober, something Hamelin accomplished just after turning the legal drinking age in Massachusetts. Six months into his sobriety, unemployed and living in his parents' basement, his father dragged him to a men's weekend retreat in Shrewsbury, Massachusetts, an opportunity for reflection, prayer, and time to make peace with the ordeals he was going through.

During a break in the program, Hamelin took part in a pickup basketball game with other attendees on a court behind the church. It was a comfortable environment for Hamelin, who'd played plenty of basketball on the streets of Spencer with the tough, hardscrabble kids he hung out with. In those games, they'd take off their shirts and bang into each other under the rim, each one trying to one-up the other's macho approach to the game. The competition at the retreat would be decidedly different from those contests. At least, that's what Hamelin figured when he caught sight of the shorter guy defending him, dressed in jeans and Teva sandals. "Who the hell is this guy?" Hamelin asked himself. He definitely didn't look like he'd pose much of a challenge. The clothes were deceiving, though. Hamelin watched his opponent block shots, dive for loose balls, try to steal the ball from him as if it were the NBA Championship, and display a competitive fire that stood out. "Honestly, he wasn't a very good basketball player," Hamelin said. But the determination and drive caught his attention. The guy was Dan Egan.

After the game, Dan introduced himself, and he and Hamelin took a walk around the retreat's campus. This was right after Dan had accepted his new job with Ski 93, and he asked Hamelin if he was a skier. Pete should come up to New Hampshire, Dan suggested. Dan would put him to work and give him a fresh start. It was quite the turn of events for Hamelin, who took the offer seriously. After all, if that guy in jeans and sandals could be so ferocious on the basketball court . . . what else could he do? That question began fueling Hamelin's imagination. "I just felt something," Hamelin said. "He inspired in me, that day, that I could do something different."

Weeks later, Dan's phone rang in the Ski 93 office. It was Pete. "He asked if I was serious about the offer to come up north to live," Dan said. "I was like, 'Yeah, come on up, crash with me if you want.' What was one more in our house? It was practically a hostel for wayward ski bums, anyway." Hamelin moved to Lincoln, New Hampshire, and got a job as a parking lot attendant at Loon Mountain, eventually moving into a $300-a-month apartment in a boarding house above a local ski shop. Soon enough, Dan hired Hamelin and tabbed him as his logistics coordinator for the NASJA conference, for which he was diligently preparing, putting Pete right to work.

"It changed my life, working for Dan," Hamelin said. "Nobody ever trusted me. I was a delinquent." Hamelin figures he skied about a hundred days that winter, leading to his making a move the following year to a job in Vail, Colorado. He eventually became the president of the Chamber of Commerce in Portsmouth, New Hampshire. Today, he's married, with two young sons. He is also the director of live music for Signature Sounds, in Northampton, Massachusetts, responsible for booking talent and promoting shows and festivals. It has all been a different path than Hamelin figured he'd go down, thanks to what he calls a divine moment in time. "From this experience, I've traveled the world," he said. "My life just went on a whole different structure. Dan showed me that anything is possible if you put your mind to it and have faith. If I hadn't run into Dan on that basketball court, who knows what would've happened to me. A lot of my friends back in Spencer are either in jail or dead. Within a year, my life had gone from this hopeless, central-Mass dropout to this kid skiing a hundred days a year with Dan Egan. It was magical, man. It was magical."

Dan hadn't considered what he does as equivalent to "working the room," so to speak, even if that was a part of his day-to-day business life, at times. He hasn't felt the need to schmooze for support, to grease up potential advertisers for his show or films. "I've made a lot of sales calls in my life," he said. "But, compared to my friends who own other businesses, I haven't made that many. 'Working the room' is kind of close to what I do, but not with that intention. I think those jobs have come from relationships I've had with people throughout the years—people who have been able to recognize my thinking."

Hamelin is one friend who witnessed this business sense. While serving as the facilitator at an outdoor education center in New Hampshire, Hamelin was able to raise grant money and invite the Romanian skiers from the New England Mountain School to a two-day program at Merrowvista, a youth camp in Tuftonboro, New Hampshire. While Hamlin was at the Portsmouth Chamber of Commerce, Dan popped up again, working to promote an online vacation search engine. That venture, ultimately, didn't work out. Not all of them do. But it may have served as an example of where Dan had latched on too late to the digital platform, failing to take *Wild World of Winter* to the World Wide Web before it got lost in a sea of advertising woes.

Dan had been all over the VHS tape revolution, using his business acumen to obtain distribution rights when others didn't see the value. He also struck at the right time to merge into cable television, when *Wild World of Winter* debuted on NESN in 1998. His failure to switch to digital at its pivotal juncture, however, meant Dan was late to the revolution and was forced to catch up when he'd normally been the one taking the lead. All of a sudden, he was behind on the digital platform which would spawn a new wave of tools long before he recognized their significance. "I was still shooting on tape when my cameramen wanted me to buy digital cameras," he said. "I was like, 'Why would we do that?'"

On September 11, 2001, terrorists leveled the World Trade Center in New York City and attacked the Pentagon in Washington, D.C. On September twelfth, Dan lost 75 percent of his advertising for *Wild World of Winter*. Thrifty Car Rentals, Red Bull, and Taco Bell all pulled out in an onslaught of uncertainty, not only for the American economy, but for every citizen's normal way of life, to that point.

Besides a desperate attempt to save his marriage, Dan's decision to take the general manager's role, seeking personal shelter at Tenney Mountain, was also because he was looking at a winter in which he'd lost all of his advertisers.

"At Tenney, I was still producing the show, but I was winging it," Dan said. "I owned so much commercial time because I had negotiated so well with cable networks when they were regional. Then they became national and I was grandfathered in. I had a ton of ad space and had sold it once, but after 9/11, I had to get new advertisers. The world had shifted and I was battling for my life, both personally and professionally." In the media world, besides the switch from analog to digital, new people moving to online viewing created the devaluation of television ad space. Dan hung on for a bit, then the 2008 recession hit.

"In 2007, I had clawed my way back," he said. "I had Skiclinics.com running again, with trips to Alaska, Europe, Big Sky, Killington, and Canada. We rebranded Egan Entertainment Network as EEN, with the slogan, 'Exploring the World is our Business.' I had a staff, an office, real estate holdings in New Hampshire, and new avenues for distribution partnerships with ski publications and clients. We were also producing content for other industries, like sailing." Dan Egan's *Wild World of Winter* was being broadcast to over seventy-five million homes and supported by regional tourism groups in Canada, France, and Switzerland. Some of the largest ski resorts in North America were also clients of his. EEN's director of sales, Mark "Smitty" Smith, an old Ski Market friend, managed to keep Dan focused and on schedule. He suggested Dan reach out beyond skiing, and so, with Smith's encouragement, Dan cold-called the U.S. Sailing Association, located just outside Newport, Rhode Island. "Smitty was like, 'You grew up sailing, you know the sport,'" Dan said. "So he gave me the name and number of this guy, Dan Cooney, the marketing director for U.S. Sailing, and told me to call him. I think he harassed me for at least three months before I finally did."

It was a call that would generate a life preserver in the not-too-distant future. "When the economy crashed in 2008, it left me barely holding on," Dan said. "The landscape had changed, yet again. Advertisers dropped out of the show, banks began cutting off the flow of credit, and we were leveraged on multiple fronts. The Skiclinics trips required large deposits to hold the lodging reservation packages, and the trips suddenly weren't selling out. So my cash flow got crunched while my payroll had grown. And on top of that, I was being sued." The lawsuit concerned a disagreement over a verbal contract for use of original music, and the lawyers suing him were after more than a settlement. "The initial lawsuit had been going on for two years and the constant lawyer fees were dragging me down," Dan said. "The other side was only in it for their fees and I knew if I lost, everything would be assigned to me to pay. So when the housing crisis hit, it was a perfect storm." Dan's financial and business world suddenly dropped like a rock.

He filed for bankruptcy and had to pare his staff at Egan Entertainment from a dozen down to zero. He simply couldn't make payroll.

The last *Wild World of Winter* broadcast ended up being a regurgitated edit from old shows. "It sucked," Dan said. "I just couldn't deliver a show. I was desperate. I couldn't even pay an editor."

There's a bittersweet taste to the beach plum, native along coastal dunes of the Northeast. They come tangled in a dense web of poison ivy and ripen beginning in August, into September, a fruitful sunset to the end of the summer season. There are eleven miles of beach plum shrubs growing in the dunes of Plum Island, the barrier peninsula off the coast of Newburyport, on Boston's North Shore. Plum Island Beach is one of the region's most visited summertime spots, a sanctuary of relaxation and serenity. It has a gently sloping beach extending out to the Atlantic, where the ocean's waves endlessly lap against the shore in mesmeric rhythm. It was here, a place with characteristics both astringent and tranquil, where Dan realized he was finished. It was bad news on top of already-swirling emotions. "It was a hard time for me," Dan said. "My girlfriend and I had just had a miscarriage. We were both devastated and had been seeking the solace of Plum Island that summer to deal with the loss. The thought of finally being a father had been a lifeline during all of the business issues." It was while on the beach, trying to clear his head and heal, that he got the call from his distributor he'd feared might eventually come.

"She called me up and said, 'Seriously Dan? This isn't a very good show. And we have new producers giving us cutting-edge stuff. I can't help you anymore.'" Egan Entertainment Network, Inc. was no more. The outfit he'd launched in the attic of his parents' house and managed for nearly twenty years had run dry. The aftermath was bittersweet. "I don't have a business. I have nothing. We lost our child, I'm going to this office every day, alone, staring at the phone in complete depression. I occasionally call a sponsor, try to sell something, and then I just . . . can't get motivated. I was sitting there one afternoon and said, you know, instead of being depressed, not many people have TV shows that run twelve-plus years. I have a lot to be proud of." He decided the best thing to do at that point would be to close it all down. He called a friend, who helped him move everything out of the office.

"My best friend, Big Dog, showed up with his pickup," Dan said. "He was a former DJ, the voice of my television show. He'd been there for me during the divorce and had even been the reservations agent at Skiclinics for a while. We emptied the place out, closed the doors, and just left. It was going to the bank anyway. The last things I grabbed out of there were my bible and the production award I'd won for my first film, back in the '80s."

Suddenly, Dan was like Peter Hamelin, seeking inspiration and a new path to guide him. He needed something, or someone, to grab his imagination just like he'd done for Hamelin that day, blocking shots and diving for rebounds, all while clad in sandals and jeans. Mostly, though, he understood that he needed to look back to the roots which had sustained him, to seek another type of shelter in the passions that had always helped define his personal character.

Chapter Thirty-nine

COLD CALL

AS DAN'S FINANCIAL WORLD IMPLODED, he took a job as the interim marketing director of U.S. Sailing, a position secured through his friend, Dan Cooney, the same person he'd cold-called just a few years earlier, who was now the associate executive director of the sport's national governing body. In its final days, Egan Entertainment Network had begun a relationship with U.S. Sailing, producing a weekly video news podcast—one of the first of its kind. It was the final project EEN would produce under its umbrella. For the next eleven months, Dan latched on to the sport's marketing role, even as he was rebranding himself and his company as "Degan Media." U.S. Sailing was interested in maintaining a relationship, even after Dan's job came to a close. They began sending Dan on the road to shoot championship events, similar to the well-produced video podcasts

Egan Entertainment had delivered in years prior. So now, here was Dan, fresh in their minds and back in his element, given the assignment to shoot and edit new material for U.S. Sailing.

There were a couple problems, though. Dan wasn't necessarily a cameraman—a role he usually left to others with a more keen eye for action. Also, since he'd always hired people to edit for EEN, he didn't know how to do that, either. "And here I was at a sailing event shooting with a camera, then having to edit same-day videos," he said. "I was Googling 'How to edit.' I was learning the software I'd once hired people to use, and I was shooting with the cameras I had bought for my company but never used myself." Even with the power of an Internet search engine, the edits, admittedly, weren't very good. In fact, the quality, or lack thereof, led U.S. Sailing to stop sending Dan on the road to deliver video segments that didn't exactly pass muster. Fortunately, though, it wouldn't be the end of his chronicling competitive sailing. "They had thrown me a bone," Dan said, "but on a small budget I couldn't keep it going, trying to learn the ins and outs of digital editing, graphics, audio mixes, and posting on YouTube. But, as in all things I had started, I was determined to figure it out. So, even after they canceled the contract, I kept at it and got better."

To make ends meet, Dan partnered with the Lake Winnipesaukee Sailing Association and launched an adult sailing school on the lake. "I loved it," Dan said. "I had a boat, a steady stream of students, and, unlike the days at the Boston Sailing Center, I was sober. And people were actually learning to sail. It just grew into private and group lessons, and I was brokering boat deals from Newport to Cape Cod. What could be better?"

In November of 2009, Sperry came calling, in a pickle. The shoe company wanted to send Dan to the World Sailing Championships in Perth, Australia, to produce promotional videos of sailors and athletes discussing the shoe brand's importance on the seas. Amory Ross was Sperry's go-to guy for onboard reporting, but, a hot commodity in the sailing world, he'd just been hired by the Volvo Ocean Race, to film the ten-month, thirty-nine-thousand-mile journey around the world, divided into nine legs. Ross would take the role of media crew member, whose main responsibilities included "daily videos and stories transmitted from the middle of the world's oceans."

Now Dan had a budget and enough lead time to hone his editing skills. "I went into production mode," he said. "I hired a graphics guy and an editor who could polish my edits, add graphics, and put the videos online. Plus, I was on my way to Australia for a month to shoot world-class athletes in a sport I love: sailing. It was a twist I hadn't seen coming."

It went well. Dan made the cut and became the official video production company of the U.S. Sailing Team. He started by documenting the team's journey to the 2012 Olympics in London. The opportunity mirrored what he'd done for *Ski Press* magazine during the 2010 Olympics in Vancouver, where EEN produced daily online videos of Canadian and U.S. athletes. "In Vancouver, I learned to navigate within the Olympic bubble, as a member of the press," Dan said. "The transportation system, the press conferences, and the on-hill maneuvering, it's all a learned skill. There, I got to interview Lindsey Vonn, Bode Miller, and Julia Mancuso, as well as the USA Hockey and Figure Skating teams. We had a distribution channel with *Ski Press*, and lots of people were watching."

For London, it would be the same thing, but focused on sailing. Sperry sponsored an international team of sailors and wanted to produce their stories while promoting its sponsorship. So they sent Dan to London for the Olympic Games, where he produced daily videos with sponsored athletes and international sailors. Sperry's studio was on the docks. "At the Games, Sperry was calling me 'Danny Oprah,' because I was getting so many emotions out of the athletes," Dan said. "But, for me, it was like, just doing what I had done for so long in skiing. And most of these people had no idea what I had done before. They just thought I was 'Video Guy.' It was refreshing."

Today, Joe Powder can still be found on the endless powder runs of Val d'Isère, skiing on straight skis, and pulling off the ultimate run.

"I don't know what I do for a living, but I know what I do for my life, and that's ski," said John in Warren Miller's *Future Retro*.

Warren Miller called the Egan Brother's the "ATV's of skiing" and featured them in films from 1979–1994.

Chapter Forty

WORLDWIDE COMMUNITY

WHAT MIGHT HIS FATHER HAVE thought, had he seen the nautical heights Dan had reached? "It would have blown his mind if he was aware of where I was and what I was doing in the sailing world. I think he would have been amazed," Dan said. "We loved to sail together. He often came up to race my Lightning sailboat, here in New Hampshire, even in his eighties. One time, we were racing, Dad was trimming the spinnaker and, 'cause he was hard of hearing, I was 'speaking loudly,' telling him to 'let it out,' and my friend who was also crewing on the boat said, 'I can't believe you're yelling at your dad!' To which my dad said, 'He isn't yelling, we are racing!'"

Robert Egan's battle with Alzheimer's disease lasted some fifteen years, but only became evident to Dan in 2008. Dan had been out West, and returned home to visit with his parents and sister, Mary-Ellen, much to the confusion of his father. At one point, Robert decided he'd had enough with the conversation and asked Mary-Ellen if he could have a word with her in the kitchen. Robert didn't go to the kitchen, though. He remained in the living room. "Who is this guy and how can I get rid of him?" he asked, referring to Dan. "All he does is talk." That sort of moment could have a crushing effect on a son, but it didn't bother Dan. He knew it wasn't personal. "He had a better time recognizing Bob, Mary-Ellen, and me because we were there the most," said Dan's sister, Sue. "Toward the end, he couldn't say my name, but he knew I was family. It was a slap in his face. Here was a guy who would have been diagnosing Alzheimer's, and now he has it."

Dan believed his father was living in the moment. "Today was his best day. And every day after that would be his best day," he said. "He could ask me a question a thousand times. I would never tire of it. I never once said, 'Dad, you've said that.' It never occurred to me. I was always surprised when others did it. I don't know what they expected from him. Because of my travels, I never felt bad being away from him, because he wouldn't know if I'd been gone three days, three months, or three years, and it took the pressure off me. I never felt guilty about the time in between visits, because, every day I saw him, it was his best day and it was going to be our best visit."

Dan felt he knew his father so well, there was nothing left unsaid between them. His father had watched him battle through sobriety, get married, and get divorced. In the wake of the divorce, in Dan's most difficult time, his father was there for him, parking cars with a crew of notable retirees (three PhDs, two MDs, and five master's degrees among them) at Tenney in 2001. "You didn't mess with any of these dudes," Dan said. "They would work every day to get one more car in that lot if they could, and it was precise. Every day I went to work, immediately after the divorce, really struggling, and seeing my dad in the parking lot, chumming it up like he had no cares in the world was so amazing. He really loved it. We skied a lot of runs that winter together."

Robert traveled to clinics at Grand Targhee and Big Sky with Dan and John, and skied with his grandkids at Sugarbush and Cannon until he was eighty-three. He was featured, sitting with Dan and John, in a segment of Warren Miller's movie, *White Winter Heat*, at Sugarbush, laughing about their antics as kids. At Blue Hills, the local ski hill, just outside Boston, he became the de facto doctor of record for the ski patrol in the early 2000s. Marlen would drop him off at the ski area where they'd gone on dates back in the 1940's. Robert would count his ski runs—eighteen a day. Between runs he could be found chatting in the lodge with other locals, and around 3 p.m., with the Milton High School team, still coached by Paul Ajemian. Marlen would pick him up at the end of the day, and they'd head home for a 5 p.m. dinner. In a 1992 *Boston Globe* article on Dan's upcoming Middle East Peace Ski, Robert was quoted as saying, "How many Americans would've had the confidence to slip into Lebanon while there were still hostages?" The writer, David Arnold, ends the story with the following statement, "And in the father's voice was not only pride, but just a hint of envy."

Dan felt a sense of peace in his relationship with his father, yet always wished he'd connected better with him during their days skiing together. But the pensive Robert wasn't one for chatting on the lift, a trait that would at times frustrate Dan, leaving him wondering. "'Why won't he say anything? God, we're here, why doesn't he want to talk to me?' Then I'd realize—'Look—I've done everything I can do. If he wants to sit there in silence and look off into the distance, I'm going to do it with him. We're doing it. Maybe this is our relationship.' From that point on, I became very patient with my dad."

As the years progressed, Robert would lose his eyesight, then his hearing. Then he lost his mind. Marlen remembers the first day she recognized something was wrong, a condition her husband denied, seeing as how he'd treated Alzheimer's patients as a neurologist. Who would better know if he was suffering from it? At least from his point of view. "He was getting up in the middle of the night and walking, so we had a cowbell on the door," Marlen said. She recalled a night when she awakened and he was not beside her, so "I went and got him, and he said, 'Where are we going?' I told him, 'Back to the bedroom.'" Once there, back in bed, Robert got up on one elbow and looked at his wife of sixty years. "Have we met before?" he asked.

"I was kind of glad he didn't know what he was like," Marlen said. "Brushing my teeth one day, he said to me, 'You're my guardian angel. Every time I turn around, you're there to help me.'"

Then, as can happen, a freak thing occurred—Marlen was walking into a store one day when she was hit by an automatic handicap door. She fell, broke her hip, then had a heart attack. While Marlen was on the mend, Dan's brothers and sisters placed Robert in a facility.

After Marlen recovered, she and Robert moved back into the family home until she could no longer care for him. It was time for a new phase, an Alzheimer's memory care unit. The facility had twelve patients per pod. And without blinking, Marlen moved into the Alzheimer's unit with her husband. She spent two years with the other residents in the wing, where they didn't let inhabitants in or out. Robert's body started to fail him and he entered a cycle of hospital visits, rehabs, and emergency rooms. The family all came to visit. Dan slept on the floor of the hospital for his father's final stretch. Robert recognized him, in his own way, in those final days. And Dan was able to reconnect with him, one final time. "Dad communicated with his eyes, in the end, and that left me understanding that there was nothing we had left unsaid," Dan recalls. "Dad loved being a doctor, as much or more than I loved to ski. He had committed his whole life to his profession and his family. He shared all that he could with us. He provided for Mom. They were married for sixty-three years. What is there to say? His life speaks for itself. All of my siblings cared for Dad; Bob, Mary-Ellen, and Sue dedicated years of their lives to both of my parents. It's a debt I don't think I could ever repay to them."

In the midst of it all, Dan was getting ready to cover the America's Cup with Sperry, in Bermuda, helping the company establish a base in order to brand itself around sailing's biggest international event. His father's dementia had long since set in, leaving Dan to only imagine the pride his father, the sailor, would have felt over his accomplishments. "Every time I pull up to the Newport Yacht Club, I think how Dad would love to see this place," Dan said. "If he knew I was working at the America's Cup, even more than the skiing, that would have been the top for him."

Robert Egan died on Nov. 28, 2017. He was eighty-nine years old. He left behind fourteen grandchildren, two great-grandchildren, and a legacy in skiing and sailing that his children, and theirs, have pushed forward. "He never complained or showed any outward frustration about losing his eyesight or his mind," Dan said. "For me, being patient with him was really just mirroring what I saw in him."

Chapter Forty-one

FINDING FLOW

JOHN EGAN MADE PLENTY OF visits home to Milton after moving to Vermont in the '70s, but one, when Dan was fourteen years old, has always stuck out in Dan's mind. The Pro Race Tour was making a stop at nearby Nashoba Valley Ski Area, in Westford, Massachusetts. John spent the previous evening at his family's home, resting up for the event. Dan was sitting in the kitchen when John emerged the next morning, decked out in his race suit, carrying his skis and boots out the door, as if for a day at the office. A unique office, for sure.

"Hey, Dan," he said. "I'm wearing my work clothes today." It was a statement that never left Dan: here was his brother, ready for a day of work, looking like he was about to go do anything but. As a neurologist, their father, Robert Egan, dressed well before leaving the house every morning, wearing a suit cut from an entirely different cloth than John's—one better accessorized with a tie than goggles. But here was John, also pursuing a career, yet eschewing the norms of a "regular" job. Moments like those helped plant the seeds that sprouted into Dan's production roots and gave him the desire to pursue a non-traditional career. It was what made Babson College, a business school that prides itself on creating entrepreneurs, an ideal landing spot for Dan.

"He was exactly what this school portrays," said Babson soccer coach Jon Anderson, who said he was most impressed by the ways in which Dan harnessed his passions into his business career, turning skiing, soccer, and sailing all into profitable ventures suited to his interests. "Dan's a risk-taker. He followed his passion and lived his dreams, without a doubt. He figured out how to make it work. He was able to make a great career, a great living, by taking chances and taking jobs that took him all over the world. But he was also doing things he loves doing. Some things may fail. But a successful entrepreneur is on to the next thing."

So, while steps like making snow during the summer months at Tenney may not have been as rousing a success as Dan had hoped, neither did any other such road bumps derail his next aspiration. It was the kind of mindset that prompted Dan to reinvent himself following bankruptcy, saying goodbye to the Egan Entertainment label which had defined him for more than two decades, and shifting his focus to Degan Media, a storytelling venture that thrived on its brand marketing. It was not a carbon copy of his former company. With Degan Media, Dan was willing to take on new endeavors and, using his strategic marketing talent, focused his experience in order to build a brand beyond the camera. "I think the jobs have come from relations I've had with people throughout the years," Dan said, "people who have been able to recognize my thinking."

Those connections helped Dan launch himself into the 2010 Olympics for *Ski Press*, the 2014 Games for the *Boston Globe*, and gigs like U.S. Sailing— which was how he found himself in London in 2012, helping Sperry with its promotions during the Summer Olympics, giving Dan the ultimate satisfaction of covering Olympic athletes at the highest level, on and off the field of competition. He rode around the docks on his bicycle, toting a backpack containing his camera and tripod, producing content for Sperry and the company's sponsored athletes. He covered all the interviews and medal ceremonies, which made him a conduit between the sailing world and the general public. "Being able to tap into all of that was just a joy for me," he said.

But, by 2016, the partnership between Sperry and U.S. Sailing was souring. London came and went without any Olympic sailing medals for the United States, and, four years later, most of those on the sailing side of the sponsorship had been let go, including Dan.

"So, the new regime had this sponsorship created by Dan Cooney and others, and they think it's going to last forever, but suddenly the team is not producing results," Dan said. "They're not winning any medals and Sperry is getting tired of the deal." It just so happened that Sperry's CEO at the time, Rick Blackshaw, had been one of Dan's best friends at Babson College. Blackshaw was a soccer teammate who'd hit it off with the "mop-headed freshman." Now, he was tasked with the challenge of connecting to a younger generation—how to redefine the Sperry brand from a one-dimensional "preppy" brand to a more diversified, authentic brand, which would appeal to millennials. U.S. Sailing wasn't helping in that regard. Blackshaw was growing tired of the money the company was spending and getting frustrated with the lack of preparedness that U.S. Sailing representatives brought to meetings. Perhaps mostly, though, he found nothing exciting about racing Lasers (small, single-hull dinghies that are the norm in Olympic sailing competitions) around buoys. Dan knew Blackshaw was a big-boat kind of guy, so when he asked if Dan might think of something else for Sperry to sponsor, its focus was an easy shift: The Volvo Ocean Race, and Vendée Globe. While the world's most prestigious yacht races should have always been Sperry's focus, first and foremost should have been the America's Cup.

"Really, the only thing anyone is watching on this planet that involves the water is the America's Cup," Blackshaw said, noting that the event can garner up to a billion views from live spectators, television, and web-based broadcasts. The idea of sponsoring a sailing event with such prestige excited Blackshaw, particularly as he was in the midst of trying to rebrand Sperry. "One of the challenges we had in turning around the business was, the boat shoe had fallen out of fashion favor," Blackshaw said. "It was white-hot, and then it wasn't. If you're a preppy New Englander, it still is. But we had a real challenge on our hands. We were known for that silhouette. But the consumer wants more experiences than things. Adventure. So, as we started to think about that and we said, 'Well, maybe the Sperry brand is this incredible, authentic brand, but it's looking a little inauthentic.'"

The goal was to capture the spirit and ignite the soul of the customer through sea-based adventure. That left one untapped avenue, according to Blackshaw. The footwear business had gone way more athletic and away from Sperry's traditional Top-Siders. The company understood it had to reinvent the product, and come up with a modern boat shoe. After making a few calls, Dan soon connected with the organizers of the America's Cup and shortly thereafter found himself in Bermuda, site of the 2017 America's Cup. He had one request from the America's Cup marketing team for when he and Blackshaw arrived: Don't pick us up in a taxi. So, there they were, whisked from the airport and across the Great Sound of Bermuda in a twin-engine America's Cup powerboat. It was a greeting that impressed Blackshaw, much more so than anything U.S. Sailing had ever brought to the table. "The minute we got on this boat, Rick was like, 'We have to do this deal. This is amazing,'" Dan said.

But if Dan had impressed his old friend with that boat taxi, it was topped later in the day when the two met with America's Cup legend Sir Russell Coutts, who was to handle the sponsorship negotiations. Coutts, a New Zealander who'd won the Cup five times and a gold medal at the 1984 Olympic Games, was CEO for the Oracle Team. Dan considered him to be the Tom Brady of sailing. "It's an honor to meet you," Dan said to Coutts. "I never thought I'd get this opportunity."

"Meet *me*, mate?" Coutts said. "I love all your movies." That prompted Blackshaw to do a double-take. "Because he knew me as his friend and a skier," Dan said, "but I don't think he ever realized how far that extended. I personally was blown away that Russell Coutts would know who I was, and so was Rick."

After some tough negotiations, the two sides made a deal. Sperry became the official footwear provider for the Oracle and SoftBank Japan teams, in order to help develop the ultimate performance boat shoe—a product that had to be lightweight, durable, and boast the serious traction upon which Sperry had built its reputation. It only made sense for Blackshaw to depend on Dan to be Sperry's person in charge of video-documenting sailors wearing the shoe company's new Flex Deck sneaker. "We really needed somebody who was on the ground, coordinated, and could build those relationships," Blackshaw said. "Dan was a master at capturing these moments that don't happen at every second of a race. He was able to capture their training regimen and capture interest beyond sailing. And oh, by the way, they're wearing this new boat shoe." Blackshaw said Sperry's campaign surrounding the launch of the footwear was ambitious and wildly exceeded expectations. Much of that success was due to his old friend, Dan. "His ability to connect with people made everything related to the marketing efforts and this new chapter of the Sperry story so much easier," Blackshaw said. "I think it's so rare that you have a guy who's so well-versed in youth culture and media content, is a world class athlete, and also gets along with people. It's a definition of skill sets required to do that job probably ten people on this planet have." Dan was able to take all the skills he'd honed from his years of skiing-related ventures and apply them to sailing. He'd done this at the World Championships in 2009 and 2016, as well as the Olympics in 2012 and 2014, in Sochi, Russia. But the America's Cup was a different level of the sport.

"It was amazing, because I always loved being around world-class sailors," Dan said. "Not being a world-class sailor myself, all of those people are amazing to me. Just getting to know those sailors on a personal level was amazing, and helping them with their footwear, PR, and marketing—but seeing the highest levels of competition was what I loved the most."

Colton Wright was about seven years old when he started watching Warren

Miller films on VHS. He would lay back in his beanbag chair in the basement of his Buffalo, New York, home, focused on the daredevil escapades of the athletes on the small screen. Wright's father, meanwhile, would use the films as inspiration for his next skiing adventure, working out to the rhythm of skiing icons as he got in shape for the upcoming winter season.

Both father and son shared the same passion for skiing; Colton competed on the racing circuit in western New York, while his father, a local contractor, was intent on taking his own skills on the slopes to the next level. That was the goal when he came across a pamphlet for the Extreme Team Clinics, which offered the promise of skiing with the same professionals he watched during his basement exercises. He signed up for a trip to California with a friend, excited by the prospect of being tutored by the Egan and DesLauriers brothers.

Colton was at home preparing for a race when his father called him one evening from Squaw Valley, California. Colton could hear the après-ski revelry in the background. "I want you to talk to somebody," his father said. He handed the phone over, at which point Colton was talking with Dan Egan, a memorable introduction to somebody the teenager had only known, at that point, on a television screen.

Six years later, their paths would cross again at Holiday Valley Resort in Ellicottville, New York, where Dan was touring with a film crew, narrating the film live, like Warren had taught him. After the show, Dan met up with Colton. By this point, Colton Wright had moved onto the freeskiing circuit and was preparing to compete in the Gatorade Free Flow, a qualifier for the Dew Tour, an extreme sports circuit. "Give me a call if you win," Dan told him, promising, in that event, to try to set him up with a laundry list of sponsors. Colton finished third overall. He never called. Fast-forward a few more years.

Colton Wright was at a crossroads. He'd had an epiphany on a hot July afternoon, while getting an oil change at Valvoline. He was twenty years old and had just learned that his girlfriend was pregnant and due in November. The news came during a lull in life, but suddenly the reality of the situation hit him. His dreams would have to shift. He'd have to give up on moving out West and skiing his heart out, in order to dedicate it to something else; he'd have to give it all up to care for his first child. How would he ski that winter? Could he even afford a season pass at Holiday Valley? These weren't necessarily questions he could answer at the moment. Sacrificing that mindset was going to keep him sane. To give himself some peace of mind, he had to put such aspirations on the back burner. "Give it up, Colt," he told himself. "Give it up."

That's when his cell phone rang.

The caller ID read, "Dan Egan."

Shortly after *Wild World of Winter* and Egan Entertainment evaporated, Dan began seeking solace in activities that kept him grounded. He joined a biking group in the late '90s, which rode every Tuesday night out of Ashland, New Hampshire, just down the street from the town park where Dan liked to catch the local youth soccer club's games.

Dan hadn't coached since his immediate post-collegiate days with Jon Anderson at summer camp, more than twenty-five years earlier. Still, when asked to get involved, he leapt at the chance to mentor third and fourth graders. "I had been riding my bike past that field for the better part of fifteen years, looking longingly at the kids playing soccer in the fall," Dan said. "Once I got started, I was meeting all of the families in the area and I slowly realized the guys I was riding with had no kids, like me. And now I was meeting friends who had children." The connection that led Dan back to the pitch was his girlfriend at the time, whose kids, Sydney and Graham, needed coaching; Dan's marriage had ended without children of his own, but he found a rewarding replacement while dating Lizzie, beginning in 2004.

Dan first met Lizzie Peoples in 1994, while he was director of Ski 93. Peoples was a sales rep for a local radio station who, like Dan, was married.

But ten years later, they were both divorced and Peoples had two young children. Sydney and Graham were the glue that kept the relationship between Dan and Lizzie alive. Even after the relationship fell apart, the two remained friends over the years, and the four of them would spend holidays together, go on trips, and plan family activities around graduations and life events. "What I would say about the four of us is, they needed me as much as I needed them," Dan said. "That relationship has been hard to maintain, like all relationships are difficult at times, yet it has been hugely rewarding." At the Hall of Fame induction in Stowe, Sydney and Graham escorted Dan to the stage and hung the commemorative medal around his neck.

"Having Liz, Sydney, and Graham in my life has been nothing short of amazing. I'm so grateful to Liz for keeping the four of us close and allowing me to be part of their lives, all these years. I could never thank her enough. We are a modern family, I guess. Not very traditional in some senses, but there for each other through thick and thin," said Dan. Sydney became a stand-out athlete at St. Paul's School, in Concord, N.H., and graduated on the dean's list from Plymouth State University. Graham played soccer at Plymouth Regional High School before spending a year at Dan's alma mater, Bridgton Academy, where he was in the top ten in the class academically, and starting center back on the soccer team. He is now attending the University of New Hampshire.

The chance to coach Sydney and Graham at the town level initially drew Dan back into soccer, which soon led to a position at the Holderness Central School, the elementary school Sydney and Graham attended in Holderness, New Hampshire.

"They were looking for a coach, and few of the parents who knew me from the soccer club got me hired without me knowing it," Dan said. He started with the fifth and sixth grade team, then moved on to the seventh and eighth. The success he had with the young coed athletes was impressive.

"After a few seasons, we were so good, we couldn't find anybody to play," Dan said. "The soccer club was having more and more success; we started making it to the state finals and winning, and my middle school team was crushing local schools. Over time, we became a bit of a soccer hotbed. Central New Hampshire, for the first time in a long time, was sending kids to other clubs and to the New Hampshire State Olympic Development Program." Looking for a challenge, Dan eventually called the athletic department at Proctor Academy, a co-ed day and boarding school in Andover, N.H. He asked if the junior varsity soccer team at the high school would want to scrimmage against his elementary-aged athletes. After all, that was the way Dan's former high school coach, Tom Herget, had taught him to aim his competitive sights—by facing off against older, more seasoned players in order to up your game.

Dan arrived at Proctor with a group of fifth, sixth, seventh, and eighth grade boys and girls, ready to face a high school JV Boys team. "It was a competitive game, but they eventually wore us down," Dan said. "But slowly, over years, Holderness started to win those games." Other JV teams were added to the schedule. "The Holderness Central School principal started to question our schedule," Dan said. "We had gone from playing local grade schools to traveling the state and a seventeen-game schedule that included three high school JV teams." The principal asked Dan if he thought it was all a bit over the top for the kids. "I was like, 'Heck no,'" Dan said. "'They can play, and we are a force to be reckoned with.'" Now, granted, they were playing JV secondary teams, and Dan freely admitted the high schoolers weren't very good. Still, it was quite the statement for a team that would go 13–1–1 in one season, beating a pair of high school teams in the process. In fact, the team's only loss came against another high-school-level team in Holderness Prep, which brought tenth graders to try and beat the up-and-coming elementary school kids, who were clearly excelling at soccer. The defeat came on an own goal.

Proctor's director of athletics, Gregor McKechnie, couldn't believe the poise and swagger the Holderness team displayed in what became an annual scrimmage with his school's JV team. It got him wondering if somebody like Dan might be able to work the same sort of magic with the Proctor freeskiing squad, a team in need of a serious attitude adjustment, according to McKechnie. Here was another chance for Dan to devote himself to the sport in which he'd made his name, and he leapt at the opportunity. He started a list of coaches who would help the freeride team move in the right direction. Proctor would go on to hire Dan as their Director of Freeride and Snowboarding. One of his first calls was to Colton Wright.

"What the hell?" Colton wondered. "Is he ass-dialing me?"

While waiting for that oil change in a nondescript Valvoline, Colton listened as Dan laid out the plan. He wanted Colton to help him coach at Proctor Academy, but first they'd have to travel to Colorado for training in November. From there, they'd take the team all over New Hampshire and Vermont, and probably out to Big Sky, Montana, where Dan had started doing his own coaching clinics, in March. Suddenly, the idea of a season pass to Holiday Valley just sort of floated away. Instead of lingering in Buffalo, Wright moved to Campton to live with Dan for a few months before the baby arrived. There, he began to understand the man's passion for the sport of skiing, as well as his understanding of how to teach it.

"Regardless of his age, you just knew that he had this inner child about him, where he was able to get it with kids," Wright said. "He got that kids make mistakes and that they're going to screw up. And that's what they do. Keeping cool, mistakes are going to be made. Kids find comfort and can be honest with him and get his advice. He had an interesting way of keeping his distance but giving advice. It gave him a sort of positive role of being a father."

Dan said having Colt as part of Proctor was awesome. "Plus, he moved me forward with my skiing and upped my social media game. He introduced me to the world of Instagram." Coaching skiing at Proctor was nothing new for Dan. Really, it was an extension of the teaching he'd been doing for years with the Extreme Team Clinics. But this was the first time the audience had been primarily teenage students. It filled a gap for him that had been open for some time.

"Not being a dad, that's a heartbreak for me," Dan said. "I feel like it was stolen away from me, and left a pain I never dealt with for future relationships." Despite this, Dan had always felt a generational pull in many facets of his life, openly seeking to tutor others—a kinship he feels not only on the soccer field or on the mountain but also in the realm of cinema, where his Warren Miller credentials bound him with a new era of skiing and snowboarding film icons.

"That's kind of the coolest thing about being part of this whole Warren Miller thing," said thirty-two-year-old Marcus Caston, a native of Salt Lake City who appeared in a half-dozen Warren Miller productions, "being part of this legacy—and Dan was a huge part of it."

Dan first met Caston at a World Cup event in Killington, Vermont, where he approached him in the parking lot to tell him how much he enjoyed watching Caston's *Return of the Turn* web video series, which celebrates the basic premise of skiing in a variety of different settings—bumps, groomers, steeps—even at the largest beer league in the world, which Caston found in Buck Hill, Minnesota.

"I was packing up my gear after shooting the World Cup at Killington," Dan said, "when I looked over and saw Marcus and another pro gearing up to catch last chair. So, I walked over to them without introducing myself and gushed over their recent feats in Warren's new film. As Marcus walked away toward the lift, he looked over his shoulder and yelled, 'What's your name, man?'" Dan just waved him off and yelled back, "Dan."

"He did a double-take and later hit me up on Insta with a DM," Dan said.

"I grew up watching him in the movies and that's how I ski," Caston said. "That's what I wanted to show off." Caston's efforts stand out from the new-school era of straight lining, flips, tricks, and other showcases that put skiing on a different level from the dance with the mountain that stands as its traditional form. "I wouldn't describe my skiing as old-school," Caston said. "Maybe that's the way it's interpreted sometimes, but it's new-school in that we're just building on top of what they were doing. But we are doing it on newer and better equipment, different equipment."

The way the younger generation is able to more easily control their maneuvers on snow really highlights the difference between the straight ski and the wide ski. In fact, "skiing is really two different sports," Caston said. "There's the skiing you see in ski movies now, but it's not the same sport you used to see on film. *Return of the Turn* was an aim to build on top of that style." So, it makes sense that Dan would find a connection with Caston based on their skiing styles and appreciation for what paved the way. "I kind of go back to the time when he was skiing, that kind of style," Caston said. "Soon after Dan was in the movies, there were shaped skis and fat skis and they changed everything. It didn't change skiing so much, but it did change the focus of what you see in movies and the magazines and what they'd like to show. So, we just wanted to showcase that same style of skiing they were doing. I think it brings him back a bit and he appreciates the people who still love to ski that way."

Many younger skiers will ask Dan what his biggest trick was, back in the day. Simple, he tells them. "Staying alive. With every generation, there's a new birth of belonging," Dan said, "a new thing to do. In belonging, you become part of the becoming. For us, the becoming was extreme. But the next generation of becoming has backward tricks and grabs. I love to ski with that young energy. Skiing is generational. That's why the sport is amazing. Because we pass it on. Somebody gave it to us, and we pass it on. That generational piece of what we're all doing is subconsciously why we're all doing it."

Chapter Forty-two

STAYING LONGER

AS HE APPROACHED HIS LATE-FORTIES, Dan's travel itinerary began to change. Instead of filling his winter calendar with as many dates and locations as he could possibly handle, he made the decision to visit fewer places and stay longer at each of them. Those frantic, globe-trotting spurts of youthful wanderlust had abated. A bit, anyway.

In addition to his home base in New Hampshire, Dan began to settle in at Big Sky, Montana, where he hosted a handful of clinics each year. It was a resort he first visited in the 1980s on a whim, after hearing rave reviews from the Egans' personal travel agent, Steve Kassin. Coming out of a camp at Targhee, on their way to cat ski in Fernie, British Columbia, Dan, John, Dean Decas, and longtime Warren Miller cameraman Tom Grissom needed a place to stay. Grissom had a crush on the marketing woman at Big Sky, so he called her up and inquired what she could do for the Egan/Miller crew. She sold her boss on Grissom and crew being from Warren Miller (not *exactly* a lie), which opened doors for complementary lodging, lifts, and food. "They were treating us like royalty," Dan said.

But there really was a Warren Miller crew due at Big Sky the following week, complete with featured skiers Scot Schmidt and Tom Jungst. Dan and Grissom knew they'd have to vacate before the real crew arrived, but they stayed until the very day Schmidt checked in, essentially sneaking out the back door as Schmidt stood at the reception desk. It was a stunt that Big Sky's COO, Taylor Middleton, who served as the resort's marketing director at the time, never forgot. "Lucky for us, he had a sense of humor," Dan said, "and he always invited us back." That relationship became more formal, beginning with the 2007–08 season, when Big Sky invited Dan to have a deeper engagement, with more frequent clinics and a bigger presence at the resort. So he dug roots there and became an employee, staying for longer stretches.

One of the other stops on Dan's ski calendar was, naturally, Chamonix, France, the purported "Extreme Capital of the World." That was the problem. Dan felt Chamonix was crumbling under the weight of its own reputation. Everybody who visited wanted to immediately transform themselves into the level of skier seen on film, the ones whose daredevil acts put Chamonix on the extreme map. In the process, Chamonix had become too complicated. It was too retro, too dangerous. "There's a lot of pressure," Dan said. "It's crowded, and the lift system is not very sophisticated." For those and other reasons, Dan's clinics in Chamonix were becoming something of a headache. His clients were demanding to ski the sort of extreme terrain they saw in films, eschewing their own abilities over the fact that they were skiing with "extreme legends Dan Egan and Dean Decas." What wasn't possible? Such was the situation when Dan brought a client and his teenage son up to one of the many grandiloquent glaciers of the resort, a place that gave visitors a treacherous look at the terrain Chamonix is known for. Yet, it wasn't enough.

"The dad is yelling at me to take his boy somewhere extreme," Dan said. "I said, 'We are. This is a glacier. This is radical. There are crevasses everywhere. This is *extreme*.'" But the client persisted. "I paid you to take me somewhere extreme, like in the movies!" The father, in his frustrated huff, skied away from Dan and his son, right into the belly of a crevasse. They spent the next hour trying to get him out of the hole. "The kid had new boots and all he wanted to do was sit around," Dan said. "He didn't want to ski at all. Then, I had to get this irresponsible clown out of the crack. He wasn't prepared to be up there."

The experience was a valuable realization, though. The pressure and folklore surrounding Chamonix had created a level of stress Dan was no longer willing to deal with. That left him seeking another European stop where he could plant himself for a few weeks to host his clinics. This made him remember his first visits overseas, including his initial visit to Val d'Isère, working for the Japanese film director who insisted the Egan brothers' faces were too ugly to be in his production. His old friend Henry Schniewind, the "proper" Newton North skier Dan had raced against in high school, had moved to the region in 1984, as had Ski Market alum Marty Heckelman, a pair of friends who made the prospect of relocating two hours south to Val d'Isère all the more appealing.

From a business and teaching perspective, Dan's initial thoughts about Val d'Isère were focused on two advantages: very little crevasse danger and superior lifts. These outweighed the obligation of holding his clinics in the radical, steep terrain of Chamonix. So he made the move and began a month-long stay.

Dan was also concerned about the Valdez, Alaska, Skiclinics, where he brought clients at the end of every April. He was beginning to sour on that locale, as well, since he couldn't control the all-too-frequent rain, which often ruined skiing. "It was hard, from a business standpoint, to tell paying clients how great it was going to be, then watch it rain for four or five days," he said. "I didn't want to do that to them." Besides, what was he doing going all the way to Alaska from Europe, anyway? "I was in all the cool spots already," he said. "I was killing myself, logistically, and I was physically exhausted." So, he figured, why not spend more time in Val d'Isère, where he was comfortable with both his friends and the atmosphere?

It is in this French town where Dan now spends the second half of his winters each year. His days there begin in a café, chatting with Schniewind, who works with Alpine Experience, a team of backcountry specialists who hold an impromptu guide meeting every morning. "It's amazing to be with such icons around the resort every day," says Dan. "Wayne Watson, with over forty years in the valley; Chris Souillac has lived there since the '60s; Andreas Bjorklund, from Sweden, has over twenty-five years of experience in the Val d'Isère and Tignes; and my good friend Henry, founder of Henry's Avalanche Talk (HAT). Every morning we chat, drink espresso, banter about sports, and discuss the conditions and weather in the region. I love it as much as the skiing itself."

Henry's Avalanche Talk has become one of the region's go-to resources for off-piste training. Schniewind was, in fact, the first American to pass the French Equivalence in mountaineering, part of which was an Alpine race. "And he beat all the French guys. That's how good he was," Dan has said of his former high school rival.

After studying at Montana State University to become a "snow scientist," as Dan puts it, Schniewind landed in France and never left. He has been endorsed by the French National Association for Snow and Avalanche Study, for running a program which has saved hundreds of lives. "For them to recognize a non-French person was amazing," Dan said. "He's part of the woodwork in Val d'Isère now, very well-respected." Schniewind runs a speaking tour throughout the U.K., on avalanche awareness, and anytime there's an avalanche in the Alps, television networks, such as Sky Sports and Euro Sports, seek his commentary. "I always think it's amazing that two Boston kids have made their living in the ski industry in France, and that our roots go back to racing against each other," Dan said. Schniewind is an important member of Dan's annual reunion within the Alps community. Each morning, as they sit with the group of mountaineers and discuss the day's conditions, Dan makes sure to listen to the expertise of the local skiers, who he cherishes for their openness and sharing of their knowledge. Then, it's off to the adventure of the day, which will likely be filled with corn snow topped with a velvet surface, for three- to four-thousand-vertical-foot runs.

"Henry, his wife Ginny, and their three children—Katrina, Jackson, and

Roscoe—became my European family," Dan said. "Roscoe is my godchild, and they all give me so much pleasure each spring."

Marty Heckleman, an author and producer of videos on ski instruction, has partnered with Dan on video since the late 1980s. "Marty spends many evenings talking about the conditions in Val and how the slopes have changed from the days of straight skis in the '80s to today's fat powder skis," Dan said. "We still sit and recap our days on the slopes and discuss where the best powder can be found."

Dan prides himself on providing long, memorable days for his clients in Val d'Isère. "When you're on it, your timing is right and you're following the sun around the resort, you can ski that velvet surface right through until four or five at night," Dan said. Val d'Isère is known for its wide-open powder runs, steeps, and couloirs. Given the right conditions, skiers can go up and ski the north face of the Grand Motte at Tignes resort, a slope that rolls away to fifty-plus degrees with cold, glacial snow, making for a dry, grippy surface. "You drop down into the north face of the Grand Motte and that's where the glaciers are, where the cracks are," Dan said. "You can still get that same sort of feel that runs throughout Chamonix, but it's in Tignes and it's a little more compressed and contained. There's still danger, but you can get out, touch it, taste it, and get home safely. I get so excited, every year I call John and tell him, 'You have to be here, I can't even explain what it's like to be here.'"

Dan's appreciation for Val d'Isère is evident in the way he presents the destination to his clients. Rather than preach in obligation, like he did at Chamonix, he instead teaches from the enthusiasm that the surroundings spark. "Skiing at Val d'Isère with Dan is a much different experience than showing up on your own," Dan's old friend Kassin said, "or even hiring a guide." It is an experience born from detail, from Dan's faith in the philosophy of centered skiing, a mix of sports psychology and realization of one's inner self integrated with mechanics on the snow. It was an element of the sport first made famous by Sugarbush skier, Denise McCluggage, whose book, *The Centered Skier*, has long been the manual for skiing with Zen, a belief in mindful presence on the snow that both John and Dan have always made part of their repertoires. "Trying to chase Dan and watching him ski—being centered—and having that prowess, age doesn't affect it," Kassin said. "It isn't about how high you can fly off a cliff, but just being one with the mountain, being smooth, and using gravity." It is a mental approach Dan's students have credited with their being able to push through their boundaries, face their fears, and feel confident in what they can do on the mountain.

"We do a lot of scenarios," said Clara Greb, a twenty-year-old skier from Shepherd, Montana, who was competing on the Freeride World Qualifier Circuit, and had trained with Dan for four years. "We close our eyes and visualize the situation we're in. Account for your immediate reaction. How to talk yourself through it. So, you're putting yourself in the face of fear, in your mind, and working through it." Greb has found the process to be invaluable, especially when she finds herself on deck in the starting gate. "For me, I get nervous," she said. "I start shaking and I have to close my eyes, take deep breaths, and put myself in the situations that put you in that mind frame. The same mind frame that you're in when you're practicing and training. Go back to that. And something just clicks. Or . . . well, it helps anyway. You stop shaking. You know that you're prepared. You've put yourself in that position many times."

Kassin maintains that those who ski with Dan will only find slight improvement in their technical aspects. It's the mental change that they should take particular note of. "Some people call him 'The Skiing Jedi,'" Kassin said. "Do things, ski places, and overcome fears, and that, all of a sudden, opens up a whole world you can topple. You'd never think, on your own, to go down the Big Couloir at Big Sky, but here you are standing on top of it. And the way he talks and gets you over that hump, you end up skiing it and realize that it was the greatest thing you have ever done in your life. And I think that buzz keeps going for people. It transcends skiing and carries over to everyday life."

As Greb put it: "There's something with Dan where you feel like you can tell him anything and he's not going to judge you. He's one of the most compassionate people I've ever worked with, yet he knows just how to push you in the right way. He knows how to push your comfort-zone bubble just enough to expand it, but not make it pop and then freak out after that."

Maybe it isn't a style that a certain father and son duo at Chamonix might appreciate, but it turned into a successful style of teaching, an instructional direction that always defined the Egans, going all the way back to Grandpa Gillis—that Boston educational icon both Dan and John credit for their unique abilities to get through to the minds of students in a different manner than your average skiing instructor. But the Egan brothers also share a common enlightenment passed down from the generations before them, one that, when applied to life, works in tandem with what they can handle on snow.

"My grandfather always told me the most things about learning, and how to learn, and how to teach," John said. "But it wasn't until my dad passed away that I understood—with his sailing, he was really the one who taught me how to navigate life, not just the storm and the islands. I got a lot of: how to navigate life, how to get through different temperatures and moods of people and work your way through so as not to belabor certain things. To highlight, in a way."

In some regard, to simplify. Which is precisely what Dan managed to do when he decided to downsize. Fewer places. Stay longer. This became the recipe for Dan's perpetual pursuit of his passion on snow.

Chapter Forty-three

AGING LIKE A FINE WINE

SATCHELL BURNS SPENT MUCH OF 2019 putting the finishing touches on a handful of promotional films with his Vail-based production company, Steep Motion Works. He'd been hired to create the films for Big Sky Resort, a place that doesn't get the credit it deserves, according to Burns, Steep's principal director.

"Jackson Hole is kind of the sexy, incredible mountain with great terrain, and gets a lot of attention—as it should. But coming here, getting blown away with the terrain and wondering why it's still sort of under the radar was really an eye-opening moment," he said. Burns's sudden infatuation with Big Sky only increased once he started to recognize how Dan's clinics played their part in that quiet, underlying specialty that goes under the radar in Montana. He immediately latched onto the idea of documenting Dan in one of the video segments, and started "annoying people until they introduced me." The fact that Dan was there, for a film crew looking for subjects, was just low-hanging fruit, Burns said. "Just seeing him in Warren Miller movies, that's a name, something we can sink our teeth into. For anyone who loves to ski and has any connection to Warren Miller movies, it is literally peeking into a time machine and connecting with one of the most iconic parts of ski history. To have that connection, for anyone who loves to ski, is something that will give you chills. Dan will gladly open that up for you and share those experiences. It's a very powerful thing to listen to him, for any skier."

Burns has filmed some of the best skiers in the world, including Lindsey Vonn, in his days behind the camera, and said that Dan, in his mid-fifties, still rips impressively on the mountain. "From that aspect, it's fun to watch a great skier, and then, from more of a philosophical standpoint, riding the chairlift with him, chatting and getting his perspective of what it means to be on the snow and connect some turns, and what it can do for your mind, that's fun to talk about."

Steep Motion Works's finished video hit the Internet in early 2020, playing as a refresher of Dan's career, highlighted with several clips from his days with Warren Miller films, as well as him directing his clinics at Big Sky.

A few months later, another film crew came knocking on Dan's door in Montana with a familiar calling—recruiting him to take part in another segment. This time, for Warren Miller Entertainment. Chris Patterson, the Warren Miller director of photography who calls Bozeman, Montana, his home, wanted to do a segment for the 2020 film, *Future Retro*, with skiers who were in the must-see Miller films of the '80s and '90s. "Chris came up with the idea of bringing in older legends of film from past days," cameraman Tom Day said. "They'll use older footage and see the evolution of the change." The experience had Dan feeling like a sixteen-year-old again, being able to ski with his three favorite skiers in the world: his brother John, Day, and Scot Schmidt. "I'm the youngster," Dan said, "four years younger than Day, so those guys have a lot of history that doesn't include me. I was honored to be with that crew. For me, it was like watching my heroes ski again."

So, when Schmidt dropped in at Yellowstone Club's Pioneer Ridge, it had become clear that, while everything had changed, absolutely nothing had changed. "He's raising the bar on the first turn," Dan said. "John is pacing around a little bit—he's the oldest one out there—and then he drops in—there's John, the same spitting image he'd been my whole life. His Spidey little self." Dan was watching in awe as two of his skiing idols performed their craft below, when Day asked him what he was going to do to follow. "I just wanted to get some popcorn and watch the show," Dan said. "Whatever I'm going to do won't be anything like what those two just did."

Dan did drop in and ski his line, but he was left again in amazement two runs later when Schmidt, at the age of fifty-nine, throttled right off a cliff. "You've got to be shitting me," Dan said to himself. "I'm not twenty-five." After several days of shooting in the new snow, trees, and off Lone Peak, the crew started to look at dropping into the Little Couloir, which, at up to fifty degrees, is one of the steepest in-bound lines in the country. "John wanted nothing to do with the Little," Dan said. "Schmidt didn't even show up. I was nervous and couldn't decide what skis to bring—my ninety-six cm or the hundred and six cm under foot. Weird to have those choices, when back in the day we just dropped in on whatever we had on our feet."

Both John and Tom commented on his choice. "Going with the narrow ones?" Day asked.

"I had made up my mind by then. I wanted a ski I could arc on and make jump turns, not skid around on," Dan said. "Plus, it had been years since I skied the Little. Like, twenty-plus years. I think, the last time, I was on straight skis."

Dan found himself at the top with twenty-one-year-old Parker Costain, who'd just won the illustrious Kings and Queens of Corbet's competition by doing a double backflip into Jackson Hole's famous couloir. "We're looking down the Little, and I'm almost three times the kid's age," Dan said. "If I don't go first, I'm never going." Most people who ski the Little, Dan said, navigate the tight entrance by side-stepping. He wasn't having any of that on film. "I wanted to go in turning," he said. Costain followed, dropping in off the top cornice, had to navigate over some rocks, and then straight-lined a section, almost crashing as he hooked a rock. But with such good balance, he was able to pull himself together and finish the run. "I think he made literally four turns," Dan said. "That's such another world. That's never been my game."

The part of his game that was present during the shoot was being able to ski that signature style with his brother, side-by-side and front-to-back, those Siamese Twins, attached at the soul, skiing in tandem for the camera once again. "It was great to be with John again and chat with him about the lines," Dan said. "I think skiing for Warren, there's an audience. It's hard to think that you're not the same as you were in your twenties. I didn't have anything to prove to anyone and I tried to take that into the shoot."

Dan and John were also featured in another film that saw its release in 2020; *Ski Bum: The Warren Miller Story* featured the Egans as two of the many voices who tied together the life story of the legendary winter sports filmmaker. Upon its release during the summer, the movie landed in the Top 10 in its category on iTunes. It was a comprehensive look at Miller's turbulent life behind the camera, as well as a documentary presenting the convincing argument that Miller was the most influential man in winter sports.

"I always thought the mistake the audience made was thinking they were going to watch a movie," Dan says during the opening credits of the film. "A Warren Miller movie is an *experience*." What *Ski Bum* might have done best, though, in addition to profiling the filmmaker (*Ski Bum* turned out to be Miller's final on-camera appearance before his death in 2018) and his importance to the sport, was also illustrating the impact Dan and John had in helping Miller deliver his product over a stretch of years. That *experience* was deepened by the mantra to "follow CNN," as Dan told Miller he wanted to do years ago, to go places where skiing might be a novelty, in order to tell a story that would go beyond a skier's form.

"When you go into Istanbul, Turkey, or you sneak into Beirut, Lebanon, it's not so much 'Warren Miller films' people are accepting," Dan said in the film. "They're more curious. *Why are you here? Why are you carrying skis and why are you wearing boots through our marketplace?* To see a skier in a place like that was amazing for them. Warren was like, 'Yeah, that's what we're after.' This isn't about going left and going right down a slope. This is about taking somebody someplace they've never been before."

That was the Egans' game when it came to Warren Miller, and while Dan and John are no longer traveling the world together, their individual and combined impact on the sport continues.

"To see Dan out there, to see a piece of history, it's really special that he's skiing at this level at his age," Burns said. "He is aging like a fine wine. Part of the mystique about skiing is that it's an individual sport. One of the things that separates it from a team sport is, you can't go play a baseball game with your buddies at Yankee Stadium and feel the grass and see the lights—but you can go to Aspen, Jackson, Big Sky. It's a timeless sport. So, to see a piece of history on the mountain performing at a really high level, it's so inspiring. That's what you aspire to be as a skier, to be able to perform like that. At a really, really, high level."

Chapter Forty-four

SWEET EMOTION

THE SONG WAS AN UNINTENDED nod to the days when, as teens, John and Dan would get high in John's Impala between USSA races. They'd sit in the car. They'd smoke, and they'd listen to Aerosmith.

Four decades later, as the Boston band's "Sweet Emotion" pumped through the speakers of the Little America Hotel's ballroom in Salt Lake City, the song evoked a different feeling. More than six hundred people gathered on that Saturday evening in early April, 2019, to celebrate the induction of the Ski and Snowboard Hall of Fame's class of 2018. Honorees included World Cup champ Bode Miller, extreme icon Kristen Ulmer, Olympic medalist Andrew Weibrecht, freestyle legend Hilary Engisch-Klein, and the late snowboarding pioneer Tom Sims.

The room was a collection of skiing and snowboarding luminaries and athletes who had helped define and grow their sports over the past fifty-plus years. Picabo Street, Suzy "ChapStick" Chaffee, Doug Pfeiffer, Bernie Weichsel, Billy Kidd, Doug Lewis, Mike Marolt, Genia Fuller, and John Clendenin were among the notable Hall Honored members on hand to witness the induction of the new group of honorees.

There was another Hall of Famer standing at the podium—class of '17 inductee Dan Egan was prepared for his first stint as the event's master of ceremonies. It was a long way from where Dan stood only two years earlier, having originally bristled at the idea of submitting his ballot. "I think he realized that this is a good thing," John said. "To see his transformation from before, trying to talk him into it to him being part of it now. It's like . . . wow."

Hall of Fame executive director Justin Koski got to know Dan through the process of his Hall of Fame selection, and was left wildly impressed by the speech he gave at his induction in Stowe. "His acceptance speech was so well-thought out and so professional," Koski said. That, coupled with Dan's decades of experience in the media realm and being a well-known name in the industry, created an ideal situation to have him host the event in Salt Lake. When Koski asked Dan, about a year earlier, he told him the crowd in Salt Lake would probably top out somewhere around 250 guests. Yet, here was Dan, staring out at a sea of heads more than twice that number, many of whom likely had followed a similar path to his own. How many, indeed, took "just one more semester off" from college, like Dan had pledged to do? How many others told their moms they would get a "real job" next winter?

Here was a room filled with fellow skiers and riders who'd made snow sports their thrill-seeking passion, enough to postpone real life, only to really end up finding themselves. It was the transformation of that belonging and becoming, as Dan put it, that gathered this like-minded "tribe of kindred spirits," an "industry of misfits" hiding out in the mountains and seeking freedom for a very long time.

"Our job as skiers and snowboarders is to complement the hill," Dan said during his introduction to the evening. "To leave our tracks, to leave our little piece of art behind. We interact with nature. I mean, who among us in this room has not cruised down an alley, driven through the mountains, looked up and thought, 'Hey, I'd like to make tracks there,' or, 'What if I jumped off that cliff?'"

It was a speech that brought out a different side of Dan than the one that normally emerged when it came to anything regarding skiing. For in the days leading up to the ceremony, Dan's preparation had a whiff of hesitancy, a slight apprehension that spoke to how important he regarded the honor of emceeing the show. In fact, in atypical Dan Egan fashion, the previous day's skiing ended right around noon, four hours before the lifts stopped shuttling skiers up the Park City slopes, in order to continue working on his speech. Sacrificing hours of skiing in order to perform better in another realm was, in some ways, the opposite of what had gotten him here in the first place.

Hours before the event, he spent the majority of the forty-five-minute trip from Park City to downtown Salt Lake City practicing and rewriting. He'd kept his bottled energy at bay as his setup continued at the hotel, the longtime director of so many on-film segments who was used to giving the go, now forced to sit and wait to participate in a show that would add a chapter to his Hall of Fame legacy.

"I think, like everything else he does, he really went way above and beyond, almost on a volunteer basis," Koski said. "Being able to see what the show would and could be, having that vision, then being able to take and work with each of the individuals being honored in Salt Lake really added to the experience for the people attending the event. He's become one of our biggest supporters here at the Hall because of what he does in that role, but, in addition, he's constantly thinking about us and making key introductions to other people who share the passion of skiing and the passion of skiing history."

Indeed, Dan had become an active proponent for the museum in Ishpeming, Michigan (a town "just a little bit bigger than this room," he noted during the ceremony), furthering the Hall of Fame's importance in an industry that has made endless tracks to its doorstep. His contribution in 2019 resulted in the Hall asking him to repeat his role in the 2020 induction of the class of 2019, at Sun Valley, Idaho. Scott Brooksbank, Kit DesLauriers, Greg Stump, Sherm Poppen, James Niehues, and Johnny Spillane were among those scheduled to be inducted before the spread of COVID-19 forced the Hall of Fame to cancel the event.

Beyond, Koski said he hopes to see Dan as the event's emcee for the foreseeable future, a recurring role that, John said, "blows me away."

At the end of the evening, the party shifted back to Park City, where a few dozen attendees gathered at the Red Tail Lounge at the base of the Canyons Village. Dan shed his tie and jacket in his disheveled room at the Grand Summit Hotel with an exhibited sigh of relief, and made his way to the Red Tail where he planned to spend only a short time mingling. There would be a wake-up call before dawn, so he could make his way back to Salt Lake in the morning to catch a flight to France for his annual month-long trip to Val d'Isère, to ski with his old friend Henry.

Less than a year after emceeing the Hall of Fame awards event, Dan gave the eulogy at Marlen's funeral. "Mary Ellen (Gillis) Egan was a silent saint with a character glued together by faith, education, and service to others," Dan said. "She was married for sixty-three years, and had eight children. She was the only girl in a family of five boys, and she outlived them all. She provided elder care for countless relatives and friends, including our dad. In the last two years of my dad's life, she lived in a locked Alzheimer's unit with him, and she was the only lucid person in the twelve-patient unit. She never complained.

"She even embraced social media, signing up for Facebook after Dad passed. She told me, 'Danny, I'm nervous, it's too public. I don't want the whole world to know what I'm doing. What if I fall in love?'

"However, the changes in technology did not change her, her beliefs, or her character. These were her structure and strength, and the backdrop for how she raised us. Her example is one of inclusiveness, kindness, and forgiveness. Being the last child to move out of the house, I got a first-hand look at how my mom and dad interacted; they were so considerate of each other. One time during breakfast, I noticed Dad place his hand on Mom's, and in that time and space I saw only one hand. It's a scene I'll never forget."

Dan wrapped up his emotional tribute with this: "We are the senior generation now. How we move forward with compassion and empathy for one another will be our legacy."

And for Dan, it is a legacy wrapped in community that stretches around the world, making stops in the mountains, across the seas, and everywhere in between.

> *Now, what I am commanding you is not too difficult*
> *for you or beyond your reach.*
> Deuteronomy 30:11

Acknowledgments

ERIC WILBUR

I DIDN'T ATTEND MY FIRST Warren Miller theater event until 2003, when I caught *Journey* at a venue near Boston University. It was one of the last of his films that Warren would narrate, so there was a certain slice of satisfaction in being able to have a late chance at the authentic experience. Not that I was a novice to the Warren Miller world, by any means. Our college townhouse in Vermont boasted its own library of ski porn, where names like Glen Plake, Scot Schmidt, Robbie Huntoon, and local legends such as the DesLauriers and Egan Brothers displayed skill and bravado that scoffed in the face of the runs we had taken earlier in the day, possibly skipping British Lit to take advantage of a powder day at Bolton Valley, Stowe, Sugarbush, or Smugglers' Notch. As Dan says in these pages, "the VHS was the original YouTube," and we would watch in awe at the feats those skiers showed on film, rewinding and pausing at pivotal sequences, pining for the day when we could, ourselves, visit those same locales and experience those same lines.

A few years ago, in order to mark the twenty-fifth anniversary of the infamous Grand Targhee cornice break, I sat down for an interview with both John and Dan Egan for a feature story chronicling the skiing passion of two Boston boys who became two of the defining extreme athletes of their generation. The stories both of them told me during the process were so rich in detail, so defining in terms of their unique approaches to their careers—and from two different points of view—it became clear there was much more to be told than a 4,500-word feature could contain.

When I approached Dan a few years later, following his and John's inductions into the U.S. Ski and Snowboard Hall of Fame, to gauge his interest in writing an autobiography, I discovered it was something he'd already been thinking about. He sent me the rough, introductory draft he'd written, as well as a table of contents already put together. It was titled, *White Haze*.

During that first meeting, one slushy January afternoon in Concord, New Hampshire, we discussed the prospects of a joint venture, and I started to understand that this project was going to be far different—deeper and more introspective than I had initially thought. This was by no means going to be an empty vanity deal, but a fascinating profile of a man who is grounded in faith and has pride in his roots. I recall walking out of the Ninety Nine Restaurant that day and calling my wife with a single conviction: I *need* to write this book.

The core of Dan's original vision remains here, in a book that dives into Alpine history as told through the eyes of a skier with a gritty Boston background. I am supremely appreciative that Dan trusted me with the ability to deliver his compelling narrative. I'm grateful for all the participants in this book, including John and the rest of Dan's siblings, as well as their mother, Marlen, who I only wish could have lived to see the finished product that she was so excited about during our interactions. It was a pleasure to speak with some of the bigwigs of the heyday of extreme skiing: Tom Day, Tom Grissom, Scot Schmidt, Gary Nate, Kristen Ulmer, Greg Stump, and Rob DesLauriers. Thank you to Bernie Weichsel and Mike Bisner for their valuable input about the business side of skiing, as well as everybody else who took the time to contribute to this book. That includes Miheala Fera for opening up and talking about one of the most turbulent periods of her life.

Thank you to John Dockendorf, Paul Ajemian, Jon Anderson, Alfred Jimenez-Segarra, Eric Charamel, Stan Woliner, Clara Greb, Pete Hamelin, Justin Koski, Satchell Burns, Colton Wright, Rich Satagaj, Steve Kassin,

Marcus Caston, Matt Pepin, Jan Kotok, Julie Kramer, Margaret Anne Fletcher (King), and everybody else who helped along the way.

Of course, the bulk of the gratitude goes to Nathaniel, Carson, and Hayden for supporting me and being patient with the many hours immersed in my laptop, especially during soccer, basketball, and baseball practices when they had to share my eyes with the manuscript. The foundation of everything that makes me a good person lies with my wife, Kathleen, who insisted twenty years ago that my first book be dedicated to her. And so, here it is—in tribute to the woman who has supported and fought for me more than should be possible (but thank God it is). Telling the story of Dan's journey has been one of the most satisfying developments of my career. I hope you enjoy reading about his life as much as I did delivering it.

"Focus on today and you'll find a way
Happiness is how
Rooted in the now."
— Trey Anastasio / Tom Marshall

DAN EGAN

WHENEVER GRANDFATHER GILLIS GAVE A speech or told a story, he'd tell his listeners, "Sit back, relax, settle in—it's going to be a while." I've always enjoyed that line, and have used it many times, myself. So, when it comes to recognizing the many, many people who've provided guidance, support, tough love, and wisdom for this book, please indulge me and "settle in"—it's going to be a while.

My parents, who were very much a team, instilled confidence and independence in us almost by default, by pushing us outside to play in the world. The baseline rule set by my mother and supported by Dad was that you had to finish what you started, no quitting. There is no real way to adequately thank your parents, except to follow their guidance, live by the principles they instilled, and pay tribute to their memory and legacy. I hope this book achieves that.

My older siblings—Mary-Ellen, Bobby, John, and Sue—ushered in the adventures, friends, and experiences that formed me. Thank you so much for including me, and for all your patience—even to this day. My younger siblings, Ned and Mike, rounded out the gang. Ned and I played countless hours of street hockey, whiffle ball, catch, and soccer with neighborhood friends. As kids we were so competitive, but outside the house we hung out together, played sports, and our friends were interchangeable. Mike and I have a special bond; he's a fortress with a big heart, love of family, and enthusiasm for life.

Thank you to the entire Ski Market extended family of friends, coworkers, product reps, and suppliers that embraced and supported me. To Mike Bisner, Bob Verge, Mike Sheehan, Walter Driscoll, Chris Leake, Mike Specian, Jim West, and the entire Bob Ferguson Family: Wow—what a world of opportunity you opened up for me and countless others. Ski

Market provided countless careers for so many, and set the standard for action sports retailers nationally for decades.

When it comes to film producers, editors, and promoters, I've been lucky to work with some of the most creative people in the industry. Eric Perlman was the brainchild behind the North Face Extreme series, and does not get enough credit for ushering in the music-video era of action sports. Blake Miller, who is truly one of a kind, edited *Return of the Shred-I* and co-produced with me *Children of the Snow* with creativity, cutting-edge animations, and impressive editing techniques. Kurt Miller, Peter Speak, Max Bervy, and Brian Sisselman, who produced Warren Miller Entertainment's *Double Exposure*, *To the Extreme*, and *Extreme Skiing*, all raised the bar in production quality and video distribution. Kim Schneider, long-time editor for Warren Miller Entertainment's feature films, stands alone when it comes to producing, editing, and choosing music to complement the effort.

When it came to television production, Rory Strunk, founder of Resort Sports Network, introduced me to television sponsorship and cable distribution. Michelle Moreau, Steve Garabedian, Tim Peterson, Jim Carroll, and Bob Sylvester and all the New England Sports Network staff who supported the *Dan Egan's Wild World of Winter* television series made it possible for me to produce countless episodes. Tim Reever and Mark Smith introduced me to the art of selling the intangible, and the amazing world of radio. To Kent Rich, Peter Adams, Corey Potter, and Harry Newell, who supported, researched, and figured out the technical side of producing live-coverage sailing events, four miles off-coast, through remote cameras, drones, and by creating bonding networks—Thank you for all your hard work and dedication. Bernie Weichsel mentored me in so many ways, and provided countless opportunities at his ski shows. And to the producers, editors, and directors of *Ski Bum, the Warren Miller Story*— Joe Berry, Patrick Creadon, Christine O'Malley, Jeff Conroy, H. Nelson Henry, and Josh Earl—Thank you for honoring Warren's life.

I'm grateful to my coaches who rallied and inspired me both on and off the slopes and soccer fields, most of whom have become lifelong friends.

To Bill Rogers, Jon Anderson, Peter Gately, David Ellis, Bill Bearse, Tom Herget, Paul Ajemian, Joe Daily, Bob Doucette, Tom Austin, and the other John Egan—Thank you on behalf of myself and all the athletes, students, and individuals you've supported and instructed throughout your careers.

I've worked with so many cameramen who take their time setting up masterly shots and aim for perfection. Tom Day, Tom Grissom, Gary Nate, Brian Sisselman, and Bill Heath all captured the epic footage for Warren Miller that brought the personality and energy of The Egan Brothers to Warren's films, as well as to mine and countless others'. To Eric Scharmer, Carter Davidson, Adam DesLauriers, Jonathan Buiel, and Matt Herriger, who made *Dan Egan's Wild World of Winter* amazing for well over ten years— Can't thank you enough. To Michael Graber, Don Hyde, Corey Potter, Colton Wright, and Satchel Burns—You are all the best of the best.

The still photographers we worked with over the years have been amazing, passionate, true artists. To Tracy Hartenstien, Sam Walsh, Hank de Vré, Wade McKoy, Ross Woodhall, Cory Silken, Daniel Foster, Steve Cloutier, Dennis Welsh, Pablo Silva, Dave Roman, Larry Prosser, Marko Shapiro, Jen Bennett, Tom Lippert, and Kathryn Costello—Thank you for capturing the fun, personality, and feats over the years.

Throughout this book, the illustrations capturing family, activities, and John and me were designed and brought to life by these incredible artists: Kimberly Robinson, Martina Diez-Routh, and Senan Gorman worked on chapter icons; The Egan Brothers' logo was designed by Blair Boettger, who had three clients in the '80s: Jerry Garcia, Jake Burton, and The Egan Brothers; Nick Lyons is the creator of Joe Powder, the legendary Val d'Isère skier who lurks in the high alpine and from time to time can be seen skiing in the Fornet sector of the Vanoise National Park; and Nancy Griswold, whose artwork and creativity is a gift to the world.

Special thanks to my many mentors, colleagues, and friends who encouraged me to keep going and persevere: Dan Cooney, Stephen and Shay Kassin, Shay Graydon, Ralph Donahue, Kirk Phelps, Diane Pepin, Matt Beck, Peter Hamlin, Brook, Rick Blackshaw, Jeff Shay, Jeff Dinsmore, Mike

Neff, Eric Foch, Ed O'Donnell, Matt Stanton, Pam Kelley, Paul Douglas, Carolyn Lynch, Beth Hennessy Magann, and all my Milton friends, Arturo Lyon, Rene Schwartz, Jeff "Big Dog" Proehl, Tom Kietz, Pam Fletcher, Ken Marisseau, Peter Sole, David Baker, Danny Caldicot, Matt Welsh, Father Leo Leblanc, Father Justin Kielhorn, Father Greg Usselmann, Father George Robichaud, Clara Gleb, Shelagh Connelly, Marty Riehs, Tim Curry, Dave Casey, Rick Rader, Karen Lanoue-Egan, Jennifer Egan, Jacqueline Egan, Jay Dieselman, Jamey Shachoy, Al Fetcher Sr., Al Fletcher Jr., Dave Seymore, Emily Hart, Stan Waliner, Billy Hickey, Dave Manning, Karen Anderson, Tom Richardson, Robert Forenza, Win Smith, Justin Koski, Ann Schroeder, Charlie Callander, Frank Chalfont, Barbara Friedsam Egan, O Jay Merrill, Garry Lavoie, Deedee Driller, Dean Decas, Lee Turlington, Tom Lane, Rob DesLauriers, Eric DesLauriers, Bob Bell, Jeff Ginnis, John Woolard, John Dockendorf, Amy and Dave Deult, Casey Cockerham, Chris Mayone, Mike Bickford, Bill Roland, Jason Levinthal, Mike Nick, Ellie Pierce, Gregor Makechnie, Dillon Mailand, Troy Nevid, Julie Anderson, Taylor Middleton, Jason Sadler, Greg Wozer, Nick Herrin, Eric Lipton, Rob Guyotte, Ben Storms, Mike Wenner, Ned Huston, Louis Joseph, Billy Roland, Jay Caldwell, Richard "Wolfgang" Groezinger, Peter Gardiner, Stuart Streuli, Andreas Bjork Lund, Julie Thompson Quinn, Chris Souillac, Wayne Watson, Marty Heckelman, Peter and Christine Bassler, Dennis Ouellette, Nikki Pitts, and Henry, Ginny, Katrina, Jackson, and Roscoe Schniewind. Thank you all!

Thank you, as well, to the many musicians who wrote and produced songs for my films, television shows, and videos. The newly released *White Haze* song, now available on iTunes and Spotify, was composed and performed by Margaret Anne King and Doug "Rock It Man" Weaver.

The editors of this book did an amazing job. Matt Pepin, who has edited work from both Eric and me as *Boston Globe* contributors, was the perfect person to keep us on track and tackle the initial edits of the story. Jack Rochester was the spark for getting this project into print, as he also was for my first book, *All-Terrain Skiing*, and did an amazing job of expanding the emotion and detail of the content while also editing, refining, and transitioning the material into book form. Courtney B. Jenkins did the final edit, and took so much care with the details and formatting. Chris Wait did the final proofread, combing over every sentence, paragraph, and page for nasty, lingering ankle-biter typos. Sammy Blair coordinated and promoted; Eddie Vincent created tasteful page design; Chris and Deirdre Wait nailed the cover design; Stephen McArthur provided wise council; Scott Riley and Kathryn Costello provided web design; and Jon Parker and Alan Guilbeault consulted on strategy and tactics for online marketing. It is an honor and I really appreciate Tony Horton's taking the time to write the foreword.

Eric Wilbur is an amazing writer; because of him the story arc came together, weaving family history and extreme skiing's roots with the personal side of my story. Telling the story in the third person, as he did, provided the space needed for all the characters in the book. What a gift to have him as co-author—Thank you, Eric.

I'm at a loss for words when it comes to Warren Miller and what he did for my career. His advice was always direct and to the point, and I owe him so much. He once told me, "there is no book that says you have to live there and do this or that. You can write your own book, live where you want, and do what you love." And he was right. Thank you, Warren.

When my brother John left home after graduating high school in 1976, to be a ski bum in Vermont, it shifted my family in ways unimaginable, affecting all my brothers and sisters, and shaping our lives in a completely different direction regarding where we live and how we ski. John was the backbone of The Egan Brothers. He hung in there with me and all my crazy ambitions and dreams. His boldness, courage, and outlook on life made all the difference. Thank you, John.

My uncle, Tom Cull, coined the phrase "The Milton Hilton," in reference to my childhood home. Tom taught, illustrated, and explained to me how the world works when humility, compassion, and empathy are applied, and that "going along to get along" creates the big picture of the most important thing in life, which is family. Tom and his wife, my dad's sister Jean-Marie, have been a constant source of wise counsel to me over the years, and their children, Tom, Ned, and Cathleen, were like three additional siblings. Thank you all.

To Liz Peoples, and Sydney and Graham Pogue—you have been my family through the past two decades. I'm so blessed to have you all in my life.

I'm sure I've forgotten more than a few who've provided help along the way, and as the saying goes, I'll see you in the future if not in the pasture.

Ski for Life,
Dan

About the Authors

ERIC WILBUR

ERIC WILBUR SPENT THE BETTER part of the past two decades immersed in New England's snow sports scene. He has a bachelor's degree from Saint Michael's College in Vermont, and a master's degree in journalism from Boston University. A former producer for Fox Sports and writer for New England Sports Network, he became a *Boston Globe* contributor, and columnist for Boston.com. His sports, skiing, and travel pieces have appeared in *Metro Boston*, and he is the online editor at *New England Ski Journal*. In addition, he has recently taken on the task of becoming a high school journalism teacher. Wilbur is a passionate sports fan, and he and his wife of twenty years, Kathleen, are the proud parents of three children: Nathaniel, Carson, and Hayden.

DAN EGAN

EXTREME SKIING PIONEER DAN EGAN has appeared in fourteen Warren Miller films, and is known for skiing the most remote regions of the world. In 2001, *Powder Magazine* named him one of the most influential skiers of our time. Egan is an award-winning video producer specializing in action sports and sailing. As a journalist, he has covered three Olympics and is a sought-after motivational speaker. He has authored two other books, *All-Terrain Skiing: Body Mechanics and Balance from Powder to Ice*, and *Courage to Persevere: The Triumph Over Tragedy of Bill Fallon*, co-authored with Bill Fallon. In the winter he can be found at Waterville Valley, New Hampshire; Big Sky, Montana; and Val d'Isère, France. Check out www.skiclinics.com for his schedule. Egan was inducted into the U.S. Ski and Snowboard Hall of Fame, along with his brother John, in 2017.

Photographed by: Barrie Fischer

Dan and John at the U.S. Ski & Snowboard Hall of Fame
Induction Ceremony in Stowe, VT.

❶	Mount Sunapee, NH	⓫	Lake Louise, Canada	㉑	Valley Nevado, Chile
❷	Blue Hills, MA	⓬	Whistler, Canada	㉒	Las Leñas, Argentina
❸	Sugarbush, VT	⓭	Valemount, Canada	㉓	Treble Cone, New Zealand
❹	Waterville Valley, NH	⓮	Fernie, Canada	㉔	Chamonix, France
❺	Mount Washington, NH	⓯	Baffin Island, Canada	㉕	Val d'Isère, France
❻	Squaw Valley, CA	⓰	Torngats Mountains, Canada	㉖	Zerrmatt, Switzerland
❼	Grand Targhee, WY	⓱	Greenland	㉗	St. Anton, Austria
❽	Crested Butte, CO	⓲	Mount Elbrus, Russia	㉘	Vogel, Slovenia
❾	Big Sky, MT	⓳	Kamchatka, Russia	㉙	Mt. Erciyes - Kayseri, Turkey
❿	Valdez, AK	⓴	Sochi, Russia	㉚	Poiana Brasov, Romania

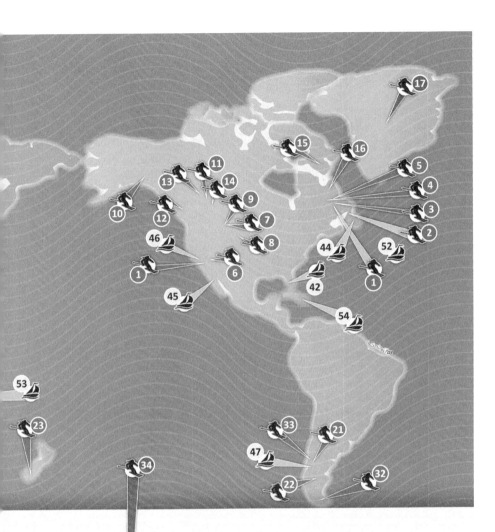

LEGEND

INDEX
Ski Films, Television, Documentaries, Live Productions, Radio, Podcasts and Books

1970–1990

1979	John	Winter Fever	Warren Miller Entertainment
1982	John	Snow Wonder	Warren Miller Entertainment
1983	John	Ski Time	Warren Miller Entertainment
1985	John	Steep and Deep	Warren Miller Entertainment
1987	John	White Winter Heat	Warren Miller Entertainment
1988	John / Dan	Escape to Ski	Warren Miller Entertainment
1988	John / Dan	How the Super Skiers Ski	Warren Miller Entertainment
1989	John / Dan	White Magic	Warren Miller Entertainment
1989	John / Dan	Extreme Skiing I	Eric Perlman Productions
1999	John / Dan	Decade of Descents	Egan Entertainment Network
1990	John / Dan	Warren Miller's Extreme Winter	Warren Miller Entertainment
1990	John / Dan	Extreme Skiing	Warren Miller Entertainment
1990	John / Dan	World Wide & Wild	Egan Entertainment Network

1990–2000

1991	John / Dan	Born to Ski	Warren Miller Entertainment
1991	John / Dan	Extreme Dream	Egan Entertainment Network
1991	John / Dan	Skiing Extreme II	Eric Perlman Productions
1991	John / Dan	Disaster on Mt Elbrus	Egan Entertainment Network
1992	John / Dan	Steeper and Deeper	Warren Miller Entertainment
1992	John / Dan	Skiing Extreme III	Eric Perlman Productions
1992	John / Dan	Return of the Shred-i	Egan Entertainment Network
1993	John / Dan	Black Diamond Rush	Warren Miller Entertainment
1993	John / Dan	Skiing Extreme IV	Eric Perlman Productions
1993	Dan	Children of the Snow	Egan Entertainment Network
1994	Dan	Vertical Reality	Warren Miller Entertainment
1995	John / Dan	Advanced to the Steep	Straight Up Films
1995	John	Skiing Extreme V	Eric Perlman Productions
1996	Dan	All Terrain Skiing - Book	Joshua Tree Publishing / World Leisure Corp.
1996	John / Dan	Double Exposure	Warren Miller Entertainment
1996	John / Dan	Skiing Extreme VI	Eric Perlman Productions
1996-97	Dan	Host of Front Row	New England Sports Network
1997	John	The Promise Land	Straight Up Films
1997	John	Home Front	Dogs of Winter
1997	John / Dan	Where the Steeps Have No Name	Egan Entertainment Network
1998-09	John / Dan	Dan Egan's Wild World of Winter	Egan Entertainment Network
1998	John	Do the White Thing	Dogs of Winter
1998	John / Dan	Baffin Island	Egan Entertainment Network
1998	John / Dan	Advanced to the Steep II	Straight Up Films
1999	John / Dan	Fifty	Warren Miller Entertainment
1999	Dan	Ski Academy	Egan Entertainment Network

2000–2020

Year	Creator	Title	Production
2000	John / Dan	20 Years of Ski Bumming	Egan Entertainment Network
2000	John / Dan	Torngat	Egan Entertainment Network
2000	Dan / Bill Fallon	Courage to Persevere - Book	World Leisure Corporation
2001	John / Dan	The Great American Freeride	Egan Entertainment Network
2001	John	Winter Never Dies	Wrecking Crew Productions
2002	John	Loud Powder	Wrecking Crew Productions
2006-09	Dan	U.S. Sailing Video Podcast	Egan Entertainment Network
2008-11	Dan	Sprint Ski Press Weekly News	Egan Entertainment Network
2010	Dan	2010 Vancouver Olympics	Ski Press
2011	Dan	ISAF Sailing World Championships	Sperry / U.S. Sailing / Degan Media
2012	Dan	2012 London Olympics	Sperry / Degan Media
2014-18	Dan	Edging the Extreme	RadioBDC
2014	Dan	ISAF Sailing World Championships	U.S. Sailing / Degan Media
2014	Dan	2014 Sochi Oympics	Boston Globe
2015-19	Dan	ICSA National Championships	Degan Media
2015	Dan	FIS World Championship	Boston Globe
2015-16	Dan	NESJ with Dan Egan	Degan Media
2016-17	Dan	Vendee Globe	Boston Globe
2016-17	Dan	America's Cup World Series	Sperry / Degan Media
2017	John / Dan	USSHOF Tribute Video	U.S. Ski and Snowboard Hall of Fame
2017-18	Dan	Volvo Ocean Race	Boston Globe / Degan Media
2015-17	Dan	Rolex NYYC Invitational Cup	Degan Media
2016-17	Dan	Rolex Big Boat Series	Degan Media
2017	Dan	America's Cup	Sperry / Degan Media
2017	Dan	50 Years of Firsts: Waterville Valley	Degan Media
2018	John	Back Country Profiles	Treasured Hieghts
2018	John	Reflections of Skiing Legend John Egan	Kulkea
2018	John	Take a Run Down CastleRock	Mountain Collective
2019	John	Beautiful Destinations: Vermont	Beautiful Destinations
2019	Dan	Flow State - Big Sky, Montana	Teton Gravity Research
2018-20	Dan	Fresh Tracks - Weekly Radio Show	Indie617
2019	John / Dan	Ski Bum: The Warren Miller Story	Lorton Entertainment
2020	John / Dan	Future Retro	Warren Miller Entertainment
2020	John	Made Back East	Vagrants
2020	Dan	Ski Talk	SkiTalk.com / Degan Media
2020	Dan	Designed by Tradition	Degan Media / Alps & Meters
2021	Dan / Eric Wilbur	Thrity Years in a White Haze - Book	Degan Media

For more information about John Egan: www.FeelTheTurn.com

For more information about Dan Egan: www.Dan-Egan.com

To Ski with Dan, go to: www.SkiClinics.com

Degan|media

Printed in Great Britain
by Amazon

14070530R00241